PALACE
POLITICS

How the
Ruling Party
Brought Crisis
to Mexico

JONATHAN SCHLEFER

UNIVERSITY OF TEXAS PRESS
Austin

Requests for permission to reproduce material from this work should
be sent to:
    Permissions
    University of Texas Press
    P.O. Box 7819
    Austin, TX 78713-7819
    www.utexas.edu/utpress/about/bpermission.html

♾ The paper used in this book meets the minimum requirements of
ANSI/NISO Z39.48-1992 (R1997) (Permanence of Paper).

LIBRARY OF CONGRESS CATALOGING-IN-PUBLICATION DATA

Schlefer, Jonathan, 1949-
  Palace politics : how the ruling party brought crisis to Mexico /
Jonathan Schlefer. — 1st ed.
    p.   cm.
  Includes bibliographical references and index.
  ISBN 978-0-292-71757-2 (cloth : alk. paper) — ISBN 978-0-292-
71758-9 (pbk. : alk. paper)
    1. Mexico—Politics and government—20th century. 2. Partido
Revolucionario Institucional—History—20th century. 3. Mexico—
Economic conditions—20th century. 4. Elite (Social sciences)—
Mexico—History—20th century. I. Title.
  F1234.S33   2007
  972.08'2—dc22
                                  2007027198

*To my parents, Mark and Marion,
who have nurtured the intellectual
and imaginative life of our family.*

CONTENTS

ACKNOWLEDGMENTS ix

LIST OF PRESIDENTS OF MEXICO, 1924–2006 xi

INTRODUCTION:
THE POLITICIANS' TESTIMONY 1

Chapter 1 11
POLITICS AT THE HEART OF THE STATE

Chapter 2 31
THE STRANGE MEXICAN STATE

Chapter 3 55
DID STRUCTURAL ECONOMIC FAILURE CAUSE THE CRISES?

Chapter 4 76
THE MACROECONOMICS OF ELITE CONFLICT

Chapter 5 94
THE CRISES THAT DIDN'T HAPPEN

Chapter 6 117
THE UNWRITTEN RULES

Chapter 7 129
THE END OF STABILITY

Chapter 8 157
STRUGGLE

181   *Chapter 9*
       SCHISM

204   *Chapter 10*
       THE INEVITABILITY OF ELITE POLITICS

227   *Appendix A*
       MEXICAN FISCAL DATA

229   *Appendix B*
       THE PRE-ELECTORAL SPENDING CYCLE

233   NOTES

265   INTERVIEW LIST

269   BIBLIOGRAPHY

283   INDEX

ACKNOWLEDGMENTS

If not for former high Mexican officials' willingness to be interviewed (I recall only one exception), I could never have written this book. The political class, as Mexicans call it, takes historical research far more seriously than could possibly be expected in most nations. Interviewees talked at length, sometimes for hours on end or continuing on several occasions. More than a few in their 80s or 90s have since died. I hope that, however my arguments may be judged, at least I have set down something about the old Mexican politics that would otherwise have died with them. I am especially grateful to the late Victor Urquidi, a distinguished Mexican economist who, though not himself an official, advised presidents and finance ministers over the course of half a century.

After fifteen years as a journalist and editor, which is to say at a stage in life when sensible people do not make such radical career moves, I undertook a Ph.D. in political science at MIT, and *Palace Politics* derives from my thesis. The excellent perceptions of my advisor, Suzanne Berger, helped focus my more useful ideas and reject false starts that did not hold up or that, when I thought about them twice, bored me. Michael Piore, as in his own work, brought his rigorous economist's training (but not mainstream economists' intellectual baggage) to bear on a political investigation. Chappell Lawson's enthusiastic, reliable comments about political science, Mexico, and writing (even editors need editing) helped again and again. The non-MIT member of my committee, the Mexico scholar Roderic Camp of Claremont McKenna College, generously read evolving drafts and reassured me that my arguments were serious. Jonathan Fox introduced me to Mexican politics before moving from MIT to the University of California.

On two separate trips to Mexico, the *Instituto de Investigaciones Económicas* (Economic Research Institute) of the National University gave me a home as a visiting scholar. Just across a grass yard from the Economics Faculty and Law Faculty, the schools that the great majority of former high Mexican officials attended, the institute helped me feel, in some small measure, part of the story too. I am particularly indebted to Professor Teresa Gutiérrez Haces, who introduced me to the institute and to Mexico; to the director, Alicia Girón; and to the head librarian, Ernesto Reyes. Ernesto's wife Susana and son, also Ernesto, transcribed massive quantities of taped interviews. Cecilia Dávila, a translator and professor of French (for a time also at the National University), with her fine care for words, helped with some particularly hard passages. I could never have managed the photo research without Rebeca Flores. And I owe a big debt to my editor at the University of Texas Press, Theresa May, for her advice through this arduous project.

The Ortiz family of Casa González, where I stayed for a year in Mexico City, made it my second home, a city I came to love for all its problems, as did the Pueblita family during an earlier stay in their house. The sustained support of my parents Mark and Marion, my sisters Kate and Ellen, and my companion Phyllis Krastanov has meant more than they can know. My cats deserve credit for enduring Mexico City, where the feline world is as fierce as the traffic.

LIST OF PRESIDENTS OF
MEXICO, 1924–2006

Plutarco Elías Calles	1924–1928
Emilio Portes Gil	1928–1930
Pascual Ortiz Rubio	1930–1932
Abelardo Rodríguez	1932–1934
Lázaro Cárdenas	1934–1940
Manuel Avila Camacho	1940–1946
Miguel Alemán	1946–1952
Adolfo Ruiz Cortines	1952–1958
Adolfo López Mateos	1958–1964
Gustavo Díaz Ordaz	1964–1970
Luis Echeverría	1970–1976
José López Portillo	1976–1982
Miguel de la Madrid	1982–1988
Carlos Salinas	1988–1994
Ernesto Zedillo	1994–2000
Vicente Fox	2000–2006

PALACE POLITICS

Palace Politics: How the Ruling Party Brought Crisis to Mexico actually
begins in the early 1950s, when the Mexican political elite resolved a
perilous internecine struggle over the presidency and consolidated what
the Peruvian novelist Mario Vargas Llosa called "the perfect dictatorship." For two decades it was a remarkably stable political system—no
mean accomplishment in a nation not yet ready for democracy. The old
Mexican regime outlived all other authoritarian regimes of the twentieth
century except the Soviet Union, and although it occasionally resorted
to repression, it was not a police state. The Mexican economic "miracle"
of sustained, rapid economic growth was spoken of in the same terms
as South Korea's economy in the 1980s or China's in the 2000s. The
success went far beyond macroeconomic statistics. Millions of Mexicans
whose fathers had been peons laboring on vast haciendas now tilled their
own fields, while a steady stream of migrants to the city found jobs in
burgeoning industries.

    Palace Politics follows that once perfect dictatorship through the
1990s, as it tore itself apart in ever-bloodier political struggles and
perhaps—so President Carlos Salinas and other members of the political
elite claimed—actual assassination. The former economic miracle now
emblematized economic failure. Mexico's 1982 crisis launched the "lost
decade" of the 1980s, a period worse than the Great Depression in much
of Latin America. Mexico's 1994 crisis led the Asian, Russian, Argentine,
and other crises, the first of a new wave in this time of expanded global
financial speculation.

    I based my research for *Palace Politics* largely on extensive interviews
with the former Mexican political elite: presidents, finance ministers,
interior ministers, and other high officials who held sway during the
second half of the twentieth century. People often ask how I managed to
get interviews with these former high officials. Were they living in mansions like mafia dons? Did they tell me the truth? And does not interviewing politicians at the top seem a distorted way of charting a nation's

history? Does my very method not regress to the old "great man" theory of history (and nearly all my interviewees were men) at a time when we increasingly recognize the importance of social movements, as well as gender and ethnic politics?

Let me start with how I got the interviews and what I found the managers of the once perfect dictatorship to be like before taking on more substantive questions. To begin with, I undertook my research, originally for a Ph.D. thesis in political science at MIT, at a fortunate historical moment. I spent two years as a visiting researcher at the *Instituto de Investigaciones Económicas* (Economics Research Institute) of the National University of Mexico, first the academic year 1996 to 1997, then the calendar year 2000: the very years when the old political system officially crumbled and collapsed.

On July 6, 1997, I watched (as a sort of political tourist, not an official observer) the voting in a precinct in Tlalpan, a former colonial town in the southeastern hills of Mexico City where I was living. Citizens lined up at the neighborhood market with their credentials, which representatives of the independent Federal Electoral Institute—as well as of the half-dozen political parties in the race—checked against the established voter list. The secret ballot was still so novel that older people had to be shown how to step into the ingenious cardboard booths, mark their ballots unseen, fold and deposit them. In the evening, representatives of each party watched as deputies from the Federal Electoral Institute tallied the totals at the precinct. Election results were reported not just in aggregated numbers but also precinct by precinct, so party representatives at the precinct level could verify the count.

The left-leaning Party of the Democratic Revolution won in a landslide, capturing the Mexico City governorship, often considered the second most powerful political post in the nation, as well as the city's legislature. The news prompted a rise in the Mexican stock market. Finance and big business had abandoned their long-standing support for the old political machine; they now saw a functioning democracy as in their best interests. The machine had all but self-destructed.

My second year in Mexico, 2000, coincided with the old regime's official demise. Oversized posters of Francisco Labastida, candidate of the long-ruling *Partido Revolucionario Institucional* (Institutional Revolutionary Party), or PRI, were draped from treetops around the Angel of Independence, the monument in Mexico City where soccer and political victories are celebrated. Then, on July 2, Vicente Fox, candidate of the center-right party of opposition, National Action, won the presidency in an amazing landslide. As Fox's supporters gathered around the Angel that evening, the spotlights played on the stage where he would appear, but the PRI's posters could still be made out hanging above, grotesque relics of a suddenly bygone era. Such an exuberant, peaceful crowd, filling the streets in all directions, I have never seen before or since.

Everyone, except maybe the mid-level PRI functionaries who had hung the posters, knew the old regime was on the way out; only the timing was in question. The street vendors, having guessed the outcome, appeared everywhere around the Angel, selling rubber masks of former president Carlos Salinas, emblem of the dead era, along with cans of celebratory foam spray. Top government officials were prepared, too. As Fox's victory celebrations began, President Ernesto Zedillo went on national television to concede the PRI's defeat. The ruling party thus announced its own demise just as it had managed the finest moments of its past: hardly democratic—to forestall possible protest and disorder among the party ranks, Zedillo conceded defeat long before the official vote was in—but astonishingly efficient.

As Mexico thus pushed toward democracy, I burrowed into its undemocratic past. This apparently odd juxtaposition actually made a certain amount of sense, quite apart from the fact that seemingly radical changes generally derive more intimately from the past than might at first appear. Many high officials from as early as the 1950s were still alive and as sharp as ever, though sometimes in their 80s or 90s. And they were increasingly willing to talk frankly about how politics really worked. As the old regime crumbled—and many interviewees saw that its time had come—so did the regime's time-honored interdiction against publicly discussing its inner workings.[1]

I started with a few references to officials from American scholars, principally Roderic Camp of Claremont McKenna College and Chappell Lawson of MIT. A mutual friend introduced me to Guillermo Barnes, a former Finance official and, in 2000, leader of the PRI's Mexico City delegation. He in turn introduced me to mentors such as Julio Rodolfo Moctezuma, finance secretary in the 1970s. I telephoned Victor Urquidi, an "insider-outsider," as he called himself, at the Colegio de México where he was teaching, and he invited me for a discussion. He had been a member of Mexico's delegation to the 1944 international conference in Bretton Woods, New Hampshire, that established the post–World War II economic system; he had been an advisor to the finance minister in the 1950s and 1960s and to a series of Mexican presidents (he knew

Carlos Salinas as "Carlitos"); and he had been president of the Colegio. I looked up Antonio Ortiz Mena, the renowned Mexican finance minister from 1958 to 1970, in the phone directory. The screech of a fax machine answered, so I sent a note, doubting it was even the right number. In a few weeks an assistant said Ortiz Mena could speak with me. We talked for more than three hours; I know by the number of tapes I recorded.

I was a little devious about the order in which I did my interviews. Many of my first were with officials who had been in the Finance Ministry and closely allied Bank of Mexico in the 1950s and 1960s. Not all were retired—Mexican politicians tend to be hardworking and little interested in a life of leisure—but they were glad to talk about their economic successes. They referred me to protégés from later administrations, typically also from Finance or the Bank of Mexico. Once I had a reasonably clear picture of the Finance–Bank of Mexico story, I began contacting officials from rival economic ministries: Presidency (an oddly named ministry that managed public investment), State Industries, and Planning and Budget. In effect, I politely implied that I had their political opponents' viewpoints and would now like to get theirs. Yet these opposing political camps were not personal enemies (except in rare cases) and were sometimes personal friends. Bank of Mexico Director Ernesto Fernández Hurtado and State Industries Secretary Horacio Flores de la Peña, anchor of opposing sides under President Luis Echeverría, each referred me to the other.

If I had been interviewing former politicians from a Central American country, I might have had to travel to Miami or other foreign destinations, but nearly all former Mexican politicians lived in or near Mexico City; many still played some role in the government. Some had moved to nearby cities such as Cuernavaca, Ortiz Mena's home. Some had taken posts in their native Mexican states. They typically lived in handsome old residences in wealthier neighborhoods, but no different from other residences on the street.

Though I could not talk with former president Salinas (then persona non grata in his own country, he had retreated to Ireland, which did not have an extradition treaty with Mexico), I spoke with his father, Raúl Salinas Lozano, industry and commerce secretary in the 1960s. He was said by some of my interviewees to have been corrupt, but he hardly occupied one of those grandiose mansions such as mafia dons do (at least on television). Having moved to the cleaner air of Acapulco for health reasons, he was living in an apartment that might have belonged to a professor at an American university—and was decorated in much the same educated taste. (Around half of high Mexican officials were, in fact, professors at one point or another.)

One of my last interviews was with President Echeverría. Former officials were glad to give me his phone number but asked that I not use their names; the Mexican president was somehow above common mortals. I sent several faxes over the course of a month. Then one day when I returned from an interview, I saw my answering machine blinking incessantly. I ran through perhaps half a dozen messages from Echeverría's assistants (I could never keep track of them all), culminating in one from the man himself. "This is Luis Echeverría," he said in a rather high voice I will not forget, "ex-president of Mexico." He identified himself as ex-president of Mexico in a tone almost of surprise, as if he had never quite gotten used to it himself. I will never know who, if anyone, had mentioned me to Echeverría. He might have just taken into his own head to grant me an interview; that was often how he made decisions.

Echeverría was known for quick action. The next morning at eight o'clock I found myself breakfasting at his house, in the hills above the Mexico City plain not far from Tlalpan (but a more fashionable neighborhood than I had lived in). I liked him. Like many experienced politicians, he was agile at dodging questions if he wanted to, but he answered others forthrightly. He said we could talk as long as I wanted the next day, but when I arrived, it turned out I had been invited to a dinner party at which the topic was U.S. immigration law. Interesting but not useful for my book. The entourage then drove to a nearby theater in San Ángel to watch a movie. If anyone in the audience recognized the former president, no one indicated it.

I interviewed high Mexican officials because *Palace Politics* looks at the way they resolved or failed to resolve their internal conflicts. I argue that "cooperation" among competing political elites helped sustain the stable, growing economy of the 1950s and 1960s, even when most of Latin America suffered repeated economic crises. The *grupo*, or clique within the political elite, whose leader won the internal party contest for the presidential nomination—and hence automatically won that public relations event, the general election—did better in the next administration. But even losing *grupos* retained key posts and the hope of winning the next time. Such a promise of political survival allowed *grupos* to defend the system's broader interests, not just narrow factional interests, and the united state repeatedly mobilized to avert possible economic crises. After 1970, increasingly all-or-nothing "struggle" among *grupos* tore the political system apart and repeatedly erupted in economic crises. Whether the regime was statist (as during its first two crises) or free-market (as during its next two crises) hardly mattered. Now *grupos* that lost a particular succession contest increasingly feared—and met with—political exile. As intra-elite power conflict turned all-or-nothing, *grupos* vied to buy support for their leader's presidential nomination via overspending, public bank lending, manipulation of the securities market, and other perilous gambles that erupted in economic crises.

To a point, changing relations among political elites are reflected in socioeconomic data, which, of course, I sought. For example, real public sector spending in Mexico often soared in *pre*-election years when the PRI's internal contest for the presidential nomination took place: by 27 percent in 1975 and 22 percent in 1981. (These figures exclude debt payments, which do not buy political support.) Real public spending was slashed in actual election years, when victory was assured and succession was not in dispute: real spending did not grow at all in 1976, and it fell 8 percent in 1982 (still excluding debt payments). But for the most part, elite politics is not visible in socioeconomic data, precisely because it matters in its own right and is not a mere reflection of socioeconomic forces.

I therefore interviewed high officials or politicians; in Mexico under the old regime, there was no distinction. Every time I cite individuals without reference to a printed source, I am relying on my interviews with those individuals. I systematically sought differing viewpoints. I made a list of all officials, living and deceased, I would ideally have liked to interview for each of the six administrations from 1952 through 1988, the era when the old political regime was most firmly consolidated. The list was as follows:[2]

- The president of Mexico.
- The finance secretary and the director of the Bank of Mexico, traditional allies.
- Secretaries of economic ministries that were often rivals of Finance and the Bank of Mexico: Presidency, not the president's office but a separate ministry that planned investment before 1976; Planning and Budget, responsible for all planning and budgeting after 1976; and State Industries, which managed a vast array of public enterprises, from steel to chemicals, electricity to oil.
- The interior secretary, the highest political official after the president, responsible for maintaining order and running the party machine, the federal police, the national spy agency, and the electoral apparatus.

- All those considered serious contenders for the PRI's presidential nomination.[3]
- All those who were a secretary of one of the principal ministries, director of the oil company Pemex, director of Social Security, or president of the PRI, for two or more administrations.

I was able to interview many of these individuals—for example, five of the six living ex-finance secretaries from the period and all four living ex-directors of the Bank of Mexico.[4] When an official was deceased or otherwise unavailable, I sought a colleague or son in politics who was likely to know his perspective. For example, for the 1952–58 administration, I interviewed the press secretary of President Adolfo Ruiz Cortines and the sons (themselves subsequent high officials) of Finance Secretary Antonio Carrillo Flores and Interior Secretary Ángel Carvajal. For the 1964–70 administration, interviewees included Finance Secretary Antonio Ortiz Mena, Interior Secretary (of course, later President) Luis Echeverría, and the deceased President Gustavo Díaz Ordaz's close ally, Health and Public Welfare Secretary Rafael Moreno Valle. I list interviewees at the end of the book.

I also relied on firsthand accounts. Emilio Carrillo Gamboa, son of Finance Minister Antonio Carrillo Flores, not only discussed what he had heard from his father and witnessed himself as long-time director of the state telephone company, but also provided a copy of his father's diary for the crucial year 1954, with some personal information excised. Published accounts such as those by Alfonso Corona del Rosal, one of the most important politicians of the 1950s and 1960s, and by Finance Secretary Antonio Ortiz Mena supplemented interviews. Many secondary sources were, of course, indispensable, but for politicians' testimony, the works of Roderic Camp and Jorge Castañeda's *The Inheritance: Archaeology of Political Succession in Mexico* stand out.[5]

I did all my interviews on the record and, usually, on tape. Where interviewees asked me to keep isolated remarks off the record, of course, I scrupulously did so. One interviewee asked that our entire discussion be off the record, and so it has remained. (His name is not in the list of interviewees.) Whenever possible, I sent all quotations, direct or indirect, to interviewees to check for accuracy. The idea was not that they could change their minds or take remarks off the record after the fact. Rather, it was that if I had misinterpreted a statement or its context— remarkably easy in a long interview, especially if it is taped—I would make changes to reflect what interviewees genuinely meant. A few were concerned about some quotes, but sometimes extended discussions led to mutual agreement about what they had legitimately meant. The quotes themselves are, I believe, about as close to hard facts as Mexican political history gets.

As a journalist for years before I began the Ph.D., I followed my usual practice of writing out questions for each interviewee ahead of time—generally the morning or night before—but barely glancing at them during the interview. I would flip through them toward the end to be sure I had not forgotten something important. At first, I also tried requesting responses on a scale of 1 to 10 to questions gauging internal elite struggle, external social pressures, and other matters. This effort was a flop. Perhaps my experience as a journalist doomed it: to get thoughtful answers, I have long been convinced, you must listen to interviewees and respond, not try to march them through some pre-established drill. In any event, Mexican officials balked: they would not even give me a number, or they would toss out one tentatively only to change it later. Instead, they would launch into long and sometimes very useful discussions.

I systematically questioned interviewees about a number of critical matters. For example, one concerned the political elite's reaction to a bloody massacre at Tlatelolco Square in Mexico City in 1968 that brought a series of anti-authoritarian protests to an end. (Responsibility for the massacre is still disputed. Although the square was full of uniformed soldiers, they appear not to have perpetrated it; the perpetrators appear to have been paramilitary "sharpshooters" not under military command. The question is who was commanding them.) It has been widely said that in the wake of Tlatelolco, political elites split irreconcilably, supporting or opposing President Gustavo Díaz Ordaz, and that that schism launched the regime's long decline. I asked every interviewee in high office in 1968 about such a split. They lamented the events of Tlatelolco but, without exception, denied that any division had occurred. Clearly, the myth of a split was constructed outside the inner circle. Such was the cloak of secrecy in which the old Mexican political system operated.

In regard to other questions about the old regime, I did find out-and-out disagreement among observers in positions to know. One such matter was whether Antonio Ortiz Mena, finance minister from 1958 to 1970, was ever a serious presidential contender. The broader question here is whether Finance was a ministry of *técnicos*, or technical experts, distinct from the *políticos*, or politicians, in other ministries. Did the political system grant an autonomous Finance Ministry extraordinary latitude to manage the economy—a task it performed extraordinarily well in those years—in exchange for shutting it out of the real contention over political succession? Ortiz Mena and several other credible interviewees said he never had been a real presidential candidate, but his economic advisors and other interviewees said otherwise. Moreover, Ortiz Mena himself concurred that Díaz Ordaz, who became president in 1964, had seen Ortiz Mena as a rival.

When I encountered such disagreements, I always report them. My interviewees doubtless tended to reconstruct the past to accord with their views and interests. Every human being surely does so, and the tendency is no doubt greater concerning a regime so secretive that one group of high officials might not know what another was doing. Journalists come to sense (however fallibly) when someone is deliberately trying to evade or lie about known facts. I rarely experienced that feeling during the interviews. With rare exceptions in the course of a few interviews, I believe my interviewees told the truth as they saw it.

When I ran up against what seemed honest disagreements, it became my responsibility to resolve them. Disagreements about Ortiz Mena's prospects for the presidency were hardly surprising. Being or not being a presidential candidate was not a binary condition, but a condition compounded of layers of ambiguity. Only the president himself knew who he was really considering as a successor and whose names he tossed out as "stuffing" to keep everybody guessing. The operative question is whether an individual was widely *perceived* to be a real candidate within a political system, it bears repeating, shrouded in secrecy. Díaz Ordaz has been accused of everything but political naiveté. If he saw Ortiz Mena as a presidential rival, Ortiz Mena was a rival, whatever he himself thought.

Palace Politics may seem out of harmony at a time when so much effort is devoted to understanding democracy and social movements—fundamentalism, whether Christian or Muslim, racial and gender politics, mass migration, community participation. This book not only looks back at relations among political elites from a bygone authoritarian regime, but also (to some inevitable extent) reflects the author's gratitude toward those individuals for generously, even bravely, discussing events they shaped.

Further, *Palace Politics* speaks well of a small group of men (and they were almost all men, though, like most Mexicans, often of mixed white and indigenous blood) who, however their regime occasionally lashed out at popular unrest, wisely guided the economy through perilous shoals in the 1950s and 1960s. At times, the argument approaches the great man theory of history: the revered ex-president Lázaro Cárdenas acted powerfully to consolidate elite cooperation in 1951; the messianic, power-hungry Luis Echeverría loosed elite struggle in the early 1970s; the failed dynasty builder Carlos Salinas brought economic and political disaster in the early 1990s.

There is a narrow answer and a broad answer to these concerns about a book on political elites. The narrow answer is that Mexican officials of the old regime lived in a different world from Mexico today, let alone a world of full democracy (if it ever existed). Those officials sometimes accomplished great good, sometimes wrought great harm, and should be understood in their own context, not against a contemporary backdrop.

The broad answer is that democracy and social movements matter greatly but never make elite politics disappear. Indeed, democracy itself rests on elite cooperation, on the American idea of a "loyal opposition"—a bargain promising political losers long-term survival in exchange for commitment to the political system. The famous "checks and balances" of the U.S. Constitution seek precisely to protect weaker political leaders, as well as to prevent impulsive policies. Even the original Constitution's terrible wrong of allowing slavery and granting Southern politicians three-fifths of a vote for every slave that whites owned was once necessary to secure allegiance to the tainted democracy of the day. When Southern politicians feared that they were politically doomed within the union—and it was they who decided, not social movements or poor white foot soldiers—the Civil War broke out. We, the people, have our interests, often ill defined, conflicting, and poorly represented. But even under the best of circumstances, our leaders define the political environment within which interests contend. They loose struggle or forge cooperation.

In 1986 the struggle for the Mexican presidency was heating up between Finance Secretary Jesús Silva Herzog and Planning and Budget Secretary Carlos Salinas. Both belonged to the ruling *Partido Revolucionario Institucional* (PRI), or Institutional Revolutionary Party. It was not a party in any ordinary sense but, in Mexico's strange political landscape, was indeed supposed to be the institutional embodiment of the 1910 Revolution. For most of the twentieth century, the PRI had always won those public relations events called elections, by fair means if possible, by foul if necessary. The fierce contest between rivals within the party for its official nomination therefore decided who would be the next president.

Silva Herzog was traveling the world as Washington's darling, advertising Mexico's economic correctness and embrace of U.S. economists' advice. This proved not the savviest political move back home. Salinas had a better idea how to build support where he needed it. Despite promises to hew to the International Monetary Fund (IMF) formula for budget austerity, he was surreptitiously financing some of the political elite's favorite projects.

For example, Silva Herzog noticed that an international airport, not in the budget, was being built in Piedras Negras, a town of less than 100,000 inhabitants along the Texas border. He phoned his rival's right-hand man at Planning and Budget, Manuel Camacho Solís: "Manuel, how can you have committed to that airport, when there isn't a single airplane that lands in Piedras Negras?" He recalls that Camacho Solís replied, "Señor secretary, we had terrible political pressure from the authorities there, and with this airport we've got them all on our side." Silva Herzog continues:

At about that time forty airports were built in Mexico, some without the least justification, but all the governors wanted them. There was Toluca, with a five-kilometer runway. At the inauguration, I asked the mayor, "Where are the planes?" "They'll come." Five years later!

In 1986, Jesús Silva Herzog (above) was locked in struggle with his opponent Carlos Salinas to be the Mexican ruling party's presidential candidate. As had so many presidential hopefuls in the past, Salinas used the public budget to buy support—according to Silva Herzog—but from other members of the political elite, not from the public. The public had nothing to do with selecting the party's nominee, who had automatically won the election for decades. Photo: Dante Bucio.

Millions of dollars were invested in an empty runway for five years. And Tlaxcala, where there still isn't a single commercial flight. We were buying political support for Carlos Salinas.[1]

Politicians are infamous for spending public funds to buy support. In democracies they try to buy votes. But often in democracies, and especially in authoritarian states, they must buy support within the political elite itself. This was the sort of politically motivated spending that mainly erupted under the former ruling party regime in Mexico. Presidential hopefuls, as well as incumbent presidents trying to strengthen their favorites' bid to succeed them, always wanted to secure as much support as possible within the highest reaches of the party for its internal nomination contest.

Political spending might be on anything—dams, roads, or schools— that made officials "shine," as it was said, in their particular arenas. Besides the government budget, there were other sources of funds, such as public enterprises that drilled for oil, generated electricity, built work-ers' housing, or invested in tourism. It was the Mexican government that transformed Cancun from a sleepy town into a resort. There were also dozens of public banks that lent money for equally diverse purposes. Foreign financing might be secured for projects, such as hospitals, that had income streams to repay the loans. When Carlos Salinas and other economist-politicians reached the top rungs of the party in the 1980s, they invented more clever techniques, such as inflating the securities market, to make themselves shine, for a critical political moment at least.

When political expenditures and other economic gambles designed to curry favor erupt on a massive scale, they can cause economic crises in any nation. Sometimes such spending did erupt under the old Mexican state, but other times the political system contained it within reasonable bounds and sustained a stable, healthy economy. Whether these pres-sures were or were not contained depended on the changing nature of elite politics. Elite politics at the heart of the Mexican state—a poli-tics played out among a small circle of high officials and not driven by broader societal factions—was for decades crucial to that nation's eco-nomic stability and material well-being.

In the 1950s and 1960s, "cooperation" within the Mexican political elite made it possible for the state to sustain economic stability. Com-peting *grupos*—cliques within the ruling party united mainly by career, educational, and family ties—abided by a live-and-let-live politics. The *grupo* whose leader secured the party's presidential nomination, and thus the general election, fared better in the next administration. But win-ners did not benefit to the exclusion of their rivals. Even losing *grupos* would survive—the defining characteristic of elite cooperation—as some prominent members retained high office, employed their followers, and contended for the presidency the next time around. The expectation of political survival forged a mutual interest in long-term success, not just narrow factional interests, allowing the Mexican state to repeatedly avert economic crises.

The resulting economic stability laid the foundation for the almost forgotten "Mexican miracle." Though repeated economic crises struck Latin American nations such as Argentina and Brazil during the 1950s and 1960s, Mexico's peso held stable. Its economy grew 6 percent, year in and year out, faster than the economic growth of any advanced nation over a sustained period, except for Japan and a few European countries reconstructing after World War II. In the wake of the 1968 Paris riots, the IMF used the Mexican peso as a part of a loan package to support the French franc. The peso held despite riots that fall in Mexico City; the franc fell. In the late 1960s, the IMF even used the Mexican peso to support the Canadian dollar and British pound.[2]

"Struggle" erupted within the Mexican political elite after 1970, sometimes causing and always contributing to economic crises that struck near the end of four successive administrations: in 1976, 1982, 1987, and 1994. Now the ruling party's internal contests over presidential succession turned all-or-nothing. As losing *grupos* increasingly feared being, and in fact were, expelled from politics—the defining characteristic of elite struggle—succession conflicts came to trump any longer-term concerns. When the presidential nomination approached in the fourth and fifth years of each six-year administration, rival *grupos* engaged in massive public spending, spending that far outran revenue, as well as other dangerous economic gambles, to buy support within the party for their leaders.[3] Once the PRI's official presidential candidate was selected, and the real transfer of power was no longer in dispute, everybody suddenly regained sense. In the sixth and final year of each administration, when elections were held, public spending was slashed and other harsh measures were taken to stabilize the economy. It was always too late.

Now the nation that had been an emblem of economic success became an emblem of economic disaster. Mexico's terrible 1982 crisis initiated the wave of crises that spread across Latin America in the "lost decade," a period worse than the Great Depression for much of that continent. Just as Mexico seemed to be recovering in the early 1990s, another collapse of the peso in December 1994 presaged a new generation of crises that struck across East Asia, as well as in Russia, Brazil, Argentina, and other countries.

Palace Politics tells the story, writ large, of elite politics and its consequences in one nation in one era. Based on extensive interviews with former presidents, finance secretaries, interior secretaries, and other high officials, it focuses on the old Mexican state. The story starts with the regime's prime in the 1950s and 1960s. A cooperative elite politics maintained economic stability, laying the basis for broad economic success. The story continues as the regime deteriorated in later decades. Struggle within the political elite caused some of the economic crises that erupted after 1970 and contributed to all of them, impoverishing the nation and ultimately bringing the regime itself down.

Elite politics mattered more in Mexico in that era than in most nations at most times, but *Palace Politics* makes a general point, too. No matter how deeply one looks within the state, one cannot find some inner core exempt from politics, some unitary leviathan that need only manage its external relations with society. On the contrary, the heart of the state has its own internal politics, its cliques that are not mere reflections of external societal constituencies but have important mutual relationships. Indeed, societal interests tend to endure and reassemble, while elite factions survive or die politically.

Even in democracies, if all-or-nothing struggle erupts among factions of the political elite, and potential losers fear for their very survival, longer-term considerations come in a distant second. A politics of elite struggle can plunge a nation into economic crisis and threaten the government's ability to sustain any sensible policies at all. Conversely, a cooperative elite politics, when competing factions expect to survive even though they lose a particular succession contest, forges a common interest in the nation's longer-term prospects. It helps sustain economic stability and generally more sensible policies.

THE ECONOMICS OF CRISES

Palace Politics is driven by a two-part question: what were the political causes of economic crisis and what were the political requisites of economic stability—avoiding crisis over a sustained period—in Mexico during the second half of the twentieth century? The best place to start is a look at what economic crises are and why they matter.

Consider an example. In the crisis that erupted in Mexico in December 1994, the peso plunged to half its previous worth. The dollar value of everyone's bank account thus sank by half. As always, precipitous devaluation ignited inflation. The reason was that essential imports, ranging from semiconductors for computers to corn for tortillas—Mexico was not self-sufficient in basic grains—now cost twice as many pesos, so firms that purchased these goods from abroad had to double the prices they charged consumers. Mexicans' spending power plummeted as price increases outpaced wages, in a cycle that continued for years after the crash. The worst increases were in basic necessities that hit the working class and poor hardest. For example, in late 1996 wages increased 15 percent, as agreed in a government-business-labor pact to control inflation, but prices rose faster. The Mexico City Metro fare went up 30 percent, and fares on the ubiquitous microbuses went up 25 to 50 percent, depending on the distance traveled. Just traveling to and from work could eat up a quarter of the daily minimum wage. Though industrial export sectors such as autos and machinery boomed, by 2000 the real

When economic crises strike developing nations, people's bank accounts lose value, the purchasing power of wages plummets, and interest rates soar. After the 1994 Mexican crisis, a debtor's movement known as El Barzón protested interest rates on mortgages and other loans that rose to more than 100 percent. The slogan on the martyred peasant says "Land and Liberty," the cry of the Mexican Revolution. Photo: Arturo López.

minimum wage was still only half what it had been before the 1994 crisis.[4]

The banks, which prior to the crisis had adopted the brilliant strategy of taking out low-interest foreign loans and relending the money at higher rates in Mexico,[5] now needed twice as many pesos to service their foreign loans. Facing that problem and soaring inflation, they raised interest rates to astronomical heights, for example, driving mortgages, all variable-rate at that time, to more than 100 percent a year. Of course, no one who could pay 100 percent interest would have mortgaged a house in the first place. Some homeowners committed suicide. Most realized that it took a bank years to foreclose under Mexican law, and the owner had a right to buy the house back at auction, so they just defaulted. So did many other borrowers; in fact, a defaulters' movement took shape. The banking system failed. Bailing it out cost Mexican taxpayers 100 billion U.S. dollars.

An economic crisis is an uncontrolled crash in the value of a nation's currency, a plunge in the exchange rate against the dollar (or other hard currency).[6] Although economists generally do not distinguish between an uncontrolled crash and a planned devaluation—they just gauge the percentage by which the value of the currency falls[7]—there is a difference. A planned devaluation, when financial authorities decide the local currency needs to exchange for fewer U.S. cents and make the new parity stick, can be harsh indeed. But there is a political difference between one government that makes a tough economic decision and another that cedes the decision, willy-nilly, to currency speculators. And there is an economic difference, too. In Mexico, a traumatic but successful planned devaluation in 1954 that laid the foundation for two decades of stable and rapid growth has never been called a crisis. The botched attempt to devalue in December 1994, which collapsed in an uncontrolled crash, has always been called a crisis. A planned devaluation is a painful measure to stabilize an economy. A currency crash, which like any financial crash exceeds all warranted bounds, is an economic crisis.

For all the diversity of economic crises, their basic mechanics share important commonalities. No matter what other causes are also involved—and a number usually are—financial panic drives the crisis per se. Although accounts of this mechanism, notably the late MIT economist Charles P. Kindleberger's *Manias, Panics, and Crashes*, are nothing new, and the phenomenon itself is as old as capitalism, only in the 1990s did economists develop formal models to show how self-reinforcing financial panic can cause an exchange rate crisis, even if nothing is fundamentally wrong with a nation's economy.[8]

A crisis that strikes a nation because of pure panic is analogous to a run on a bank that is solvent, in that it has sufficient income to pay depositors in the long term, but is illiquid, in that it cannot pay them all tomorrow.[9] Actually, all banks are illiquid in this sense. Banks accept short-term deposits, in checking and savings accounts, and issue long-term loans such as mortgages. Since they cannot call those loans if there is a run, they would continually risk collapse did not the Federal Reserve (or some other central bank) stand behind them as a lender of last resort. The Fed can always rescue the U.S. banking system because it has the authority to print dollars.

In effect, developing nations have no lender of last resort. Of course, their central banks can act as lenders of last resort for domestic debts in their own currencies, but not for public or private debts in hard currencies, which can run into the hundreds of billions of dollars. They do not have access to unlimited dollars. The IMF sometimes lends a certain amount of hard currency if a nation agrees during negotiations to accept a string of "conditionalities," as they are called. To stop a run, however, a lender of last resort must lend immediately and unconditionally.

In such a precarious situation, panic can cause an economic crisis. Because of some impetus, rational or irrational, a core of speculators starts selling stocks or bonds denominated in pesos (or other local currency) and turning their pesos in for dollars (or other hard currency) at commercial banks. The banks exchange their pesos for dollars at the central bank, and its dollar reserves decline. If the decline starts to look serious, other speculators will quite rationally fear that the central bank may soon run out of reserves—as in any run, whether the nation would be solvent in the long run is irrelevant—so they demand dollars. Panic builds on panic, and the central bank does run out. Now anyone who wants to trade pesos for dollars must go to international money markets, which will give a rock-bottom exchange rate. The peso has crashed.

Purely political shocks can provoke panic and economic crisis. For example, when Mexican President Adolfo López Mateos declared in 1960, shortly after the Cuban Revolution, that his was a government "of the extreme left within the Constitution," he meant to placate leftists who supported Fidel Castro and, at the same time, calm the private sector by promising no constitutional change. But the private sector, hardly reassured by fine points about a rather malleable Constitution, published a broadside demanding to know "which road" the president was on, capitalism or socialism. Some $200 million of capital fled the country. The Harvard economist Raymond Vernon, in Mexico at the time, said economic crisis was barely averted.[10] Helped by a loan from the U.S. Export-Import Bank, the government spent months restoring business confidence.

In today's world, where speculative capital surges across borders—such flows dwarf trade, approaching 10 percent of the world's annual output every day[11]—footloose finance can cause crises. The Asia crisis of the late 1990s has been blamed (though not by all economists) on international financial panic. As Steven Radelet and Jeffrey Sachs write, "International financial markets demonstrate a high degree of intrinsic instability, or to put things another way, the East Asian crisis is as much a crisis of Western capitalism as Asian capitalism."[12] The idea is that a crisis erupted in Thailand, which arguably did have some underlying economic problems,[13] but then nervous investors fled other essentially sound economies just because they were nearby. This panic wrought enormous damage: Indonesia's crisis was perhaps the worst anywhere since the Great Depression.

Because unstable international financial markets can allow economic crises to occur, a better global financial architecture could help prevent them.[14] Economist Barry Eichengreen, who has written extensively on the topic, notes that there is no shortage of such proposals: "The French government has one, the German government has one, the Canadian government has one, the US government has one,"[15] as do the IMF, the Group of Eight industrial nations, and Barry Eichengreen. Proposals include better financial regulation and "transparency," controls to reduce capital flight—panic-driven capital flight is so dangerous that merely slowing it may actually prevent a crisis—and a global lender of last resort. Though regulation and transparency rarely get attention until after crises erupt, capital controls are opposed by financial interests, and a global lender of last resort is nowhere in sight, these proposals could make a real difference if they were implemented. The international financial architecture adopted by the allied powers in Bretton Woods, New Hampshire, in 1944, sustained unusual stability in the 1950s and 1960s. Since the erosion of the Bretton Woods system in the early 1970s, world growth rates have fallen by at least a third.[16]

However, global financial architecture is a limited instrument. Neither Bretton Woods nor the pre–World War I gold standard, the most successful such architectures, was able to prevent repeated crises in developing nations. Though there were none in Mexico in the 1950s and 1960s, failed efforts to stabilize the economy in Argentina ended in four military coups (against Juan Perón in 1955, Arturo Frondizi in 1962, Arturo Illia in 1966, and Juan Carlos Onganía in 1970) and, in Brazil, such failures culminated in a president's suicide (Getúlio Vargas in 1954), another's resignation (Jânio Quadros in 1961), and a military coup (against João Goulart in 1964). Conversely, Mexico erupted in crisis in 1982 even though its oil revenues cushioned it from the worst economic shock (they continued to soar despite a modest price dip), while South Korea, an oil importer hit by powerful external shock, avoided crisis.[17]

Crises tend to strike nations that have adopted dangerous macroeconomic policies, falling into a "zone of vulnerability," as Eichengreen puts it.[18] This unhappy condition comes in variations, but the textbook case arises when governments find it convenient to spend substantially more than they collect in revenue. To cover the shortfall, they may "print" money. In part, they literally print bills. More important, they abuse their power to write checks on their accounts at the central bank in amounts exceeding their deposits. As a result, the quantity of money in circulation grows rather faster than the quantity of goods. When the money supply, the monetary promise to people that they can purchase output, vastly outstrips the actual capacity to produce output, the disparity will somehow be closed. Inflation is the typical way to break the promise: people get the money—paper wages, paper profits—but its value erodes, so they do not get the goods.[19]

Moderate inflation is not a mortal problem, but it can lead to one: overvaluation. The route from inflation to overvaluation was the same in Mexico during the era discussed here as in many other underdeveloped countries. The Bank of Mexico pegged the peso to the dollar, promising to exchange the two currencies at a fixed rate, or at least within some narrow band. Anchoring the local currency this way helps sustain investment. Firms can plan how many pesos they need to import capital equipment or industrial inputs; savers know what interest they will receive on domestic bonds compared with foreign bonds.

But trouble arises if prices of domestically made goods rise because of inflation, while the pegged exchange rate holds prices of imports steady. Perhaps the price of Tehuacán mineral water from Mexico rises from 3 to 5 pesos, but a relatively fixed exchange rate against the euro keeps the price of Perrier at 4 pesos. Everyone now gets a better deal by buying imports than domestic goods. As one former finance secretary is said to have joked, dead seriously, the overvaluation of the peso can be gauged by the length of the line to cross the border in Tijuana and shop in the United States. If it is half an hour, the exchange rate is fine; if it is two hours, the peso is overvalued; if it is three hours, economic crisis is imminent.[20]

As the peso becomes overvalued, and Mexican firms stock up on imports, they must exchange their pesos for dollars or other hard currency at banks. Banks exchange their pesos for dollars at the Bank of Mexico, and its reserves dwindle. At some point, panic strikes. Speculators fear that the Bank of Mexico will run out of reserves, so they turn torrents of pesos in for dollars to stash in Miami or Switzerland. When they thus attack the peso, the Bank of Mexico's hard currency reserves really plummet. Before long it can, indeed, no longer secure dollars to continue exchanging for pesos. The peso crashes.

External economic shocks, as surely as dangerous domestic macroeconomic policies, can lead to crises. When the U.S. Federal Reserve precipitously doubled or tripled interest rates in 1979 to attack inflation, the effects swept across the developing world. As if a credit card company had suddenly decided to jack up interest rates, those nations' external debt payments, which had often been reasonable, became unsupportable, and they hemorrhaged dollars. Likewise, if the world price of a poor nation's major export—perhaps oil, coffee, or some other commodity—plunges, it will be squeezed for hard currency and may succumb to economic crisis.

Debates about the economic causes of crises do not center so much on which generic mechanisms can produce them as on which mechanism contributed most in any given case.[21] Each culprit carries a political agenda. Speculative panic racing across borders indicts an inadequate international financial architecture, hence financial interests of advanced nations that resist strengthening it. Specific external shocks may be caused by obvious actors such as the Federal Reserve. When national governments massively overspend, domestic politicians may be at fault. Everyone can usually find someone else to blame. For example, many charged that the IMF caused the Asia crisis by pushing financial deregulation too fast, but the IMF pointed to Asian nations' own inadequate financial supervision.[22] When domestic financial bubbles burst, the resulting panic can erupt into exchange rate crises as speculators flee the currency.

THE POLITICS OF CRISES

When crises do result from national governments' dangerous macroeconomic policies, what are the ultimate political causes? Those who study the matter—political scientists, economists stepping into political economy, and (it should be said) many Mexican intellectuals—tend to discover powerful socioeconomic forces at work. What else, they seem to suppose, could possibly cause such powerful socioeconomic disasters as crises?

The idea is that governments face "distributive" conflicts. Business lobbies, middle-class groups, and public sector unions (the most important unions in many developing countries, including Mexico) press the state for more subsidies, stronger social welfare programs, and higher wages. Even in the absence of explicit demands, politicians know they can boost their popularity by overspending all around.[23] As well, underlying "structural" industrial problems—excessive protectionism and inefficient state-owned enterprises—are said to cause spending pressures. Because of these problems, the argument goes, growth stagnates, and interest groups protest their eroding economic fortunes. Politicians then overspend to persuade everyone that things are okay. The resulting budget deficits, inflation, and overvaluation cause a crisis.

Why do some political systems have the capacity to resist such distributive pressures while others succumb? One line of thought looks at institutions to manage social conflict. A popular argument is that democracy works best. The economist Dani Rodrik argues that "democratic institutions are the institutions of conflict management par excellence."[24] Democracy provided the foundation allowing some nations to weather the Asia crisis better than others, he says. Among other things, it "imposed mechanisms of participation, consultation, and bargaining, enabling policymakers to fashion the consensus needed to undertake the necessary policy adjustments decisively."

Oddly, until the 1990s—the fall of the Eastern Bloc seemed to mark a shift in attitude—the usual thinking was that democracy destabilizes economies by giving voice to distributive conflict.[25] While not entirely subscribing to the thesis, Stephan Haggard, a political scientist, sums it up: "Distributional coalitions flourish in democracies; only strong states can tame them."[26] Certainly, many seeming democracies—Chile before its 1973 military coup, Russia in the 1990s—have plunged into economic crisis, while many authoritarian states—South Korea in the 1970s and 1980s, Mexico in the 1950s and 1960s—have sustained economic stability.

Democracy is simply too broad a category to be useful here, but particular types of democratic institutions may, indeed, do a better job of resolving distributive conflict. In the 1970s, when the tug and pull of American pluralism was thought to cause inflation, the "democratic corporatism" of nations such as Sweden, Norway, or Denmark, where encompassing "peak associations" represented labor and business in centralized bargaining, was seen as the successful way to manage conflict in general and avoid economic crises in particular.[27] Such peak associations, it is thought, understand their broad responsibility for economic success. Labor and business are likely to agree to real wage increases in line with productivity growth, so monetary promises of output rise with real output. Conversely, multiple competing unions and interest groups that vie to boost wages, profits, welfare, and subsidies are seen as exerting powerful distributive pressures. No particular wage bargain or business subsidy has discernible effect on the national economy, so no one group cares much, or even can do much. Leaders that win smaller benefits are just blamed as ineffective.

Because corporatism channels societal pressures through centralized associations likely to be unresponsive to members, it may improve governability at some sacrifice of democratic norms of citizen participation.[28] Indeed, several authoritarian Latin American nations have been seen as organized along "state corporatist" lines, legally requiring societal groups to be incorporated under the aegis of the state.[29] In particular, the Mexican Workers Federation, National Peasants Federation, and National Federation of Popular Organizations (the last including middle-class and professional associations), official sectors of the ruling party founded in the late 1930s, are widely thought to have improved the government's ability to control distributive conflicts and sustain more stable macroeconomic policies.[30]

In short, it is not always necessary to resolve conflicts: quashing them can work, too. South Korea, hit in the early 1980s by severe external shocks as oil prices and interest rates soared, took harsh measures. The state slashed government spending, fired large numbers of public sector workers, eliminated farming subsidies, broke national unions, cut real manufacturing wages 10 percent, and, in case anyone objected, jailed its political opponents.[31]

Thus the other line of thought about the politics of macroeconomic stability: even if political institutions do not in any real sense resolve distributive conflicts, is the state "autonomous" enough to suppress them?[32] Strong authoritarian governments that can "establish dominant party systems"—the Mexican PRI being a prime example—or "proscribe electoral politics entirely over extended periods of time" are better at maintaining stability, Stephan Haggard and Robert R. Kaufman argue.[33] A degree of autonomy can be built into democratic political systems, too. Hence economists' perennial call for central banks to be politically independent so they can resist inflation.

THE CASE OF MEXICO

These approaches to understanding the politics of economic crisis make sense for many countries at many times, but they miss a crucial piece of the picture for other countries at other times—in particular, for Mexico in the second half of the twentieth century. Why was it so stable in the decades before 1970, and why did it suffer repeated crises afterward?

Many would argue that changes in the international financial architecture caused this stark reversal in Mexico's economy, an idea that seems quite sensible at first glance. The workable Bretton Woods system, which supported the fastest growth capitalism has ever known in the post–World War II era, might have helped sustain Mexico's stability in the 1950s and 1960s. Its demise circa 1970, as financial speculation increasingly surged across borders, might account for Mexico's crises in 1976, 1982, 1987, and 1994.

Graph 1.1: Stability of Mexican peso, 1950-70

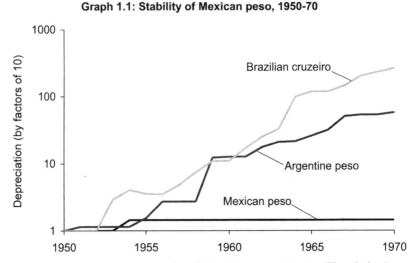

The Mexican economy was unusually stable in the 1950s and 1960s. Though the Argentine and Brazilian currencies repeatedly sank in value, the peso held stable except for one planned devaluation in 1954. Data: Skidmore 1977, 159.

But the closer one looks at Mexico, the less this explanation works. Poor nations have always suffered economic crises, even under Bretton Woods. Why did the Mexican peso hold steady during the 1950s and 1960s, while, for example, the Argentine peso and Brazilian cruzeiro sank to about a hundredth of their initial values (Graph 1.1)? The international economic system alone cannot explain the difference.

What is more, the Mexican peso was stable in the 1950s and 1960s despite unusual, arguably unique, vulnerability to crisis. The peso was freely convertible to the dollar, and the government never controlled financial flows, even during the Bretton Woods era when most advanced nations such as France and Germany, let alone nearly every other underdeveloped nation, did control them. The reasons why Mexico allowed free financial flows are debatable, but it did.[34] The country therefore always faced dangers of capital flight that have worsened across the rest of the world since the 1970s. Ernesto Fernández Hurtado, a Bank of Mexico official since the 1940s and its director from 1970 to 1976, says of the period before 1970, "Any international crisis or internal crisis of confidence could affect us. We had to manage the economy with exquisite care."

Only the Mexican government's deft action averted half a dozen crises that could have erupted in the 1950s and 1960s. Sometimes external economic pressures could have caused crises. In the early 1950s, Mexican exports to the United States mushroomed 20 percent a year to supply the Korean War effort, then plummeted as the war ended. This reversal, along with others, such as poor cotton exports—Mexico's petroleum of the 1950s—drained hard currency reserves. Reserves fell by $42 million in 1953, then $43 million in just the first quarter of 1954—serious numbers for Mexico at that time. Finance Minister Antonio Carrillo Flores became convinced that if he did not act, the economy was headed straight for crisis. He carried out a successful devaluation, and the president rallied the force of the state behind him. The interior minister controlled political protests; the labor minister held wage increases to almost trivial levels. The economy stabilized and prospered.

Other times Mexican social protests could have caused financial flight and economic crisis had the government not controlled them. In 1958, the most powerful Mexican grassroots movement since the 1930s erupted. Waves of wildcat strikes by railroad and other public sector workers across the nation brought the transport system to a halt just as presidential elections were approaching. After negotiating and granting selective concessions for the better part of a year, the state finally resorted to massive repression, jailing 10,000 workers and firing 20,000. But however ugly its tactics, it acted in unison to avert economic crisis and sustain buoyant growth.

International economic forces no more caused Mexico's crises after 1970 than its earlier stability. The government's own bungling brought on crisis during these years, even as its agile management had sustained earlier stability. Theories abound about the causes of the 1976 and 1982 crises—structural "exhaustion" of the industrial model, the government's overspending to buy political "legitimacy" after repressing anti-authoritarian protests in 1968, irresponsible "populist" politicians—but they accuse internal culprits.[35]

Though external economic pressures, notably the Federal Reserve's precipitous 1979 interest rate increase and falling prices of commodity exports, were important causes of crises that spread across many Latin American nations in 1982,[36] Mexico enjoyed a uniquely favored position. Between the late 1970s and the mid-1980s, thanks to recently discovered oil fields, the real purchasing power of its exports increased 11 percent a year, a good fortune not even remotely approached by any other Latin country.[37] Mexico was not caught with dangerous debt levels when the Fed ratcheted up interest rates in 1979: it only took on dangerous debt levels in 1981[38]—despite the fact that its oil export revenues climbed almost 50 percent that year alone. And Mexico's 1982 crisis could hardly have been caused by financial contagion from other countries because its crisis was the first.

In the late 1980s and early 1990s, Carlos Salinas and his *técnicos*, as Mexicans called his team of economist-politicians, used more sophisticated tactics to push the economy toward crisis. Even under the IMF's watchful but naïve eyes, they managed to deploy public spending to political advantage—in many ways, as Silva Herzog noticed, including the building of airports—as well as distributing huge, less visible public bank loans. They also invented dangerous new gambits, such as inflating the stock market 500 percent in the nine months leading up to the PRI's 1987 presidential nomination. Two days after Salinas won that nomination, a Mexican market crash started. Two weeks later, the October 1987 U.S. stock market crash further shook Mexico's economy. This external shock contributed destructive momentum to the peso crisis in November, but Mexican politics had set the peso up for crisis.

In the early 1990s, now as president, Salinas and his *técnicos* devised yet more clever macroeconomic schemes. They privatized government banks, protecting them from foreign competition (one of the many anomalies in the North American Free Trade Agreement) while leaving them almost free from domestic regulation. On the one hand, this juicy sale won private sector support as business conglomerates grabbed the banks; on the other hand, it yielded Salinas $12 billion to fund Solidarity, an anti-poverty program with 70,000 offices across Mexico designed to construct his own party machine. The newly private banks expanded their loans at the blazing rate of 35 percent per year, as middle-class Mexicans charged up their credit cards in the so-called "home appliance boom." Salinas' *técnicos* also overvalued the peso by virtually the same amount as protectionist politicians of the past, yet again encouraging Mexico to live beyond its means. And all the while, the *técnicos* garnered cheers from the IMF, the U.S. Treasury, and the business press—until the nation sank in crisis in December 1994.

Why did Mexican politicians repeatedly gamble so desperately after 1970, and why did they manage the economy so sensibly before 1970? The usual answers point to underlying socioeconomic forces. It is argued that, as socioeconomic development gave interest groups and labor unions more clout to assert distributive demands, the Mexican state lost its powerful grip on society in about 1970. Then, after anti-authoritarian protests in Mexico City in 1968 were ended by the slaughter of perhaps hundreds of demonstrators in Tlatelolco Square (the numbers are still not known), the government is said to have overspent to buy back political "legitimacy." Or it is argued that the protectionist economic regime suffered from structural industrial failure by 1970, and subsequent administrations overspent in a desperate effort to inflate growth.

These arguments are wrong. Pressures on the Mexican state after 1970, to the extent that they existed at all, did not cause economic crises. Indeed, external societal demands on the state were in many ways stronger during the 1950s and 1960s. Academics just started studying them after 1970. If there was one moment when the Mexican ruling party nearly lost its grip on society—and should have been vulnerable to crisis, according to the usual thinking—it was the powerful grassroots strike wave in 1958 and 1959. But there was no crisis; those events only ushered in a period of remarkable stability and growth. The so-called "labor insurgency" of the early 1970s was a feeble echo of the 1958–59 strike wave. It was manipulated by none other than President Luis Echeverría. He tried to help several unions break free from the ruling party's labor apparatus—in an effort to oust long-time labor boss Fidel Velázquez and thus gain direct control over the unions. When Echeverría decided he needed Velázquez after all, the supine "labor insurgency" collapsed. But economic crisis erupted in 1976.

After 1970, as earlier, the PRI continued to literally incorporate within itself, and control, the most important social organizations, from workers to peasants, architects to economists. It won national elections by landslides. True, the vote count was corrupt, but it would have won anyway. Besides, civil society was so thoroughly manipulated that, until the late 1980s, it was incapable of even protesting electoral corruption. In 1982, just after the presidential election, as economic crisis struck, *The Economist* noted:

> Even though [President-elect Miguel] de la Madrid faced six opposition candidates in the July [1982] election, none of them looked credible. . . . The urban middle classes voted en masse for the conservative National Action party; even so, it won only 14% of the vote. The left-wing parties did even worse. . . . [T]he government so thoroughly dominates the Confederation of Mexican Workers and the National Peasant Confederation that they are ineffective lightning rods of dissent.[39]

The PRI did suffer an electoral debacle in 1988 when an opposition movement, the Democratic Front, nearly won the presidential election, or perhaps won it but for electoral fraud. But that debacle, not even

*For decades, the Mexican ruling party won national elections without any real
contest. One reason was that it incorporated within itself the most important social
organizations—whether groups of workers or peasants, architects or economists.
Fidel Velázquez led the party's principal labor union federation from 1940
until his death in 1997.*

envisioned by party leaders until the very night the vote came in, could hardly have caused the 1987 crisis the previous fall. Moreover, like the "labor insurgency," the Democratic Front resulted from a power struggle within the PRI itself: an older generation of left-leaning politicians, after being exiled from the ruling party by Salinas' younger generation of *técnicos*, broke off and launched the opposition campaign. Once Salinas became president, he gained huge popularity and repaired much of the damage. In the early 1990s, Haggard and Kaufman still maintained, the Mexican state remained the type of dominant-party system "conducive to stable macroeconomic policy." [40]

Though Mexico's essential change in about 1970 had little to do with relations between state and society, it had everything to do with relations among *grupos* at the heart of the state. Indeed, much discussion of Mexican politics, from a body of academic work [41] to the newspapers to street gossip, has placed *grupos* squarely at center stage. Scholars often use the term *camarilla*, but it connotes more nearly a mafia than a political group, [42] so *grupo*, the everyday Mexican word used by politicians themselves, journalists, and taxicab drivers, seems preferable. If *grupos* were central to political power struggles, why not also to economic policymaking?

A few authors say they were. In *Democracy within Reason*, the U.S. political scientist Miguel Angel Centeno argues that the ascent of Carlos Salinas' powerful, cohesive *grupo* within the PRI was the reason the state could transform the economic regime from protectionist to free-market almost overnight. Starting his essential story in about 1970 and ending in the early 1990s, Centeno paints Salinas' *grupo* as a successful engine of policy transformation. He omits its collapse in political and economic crisis in 1994 because that crisis had not erupted when he was writing. Jorge Castañeda, a Mexican intellectual and former foreign minister, tells in many ways an opposite story in his fascinating *La Herencia* (*The Inheritance*), which details how Mexican presidents were chosen from 1970 through 1994. His is a story of the state's deepening failure, as the self-destroying machine of *grupo* struggle inexorably brought the regime down.

Both these accounts have important elements of truth, but both are oddly static in opposite ways. Because they begin in about 1970, neither discovers fundamental changes in elite politics, quite why it worked, or quite why it failed. *Palace Politics* does. It looks for fundamental change in *grupo* politics by starting in the 1950s and 1960s, when the ruling party system worked and worked well, if undemocratically, and then watching that politics deteriorate through succeeding decades. The state within which *grupos* contended for power, in some real measure, continued to dominate Mexican society, but internally it slowly broke apart. The important question was how *grupos* managed or failed to manage their mutual conflicts: whether they resolved them through elite cooperation or elite struggle.

For most of the twentieth century the Mexican ruling party seemed eternal. Elections came and went, but they did not determine political succession because the PRI always won. It controlled the presidency, the Congress, and the courts. It did not even lose an important state office until 1988. The ruling party was the arena within which the real contest over political succession occurred.

If the Mexican state had been different—if it had been like almost any other twentieth-century state—elite politics at the heart of it would still have mattered, but might not have been so decisive or stood out so vividly. A clear picture of this former state is therefore essential.

Many Mexican scholars have drawn this picture, differing only in details. The main thing some have missed is how strange it looks if viewed afresh. It must seem strange even to those who played roles within it. Mexicans are, arguably, a revolutionary people: since Spanish rule, Mexico has seen three full-scale revolutions and more lesser uprisings than could reliably be counted.[1] Labor insurgency for democratic governance has repeatedly erupted despite terrible costs: death, jail, impoverishment. Peasants have repeatedly invaded private estates to claim some land, also sometimes at terrible cost.

Against this backdrop, how did the ruling party incorporate within itself and control major social organizations? How were political elites forged? How did *grupos* of political elites emerge as an essential political structure in a state where few formal rules counted for much? How did the president come to stand atop a virtual Aztec pyramid of power?

CENTRALIZATION OF POWER

The Mexican president for his six-year term, and the national bureaucracy directly under him, virtually were the government. Though called the ruling party, the PRI per se—its National Executive Committee and the rest of its apparatus—had no independent power. As Octavio Paz wrote in a 1985 essay, it gave "blind obedience to each president in turn. . . . The party has not produced a single idea, not a single program, in [all its] years of existence!" The corporatist sectors—labor unions, peasant associations, and even middle-class groups such as the College of Architects, all legally incorporated in the party—were also dominated by the president and bureaucracy and had as their mission "the control and manipulation of the people." As for the Senate and Chamber of Deputies, they "have been, and still are, two groups of chatterers and flatterers who never offer any criticism whatsoever; . . . the judicial power is mute and impotent; . . . freedom of the press is more a formality than a reality."[2]

No serious observer disputes how centralized the old Mexican state was.[3] Even if revisionist scholars question the conventional account as to how the central bureaucracy dominated society, they do not question that it did. For example, Jeffrey W. Rubin writes that "while social scientists in the 1970s were right to characterize the post-revolutionary Mexican regime as authoritarian and hegemonic, they were wrong about the nature of that hegemony." There was no single "triumph of state building."[4] In studying Mexicans' struggle to defend grassroots interests rather than be manipulated by the state, Jonathan Fox notes that, even as late as the 1990s, the overall system remained "still largely dominated by an authoritarian corporatist brand of machine politics."[5]

Two historical legacies begin to explain why the Mexican state was able to concentrate so much power in the national administration and president. First, although all Latin America experienced centralized Spanish rule, in Mexico it overlaid a centralized Aztec empire. The Mexican president's authority has rested in part on "the Aztec archetype of political power: the *tlatoani*, or ruler, the pyramid," to quote Paz again. "The *tlatoani* is impersonal, priestly, and institutional—hence the abstract figure of the president corresponds to a bureaucratic and hierarchic corporation like the Institutional Revolutionary Party. . . . The president is the Party during his six-year term; but, when it ends, another president appears, and is only another incarnation of the Party."[6] (The "party," in this sense, is a common but somewhat confusing shorthand for the entire political system, not the subordinate electoral apparatus.)

The second historical legacy was the 1910 Revolution—always with a capital "R"—bequeathing, on the one hand, broadly shared ideals, and, on the other, deep-seated fears of societal violence. Wayne A. Cornelius and Ann L. Craig write:

A residue of the widespread violence of [the 1910 Revolution and its aftermath], which killed one of every seven Mexicans, is a general fear

Burying the dead, Mexicans never forgot the pervasive violence of the 1910 Revolu-tion. Deep-seated fears that political contest might again erupt in violence helped persuade the political elite and citizenry alike to accept presidential authority. Photo: W. H. Horne (Library of Congress).

of civil disorder and uncontrolled mass mobilization. The prospect of another wholesale disintegration of the social and political order is viewed with alarm not just by Mexico's elites but also by a majority of the poor. Their personal economic risks in a period of protracted political violence would be much greater than those of the elite.

An even more important legacy of the 1910 to 1940 period was the symbolic capital that accrued from events and public policies pursued during those years: the Revolution itself; the radically worded Con-stitution of 1917; the labor and agrarian reforms of [President Lázaro Cárdenas in the 1930s]; and Cárdenas' expropriation of foreign oil companies in 1938.[7]

A 1963 survey of political culture in several democracies (a category to which many political scientists at the time imagined Mexico belonged) discovered a dichotomy that every subsequent study on the matter con-firmed: Mexicans' pride in their national political institutions coupled with cynicism about their government's actual performance.[8] Faith in the Revolution and the president endured despite a bureaucracy that was often arbitrary and corrupt, at least on the lower levels that interacted with the population. Asked to respond in 1969 to the statement that "the individual owes first loyalty to the state and only secondarily to his personal welfare," an astounding 92 percent of Mexicans agreed; of all other nationalities surveyed, Italians were second likely to agree, at 48 percent.[9]

The violence of the Revolution also helped persuade the political elite to accept presidential authority. In extensive interviews with high officials of the 1950s and 1960s, Roderic Camp found their "most striking universal belief" to be an "emphasis on peace and order."[10] If they had not participated in the Revolution itself, they had seen firsthand how its violence had engulfed Mexico. As one said:

> I helped my father take pictures of men who were to be executed by the various sides during the revolutionary period. As a young boy, I saw and talked to men who were brave, melancholy, or crying just before they were killed. I also helped my father . . . pick up the dead men in the streets after an engagement by opposing forces. All of this made a lasting and profound impression on me, and is something I would never want my children to witness.[11]

Even after the Revolution, really a civil war among shifting factions, officially ended in 1920, democracy did not bring peace and order. Elections were always followed by revolts, and losers were executed. The ballot box failed as a real means to decide political contests, instead serving only as the first step toward more violence.

Forging a dominant party was a strategy to shape a workable political system under these circumstances. In 1929, President Plutarco Elías Calles brought together the factions that would join one ruling party and defeated in battle those that would not. A president presiding over a centralized political system served as a practical alternative to democracy. Pablo González Casanova, whose *Democracy in Mexico* eloquently indicted the authoritarian state, carefully qualified himself by noting that trying to apply democracy after the Revolution would have been "senseless"; it would only have meant "respect for the conspiracies of a semi-feudal society."[12]

The state that emerged from the Revolution fought under the banner of democracy, but in a society unprepared for democracy, looked one way on paper but worked another. According to José Andrés de Oteyza, former state industries secretary, "The PRI was called a political party, but it wasn't a political party, it was a whole political system. It is said that there were three powers, but there was only one. The system was called federal, but it was centralized."

On paper, the Mexican Constitution of 1917 derives from the U.S. Constitution, resting sovereignty in the people; dividing power among executive, judiciary, and legislative branches; and providing for checks and balances.[13] Indeed, under Vicente Fox's administration from 2000 to 2006, the first time one party did *not* control all branches of government since 1929, those provisions turned out to matter. The checks and balances even began to edge perilously close to stalemate. But as long as the PRI dominated the state, the executive was in firm control. On entering office, presidents would use their overwhelming majority in Congress to pass a flurry of constitutional amendments, adding up to several hundred over the course of seventy years.[14]

Some of the president's power was de jure. The Constitution and laws gave him control over the executive branch and state-owned enterprises.[15] He could appoint and dismiss, without congressional approval, all cabinet secretaries, from Finance and Interior to Justice and Tourism, as well as the governor of Mexico City.[16] He had equal power over state enterprises: the oil company Pemex and electric utilities; railroads, airlines, and telecommunications; industrial giants from steel mills to chemical plants. As President Miguel de la Madrid wrote, cabinet secretaries and directors of state enterprises, along with everyone under them, were mere "auxiliary collaborators dependent on the unique office-holder, the president."[17] Victor Urquidi, advisor to the finance secretary in the 1950s and 1960s and president of the Colegio de Mexico for two decades, wryly notes: "The MacArthur Foundation once asked me how to develop a program that would interest policymakers in Mexico. I said, 'There's only one policymaker in Mexico. He's the president.'"

Even more important were the president's extra-constitutional powers as de facto head of the ruling party. He dominated it, and it dominated Mexican politics. As de la Madrid wrote, "Even though the party has its own bosses, it recognizes the incumbent president of Mexico as its highest leader."[18] Fernando Solana, a former professor of political science who held four posts as cabinet secretary, broke off an interview to correct the misusage (the same that Paz committed) of referring to the regime itself as the PRI: "The PRI was not important. I never was in the PRI. The correct term is the political system." The PRI's National Executive Committee was appointed and dismissed by the president, and its financing came from the Interior Ministry.[19] Legal authority to certify opposition parties and run elections was likewise under Interior.[20]

The president's dominance of the party translated into control over the legislature, courts, and (less easily) state governments. The PRI supplied every governor and senator and more than two-thirds of federal deputies until 1988. That year it lost its super-majority in the lower house of Congress, the Chamber of Deputies, and thus for a time its unconditional ability to pass constitutional amendments, but regained it in 1991. The Constitution still prohibits elected officials from serving successive terms—talk about term limits—making an elective career impossible. Legislators owed their nominations, and hence elections, to the president and his entourage; their advancements depended on him or his successor, always a cabinet secretary appointed by him.[21] Thus, bills were approved almost automatically.[22] Since governors did manage states, they were by far the most important officials outside the central administration, but the president could unseat them, too. Through informal pressure or formal "withdrawal of powers," the president could remove the governor, legislature, and other authorities all at once.[23] Typically, governors were deposed if they failed to maintain order, as when Eduardo Angel Elizondo of Nuevo Leon was unable to handle student riots and "the federation"—but in fact it was President Luis Echeverría—decided he should resign.[24]

Supreme Court judges, appointed and dismissed by the president thanks to automatic Senate approval, were politically irrelevant.[25] Three presidents, including Ernesto Zedillo in 1994, dismissed the entire bench. Though in theory the court could challenge a law's constitutionality, a decision applied only to the particular defendant whose case had been heard and set no precedent, so that if others disobeyed the now supposedly unconstitutional law, they could be prosecuted anyway.[26] And the court had a staggering workload, for example, issuing 6,573 rulings in 1999.[27]

Presidential authority rested on force, too. Mexico was not a police state, but it had its dark side: its approach was said to be "two carrots, then a stick."[28] Interior managed the infamous Federal Security Directorate, the secret police. Particularly in crisis moments, such as the 1968 Tlatelolco Square massacre in Mexico City, "they had spies everywhere," says Urquidi. He was president of the Colegio de Mexico at the time and Interior knew more about student activities there than he did. "The force of the Mexican president had two sources: legitimacy and the legitimate use of force," says Victor Bravo, advisor to a former presidential contender and son of a cabinet secretary. Bravo explains what he means by the "legitimate" use of force:

I am not talking about the atomic bomb—no—the police, the public prosecutor, intelligence services, hidden tape recorders. If someone was homosexual, I mean photos taken of him with a friend. J. Edgar Hoover didn't have the atomic bomb, but files on individuals, no? Suppose in the fourth year of Echeverría's administration my father, the education secretary, had asked his friends who were rectors of universities to support [the presidential contender he favored, Interior Secretary] Mario Moya Palencia. If Echeverría had found out, he would have gotten rid of my father. He would have driven him out. Suppose my father had said, "I'm not going; no one who replaces me will be as good an education secretary." "Oh yes? Well, then, it seems you didn't pay your taxes." If it wasn't by fair means, it was by foul.

Big business and the Catholic Church had real political bases and could negotiate with the executive branch,[29] and the U.S. government could never be ignored. But the ruling party incorporated and regulated the most important other societal organizations, notably the Mexican Workers Federation, the National Peasants Federation, and the National Federation of Popular Organizations (professional and middle-class associations).

This corporatist apparatus depended in part on the kind of informal patron-client relationships that pervaded much of Mexican society. For example, the ubiquitous street vendors in Mexico City paid a local boss to occupy space, as if public sidewalks were for rent, while the boss kept the authorities and rival vendors at bay. Mafioso-like *caciques*, often accompanied by armed guards, dominated many poor communities, collecting "donations," ostensibly for bribes and other costs of doing business with the government. For all their inflated commissions, they did secure benefits such as land titles, water service, or street grading from politicians. Those politicians, in turn vying with each other to prove their effectiveness to higher authorities, required the *caciques* to produce masses of supporters at rallies, prevent social unrest, and avoid building alliances with other communities.[30]

State control over social organizations rested not just on informal patron-client relationships but also on corporatist sectors carefully constructed after the Revolution.[31] In the 1930s, President Lázaro Cárdenas, a champion of land reform and worker rights, drew on his popular image to officially incorporate labor and peasants into the PRI.[32] Unions had been splintered when his administration began, but labor leader Vicente Lombardo established the primacy of his umbrella group, the Mexican

Workers Federation, and cemented its ties to the state.[33] The story had its odd twists, as when Moscow rescued his federation by ordering powerful Communist unions, such as rail and electrical workers, to join it. Lombardo's belief that unions should ally with progressive, Revolutionary currents in the state was crucial.[34] The Cárdenas administration did not forget to repay Lombardo, giving his federation financial subsidies and installing labor leaders in office, including thirty in the Chamber of Deputies. Peasants who benefited from agrarian reform were organized in *ejidos*, communities that jointly managed expropriated lands. They were split from Lombardo's urban workers and required to join the official National Peasants Federation.[35] Government employees, cordoned off from other workers, were later incorporated in the "popular" sector.

As Alfred Stepan argued in the late 1970s, this corporatist structure assured that Mexican worker and peasant organizations "do not, and cannot, exercise group sovereignty, but rather perform the role assigned to them" by the political elite.[36] Diverse features of the system contributed to that end. Fragmented unions, covering only 16 percent of the workforce in the 1990s and often representing employees of only a single firm[37]—the average union in the Mexican Workers Federation had fewer than 150 members[38]—faced enormous obstacles to collective action. They were supported by government subsidies rather than by membership dues.[39] Though in theory workers could vote to be represented by whichever union they chose, in practice, if official corporatist leaders were threatened, they could postpone votes, get ringleaders fired, and sink the process in the state-controlled courts.[40] Strikes had to be recognized as legal by so-called conciliation and arbitration boards, with one member from the government, one from the official labor movement, and one from management—in short, by state-controlled boards—or workers who participated could be fired.[41] Between 1963 and 1993, a mere 2.2 percent of strike petitions under federal jurisdiction, covering the most important industries, were recognized as legal. During the economic depression of the 1980s, real Mexican wages fell nearly twice as fast as the Latin American average, yet there was not a single general strike in Mexico, as compared with eight in Argentina and two in Brazil.[42]

Corporatist labor leaders had every incentive to control rank-and-file demands and mobilize the workers to rally behind the PRI at elections because their careers advanced within the political system, not the labor movement per se. They were called *charros*, cowboys. Francisco Pérez Arce, an anthropologist, writes that in workers' eyes, "a *charro* is some-

Lázaro Cárdenas, a champion of worker rights and land reform, was perhaps the best-loved Mexican president of the twentieth century. During his administration in the 1930s, he drew on this popularity to officially incorporate labor unions and peasant organizations into the ruling party. Photo reproduced with permission of the General Secretariat of the Organization of American States.

one who has an office (the union's office) and has a political career (in the PRI) and will probably become a congressional deputy, or is one, or already was one." [43] Even if national and state legislatures had no real legislative power, lucrative legislative seats rewarded labor, peasant, and popular sector leaders for maintaining discipline. [44] And troublemakers could be sacked, [45] as, for example, when President Carlos Salinas ostentatiously jailed the Pemex union leader, Joaquín "La Quina" Hernández Galicia, a corrupt *cacique* who at least defended workers, to replace him with another corrupt *cacique* who did not even defend workers.[46] The Mexican Workers Federation consistently opposed efforts to democratize, from anti-authoritarian protests in 1968 through an opposition electoral campaign in 1988, as democracy might threaten leaders' own careers.[47]

Though state control over society was never complete—there were eruptions—it was pervasive. Peasants and unorganized workers were notoriously the easiest to manipulate,[48] but even presidents of professional associations, such as the College of Architects, could be bought off by being inducted into government.[49] Incidents could be manufactured to control dissent, too. Although proving any given case is difficult, the technique was widely recognized. For example, in 1966 President Gustavo Díaz Ordaz told the rector of the National Autonomous University of Mexico (UNAM), Ignacio Chávez Sánchez, "You are going to make a terrific ambassador to France when you have finished at the end of the current year." Ambassador to France would be a pleasant but less important post. Chávez Sánchez said, "Thank you, but I am considering running for a second term." Díaz Ordaz turned to the person on his left and muttered, "This idiot doesn't understand." The government shortly organized a little riot that ended Chávez Sánchez' career as rector.[50]

Media control was critical in containing dissent: protest did not spread because one pocket could not even learn that another existed. Here the state's principal leverage was economic. It bought print coverage by strategically placing government, state enterprise, and party advertisements, which accounted for an astonishing half of all newspaper ad revenue, while agencies that reporters covered often handed them monthly cash payments larger than their salaries. The state paper manufacturer, which controlled the importation as well as production of newsprint, could ignore accounts payable by friendly outlets and, on rare occasion, shut off supplies to unfriendly outlets.[51] On June 22, 1966, when new monkeys arrived at the zoo and the president inaugurated a public works project, someone with a perilous sense of humor in the layout department of the newspaper *El Diario de México* switched captions, so the one under the photo of President Díaz Ordaz read, "The zoo has been enriched." The newspaper was forced to publish news of its own demise.[52] Journalists could mouth Marxist rhetoric, providing a façade of diversity, but reporters who discovered damaging facts could, as a last resort, be murdered. Emilio Azcárraga Jr., owner of the sole private television network, Televisa, famously proclaimed that Televisa considered itself "part of the government system."[53]

THE POLITICAL ELITE AND *GRUPOS*

Though Mexican society was organized in a corporatist structure controlled by the state, the heart of the central state itself was organized
along very different lines. *Grupos* of political elites competed more or
less equally to influence the incumbent president and, especially, his
choice of successor.

A sociological portrait of political elites is the best place to start.
Particularly the old-time "dinosaurs," as the technocratic generation of
Carlos Salinas dubbed its predecessors, have been caricatured out of all
proportion. A typical example was Augusto Gómez Villanueva. In his
private office in an old Mexico City row house—many politicians maintained law firms, consultancies, or other businesses to support themselves when not in government—he kept, beside his ornate wooden desk,
a three-foot-tall plastic dinosaur. Son of a railroad worker and small-time
politician, he attended the National Preparatory School by taking night
classes, received a political science degree from the National University
at age thirty-five, and later taught at the university. He rose to become
secretary of Agricultural Reform in the 1970s, the ministry overseeing
redistribution of land from large hacienda owners to peasants. He met
initially with the Democratic Current, a group of politicians on the left
that split from the PRI in 1987 to run a powerful opposition campaign,
but his sense that the group was plotting behind President Miguel de la
Madrid's back angered him deeply, so he abandoned it. In the 1990s, he
continued to represent his state in the Chamber of Deputies and seemed
quite unwilling to forsake politics.

The political event of overarching importance, at least for elites who
dominated high office through the early 1980s, was the Revolution and its
violent aftermath, roughly the years from 1910 through 1930.[54] Numerous interviews with officials from the 1950s and 1960s persuaded Roderic
Camp that the most powerful lesson drawn from that experience was the
importance of "nonviolence and the need to promote cooperation."[55] One
thing the Mexican Revolution did *not* bequeath, unlike social revolutions
in France, Russia, and China, was any requirement for ideological homo-
geneity.[56] One could espouse beliefs ranging from nineteenth-century
liberal to socially-oriented Catholic to "heterodox Marxist," as Finance
Undersecretary Jesús Silva Herzog (father of the finance secretary who
contended with Carlos Salinas for the presidency) called himself.[57]

If political elites had any unifying ideology, it was a fervent nationalism.[58] They saw themselves as intensely Mexican. Their homes and

offices displayed a devotion to Mexican art, which in some real measure they created. There would have been no public murals from Diego Rivera, Rufino Tamayo, José Clemente Orozco, or David Alfaro Siqueiros had the political elite not commissioned these works.

The National University, particularly the Law Faculty and the Economics Faculty, situated side-by-side on the campus, forged the political elite. More than 70 percent of high officials in the 1960s and 1970s had graduated from "the university"; one did not even bother to mention its name. In a country where no more than 2 percent of the population had a university education,[59] the *licenciatura*, or primary professional degree, was a requisite to enter the political elite. It carried such distinction that even former presidents of Mexico were properly addressed as *licenciado*, holder of that degree.

The professor-politician, a product of the revolving door between government and academia, was identified by political elites contacted by Camp as their most important professional influence: one generation taught and recruited the next.[60] Of the thirty-four most influential Law Faculty professors identified, twenty-four had held high public office, including three finance ministers, and only three had held no government post. Of the twelve most influential Economics Faculty professors identified, eleven had held public office. To look at the political-academic relationship from the other side, half of all high officials were professors at one time or another.[61] Mexican presidents, the apex of the political elite, spoke clear, formal Spanish, serving as both symbolic sovereign and working chief executive.

The "political class," as that common Mexican phrase suggests, was essentially self-contained. There was no unified power elite in Mexico; there were separate political, business, and church elites. Among the two hundred persons Camp identified as members of Mexican political or business elites, only one individual belonged to both groups.[62] Indeed, the public and private sectors interacted "within an atmosphere of uncertainty, distrust, suspicion, and even disdain," Peter Smith concludes, in part because of their different backgrounds.[63] More than 80 percent of high Mexican public officials were middle class, from families of teachers, lawyers, doctors, and the like, and essentially all were native-born. If not the National University, they attended other public universities. By contrast, more than half of entrepreneurs were upper class, from families of entrepreneurs or large landowners, and almost half were of recent foreign origin,[64] largely from Spain, Germany, or other European nations. They tended to study at the few private universities, such as the Catholic

Ibero-American University in Mexico City or the Technological Institute of Monterrey.

Political *grupos* constituted an informal but essential structure principally within the central administration. Forged from contending battlefield factions during the Revolution, though antecedents go back earlier,[65] they came increasingly to be bound together by family, career, and—especially—educational ties, principally from National University.

A body of work by scholars such as Peter Smith, Marilee S. Grindle, Roderic Camp, Rogelio Hernández Rodríguez, Joy Langston, Francisco Suárez Farías, and Miguel Angel Centeno, sees *grupos* as a rational response to the political and social environment. An important societal characteristic underlying their formation is Mexicans' comparative lack of diffuse social trust. One author writes: "Whether or not circumstances justify it, there is nothing in the universe which the Mexican does not see and evaluate through his distrust. It is like an *a priori* form of his oversensitivity. The Mexican does not distrust any man or woman in particular; he distrusts all men and all women."[66] Even if this characterization may be exaggerated, surveys have consistently found low levels of social trust in Mexico.[67] The society-wide response is to entrust critical tasks to people intimately known and thus trustworthy, *de confianza*. Both villain and hero in the soap operas have their circles of trusted men, *hombres de confianza*, usually armed. If one goes home late at night in Mexico City, one's middle-class friends insist on calling their taxicab driver *de confianza*. This sort of trust, *confianza*, is the basis of *grupos*.[68] For example, when a new manager was appointed in 1970 to run one subsidiary of the vast state enterprise that sold basic foods, he installed his trusted team: "I found that although I had many friends, there were few I trusted enough to invite them to help me. There are three people I brought here whom I trust blindly . . . . I trust them with my prestige, with my signature and with my honor."[69]

In a political system where elections did not decide who held power, there was no civil service to determine advancement through the bureaucracy, and formal rules counted for little, if *grupos* had not existed, they would have had to be invented. They made sense for leader and followers alike.[70] In a mere collection of atomistic individuals, how could job aspirants, especially at an intermediate or lower level, establish their good reputation? *Grupos* solved the problem. They were tight-knit enough for individuals to prove their capacity for hard work—sixteen-hour days were not uncommon for high Mexican officials—competence, and trustworthiness.[71] Likewise, without *grupos*, how could top officials, confronting queues of job aspirants, have the remotest idea who would be competent, let alone trustworthy?

Developing an effective *grupo* gave the leader an advantage because his prospects depended on how well his area of government ran.[72] For example, President de la Madrid says that President José López Portillo nominated him as the next president in good part because he had built an efficient and cohesive *grupo*. In exchange for followers' good performance, the leader was responsible for their advancement.[73] Thus, when he went from one post to another, they followed him or moved, on his recommendation, to work for an ally.

This system could produce enormous turnover as a new secretary moved in with his team and another moved out. For example, when Ernesto P. Uruchurtu was deposed as governor of Mexico City in 1966— he lost control of a squatters' riot,[74] probably instigated by President Díaz Ordaz himself in a scheme to oust him—his successor in this key cabinet post, Alfonso Corona del Rosal, replaced almost the entire top management. Born before the Revolution broke out, general and *licenciado* Corona del Rosal, who always emphasized that he had graduated from both the Military College and the National University, had enjoyed an unusually varied political career during the period when the regime was being consolidated. As army officer, state bank director, political campaign manager, federal deputy, senator, state governor, president of the PRI, and secretary of State Industries, he developed unusually diverse contacts.

On September 20, 1966, out went Mexico City's second-in-command, *licenciado* Arturo García Torres—"whose resignation the President of the Republic accepted," notes Corona del Rosal in his political memoirs[75]— to be replaced by *licenciado* Rodolfo González Guevara, Corona del Rosal's second-in-command from State Industries. Out went the chief administrative officer, *licenciado* Luis Coudurier, to be replaced by Corona del Rosal's candidate, *licenciado* Guillermo Lerdo de Tejada.[76] Corona del Rosal installed a colleague from the National Bank of the Army and Air Force to be the comptroller who would monitor expenditure; as labor director, a long-time friend from the Law Faculty; as public works director, a Pemex engineer he knew from State Industries; as medical director, a doctor who was also a personal friend; as director of social action, an orator whose ability to express "the spirit of the Revolution" he had admired in the PRI. The directors of interior, transit, administration, and markets were likewise replaced by allies. The police chief, a general fortunate to have known Corona del Rosal from the Military College, stayed on. Corona del Rosal only kept two individuals

When a high Mexican official moved into a new office, he brought his entire grupo, *his trusted team, with him, producing enormous turnover. On becoming governor of Mexico City, often considered the most important post after the presidency, Alfonso Corona del Rosal replaced the managers of virtually every municipal department. This system was not necessarily inefficient. Among other things, in only a little more than two years, Corona del Rosal's team planned and built the initial portions of the Metro. Above: Corona del Rosal at the center, President Gustavo Díaz Ordaz to the right, inaugurating the first Metro line in 1969. Photo: courtesy of Corona del Rosal family.*

in key posts with whom he does not mention a prior connection: the "honest and capable" treasury director (who collected revenue, but did not spend it) and the director of the Mexico City judiciary.

The wave of personnel change when a new cabinet secretary or state enterprise director installed his team would reverberate, as his appointees in turn brought in their teams. When Jorge de la Vega Domínguez, who had parlayed his presidency of the College of Economists into political office, followed his former boss Carlos Hank as director of the food distribution company, even though he was Hank's man *de confianza*,[77] he appointed a new team of twenty-eight directors and managers, who in turn brought in their teams. By the time all the shuffling was over, of seventy-eight mid- to high-level administrators interviewed for a study of careers in that enterprise, only twelve had survived, and even they were in different positions.[78] Bureaucrats below the managerial level were generally protected by law and union contracts,[79] but they did not cross the great divide marking authority, education, and income.

Unlike factions of the Japanese Liberal Democratic Party, which required career-long commitments, published official membership lists, and maintained established headquarters,[80] Mexican *grupos* were fluid, defined by degrees of friendship, trust, and mutual benefit, not a binary mathematical function. The leader had his *equipo*—his team of immediate subordinates—but over time he placed *equipo* members in other areas of the administration, creating a broader and somewhat less tight-knit *grupo*.[81] *Grupos* overlapped somewhat, and all successful politicians belonged to several different *grupos* during the course of their careers.[82]

Followers were allowed to abandon one *grupo* and join another if the leader's career was blocked.[83] Jorge Gamboa de Buen, former director of Mexico City development, confirms, "One is with a leader as long as he keeps rising and opening new opportunities; when he ceases to, one has to look elsewhere." For example, after Luis Echeverría won the presidential nomination in 1969, he invited the losing Corona del Rosal's second-in-command, González Guevara, to accompany his electoral campaign, apparently to mend bridges. Knowing that he could no longer promise advancement, Corona del Rosal urged his long-time collaborator to accept, but González Guevara said that doing so would be "opportunistic."[84] The refusal, writes Corona del Rosal, "demonstrated his rectitude and loyalty, but I continue to think he made a political error."

López Portillo avoided that error in 1969. Though a boyhood friend of Echeverría, he had supported his boss, one of Echeverría's rivals, for the nomination. As a result, he had to take a demotion, but he did accept a post, and soon Echeverría began to resurrect his career—right up to the presidency of the republic. Was López Portillo in his boss's *grupo* or Echeverría's? *Grupos* were not mathematically defined. First López Portillo was in one *grupo*, and when it could get him nowhere, he joined the other. Then when he became president, he reached back to appoint his old boss as secretary of health.

Politicians were somewhat secretive about *grupos*. In the course of research on them, when the political scientist Joy Langston informally raised the topic with a Mexican graduate economics student at MIT—particularly since the 1970s an advanced economics degree from a prestigious U.S. university has been an excellent route into the political elite—he blushed, told her to read Roderic Camp, and left the room.[85] More experienced politicians will talk about *grupos*, but precisely because of their fluidity and partial secrecy, they cannot give a complete picture of who belonged to which one.

The political *grupos* that mattered were concentrated in the national administration, both ministries and state enterprises. Just as there was a division between public and private sectors, so there was one within the state between the political elite in high administrative office and the electoral and corporatist apparatus. This division was deep and powerful, even if *grupos* did spill over into a few top party posts such as president of the PRI or elected offices such as governor. Among all cabinet secretaries from 1946 to 1982—that is, the highest officials after the president and the only individuals eligible to succeed him—60 percent had *exclusively* administrative careers (often along with professorships or other outside positions), and the rest combined administrative with electoral or party experience. Only one had just electoral experience, and none at all had just party experience.[86] A study of public careers suggests that a background in elective office was "something of a liability in the quest for admission to the upper-level circles of power and prestige."[87]

The administrative political elite, where *grupos* were concentrated, dealt with top brokers in the corporatist sectors.[88] Those sectors provided careers for labor and peasant leaders, with money and opportunities for graft, but on a separate track, requiring effective work in the trenches to mobilize support and control unrest, rather than a *licenciatura*. And here the electoral branch served its useful function within the Mexican state; a term as deputy or in some other electoral post would be awarded to corporatist leaders.[89] There were even informal quotas for each sector in the Chamber of Deputies, which changed over time with the sectors' perceived importance.

THE MOST DANGEROUS MOMENT

The determination of presidential succession was the political system's most dangerous moment and greatest mystery. Here there is some disagreement among scholars. Daniel Cosío Villegas, who taught a quarter of a century's worth of Mexican presidents at the National University, marveled at U.S. political scientists' brave theories about how the PRI nominee was selected—which is to say, how the next president of Mexico was selected—behind the shadows of the political system's innermost sanctum. Frank Brandenburg, he quipped, "sees the process so clearly that he animatedly describes it in nine steps."[90] Cosío Villegas saw nothing more in those theories than "pure imagination or common sense, something we Mexicans do not entirely lack."[91] As of 1975, only one Mexican, in an undergraduate thesis at the National University, had even seriously attempted to explain the mystery, Cosío Villegas noted. The best wisdom Mexico could offer was street gossip, which agreed that the president chose a successor who was personally loyal to him, shared a certain affinity in ideas ("if any"), and had as few enemies as possible.[92] Even if the president decided early on whom to name, he would keep quiet until the last moment for good reasons, "among them the entertainment value of watching five or six aspirants do pirouettes trying to divine his thinking." Street gossip conceded that everything everyone imagined was precisely that, imagined, "since the drama, or comedy, of the selection plays itself out within the president's head." Moreover, "when the president does offer some little tidbit or gesture indicating a possible preference, his only real purpose is to deceive and hide what he knows inside."

Cosío Villegas' astute cautions notwithstanding, political scientists' arguments, as well as statements by former officials after the old regime began to collapse (and decades after Cosío Villegas died), make it possible to credibly outline the politics of presidential succession. The outline begins with an important negative point: political elites could not even openly declare which presidential hopeful they preferred, much less mobilize to support him.[93] Recall the chilling scenario that, according to Victor Bravo, would have befallen his father, education minister under President Luis Echeverría, had he openly pressed for his presidential favorite in 1975. Francisco Labastida, governor of Sinaloa in 1987, when asked if he would have directly told the president, then Miguel de la Madrid, that he supported one contender or opposed another, replied, "No, no, no, no, no." If he had done so and picked the wrong candidate, it would have been devastating not only to his own political career but also to the state of Sinaloa. And de la Madrid himself concurs that no high official would dare point-blank express support for or opposition to any nominee.

If expressing political support for a presidential candidate was a venial sin, openly campaigning to nominate one was a mortal sin—either to the campaign or to the political system itself, depending on the outcome. Two great events underline this point. In 1951, when former Revolutionary military officers and some labor and peasant groups overtly sought the nomination of General Miguel Henríquez Guzmán, they were expelled from the PRI, and the opposition party they formed was destroyed. In 1987, when a coalition of left-leaning political elites split off and overtly sought the nomination of Cuauhtémoc Cárdenas, son of Lázaro Cárdenas, they were also expelled from the PRI. However, the opposition party they formed fared better than that of Henríquez Guzmán. They nearly won the 1988 presidential election, or perhaps actually won it but were foiled by massive voter fraud. Over the longer term, they pushed the old political machinery a long way toward destruction.

Between these events no presidential hopeful was naïve enough to mobilize support for his nomination, but there were lower level reminders of the prohibition. Having gained popularity in the relatively unimportant post of mayor, in 1961 Dr. Salvador Nava began openly campaigning to win the PRI's nomination for a position that mattered: governor of the state of San Luis Potosí. He was called to Mexico City to talk with Alfonso Corona del Rosal, at the time president of the PRI. The following dialog took place:

CORONA DEL ROSAL: Doctor, you are not going to be the PRI candidate for your state's governor.

NAVA: General, you must be mistaken; the party hasn't even held its convention yet in San Luis Potosí.

CORONA DEL ROSAL: With or without the convention, doctor, you are not going to be the party's candidate . . . because in addition to votes, you need something else.

NAVA: What else? The President's benediction?

CORONA DEL ROSAL: No, doctor, the President doesn't need to get mixed up in this.

NAVA: Then I need your good graces?

CORONA DEL ROSAL: Let's suppose so, doctor.

NAVA: I don't accept that, because you are not the party; the party is its members, and it is their votes I seek.

CORONA DEL ROSAL: Wait a bit, doctor, and later it will be another matter. For the moment, I will make you federal deputy from the first district, and I will give you back the money you spent on your campaign.

NAVA: General, I am not looking for employment. The people called me to seek the candidacy for governor because they have confidence in me.[94]

Nava was backed into running an opposition party campaign and fraudulently defeated. Some of his supporters were killed in violence provoked by federal agents,[95] others were jailed, and the group that had supported him was destroyed.

There was an important logic to the old Mexican political system's ban on overt mobilization. If mobilization once gained hold, since in Mexico in that era the ballot box had proven incapable of resolving matters, it could only culminate in violence. The state turned to violence as an unfortunate last resort to destroy one threatening candidacy in San Luis Potosí, but nationwide violence over a national political succession might well mean another Revolution. Therefore, any mobilization that might lead to mass violence had to be quashed. Much the same logic underlay the quasi-secrecy of *grupos* within the political elite. Because the next president was not going to be chosen by vote, political elites could not start lining up to be counted. By contrast, Japanese Liberal Democratic Party factions could publish membership lists because a vote of listed faction members did choose the candidate for prime minister.[96]

Though *grupos* could not openly mobilize, scholars widely agree that they did work covertly to win support within the political elite for their preferred candidate.[97] Luis Enrique Bracamontes, a cabinet secretary and undersecretary for eighteen years, describes how *grupo* members proselytized for their candidates "with great discretion, through intimates, friends *de confianza*, no? Someone would say to me, 'I would like to introduce you to [Agriculture Secretary] Gilberto Flores Muñoz.' I would say, 'Thank you, but I already know him.' Since he was a secretary and I was an undersecretary, I had had dealings with him on occasion. Or partisans of [Public Health Secretary] Ignacio Morones Prieto would say the same. The idea was to keep building supporters."

Rafael Moreno Valle, the PRI's secretary of political action from 1962 to 1964, describes how he helped prepare the way for Interior Secretary Gustavo Díaz Ordaz's presidential nomination in 1963. Beginning in 1962, a group of politicians inclined toward Díaz Ordaz met every week in Moreno Valle's house. He was not then in a position to deal with cabinet secretaries, but rather leaders of the party's corporatist sectors:

> It fell to me to converse with the secretary general of the Regional Federation of Mexican Workers, *señor* Antonio José Hernández, and [another leader], so that when the federation was asked at high levels about its sympathies, they would support *licenciado* Díaz Ordaz. They made a commitment to me to do so. I conversed with *señor* Manuel Rivera Anaya and [another leader] of the Revolutionary Federation of Workers and Peasants, and they also made a commitment that, when those at high levels talked with them, they would support *licenciado* Díaz Ordaz' candidacy. And *licenciado* Javier Rojo Gómez, secretary

general of the National Peasants Confederation, also committed his group to support *licenciado* Díaz Ordaz when the matter was decided at high levels. Only the Mexican Federation of Laborers and some minor corporate labor groups remained uncommitted.

Moreno Valle's effort conspicuously focused on quietly obtaining support from one or two top leaders, not on mobilizing the rank and file.

The sub-rosa campaign for presidential nomination was not always so polite. *Grupos* would deliver *golpes bajos*, low blows, as they were called, to try to destroy their competitors. News leaks were a favorite form of *golpe bajo*, as when a report detailing corruption and administrative chaos in Pemex, managed by the unsuccessful presidential contender Jorge Díaz Serrano, made its way into the feisty weekly *Proceso* in 1981.[98] The report had been prepared by the Planning and Budget Ministry, run by the successful presidential contender de la Madrid. And presidential hopefuls and their *grupos* notoriously used public spending to buy support among the political elite. Former finance secretary David Ibarra says, "If I have a governor who sympathizes with me, I give him more to spend, or if I'm the finance secretary, I increase his credit line. There are any number of different methods, the same as in any country." Except, of course, that what mattered in Mexico was not votes but quiet support within the political elite.

This stealth campaign was very much a *grupo* effort—*grupo* members launched initiatives on their own, not just under the leader's orders—because the outcome mattered enormously to them. Recall the massive turnover of managers by Corona del Rosal when he took over the reins in Mexico City, or how Jorge de la Vega Domínguez replaced managers at the government's food distribution firm. The same phenomenon, on an even broader scale, occurred each six years when a new president of Mexico took office. As a member of his *grupo* said, if de la Vega Domínguez supported the winning presidential candidate and thus became a cabinet secretary, "we'll all have positions in the Ministry."[99]

If intra-elite campaigns to build support for candidates were so covert, how could the president tell which candidates were more popular and which less, and why did he even care? The president had long tentacles to gather information, which he used subtly, so as not to stir up unwanted opinions or pressures. For one thing, in regular meetings with the most important officials across the political system, he discreetly sounded out opinions, performing what political elites called an *auscultación*, the medical procedure of listening to a patient's heartbeat. De la Madrid says that prior to his nomination, President López Portillo had not explicitly asked opinions of political groups, but "he had been checking the lay of the land, making an *auscultación*, asking."[100] The president had plenty of assistance with his *auscultación*.[101] As Moreno Valle explains:

> I believe that the president of the PRI [based on discussions with political *grupos*] exchanged opinions with the president. As well, the Interior Ministry had agencies to investigate political questions and provided reports to the secretary, who passed them on to the president: there are political currents in this state leaning this way, in another state leaning that way. In other words, they would go along performing an *auscultación* of national opinion.

In the 1950s and 1960s, it appears that the most popular candidates for the presidency—Adolfo López Mateos in 1957 and Gustavo Díaz Ordaz in 1963—in fact won the nomination.[102] After 1970, the most popular candidates often did not win. For example, in 1975, Interior Minister Mario Moya Palencia was widely regarded as favored. When President Luis Echeverría instead nominated José López Portillo, a joke made the rounds that the initials JLP stood for *Jamás Lo Pensé*: I never imagined it.[103]

But even when the president did not necessarily nominate a candidate who was the most popular across political currents, he always, always, feared picking a candidate who might be deeply hated by some important political current. To put it another way, winning broad support often mattered less than assuaging bitter opposition. Even the president could not be sure what grave dangers a hated candidate might bring, so covert was the nomination process. But the worst case was clear: the destruction of the political system.[104]

Though the president's choice of successor was limited, the boundaries were not clearly marked. "I reiterate my thesis," says de la Madrid— an odd way to speak, as if even a former president could not quite be sure about the political succession process he himself managed—"that it is not true that the president could designate a candidate without limitation, according to his own fancy. I think that a president could not impose a candidate against the will of his party or one of its sectors: labor, peasant, or popular. The party would simply rebel." By "the party" he surely meant political elites. The rank and file were so far from the covert internal nomination process that they heard only muffled rumors about it.

De la Madrid and other officials[105] also noted that the president could not impose a candidate opposed by the private sector, Catholic Church, or United States. These external interests, never brought under the umbrella of the ruling party system, might not have been so bashful as *grupos* were about stating their views to the president.

But it was political elites, not external interests, that the president had to worry about. Twice, in 1951 and 1987, Mexican presidents tried to nominate successors hated by significant currents of the political elite. Both times they thrust the worst possible danger upon the political system: overt mobilization by factions that saw submission as sure political death. In 1951, President Miguel Alemán tried to nominate a crony whom leftists and former Revolutionary generals feared would forever end their political careers. They mobilized under the banner of Miguel Henríquez Guzmán, and the political machine destroyed their movement. In 1987, de la Madrid ignored his own advice by nominating a candidate deeply hated by party factions. Carlos Salinas and his team of young, U.S.-trained economists seemed certain to forever end the political chances of an older, left-leaning generation of officials. They split off under Cuauhtémoc Cárdenas, mobilized civil society with difficulty, and ran a more successful opposition campaign. The harm they wrought to the political system helped push it toward its destruction.

The ritual in which the incumbent president revealed his successor—the *destape*, or uncovering—was ingeniously designed to prevent this ultimate nightmare, a fracturing of the political elite. The president guarded his decision until the last moment, not for entertainment value—he cannot have enjoyed hurting close collaborators and friends by doing so—but to keep all contestants playing at the internal game of presidential succession, rather than fatally splitting from the party. In his *Political Memoirs*, Corona del Rosal describes the classic *destape* that revealed the 1963 winner, Gustavo Díaz Ordaz. Then president of the PRI, Corona del Rosal says he discussed with President López Mateos "some members of his cabinet whom the public [a euphemism for political elites] considered possible candidates. I will say that I presented my viewpoint with care, because we were talking about persons who merited my respect."[106] He proceeds to list practically the entire cabinet, as if, thirty years later, it were still necessary to avoid casting his lot with a losing candidate. But, political survivor that he was, he ferreted out the successful candidate's identity:

> As for the interior minister, Gustavo Díaz Ordaz, I remembered that years earlier, when we were senators, *licenciado* López Mateos called him "Gustavito" and, along with other members of the Senate, used to

comment on his intelligence and ability. . . . President López Mateos kept indicating his recognition of and affection toward *licenciado* Díaz Ordaz, that master of juridical knowledge and culture, whom he tacitly indicated as his successor.[107]

The public *destape* was a strange dance of president and political elites, all aware that things could go terribly wrong if some line were crossed, no one quite sure just where that line was. President López Mateos called into his office Luis Gómez Z., a Railroad Workers leader who had tried to foment an independent federation but had been defeated and brought back into the system, along with Napoleon Gómez Sada, leader of the Mining and Metalworkers, and asked them to make speeches lauding the winning candidate at the *destape*. They emerged from the president's office brimming with enthusiasm—but unsure who the candidate was.[108] Corona del Rosal announced the name before the National Executive Committee of the PRI: "The majority of statewide party committees, labor leaders, and labor federations," he intoned, "have expressed their solidarity for *licenciado* Gustavo Díaz Ordaz." Of course, there had been no actual vote. Corona del Rosal adds: "My words were received with a unanimous public approval: the whole [executive committee] and all who had come as spectators stood up and applauded."[109]

The executive committee and spectators had no other option. Suppose opponents had wanted to organize so much as an informal chat about the winning candidate or the *auscultación*. They would have had to read each others' minds instantly. Anyway, members of the executive committee did not even occupy the second rung of power below the president, but the third or fourth, and were in no position to object. When that committee later announced the result to the much larger party convention, it also had no alternative but to applaud. Immediately the *cargada*, or cavalry charge, of all important groups in the PRI—and above all the losing candidates—had to hail the new dauphin.[110] Now the danger of an elite fracture and political succession crisis had passed.

Many Mexicans, as well as many foreigners who study Mexico, share the conviction that underlying socioeconomic forces caused the nation's economic crises. Although Mexico was seen as an economic miracle in the 1950s and 1960s—especially from 1958 to 1970 under the guidance of Finance Minister Antonio Ortiz Mena—it is argued that the economy and society suffered from deep, structural flaws. The view that these flaws inevitably produced economic crises comes in several variations. They are all wrong.

"Structural" industrial failure has been blamed for economic crisis in diverse times and places. In the 1950s and 1960s, for example, inefficient agriculture in Latin America, seen as a legacy of colonial exploitation, was blamed for failing to produce enough food to consume at home or crops such as cotton and coffee to export, and thus causing economic crises.[1] After the Asian crisis of the late 1990s, though not a single Western economist had predicted it,[2] some claimed that it had inexorably resulted from "crony capitalism"—in the words of Jeffrey A. Frankel, a former member of the President's Council of Economic Advisers, "patterns of corruption, industrial policy and other excessive government interference in the economy."[3] The 1976 and 1982 crises in Mexico were blamed on quite similar sorts of structural problems. At least, in this case, the problems were discovered before the crises—a point in favor of the argument because if structural problems exist, somebody should notice them before crises send everyone looking for them.

Mexico's supposed structural economic problems proved a popular culprit in part because, beneath some ideological differences, free-market and Marxist views could essentially agree about them. In somewhat eclectic versions, both views were important in Mexico in the 1970s and 1980s. The Economics Faculty of the National University taught "60 percent Marx and 40 percent Keynes," as one former Bank of Mexico official joked.[4] Like many other Bank of Mexico and Finance Ministry officials, he had not only attended the National University, but also had

Antonio Ortiz Mena, finance secretary from 1958 to 1970, presided over the "Mexican miracle": a stable, rapidly growing economy, widely benefiting the populace. One theory after another has suggested that beneath the apparent success was structural failure. None of the theories hold up. Photo: Archivo General de la Nación, Fondo Hermanos Mayo.

later studied graduate-level economics at a prominent U.S. university, in his case at the University of Chicago's famously free-market economics department. Strands of these seemingly opposite lines of thought tended to intertwine.

The "neoliberal," free-market critique of Third World structural problems originally did not focus on economic crises, but instead argued that excessive protectionism and other statist intervention undermined industrial efficiency.[5] When crises erupted, this argument about industrial efficiency provided a ready-made explanation. Clark W. Reynolds, author of a prominent economic history of Mexico, blamed the 1976 crisis on "artificial" trade protection and government subsidies for electricity, fuels, and even roads.[6] When Mexican presidents of the 1980s and 1990s with advanced economics degrees from U.S. universities—Miguel de la Madrid, Carlos Salinas, and Ernesto Zedillo—blamed economic crises on the old economic model, they meant the same thing as Reynolds.[7]

Marxist "dependency" theory, taking shape during much the same period as the free-market critique, also initially focused on industrial efficiency, seeing the capitalist "core" in advanced nations as undermining development in "dependent" Third World economies.[8] This theory about structural industrial problems likewise provided a springboard to explain crises once they erupted. For example, E. V. K. Fitzgerald argued that foreign and large-scale domestic capital wielded international connections and threatened divestment, demanding public subsidies and avoiding commensurate taxes. The resulting massive budget deficits created the "fiscal crisis of the state,"[9] hence crises.

Ideological disputes about culprits should not obscure the parallels between these arguments. Both sides said big business got excessive subsidies and tax breaks, even if neoliberals blamed heavy-handed governments and dependency theorists pointed to domineering capital. Neoliberals especially attacked protectionism, but so did dependency theorists such as the Brazilian sociologist Fernando Henrique Cardoso.[10] When Cardoso became president of Brazil in the 1990s and pushed through free-market reforms, he quipped that everyone should forget everything he had ever written. Yet aside from ideological coloring, his views did not change so radically.

Indeed, the idea that underlying structural economic problems caused Mexico's economic crises has been espoused by economists across the ideological spectrum.[11] In his important analysis of the Mexican economy almost throughout the period of one-party rule, Enrique Cárdenas makes one of the most careful, centrist arguments about protection-ism and fiscal crisis.[12] And many political scientists have accepted these arguments.[13]

THE "EXHAUSTION OF IMPORT SUBSTITUTION"

The more free-market view about structural problems sees Latin American economic crises as caused by the "exhaustion"—increasing inefficiency—of "import substitution." Import substitution used protec-tionism to block imports and provided subsidies to stimulate domestic industry. (The phrase sounds odd in English; it should be "import re-placement" because the goal was to replace imports with home produc-tion. But it makes sense in Spanish: *sustitución*, a false cognate, means "replacement"; *sustitución de importaciones* means "import replacement.") Import substitution policies were a legacy of the Depression when Latin America was cut off from trade and of World War II when industrial goods were scarce. After the war, these policies were officially adopted by governments and promoted by the U.N. Economic Commission for Latin America (ECLA). They seemed to be working through the mid-1960s, and many economists supported them.

Economists began to criticize import substitution in the mid-1960s.[14] Initial import substitution to stimulate domestic manufacture of ba-sic consumer goods such as textiles and processed foods was said to be "easy": the technology was known, investments moderate, economies of scale limited, and a small market adequate. But import substitution might become exhausted once nearly all such goods were already made at home. Viable strategies to continue industrial development were deemed "hard." For example, lowering trade barriers to make domestic produc-tion more efficient and encourage manufactured exports would, at least initially, threaten profits and wages. Alternatively, "deepening" import substitution to produce industrial inputs like chemicals or durable goods like autos at home would require more advanced technology and more extensive markets than existed in developing countries, so the state would have to shift policies to favor multinationals.

Now a political argument enters to bridge the gap between indus-trial problems, in the real economy, and economic crises, in the financial economy. Any viable restructuring would hurt Latin American politi-cians' major bases of support—domestic business and labor—so instead they resorted to overspending (letting public expenditures far outrun revenues) and other short-term expedients to inflate growth. These short-term expedients, erupting in the financial economy, put the nation on the road to economic crisis.[15]

Intriguing as such ideas sound, there are three reasons why exhaustion of import substitution did not cause Mexico's 1976 and 1982 crises. The first is just based on observation: a look across developing nations reveals no convincing evidence that high levels of protectionism are correlated with economic crises, much less that one causes the other. The second reason is a little unconventional: Mexico did not suffer broad-based exhaustion of import substitution (though some countries may have). Even this argument is not very unconventional: Deepak Lal, an economist notably critical of import substitution, concedes that "total-factor" productivity growth, the standard measure of economic efficiency, remained "quite respectable by international standards" in Mexico as it headed into its crises.[16] The third reason is utterly conventional: even if Mexico had suffered from exhaustion of import substitution, structural industrial problems could not have caused its economic crises. Mainstream economics proposes no clear argument why industrial problems should cause economic crises at all.[17] Economists' statistical efforts to identify factors that cause crises consider financial variables such as printing too much money and overvaluing the currency, not protectionism or subsidy.[18] The idea that protectionism and subsidy might cause industrial inefficiency, hence low growth, hence political pressures, hence financial and monetary problems, hence crisis is perilously intricate. It might work sometimes, but it utterly breaks down for Mexico.

Start with the first reason why exhaustion of import substitution did not cause Mexico's 1976 and 1982 crises: there is no systematic evidence across nations tying protectionism to economic crisis. Of course, some countries with high levels of protection, such as Argentina from the 1950s to the 1980s, suffered economic crises. Yet, Colombia, which also maintained high levels of protection through the 1980s, was the most economically stable major Latin American economy during most of the twentieth century, and the only one to avoid crisis in the 1980s. In a study of all developing countries for which he could obtain data, Dani Rodrik showed that those with large "microeconomic distortions"— protectionism and industrial subsidies—did not suffer economic crises any more than those with small distortions. In fact, countries that avoided the devastating 1982 wave of crises actually had slightly *larger* "distortions" than those that succumbed to it.[19]

This evidence is powerful. No doubt, among some sample of countries over some time span—perhaps among Latin American countries in the 1970s—those with large microeconomic distortions might have been likely to suffer crises. But the fact remains that many countries such as Colombia—or India or Pakistan—that were nobody's idea of free-market nevertheless avoided crises. These examples break any inherent link between industrial policies (whether good, bad, or indifferent—they can range across the spectrum) and economic crises. The supposed tragic plot whereby underlying structural problems inevitably erupt in crises lacks any logic.

Turn next to the point that Mexico did not even suffer from exhaustion of import substitution before its 1976 and 1982 crises. Of course, Mexico had some industrial problems (few nations avoid them altogether), but on the whole it made rather successful transitions from "easy" to "hard" import substitution and then to export promotion.

Mexico completed the easy stage of import substitution, manufacturing basic consumer goods at home, not by 1970, when it should have if that supposed impasse set it on the road to economic crisis, nor even by 1960, but by 1950. In 1950, Mexico imported only 7 percent of basic consumer goods, and there the level stayed.[20] But the end of easy import substitution hardly triggered economic crises. On the contrary, it ushered in the Mexican miracle: stable 6 percent growth, year in and year out.

Mexico continued to develop after the end of easy import substitution, in part because economic officials adopted policies to move toward hard import substitution. Though academics would only invent that term later, officials interviewed by the Harvard economist Raymond Vernon in 1960 already understood the substantive issue: Mexico had to push beyond consumer goods to more advanced production—manufacturing aluminum instead of kitchen pans, engine blocks instead of assembled cars—and this more advanced production required larger investments and more sophisticated technology.[21] "Fabrication programs" provided trade protection and tax incentives for heavy intermediate goods such as steel and chemicals and some capital equipment, helping transform those advanced sectors into the motor of the economy. They grew, on average, more than 11 percent a year during the 1950s and 1960s (Table 3.1).[22] So much for the impossibility of moving beyond easy import substitution.

Surely, Mexican trade protection was not always optimal (if that level could ever be determined), but neither was it inevitably increasing, as critics of import substitution imply. "Effective protection," a comprehensive gauge of trade barriers including quotas as well as tariffs, was reduced for established consumer goods industries from 28 percent in

TABLE 3.1. REAL MANUFACTURING GROWTH (PERCENT PER YEAR)

	1954–64	1964–72	1972–79	1979–84	1984–90	1990–94
Manufacturing	8.0	8.9	6.5	1.2	3.3	2.3
Consumer goods	6.0	7.4	5.0	1.6	1.7	0.8
Light intermediate	8.5	7.9	6.8	1.6	2.2	–0.9
Heavy intermediate	11.0	11.3	7.6	3.3	3.7	2.2
Capital/durable	12.5	11.7	8.9	–2.2	6.6	5.9

Import substitution—the replacement of imports with domestically manufactured goods—is often said to have become "exhausted" in the 1950s and 1960s. But it advanced rapidly as industry pushed into heavy intermediate goods such as concrete and steel, consumer durables, and capital equipment.

Growth is measured from business cycle peak to business cycle peak, a standard method to smooth out annual fluctuations. Data for 1954–64: manufacturing output in 1960 pesos, Ros and Vázquez 1980. Data for 1964–94: manufacturing output in 1980 pesos, Nacional Financiera 1990 and 1995.

1970 to 5 percent in 1980.[23] Some firms, of course, always had to purchase industrial inputs, and they sought to limit protectionism, notes
Luis Giménez Cacho, an entrepreneur who bought steel to fabricate
products for the construction industry. Committees consisting of officials from the Finance Ministry, the Ministry of Industry and Commerce, and business chambers would meet to debate levels of protection.
"If the users said the domestic product was bad," says Giménez Cacho,
"the government would allow imports—without tariffs, without quotas."
Gilberto Borja Navarrete, president of Grupo ICA, one of the largest
Mexican industrial and construction consortia, agrees that officials, after meeting with representatives from diverse industries, allowed protection "only up to a certain limit." Tariffs on earth-moving equipment
manufactured by Grupo ICA averaged around 15 percent in the 1970s,
and if domestic firms charged more than that margin above world prices,
the government would allow imports.

In the 1970s, the Mexican state turned to promoting manufactured
exports.[24] In particular, the government gave advanced industries protection and duty-free access to inputs in exchange for export commitments.
Effective protection for heavy intermediates increased from 41 percent
to 53 percent over the decade, and from 77 percent to 109 percent for consumer durables and capital equipment.[25] Surely some of these levels were
excessive, and the favored industries did not always meet their export
commitments, but overall they did rather well. They led manufacturing
exports, which grew, on average, 10 percent per year from 1972 through
1984—before any trade barriers came down (Table 3.2).[26] The state also
targeted key sectors, for example, strong-arming U.S. automakers into
building modern factories in northern Mexican states in the late 1970s.[27]
Those factories became major sources of industrial exports.

Productivity figures likewise paint a picture of overall industrial success.[28] Total-factor productivity (as mentioned, the usual gauge of efficiency) grew 3.5 percent annually from 1973 through 1980 in capital and
durable goods, faster than in the large advanced nations except Japan. It
did extremely well in heavy intermediate goods: 2.5 percent annually in
chemicals and 3.2 percent in non-metallic minerals such as glass and clay,
in both cases faster than in any large advanced nation, Japan included. It
fell 1.3 percent in basic metals such as steel, a bad record (though not as
bad as that of the United States). Total-factor productivity across Mexican manufacturing grew 1.2 percent annually in 1962–73, then picked up
to 1.5 percent annually in 1973–80. Where was the collapse of industrial
efficiency circa 1970? The Mexican industrial record was solid.

TABLE 3.2. REAL GROWTH OF MANUFACTURED EXPORTS
(PERCENT PER YEAR)

	1964–72	1972–79	1979–84	1984–90	1990–94
Manufacturing	8	10	10	12	13
Consumer goods	7	8	–2	6	12
Light intermediate	9	10	2	7	2
Heavy intermediate	8	9	10	12	8
Capital/durable	10	11	15	20	18

Under the protectionist economic regime, Mexico's manufacturing exports rose rapidly and steadily, becoming an important source of foreign exchange. Growth is measured from business cycle peak to business cycle peak, as in Table 3.1. (All figures *exclude* mostly foreign-owned *maquiladoras*, or export assembly plants.)

Real exports (1960 pesos) in 1964–72: Ros and Vázquez 1980. Exports in current dollars, 1972–81: Lopez Portillo 1982. Exports in current dollars, 1982–90: INEGI 1996. Exports in current dollars, 1991–94: Banco de México, *Indicadores del Sector Externo*, various issues. (All export figures derive from this same Banco de México series.) Exports in current dollars for 1972–94 are then deflated by producer price index (1982=100) from *The Economic Report of the President 1995.*

These results sound surprising if one listens to mainstream economists' public encomiums on trade, but less surprising if one looks at their actual calculations. Calculations based on standard trade theory show that protectionism has remarkably small net economic costs, or "welfare losses." The main effect is to transfer resources from consumers, forced to pay high prices, to protected firms, which reap high profits. Once economists noticed the trivial size of these welfare losses, free-trade advocates had to invent supposed ancillary costs of protectionism such as corruption and influence buying to sustain the case against it.[29] Of course, corruption and influence buying are hardly exclusive to protectionist regimes, as Mexican administrations in the 1990s so vividly demonstrated. And as long as firms face reasonable market competition, higher profits from protectionism may boost long-term growth by providing resources to invest. Again in the words of the anti-protectionist Deepak Lal, "The vigor of the [Mexican] private sector helped to maintain competition."[30] Even the most concentrated sectors could count on four major firms.[31]

Protectionism did have its problems. Manuel Suárez Mier, a former Bank of Mexico official and professor at the Technological Institute of

Mexico, doubts the figures on effective protection; import quotas and other non-tariff barriers make them hard to gauge. "As a consumer, I can tell you that all of us waited until we had a trip abroad to shop for clothing," he says. "And those industries—textiles and apparel—didn't survive well." Sergio Ghigliazza, director of the Center of Latin American Monetary Studies, says, "Mexico produced sheet iron at 60 or 70 percent above world prices. And the quality was so bad that 30 percent of it had to be thrown out. Suddenly, when it could be imported from the United States or Japan, the cost of stoves and refrigerators fell 50 percent."

Moreover, only larger firms could manage the bureaucratic procedures to import duty-free materials and components that they incorporated in exports.[32] Only they had the clout to bargain with officials about tariffs and quotas. Partly because of this fact, by far the worst industrial problems afflicted sectors of smaller, more competitive firms producing traditional consumer goods. Battered by the string of crises from 1976 on, and starved for capital, they were unable to invest, and many folded. Suárez Mier notes that after trade barriers came down, multinationals such as Levi's bought some of the very same manufacturing plants and restored them to efficient production.

Nevertheless, 10 percent real annual growth of manufactured exports and respectable total-factor productivity improvement through the 1970s is not a picture of massive failure. Moreover, had the heavy-intermediate and durable-good industries favored by industrial policies been so inefficient, they should have collapsed when trade barriers were slashed from 1985 through 1987—this period, when Mexico entered the General Agreement on Tariffs and Trade (GATT), saw a much more dramatic trade opening than when it entered NAFTA in 1994. Factories cannot be transformed from industrial failures into export miracles overnight. But far from collapsing, these advanced industries prospered. Their annual export growth increased, to 12 percent annually in heavy intermediates and 20 percent in consumer durables and capital goods. As the Mexican economists Juan Carlos Moreno and Jaime Ros argue, "The outstanding export performance of Mexico's manufacturing . . . [was] to a large degree, a legacy of the import substitution period."[33]

If Mexican manufacturing progressed so well, why did manufacturing trade deficits, typically gauged at business-cycle peaks to smooth out ups and downs, rise from $0.5 billion in 1972 to $7.8 billion in 1979, fall to $3.5 billion in 1984, then explode to $30 billion in 1994?[34] This last gargantuan deficit, occurring almost after a decade under the free-market regime was in place, could hardly have been caused by protectionism.

Graph 3.1: Peso overvaluation and manufacturing trade balance

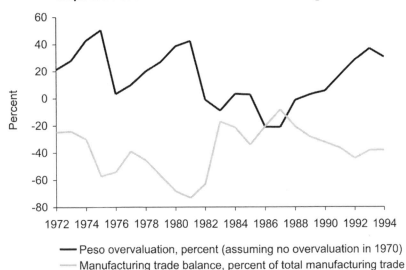

— Peso overvaluation, percent (assuming no overvaluation in 1970)
— Manufacturing trade balance, percent of total manufacturing trade

Why did Mexico sometimes run large manufacturing trade deficits? Not because of protectionism—the largest deficits were actually under the free-trade regime after 1986—but because the peso became overvalued. As in other trade data, maquiladoras, *or export assembly plants, are not included.*

Trade data for 1972–79 are from López Portillo 1982, 57, 68. Data for 1980–81 are from INEGI 1993, Tables 17.6 and 17.7. Data for 1982–90 are from INEGI 1996, Tables 17.6, 17.7. Data for 1991–94 are from Banco de México, Indicadores del Sector Externo, *numbers 152, 155, 173. Index of peso overvaluation is from Cárdenas 1996, 213 (1970 value = 100).*

There is an utterly conventional and correct reason why trade deficits sometimes swelled under protectionist and free-market regimes alike: they were caused by overvaluation of the peso, not protectionism. The peso appreciated 50 percent in value against the dollar from 1970 through 1975. The 1976 crash brought it back to its 1970 level, but it then proceeded to appreciate 40 percent through 1981. After an erratic course in the troubled 1980s, it rose 40 or 50 percent again through 1994.[35] Each time the peso thus came to buy 40 or 50 percent more foreign goods, imports reached insane levels. Trade deficits thus swelled as the peso became overvalued: the phenomena moved in lockstep (Graph 3.1). Overvaluation of the currency on this scale can swamp domestic industries with imports, and once factories close, as "strategic trade" models from mainstream international economics demonstrate, subsequent devaluation may not revive them.[36] The surprise is how resilient Mexican industry proved *despite* macroeconomic chaos. Macroeconomic chaos itself was the problem, not industrial efficiency.

Turn now to the third reason why exhaustion of import substitution did not cause Mexico's 1976 and 1982 crises. Suppose, for the sake of argument, that import substitution had, after all, become exhausted in Mexico circa 1970. The idea that import substitution can become exhausted is not inherently illogical. Overprotection can surely make industries inefficient. So suppose some economists argued, despite the evidence just given, that such inefficiency mattered enough in Mexico in 1970 to create broad structural problems.

Even if structural economic problems existed in Mexico, they could not have caused the 1976 and 1982 crises. Structural problems occur when manufacturing or other major sectors of the real economy become inefficient.[37] Economic crises occur when the exchange rate crashes in the financial economy. No standard economic models connect the one kind of problem to the other; some political link is required. The structural problems must visibly erupt, cause a sustained economic slowdown, and give rise to political protest. This pressure forces politicians to borrow and spend excessively or adopt other short-term expedients to inflate the economy. The political links in this overly long deductive chain break apart in the case of Mexico.

Even though some argue that Mexico suffered from long-term industrial problems in 1970, the economic data show that there was not yet any actual slowdown to force politicians to borrow and spend. What contemporaries called the "weakness" of 3.8 percent growth in 1971 [38]—imagine that level of growth being considered weakness!—was only the norm for the year that a new administration took office and began to plan new investment projects.[39] And that normal growth was achieved despite the fact that the Finance Ministry slashed public investment excessively, even in the opinion of some fiscally conservative officials.[40] If such a modest weakness could force the state to borrow and spend its way to crisis, why did zero growth in 1953, the first full year President Adolfo Ruiz Cortines held office, not do the same? Despite the 1976 crisis, growth under President Luis Echeverría, from 1970 through 1976, slowed only slightly, from the 6.6 percent average of the 1950s and 1960s to 6.2 percent.[41]

Then, under President José López Portillo, oil exports surging from nothing in 1976 (new reserves had been discovered a few years earlier) to more than $16 billion in 1982 [42] would have swamped any manufacturing troubles, even if they existed. Not only was there no economic slowdown, but growth exceeded 8 percent a year, some 2 percent above the norm, in the years leading into the 1982 crisis. World oil prices did dip moderately in 1981, a point some Mexican officials belabor, but Mexico's oil export revenues kept surging: almost 50 percent in that year alone. Mexico's total exports grew 28 percent a year in the 1970s, not far behind South Korea's meteoric 35 percent a year.[43] How could industrial exhaustion have forced politicians to borrow and spend?

Angus Maddison, an economist widely known for studies of long-term growth, concludes that Mexico's economic problems were not caused by the "inefficiency of *dirigisme.*" They resulted from "major errors in macroeconomic policy—attempting to push growth too fast and ignoring the canons of fiscal responsibility and sound money."[44] The political question is why Mexican officials adopted hazard-prone policies.

THE "FISCAL CRISIS OF THE STATE"

The theory of the "fiscal crisis of the state"—or what in Mexico is more concretely called the "Pact of 1958," after an implicit government-business-labor bargain solidified in the wake of a powerful 1958–59 grassroots strike wave—takes a somewhat different tack on structural economic failure. It holds that subsidies and tax breaks demanded by business to support healthy investment inevitably caused deepening public sector deficits. Thus, the very effort to sustain growth forced the state to borrow and spend its way to fiscal ruin and economic crisis.

The argument proceeds as follows in the case of Mexico: Adolfo López Mateos faced the powerful strike wave first in 1958 when he was labor secretary and then in 1959 when he became president. He believed that earlier peso devaluations in 1938, 1948, and 1954, by eroding wages, had helped radical labor leaders mobilize rank-and-file support, and he wanted to end that cycle.[45] On assuming the presidency, he told his finance secretary, Antonio Ortiz Mena, that political stability required, on the one hand, sustaining growth, and, on the other hand, avoiding inflation that could lead to another devaluation.[46]

To support investment while holding prices down, the argument continues, the government offered an array of business incentives. For example, state-owned enterprises provided firms with electricity, fuel, and rail transport at below cost; "new and necessary" industries (those pushing beyond easy import substitution) received subsidies and tariff protection. At the same time, taxes remained very low, less than 10 percent of GDP, and could not be raised because the lack of capital controls (unusual among developing nations at the time) would have allowed wealthy Mexicans to send their money abroad to evade taxation. Threats of capital flight are said to have foiled repeated attempts, beginning in 1960, to close loopholes and increase taxes.[47]

Nothing could budge, it is argued. To sustain investment and avoid inflation, the state had to continue providing business subsidies without raising taxes. To cover the resulting budget gap, it could only keep borrowing, from the Bank of Mexico and then from abroad, until at some point lenders balked, and the fiscal scaffolding collapsed in crisis.

This is another intriguing argument that what happened had to happen—the 1976 and 1982 crises were inevitable—but it, too, is unconvincing for two reasons. The first is that taxes could have been raised. In part, this argument is hypothetical, though no more than the argument that they could not have been raised, but it also turns out that taxes actually were raised significantly. The second reason is entirely matter-of-fact. Public sector deficits were *not* increasing in the 1960s. In fact, they were declining. Where was the inevitable fiscal crisis? (It is remarkable how people can cling to theories in the face of contrary evidence.) Of course, public sector deficits exploded before the 1976 and 1982 crises (a point nobody disputes), but they exploded because Presidents Echeverría and López Portillo sharply broke with the Pact of 1958, not because they were captives of it.

Start with the point that taxes could have been raised. Those who argue it was impossible to raise them have made much of a failed 1972 tax reform effort.[48] In 1971, President Echeverría's advisors persuaded him that tax reform was essential to his plan for "shared development"—not just growth but equitable growth—according to Javier Alejo, head of the working group that drafted the tax proposal. State Industries Secretary Horacio Flores de la Peña, the leader of the economic left, strongly supported the reform.[49] The more conservative finance minister, Hugo Margáin, supported it with some cautions; only some Bank of Mexico officials may have opposed it.[50]

The aim was to make the taxes more equitable and reduce evasion. The existing code abetted evasion by compartmentalizing different types of income, such as salaries, business profits, rent on real estate, and interest on bonds. The authorities literally could not tell if one return on interest and another on a salary came from the same person. The fact that bonds and shares were held anonymously likewise abetted evasion. The administration agreed on a measure that required all income to be reported jointly, except on interest and dividends, but bonds and shares could no longer be held anonymously.[51]

Finance Minister Hugo Margáin and other officials met twice in December 1972 with leading bankers, industrialists, and their retinue of attorneys. Leopoldo Solís, director of economic planning under the president, recalls that "private sector representatives were very critical and presented a common front against both bills."[52] Their principal argument, seconded (if not supplied in the first place) by Bank of Mexico officials, was the perennial complaint: tax reform would precipitate capital flight.[53] The administration replied that if wealthy Mexicans sent their capital to the United States or Europe, they would only have to pay higher taxes there.[54] A former ambassador to Washington, Finance Minister Margáin, according to Solis, "showed all his diplomatic skill in overlooking the carping tone of the private sector representatives and went on to explain the bills point-by-point."[55] He apparently did not win them over. A few days later the Mexican Council of Businessmen, an elite group of business leaders, is said to have met privately with Echeverría.[56] He dropped the bill.

Why did Echeverría drop the tax proposal? In response to the question, he talks in circles. He says the private sector did not even meet with him privately, as opposed to formally with him and other economic officials. But he says that though some cabinet members promised that fiscal reform would "solve all Mexico's economic problems," adopting it would not be so easy as they imagined. Theirs were only "partial views." But what had they supposedly missed? "Theorists who write lovely books but never get out of their libraries [do not realize that] nobody invests just to create jobs and pay taxes. Capital needs to reproduce itself and make profits in order to invest more. The capitalist's efforts have to be rewarded." Such pearls of wisdom surely did not escape Leopoldo Solís, Javier Alejo, Hugo Margáin, or other officials involved in the tax reform effort.

Does this episode demonstrate the impossibility of any reform to tax wealthy individuals more? Some academics believe so.[57] Suárez Mier, who worked on tax reform under Alejo, says it never passed because "there were too many interest groups, both in the cabinet and in the private sector close to the government, such as bankers and industrialists." Ortiz Mena says that tax reform was possible—and indeed that some occurred while he was finance secretary in the 1960s—but argues that the danger of capital flight did limit the possibilities: "The idea that you could just tax capital from one day to the next and nothing would happen is the gravest error. If you impose harsher conditions on capital here than in the United States, it will go to the United States. You have to carry out fiscal reform gradually." If he had continued as finance secretary in the 1970s, he says he would not have substantially raised taxes, particularly not on capital. Given Pemex's increasing oil income, he argues, public sector revenue was adequate to support sustained, broad-based development.

Other former officials, including Ortiz Mena's advisors Victor Urquidi and Rafael Izquierdo, think substantial tax reform was entirely feasible. Alejo says that Echeverría and Margáin should not have done what the Finance Ministry always did—bargain with business—but instead should have just sent the bill to the Chamber of Deputies.

Solís is persuasive that the 1972 failure was a mere political bungle on Echeverría's part. The president's strident leftist rhetoric frightened businessmen who, according to a survey commissioned at the time by Solís, expressed "fears that the country was being led to socialism."[58] They therefore reacted to the tax proposal "purely on ideological grounds . . . rather than as managerial personnel who would have assessed the issue in strictly rational terms."[59] Moreover, Solís notes, Echeverría failed to mobilize workers to support tax reform, though they would have benefited as it affected mostly unearned income, but then when inflation took off as a result of budget deficits, he did mobilize them to support wage increases that only caused more inflation. Pushing these wage increases against business opposition required at least as much political clout, Solís is convinced, as would have been required to pass the far more sensible 1972 tax reform.[60]

Rafael Izquierdo, economic advisor to President López Portillo from 1976 to 1982 as well as to Finance Minister Ortiz Mena in the 1960s, concedes that a tax reform would have caused capital to leave Mexico but says it would have returned. Capital had fled several times in the 1950s and 1960s but returned soon enough to Mexico's favorable business climate. Why should it not do the same when wealth holders saw that public finances were sounder and a growing economy offered good investment opportunities?

Another reason to suppose that tax reform was possible is that it actually passed in 1974 and 1981, a fact strangely omitted from debates on the topic.[61] The 1974 legislation required all forms of income, except interest, to be reported jointly.[62] Bonds were taxed at 12 percent if the owner was identified, 16 percent if not.[63] Also, gasoline prices were doubled.[64] This last measure was intended partly to raise short-term revenue, partly as a decoy to stir controversy and draw attention from the rest of the package, Alejo says. The gasoline prices created the predicted storm, the legislation passed, and Echeverría is widely considered to have continued to be one of the most powerful Mexican presidents until the 1976 crisis broke two years later. Between a small excise tax increase in 1973 and the 1974 reform, total tax revenue rose from 8.1 to 10.3 percent of GDP, a far from trivial amount.[65] The 1981 tax reform under López Portillo abolished volumes of paperwork on some 36 federal and 660 local taxes[66] and established new value-added and corporate income taxes. Taxes collected from low-income brackets (between one and five minimum wages) fell 50 percent, while those collected from high-income brackets (more than 15 minimum wages) tripled.[67] This was hardly a trivial reform, either.

The more direct argument against the theory that the Pact of 1958 produced inevitably widening public sector deficits is that, simply, the data do not show them as widening. Poor data provide fertile ground for imaginative theory. The data on federal government debt payments in the 1950s are poor (appendix A), and there are no data at all on state-owned enterprises—the oil company Pemex, electric utilities, railroads, and many other firms that accounted for half of all public spending. If debt payments are excluded, the federal government's balance shows a slightly deteriorating trend from a budget surplus of 0.3 percent of GDP in the 1950s to a deficit of 0.8 percent of GDP in the 1960s—a stellar performance in any case.[68]

The only useful data cover the entire public sector, including the federal government and the state enterprises, debt payments as well as current expenditures. These data, available only since 1960, point to noticeably *decreasing* deficits. They fell from an average of 3.3 percent of GDP in 1960–64 to an average of 2.1 percent of GDP in 1965–70 (Table 3.3).

Anyway, a deficit of 2 or 3 percent of GDP in an economy growing 6 percent a year is a long way from disaster. Deficits remained "very moderate" throughout the 1950s and 1960s, according to Francisco Gil Díaz, Mexico's economically conservative finance secretary from 2000 to 2006.[69] Mexico's fiscal performance throughout the 1960s met the Maastricht Treaty's requirements for European monetary union[70]— better than several European nations have done since joining it.

The Pact of 1958 also could not have erupted into deficits in the 1970s because Echeverría and López Portillo sharply broke from the economic policies of the 1950s and 1960s. These were not just a matter of tax rates and subsidies, but of maintaining something perhaps more critical to investment: business confidence. Echeverría was unprecedentedly and gratuitously acrimonious toward the private sector. For example, he de-

TABLE 3.3. PUBLIC SECTOR BUDGETS, 1960–70 (PERCENT OF GDP)

	Public sector	Federal government plus state enterprises			Federal government alone		
	Surplus or deficit	Revenue	Spending	Surplus or deficit	Revenue	Spending	Surplus or deficit
López Mateos							
1959	NA	NA	NA	NA	7.4	8.1	-0.6
1960	-2.9	14.8	17.4	-2.6	8.1	9.6	-1.6
1961	-2.5	14.5	16.8	-2.3	7.1	8.5	-1.5
1962	-2.7	15.1	17.2	-2.1	7.5	8.8	-1.4
1963	-3.7	15.6	18.5	-2.9	7.9	9.5	-1.6
1964	-4.8	15.0	18.9	-3.9	7.6	9.4	-1.8
Díaz Ordaz							
1965	-0.9	17.5	18.4	-0.9	8.2	9.8	-1.6
1966	-1.2	16.7	17.9	-1.2	8.2	9.1	-0.9
1967	-2.4	17.0	19.0	-2.1	8.4	10.0	-1.6
1968	-2.2	17.1	18.7	-1.6	8.8	9.8	-1.0
1969	-2.2	17.5	19.0	-1.5	9.0	10.2	-1.2
1970	-3.8	17.3	19.4	-2.1	9.1	10.9	-1.8

Contrary to the assumption of those who see structural problems in the Mexican economy, public sector budget deficits were not increasing during the 1960s. In fact, they were decreasing, averaging 3.3 percent of GDP under the López Mateos administration in 1960–64 and 2.1 percent of GDP under the Díaz Ordaz administration in 1965–70. The Public sector includes the federal government, state enterprises, Mexico City, net deficit of public banks, and other off-budget items. All spending data include interest payments.

Federal government data are from Izquierdo 1995, Table VII.15; state enterprise and public sector data are from Table VII.22. The 1960–64 data were originally reconstructed by a Finance–Bank of Mexico working group and should be treated with a little caution. GDP is from INEGI 1994, Table 8.1.

TABLE 3.4. PUBLIC SECTOR BUDGETS, 1970–82 (PERCENT OF GDP)

	Public sector			Government			Pemex
	Revenue	Spending	Surplus or deficit	Revenue	Spending	Surplus or deficit	Net revenue to the state
Díaz Ordaz							
1970	18.9	22.3	-3.8	8.7	9.7	-1.0	0.6
Echeverría							
1971	18.4	20.5	-2.5	8.4	8.8	-0.4	0.2
1972	18.7	22.9	-4.9	8.6	11.6	-3.0	0.4
1973	20.2	25.8	-6.9	9.3	12.4	-3.1	-0.2
1974	21.1	27.0	-7.2	8.8	11.6	-2.8	0.8
1975	23.1	31.9	-10.0	10.0	13.3	-3.3	0.0
1976	23.8	32.0	-9.9	10.7	15.5	-4.8	0.4
López Portillo							
1977	24.2	29.5	-6.7	10.2	13.6	-3.3	1.0
1978	25.5	31.0	-6.7	10.5	14.2	-3.7	1.0
1979	26.2	32.2	-7.4	10.1	15.2	-4.9	1.9
1980	27.8	34.6	-7.9	7.5	16.7	-9.2	6.3
1981	27.7	41.3	-14.7	8.3	20.8	-12.5	4.1
1982	30.1	46.4	-17.6	6.2	26.5	-20.2	8.3

If the Mexican economy had inevitably driven the public sector to run deficits, as those who see structural problems in the economy argue, an effort to contain spending and the failure to raise revenue should have caused the budget squeeze. Quite the opposite happened. Revenue increased substantially, but public spending exploded under President Luis Echeverría, then redoubled under President José López Portillo.

Government spending and revenue includes the federal government and Mexico City. The public sector includes the federal government, Mexico City, state enterprises, and off-budget items. All spending data include interest payments. The public sector deficit also includes the deficit of public banks and is thus slightly larger than the difference between revenue and spending. The data are from Buffie 1990, 422–423, 435–436.

parted from the text of his 1973 state of the union message to improvise an attack on "little rich men" who engaged in capital flight, were "despised by the people," and led their sons "to social inadaptability, to drug addiction, to irresponsibility."[71] When a nervous private sector formed the Businessmen's Coordinating Council, Echeverría's finance secretary and close friend José López Portillo, soon to be president, proclaimed its rather innocuous principles to be "an impossible admixture of Saint Thomas Aquinas' ideology, the Manchester School, eighteenth-century utilitarianism, Ayn Rand's execrable literary productions, and ideas of the Mexican Revolution. . . . [F]rom there to Nazi-fascism is one mere step."[72]

Budget data also show how sharply Echeverría and López Portillo broke from the economic policies of the 1950s and 1960s. If the Pact of 1958 had been the problem, a struggle to contain spending and the failure to raise revenue should have caused a budget squeeze. Nothing of the sort happened (Table 3.4). Public spending exploded from 22 percent to 32 percent of GDP under Echeverría, and even substantial revenue increases could not keep pace. As the economist Edward F. Buffie notes, the government's revenue growth was "relatively strong," rising 2 percent of GDP (thanks to the 1974 tax reform), but "enormous" spending increases, rising 6 percent of GDP, swelled deficits.[73] If state-owned firms are added to the picture, revenue grew by 5 percent of GDP, while spending soared by 10 percent of GDP. And it would be a very odd argument that business pressure forced the state to increase expenditures. The private sector incessantly and clamorously opposed rising expenditures.

López Portillo redoubled Echeverría's performance, increasing public spending from 32 percent to 46 percent of GDP. And after 1977, when new oil fields came on line, there was surely no lack of revenue. The net revenue Pemex provided to the state (excluding all its own expenditures) rose from 0.4 percent of GDP in 1976 to 8 percent of GDP in 1982. At this point, revenue from Pemex alone was almost as large as total federal government revenue had been in 1970. The question is not why the Mexican state faced some inevitable revenue squeeze but why it spent so profligately.

STRUCTURAL PROBLEMS VERSUS PERCEPTIONS

There is a common problem with structural theories about Mexico's crises. Suppose structural industrial problems were at work beneath the surface of things. Still, they had not manifested themselves in 1970. With a sustained 6 percent growth, there had been no economic slowdown. Budget deficits had shown a marginally decreasing trend, and current-account deficits (the net amount Mexico had to borrow from abroad, largely to pay for imports) were a "moderate" 2.8 percent of GDP, again in the judgment of the Mexico's economically conservative finance secretary Gil Díaz.[74]

What is more, everyone thought the economy was doing very well, except for a small intellectual current on the left. Even those who saw structural problems beneath the surface concede that the dominant view of the economy was "triumphalism."[75] Officials across the institutional spectrum of government saw excellent economic prospects.[76] The president of the Federation of Business Chambers delivered encomiums on the economy.[77] Octavio Paz, unflinching critic of his nation, wrote in 1972 that its "economy has made such strides that economists and sociologists point to Mexico as an example for other underdeveloped countries."[78] Fausto Zapata, a close Echeverría advisor, says:

> For many lucid thinkers, with an ability to see into the future, such as Pablo González Casanova in his book *Democracy in Mexico*, the economic model had failed by creating many more poor people than rich. . . . But they were a critical minority. The majority of us lived in total self complacency. In the eyes of the majority, the economy was a marvel. . . . This sort of self complacency was morally reprehensible, but businessmen, social leaders, labor leaders, government, church, and all the great institutions were convinced that, as things were, the country was working very well.

The point is not to minimize Mexico's severely inequitable income distribution (though it was improving slightly), but rather that the broad consensus saw the economy as doing excellently. The consensus did not see structural problems, nor were they evident in data on growth, budget deficits, or foreign borrowing.

How then could invisible structural problems force the Echeverría administration to suddenly loosen spending? In political terms, those problems did not exist. Some economists might warn that grave troubles would surface—surely no economy can continue on a dead reckoning course forever—but these were unproven theories about the future. Politicians do not turn economic policymaking around because of such theoretical arguments. In Mexico, there was no manifest economic failure.

Chapter 4

THE MACROECONOMICS

OF ELITE CONFLICT

The idea that Latin American crises were caused by the "macroeconomics of populism" (the late MIT economist Rudiger Dornbusch's phrase) is a lot simpler than intricate arguments about how structural industrial problems might work their way through the political system to erupt in the financial economy. It is no secret that "populist" politicians (whatever that label means; it could be applied rather broadly) often seek to strengthen their base of support by granting welfare benefits and allowing wage increases far beyond sustainable levels. Such policies can cause budget deficits and inflation and thus lead to crises.

Yet populist pressures on the state did not cause Mexico's crises. The state did not face significant populist pressures because the ruling party so powerfully controlled peasant, labor, and middle-class organizations, and national electoral competition was so trivial. Particularly in the 1976 and 1982 crises, both sometimes blamed on the macroeconomics of populism, the very pattern of public spending shows that it had nothing to do with securing external political support. Public spending and budget deficits (excluding debt payments, which do not buy political support) plunged in actual election years. They surged in *pre*-election years when power was really in dispute, as rival *grupos* within the ruling party sought to gain backing among political elites for their leaders' presidential nomination. This internal contest to be the PRI's official nominee was the principal political cause of economic crises.

LABOR INSURGENCIES REAL AND SUPPOSED

If pressure from social organizations had caused economic crisis in Mexico, it should have done so in the late 1950s, not after 1970. In the authoritative *History of the Mexican Revolution*, José Luis Reyna says that the 1958–59 strike wave led by the railroad union "was the first important proletarian social movement that, momentarily, reached the point of putting the political system in crisis. It is without doubt the most important movement that has arisen since 1935," that is, since the ruling party's corporatist system was consolidated.[1] Reyna could not have forgotten to compare 1958–59 with the so-called labor insurgency of the 1970s because he wrote those words in 1978, shortly after it collapsed. But the powerful 1958–59 grassroots movement, far from provoking the macroeconomics of populism, only ushered in the most stable, rapid growth Mexico has known.

The strike wave began with pocketbook demands and only later threatened the political system. Initial labor protests arose in 1956 among electric utility workers and Mexico City teachers.[2] In 1957, after wages of the 60,000 railroad workers had been eroding for some years, especially as compared with those in other key industries, several sections of the union successfully pressed corporatist leaders to convoke a commission to study the matter. The commission proposed to raise salaries 350 pesos a month, a 38 percent increase for the average worker intended to restore purchasing power to what it had been in 1948.[3] In May 1958, railroad union leaders rejected the commission's advice and asked for only 200 pesos.

With presidential elections approaching in July 1958, Mexico City teachers, along with oil and electric utility workers—all public sector unions except for some of the electric workers—were already petitioning for raises. But rail and telegraph workers had unusual capacity to organize on a national scale outside the corporatist union structure because they controlled communication lines. A supine media could and would lambaste them, but press censorship could not prevent local sections from keeping each other abreast of developments.

A group in the railroad workers salary commission led by one Demetrio Vallejo of Oaxaca not only sought the 350 pesos raise but also began to take moves that threatened the corporatist leadership. They telegraphed a wildcat strike plan to all sections: work should stop at ten o'clock on June 25 for two hours, two more hours the next day, and so on until their demands were met. Otherwise, they would paralyze the nation on the eve of presidential elections. The government and corporatist union bet the wildcat strike would not happen, but they bet wrong. It spread across the nation, stopping transport. On June 30, President Adolfo Ruiz Cortines offered 215 pesos, and the insurgents accepted. They had won—the first round.

After more strikes, the government let railworkers call a leadership vote in August, and Vallejo was elected, 59,759 votes to 9. But the union did not know when to quit. It made more demands: a 32 percent raise for train dispatchers, another 16.7 percent for all railworkers, 10 pesos a day for rent. It even petitioned to improve inept rail management, for example, not charging U.S. mining companies 20 percent less than Mexican farmers. The "railroad workers effect" spread: electric utility workers attacked their corporatist leadership; Pemex workers proposed to install "authentic labor democracy"; telephone workers cut off service briefly. Even Fidel Velázquez, perpetual boss of the official labor movement, noticed the discontent and announced that social justice was just a "myth" in Mexico.

When the railworkers' union threatened more strikes before Easter 1959, the Federal Arbitration and Conciliation Board took the usual step of declaring them illegal, but this time the government, under the new president Adolfo López Mateos, meant it. On Holy Thursday, 13,000 workers were fired; on Easter Sunday, 10,000 workers were jailed. In the end as many as 20,000 lost their jobs, means of subsistence, and, in many cases, company-supplied homes. Charged with "social dissolution" (whatever exactly that meant, it was on the law books), Vallejo was locked up until 1971. The upshot was, as the historian Enrique Krauze says, "the subordination—complete or partial—of virtually all groups within the society."[4]

Facing powerful strikes, wage demands, and a presidential election, which could not be allowed to descend into chaos even if a loss was inconceivable, the government spent heavily in 1958. Real expenditures, excluding debt service, grew 14 percent (Table 4.1) that year. But long before the fateful Easter weekend that ended the strikes, López Mateos and his finance secretary, Antonio Ortiz Mena, agreed that inflation must be stopped.[5] As they cut spending 5 percent in real terms in 1959, inflation fell to a mere 2 percent, incredibly low for a developing country, and averaged about that level for the next five years. How a cooperative politics among *grupos* in the central administration allowed those cuts to be enforced is a story for later chapters, but the data show that they were enforced. The only real, if temporary, grassroots threat to the political system since its consolidation in the 1930s produced no economic crisis.

Might the labor insurgency of the 1970s, as it is called, even if less powerful than the 1958–59 strikes, have contributed to the 1976 crisis? There are two problems with the idea. First, in contrast to much union activity in other Latin American nations such as Brazil and Chile, Mexico's so-called insurgency was largely instigated by the administration, indeed by the president, and never overwhelmed the state's resources to control it.[6] Second, unlike the 1958–59 strikes, the disputes in the 1970s

If societal pressure had caused economic crisis in Mexico, crisis should have erupted after the most powerful grassroots protest since the 1930s, the 1958–59 strike wave that Adolfo López Mateos faced, first as labor secretary and then as president. But the following decade ushered in Mexico's most stable, rapid growth of the twentieth century. Photo reproduced with permission of the General Secretariat of the Organization of American States.

did not even concern wage demands that could cause macroeconomic problems, but rather union democratization, or at least the ousting of *charro* leaders. The lack of wage demands is not surprising, as the economy had been growing rapidly for years, and organized labor, corporatist though it was, had benefited handsomely from that growth. Indeed,

	Real spending growth (percent per year)	Surplus or deficit (percent of GDP)	GDP growth (percent per year)
Alemán			
1947	12.2	0.9	3.5
1948	27.8	−0.2	4.1
1949	32.2	1.9	5.5
1950	−14.0	1.3	10
1951	12.0	1.6	7.7
1952	32.5	0.7	4.0
Ruiz Cortines			
1953	−15.2	0.2	0.3
1954	32.4	−0.6	10.0
1955	−8.0	0.9	8.5
1956	13.7	0.6	6.8
1957	1.0	0.3	7.6
1958	14.1	0.5	5.4
López Mateos			
1959	−5.3	−0.4	3.0
1960	26.5	−1.1	8.2
1961	−14.2	−0.4	4.9
1962	9.9	−0.4	4.6
1963	10.8	−0.2	8.0
1964	20.3	−1.1	11.7
Díaz Ordaz			
1965	22.7	−1.8	6.5
1966	−8.5	−0.4	6.9
1967	10.6	−0.6	6.3
1968	8.3	−0.1	8.1
1969	18.4	−1.0	6.3
1970	4.9	−0.7	6.9

As nationwide strikes erupted and a presidential election approached in 1958, the
Mexican government rapidly increased spending. But the next year it slashed spending, bringing inflation down to 2 percent and keeping it about there—an incredibly
low rate for a developing country.

All spending excludes debt payments. (Data on them are not available for most
of these years, and debt payments do not buy political support anyway.) For 1953–58
spending data are from INEGI 1994, Table 17.10, revenue from Table 17.6. For
1959–70 spending is from Izquierdo 1995, Table VII.5, revenue from Table VII.8.
GDP in current and 1970s pesos is from INEGI 1994, Table 8.1.

today all studies agree that income distribution was improving at least slightly in the 1960s, and migration studies indicate that new arrivals to Mexico City found jobs quickly, more than half of them in the formal industrial sector.[7]

Odd though it may seem, President Luis Echeverría cultivated the labor insurgency, and it petered out when he abandoned it. Though he had been interior secretary when President Gustavo Díaz Ordaz suppressed anti-authoritarian protests at Tlatelolco Square in 1968, Echeverría sought to distance himself from Tlatelolco during his campaign, promising "democratic opening" and "shared development." In December 1970, just after taking office, he proclaimed, "How are we going to talk of democracy in Mexico if, when union leadership is chosen, the process is not democratic?"[8] He passed a new labor law that theoretically allowed only twenty workers in a plant to demand a revote to determine which union should represent them. More important, since the law could always be skirted, in 1972 Echeverría appointed an anti-*charro* labor secretary, Porfirio Muñoz Ledo, who began recognizing important unions outside the corporatist federation, such as the National Iron and Steelworkers representing employees at the Spicer and Zapata Consortium factories.[9]

The core of the labor insurgency was the Democratic Tendency, a movement of electric utility workers. Its history went back a decade. After the government nationalized American Foreign Power in 1960, really a takeover via the U.S. stock market, its relatively democratic union (the corporatist bureaucracy often let multinationals deal with their own labor affairs) and the larger *charro* union within the state-owned Federal Electricity Commission were legally required to combine.[10] But the vote was delayed repeatedly because the more democratic union, led by Rafael Galván, did not want to be swallowed up, and the *charro* union, which was allowed to continue signing up more workers, wanted to be sure it would have an overwhelming majority.

As Echeverría turned up the democratic rhetoric, so did Galván, and the corporatist Conciliation and Arbitration Board announced union elections. The *charro* union, led by Francisco Pérez Rios, easily won, but Galván protested, saying the ballots had asked which union workers belonged to, not which one they wanted to represent them. He fought the vote all the way the Supreme Court, of course losing. Believing as the labor leader Vicente Lombardo had under President Lázaro Cárdenas in the 1930s that labor should ally with progressive, Revolutionary currents within the state, Galván petitioned to strike, hoping that the president

Societal demands did not cause Mexico's 1976 crisis. For one thing, the so-called labor insurgency of the early 1970s was actually sustained by none other than President Luis Echeverría (left) himself, in a bid to usurp control from the union boss Fidel Velázquez (right). When Echeverría decided he needed Velázquez' support after all, he abandoned the labor insurgency and it collapsed.

would step in. But the Conciliation and Arbitration Board declared the strike illegal, and the *charro* union signed a contract with the electric utility to represent all workers.

Then Echeverría decided to enter the fray to rescue the Democratic Tendency. He called a congress to decide the matter—even if it had already legally been decided—but then he personally worked out a pact creating the Unique Electrical Workers of Mexico. Pérez Rios of the *charro* union would have the highest post, general secretary, and Galván of the Democratic Tendency would be second-in-command.

Thus, only the president's extra-legal, if not illegal, intervention—after Galván lost the vote, the Supreme Court confirmed the loss, and the proposed strike was defeated—kept the Democratic Tendency afloat. This was not a powerful grassroots revolt from below, like that of the railworkers in 1958–59, but rather the powerful hand of Luis Echeverría from above, reaching down to manipulate the action like a puppeteer.

Emilio Carrillo Gamboa, director of the telecommunications giant Teléfonos de México (Telmex), which faced the largest actual strike under the administration, also over union control rather than wages and also decided by Echeverría rather than by established procedures, says the president and labor secretary supported dissidents because they wanted "to get rid of" Fidel Velázquez: "They felt that the real leader of the labor movement in Mexico should be the secretary of labor."[11] The labor secretary served at the will of the president, so Echeverría would have gained control.

But by 1973, facing rising inflation and presidential succession, Echeverría backed off from supporting the Democratic Tendency.[12] The corporatist labor structure destroyed it by 1976, then cleaned up the rest of the so-called labor insurgency within a couple of years.[13] Under the conservative Díaz Ordaz, 3.0 percent of strike petitions had been recognized as legal, but only 1.9 percent were under Echeverría.[14] There were no remotely powerful enough "populist" economic demands to cause an economic crisis.

Under President José López Portillo (1976–82), unions continued to be dependent on the state. No one recognized this better than Carlos Tello, the leftist secretary of State Industries whose nationalist economic project sought union support. He wrote in 1981:

> On the one hand, union leaders say they will put organized labor at the service of the development project of the state. . . . On the other hand, . . . the labor movement has wandered off course, suffered bureaucratization, lost the impetus it had [in the 1930s], grown more

slowly, failed to advance in its organizational structure, become de-politicized and divided, generally succumbed to antidemocratic and repressive practices, and allowed workers' real salaries to fall.[15]

Workers' real earnings suffered declines under López Portillo, ranging from 7 percent in manufacturing to 20 percent in the public sector.[16] After peaking in 1978 and 1979, federal jurisdiction strikes (those in major national industries) fell sharply, long before the 1982 crisis approached.[17] Under the administration of de la Madrid in the 1980s, even as real minimum wages fell by half,[18] the percentage of legally recognized strikes continued to decline.[19] Mexican labor quiescence contrasted with protest in other large Latin American nations.[20] This is not the way that populist demands cause economic crises.

THE SPENDING CYCLE OF ELITE POLITICS

Electoral spending in developing nations, as politicians vie to buy support at the polls, is often supposed to cause macroeconomic instability that can lead to crises.[21] Stephan Haggard and Robert R. Kaufman argue that even authoritarian regimes often see elections as referenda and use spending to "legitimate their rule."[22] Korea shows evidence of such an electoral cycle.[23] A study of politically motivated spending across Latin America concludes that politicians there, like their counterparts elsewhere, used public expenditure—building infrastructure, recruiting state workers, providing welfare benefits—as "a weapon for survival."[24] Spending increased significantly during election years "because governments running for reelection sought to buy support."[25]

This argument does not fit Mexico. From 1952, when a strong opposition presidential campaign led by Miguel Henríquez Guzmán was defeated, until 1988, when Cuauhtémoc Cárdenas again seriously challenged the ruling party, the PRI faced no meaningful electoral competition. Opposition parties never got more than 15 percent of the official vote.[26] Moreover, the state controlled social organizations so well that they could not even seriously protest electoral fraud. As González Casanova noted in *Democracy in Mexico* (democracy was for him a hope, not a fact), "Civil life has not reached the level at which authorities become compelled in their own interest to register carefully the votes of the opposition—that is, the level at which not doing so would provoke serious conflicts."[27] Even in 1988, when the official count showed the ruling party getting a bare 50 percent of the votes cast,[28] the PRI was not concerned that things would go badly until election night itself.[29]

Ames suggests that there might have been an electoral spending cycle in Mexico anyway because the margin of victory mattered to "a host of lower-level politicians on their way up."[30] But they did not control any significant portion of public spending. Why should the president, constitutionally prohibited from reelection, hazard massive expenditures on lower-level politicians? (A little for some favorites would hardly matter.) As for cabinet secretaries who played an important role in approving expenditures, they rose through the central administration, not through elected posts. What would they care about armies of politicians running not only for electoral posts but also for lower-level ones?

Political succession was never decided in elections; the transfer of power was never in play then. The contest for the party's nomination was the real one, no matter what the office. A precandidate for the nomination had to demonstrate support not because the party feared it might lose the election but because it wanted him to prove he could maintain order. Braulio Maldonado, a governor of Baja California who may have provided the only inside account of the political system prior to the 1990s (and was duly ostracized), described the candidate who secures the president's endorsement:

> [T]he contender has . . . given the shirt off his back, he has made countless promises, often at the price of his own dignity. He has been mercilessly exploited by hundreds of politicians, labor bosses, peasant leaders, and by mercenary journalists. . . . He has already made arrangements for the disbursement of the public budget, or even for his own salary, for the period of his incumbency. [But once he has secured presidential approval] the process is exceedingly easy, and battle is won, victory having been secured in governmental anterooms. Now the labor unions, the peasant organizations, the popular sector and the party declare him to be the Official Candidate.[31]

Much as with this gubernatorial hopeful, cabinet secretaries vying in the big race, the presidential nomination, sought to gain support among political currents—other high officials, governors, labor—to show that they could maintain national political order.

The Mexican pattern of political spending reflected the mechanism of political succession: it generally peaked in the pre-electoral year, when internal party competition for the presidential nomination determined the real transfer of power, and it was cut back during the year when elections, essentially public relations events, were staged. The decade of the 1950s may have been an exception (Table 4.1). The data are bad for those years because they only track government spending—not state enterprise spending, which constituted half of the total public sector budget and, according to Finance Ministry sources, was often the place where politically motivated spending was concentrated.[32] But the state might well have increased spending during the two presidential election years in the 1950s for logical political reasons.

In 1952, General Miguel Henríquez Guzmán mounted the last serious opposition presidential campaign before the political system was fully consolidated. Real government spending soared 12 percent in 1951 when Henríquez Guzmán's party split off, then 32 percent in the election year 1952. (Again, spending data exclude debt service to highlight their current political uses.) Spending was tightened after the election, falling 15 percent in 1953. In 1958, though the election was not in doubt, the powerful strikes by rail and other public sector workers were managed via raises as well as repression. The raises were mostly borne by state-owned enterprises, such as railroads, not in the federal budget, but teachers' salaries were in the budget, and other spending on the budget might have been used. Having inched up 1 percent in 1957, real expenditure swelled 14 percent in the election year. Again, it was tightened the next year, falling 5 percent as the strikes ended. In any event, budget deficits (deficits, not spending, are what can cause crises) were less than 1 percent of GDP during both election years. And there was no crisis.

In the 1960s, the pre-electoral spending cycle began to emerge, peaking in the year when *grupos* vied within the ruling party for its official presidential nomination and falling off in actual election years. The data from the first half of the decade are still poor. A Bank of Mexico–Finance Ministry working group later reconstructed complete public sector budgets, including state enterprises as well as the government, but it is impossible to separate out debt payments, which lag behind spending on actual programs. The data, such as they are, show the biggest increase of 16 percent in the pre-electoral year of 1963 and a slightly lesser increase of 14 percent in the election year of 1964 (Table 4.2).

But this is a case where anecdotes are better than data. Finance Minister Ortiz Mena says that presidential hopefuls used public spending to curry favor in their efforts to win the 1963 presidential nomination. For example, Donato Miranda Fonseca, secretary of Presidency—an oddly named ministry, distinct from the president's actual office, that allocated investment funds—let the secretary of Public Works and the secretary of Communications and Transport undertake large construction programs, hoping to gain their support for his candidacy.

TABLE 4.2. PUBLIC SECTOR SPENDING GROWTH AND BUDGET
DEFICITS, 1960–70

	Real spending growth (percent per year)	Surplus or deficit (percent of GDP)	GDP growth (percent per year)
López Mateos			
1960	NA	−2.6	8.2
1961	1.0	−2.3	4.9
1962	7.3	−2.1	4.6
1963	15.9	−2.9	8.0
1964	14.3	−3.9	11.7
Díaz Ordaz			
1965	3.7	−0.9	6.5
1966	4.2	−1.2	6.9
1967	12.8	−2.1	6.3
1968	6.3	−1.6	8.1
1969	8.0	−1.5	6.3
1970	9.3	−2.1	6.9

Data from the 1960s do not show a clear cycle of increased spending in the year before elections, as presidential hopefuls tried to buy support from other political elites, and reduced spending in actual election years, when the winner was no longer in doubt. In part, lack of evidence for this cycle may be due to poor data. The data include debt payments (none other are available), which often surged after current expenditures (as, for example, under the López Portillo administration—see Table 4.3). In any event, Finance Ministry officials say some presidential hopefuls were already beginning to spend heavily in the pre-electoral years.

The public sector in this table includes the federal government and state enterprises but not Mexico City or off-budget items, for which total spending data are unavailable. All spending includes debt payments. Federal government data are from Izquierdo 1995, Table VII.15; state enterprise data are from Table VII.22. The 1960–64 data were originally reconstructed by a Finance–Bank of Mexico working group and should be treated with a little caution. GDP is from INEGI 1994, Table 8.1.

The most flagrant case was Benito Coquet, director of Social Security, the principal social welfare program for workers.[33] A long-time ally of the president—indeed his former boss in the Education Ministry in the early 1940s—Coquet sought to build support for his presidential candidacy by taking out massive "floating" loans, contracted with foreign banks but kept off the books and unknown to the Finance Ministry, to speed construction of a national network of medical centers, housing complexes, movie theaters, and other projects. The loans came to light shortly after Victor Urquidi, the finance minister's economic advisor, had painted a rosy picture to Washington financial circles of Mexico's modest foreign borrowing requirements. The disclosure embarrassed Urquidi, making him appear deceptive or incompetent.[34]

The Social Security budget, after averaging 225 million pesos annually from 1959 through 1962, soared to 892 million in 1963 and then 2,176 million in 1964,[35] a $200 million increase for the two years, amounting to nearly a fifth of Mexico's total accumulated foreign debt.[36] In 1965, authorized foreign borrowing jumped from $92 million to $360 million, as the "floating" loans were, perforce, put on the books.[37] This borrowing and spending was a principal factor posing a threat of economic crisis in 1965, according to Finance sources.

Social Security spending appears to have followed an electoral as well as a pre-electoral cycle, quadrupling in 1963 during the PRI's internal nomination contest, then doubling during the election year 1964. The timing cannot be completely wrong: even if Coquet was trying to build support for his nomination, medical centers and other construction could not be stopped dead when he lost. But, as well, much of the money registered as public spending during the election year 1964 could well have actually been paid during the pre-electoral year 1963,[38] because Mexico's public sector financial system had mechanisms to delay putting spending on the books. For example, President Díaz Ordaz once asked Julio Rodolfo Moctezuma, then director of public investments, how much several recently built schools had cost. A *fideicomiso* for the schools, an ad hoc construction fund backed by a public bank, paid the contractors, but the Education Ministry, still lacking funds for the schools, paid nothing. Eventually the ministry would reimburse the *fideicomiso*, with interest, but it had not yet done so when Díaz Ordaz asked Moctezuma how much the schools had cost the government. Thus, his answer was: so far, nothing.

The fact that some significant portion of investment, though just what proportion cannot be determined, was made substantially earlier than indicated by fiscal data only reinforces evidence for a pre-electoral political spending cycle. Actual spending during the election year was less than budgets indicate since some of the funds were really paid out earlier. Likewise, some spending registered in the pre-electoral year was paid out even earlier. The nomination contest simply started somewhat before the fiscal data suggest, in an administration's fourth or even third year.[39]

The data from the mid-1960s through the mid-1980s are good, and the pre-electoral spending cycle is clear and powerful (see Table 4.3). The pattern can be corroborated by a regression to isolate the political cycle of public spending from economic factors such as GDP (increases provide more resources) or foreign reserves (increases provide external funds). The result is that from 1961 through 1988 public spending typically rose 11 percent in the fifth year, during the party's internal contest for the presidential nomination, and fell 12 percent in the sixth year when actual elections took place (appendix B). If the regression is done in different ways, the precise numbers vary, but the basic results are always the same.

Under Díaz Ordaz, public spending rose 13 percent in the pre-election year 1969 and only 1 percent in the election year 1970 (excluding debt payments). The largest deficit, though only 0.7 percent of GDP, was in the pre-election year. Under Echeverría, public spending rose 27 percent in the pre-election year 1975, and none at all in the election year 1976. Again, the largest deficit, now very serious at 6.5 percent of GDP (still excluding debt payments), was in the pre-election year.

The worst case was López Portillo. Public spending rose rapidly, topping out at a 22 percent increase in the pre-electoral year 1981. The deficit was also by far the worst that year, at 7.2 percent of GDP. De la Madrid, then the planning and budget secretary in charge of monitoring expenditure, was known as a fiscal conservative but did not enforce cuts that the economic cabinet had agreed to.[40] On the contrary, concludes José Ramón López Portillo, son of the president and an official under de la Madrid, his boss "proved to be flexible enough to . . . disguise his own economic position in order not to endanger his political future."[41]

The Planning and Budget Ministry even concealed spending data. As late as August, Planning and Budget's statistical director, one Carlos Salinas, continued to estimate the budget deficit based on April data. After his boss, de la Madrid, won the presidential nomination in September, the estimate suddenly increased by two-thirds.[42] Had he admitted the budget problem and slashed spending earlier, even supporters agree, de la Madrid would have undermined his candidacy.[43] Budget cuts began immediately after the nomination. Public spending was slashed 8 percent during the actual election year 1982, and the deficit, excluding debt payments, was a mere 0.6 percent of GDP. But because of massive accumulated debt, the total deficit was 14.7 percent of GDP: catastrophe level.

During de la Madrid's administration, Mexico's budgets were intrusively monitored by the IMF and its economy was mired in recession.

TABLE 4.3. PUBLIC SECTOR SPENDING GROWTH AND BUDGET DEFICITS, 1966–88

	Real spending growth (percent per year)		Surplus or deficit (percent of GDP)		GDP growth (percent per year)
	Total	Excluding interest	Total	Excluding interest	
Díaz Ordaz					
1966	4	3	−1.4	−0.3	6.9
1967	9	9	−1.9	−0.7	6.3
1968	7	7	−1.5	−0.2	8.1
1969	13	13	−2.1	−0.7	6.3
1970	3	1	−1.4	0.2	6.9
Echeverría					
1971	6	7	−2.0	−0.5	3.8
1972	21	21	−3.5	−1.8	8.2
1973	23	25	−5.2	−3.5	8.5
1974	11	10	−5.2	−3.3	5.1
1975	26	27	−8.5	−6.5	5.7
1976	2	0	−6.8	−4.2	4.4
López Portillo					
1977	0	−2	−4.6	−1.8	3.4
1978	12	12	−4.5	−1.6	9.0
1979	17	17	−5.0	−2.0	9.7
1980	21	21	−5.6	−2.4	9.2
1981	26	22	−12.0	−7.2	8.8
1982	18	−8	−14.7	−0.6	−0.6
de la Madrid					
1983	−16	−17	−7.4	6.1	−4.2
1984	−4	1	−5.8	5.9	3.6
1985	−3	−7	−6.8	5.4	2.6
1986	0	−13	−12.3	5.0	−3.8
1987	10	−1	−13.4	7.4	1.9
1988	−13	−9	−9.9	8.4	1.2

After 1970, public sector spending surged in the year before elections, as presidential hopefuls vied to buy support from other political elites, and fell in actual election years, when power was no longer in dispute.

Data include federal government and state enterprises but not Mexico City or off-budget items that are unavailable in consolidated figures. All figures are net of amortization, the correct method (see appendix A). Revenue is from Salinas 1992, 161. Spending is from Salinas 1992, 168. GDP in current and 1980 pesos is from Cardenas 1996, 214–215, Table A.4.

Nevertheless, the pre-electoral spending pattern appeared to continue. Real public spending practically held its own, falling only 1 percent, in the pre-electoral year 1987, then was cut 9 percent in the electoral year 1988. Here some caution is in order. The economy had been such a mess for the entire administration that this spending may well have been the least of the problems. And excluding debt payments, the budget was in substantial surplus.

In any case, sophisticated economist-politicians of the late 1980s found more innovative, less visible ways to inflate the economy in the pre-electoral year. The total volume of public development bank loans, which can cause inflation and overvaluation just as surely as budget deficits, soared from 22 percent of GDP in 1985 to 33 percent of GDP in the pre-electoral year 1987[44]—an enormous increase conveniently invisible in the fiscal accounts scrutinized by the IMF. As economic czar since eliminating his rival in 1986, Carlos Salinas effectively controlled that lending. He and his *grupo* also contributed to inflating the securities market 500 percent from January through September 1987[45]—and thus expectations about their economic management abilities, according to sources including State Industries Secretary Francisco Labastida, not part of the nomination fray that year.[46] Beginning October 6, two days after Salinas won the presidential nomination and two weeks before the 1987 U.S. market crash, the Mexican securities market broke, ultimately sinking further than any other in the world.[47]

THE ECONOMIC PERILS OF ELITE POLITICS

Candidates for the ruling party's presidential nomination not only used spending, but also hid it; the data itself, hard enough to analyze in a developing country before the advent of computers, became politicized. For example, in 1973, President Echeverría made his boyhood friend López Portillo finance minister. Sensing what this promotion meant, López Portillo boldly remarked in his first conversations with Bank of Mexico Director Ernesto Fernández Hurtado, "You understand that I am on a direct road to the presidency of the republic."[48] Before long López Portillo's extravagant spending habits, helping him along that road, clashed with the Bank of Mexico's customary fiscal conservatism. Sergio Ghigliazza, then a third-ranking bank official, recalls that he became the primary liaison with Finance because higher-ups stopped talking to each other. In one meeting, López Portillo named a figure for the public sector deficit that Ghigliazza knew to be half the size of the real deficit because all government revenue was deposited in Bank of Mexico accounts and all spending was withdrawn from them. Ghigliazza kept raising his hand to make this point, but the finance secretary refused to call on him, so he finally stood up and blurted it out. López Portillo banged his fist on the table and ended the meeting. Thus was the Finance Ministry's figure for the deficit determined.

Not only presidential hopefuls but also the president himself had motives to inflate the economy as the nomination approached. The better it appeared to be doing when he designated his preferred successor, the less opportunity any potential opposition had to organize. This was a consideration of utmost gravity. Serious threats to the political system never came from below; they always arose when a disgruntled faction of the political elite rebelled, mobilized societal sectors, and waged an opposition campaign, as Henríquez Guzmán did in 1952 and Cárdenas in 1988.[49] Salinas, who had grown up inside Mexican politics, says that the president's greatest responsibility during succession was "to keep confrontation between different *grupos* and currents from tearing the ruling party apart."[50] An inflated economy discouraged factions from splitting off—they would have had a harder time mobilizing support—and gave the president latitude to designate his preferred successor. Gustavo Carvajal, a former president of the PRI whose father was interior secretary, observes:

> The moment of greatest spending was an administration's fourth and fifth years [not the sixth year when elections were held]. That was its strongest moment, when it consolidated projects; the whole government structure was involved in public works—ports, dams, irrigation. Investment strengthens the party; there is plenty of work to go around; the private sector has good profits. As a result, the nation is generally free of conflicts when the presidential candidate is named.

As soon as the presidential successor was "revealed," the traditional brigade of party officials, labor bosses, peasant leaders, and anyone else who mattered—especially the losing candidates—was obliged to congratulate the winner. Now political schism and an opposition campaign became hopeless; everyone important had endorsed the winner, and anyone who broke off would look like a spoiler. Cárdenas and Henríquez Guzmán both initiated their splits before the nomination—and in conditions when important economic sectors had been hurt. It was the period before the nomination when economic troubles must not surface.

Presidential succession was perilous because the logic of the system was grim. Hopeful presidential candidates had incentives to build support by spending and hiding spending, but even more than the candidate, the *grupo* had to wage struggle. The candidate had already achieved the normal pinnacle of a political career as cabinet secretary, but his followers' still incomplete ambitions depended on his advancement.

For example, David Ibarra, finance secretary and a presidential contender in 1981, charges that it was particularly subordinates of his rival Miguel de la Madrid, such as Carlos Salinas, who spent massively to recruit governors and other political elites to support their boss's ambitions.[51] De la Madrid says that members of Ibarra's *grupo*, such as Óscar Levín, orchestrated "low blows," such as press calumnies, against him. Finally, de la Madrid asked Ibarra, "Isn't there some way to smooth things over? Why should you and I be fighting if we're good friends?"[52] Perhaps the two of them could have smoothed things over. The problem was that their subordinates had more to win or lose than they. Compare the political careers of Carlos Salinas and Óscar Levín. How many have even heard of Levín?

The president, supposedly in charge, thus found himself atop a dangerous terrain of struggling *grupos*. He could not even trust economic data from them. Anyway, he had good motives to spend or let *grupos* spend, if only to make all of them think they were really playing in the presidential race. In this way, he ensured that none of them would split off, launch an opposition campaign, and tear the political system apart.

Such intra-elite conflict did not inevitably cause crisis in Mexico, any more than incumbents' spending to buy votes in democracies inevitably does. But it was the political system's inherent vulnerability, the peril that could lead to economic crisis. The critical issue was controlling intra-elite conflict, rather than relations between state and society. The next two chapters take up the question—a puzzle in its own right—as to how the political system did repeatedly manage to control internal conflict and avert crises in the 1950s and 1960s.

Chapter 5

THE CRISES THAT

DIDN'T HAPPEN

Having put to rest socioeconomic accounts about Mexico's crises, the argument now turns to palace politics: how elite cooperation was requisite for economic stability, and how elite struggle caused crises. The first question concerns stability. Why was Mexico so stable in the 1950s and 1960s?

A principle of social science requires that an explanation of why something happens should be accompanied by an explanation of why it does *not* happen. Otherwise, how can the changes that made the difference be identified? A problem with many theories about economic crises is that they do not even attempt to explain stability, except as a seemingly natural state that would obtain, barring specific problems.[1] The very names of the usual theories suggest that all nations need to do is avoid problems—the "exhaustion of import substitution," the "fiscal crisis of the state," the "macroeconomics of populism"—to maintain stability. But periodic crises are almost the normal state in underdeveloped countries. These countries averaged 4.4 crises each from 1976 to 1995—one every four and a half years.[2] It is a little too easy to discover favorite problems in underdeveloped economies and blame crises on them. The unusual situation—the situation that might point to critical political factors—is sustained stability.

There is another reason to try to understand economic stability. A series of crises could be caused by various different pressures—financial contagion from nearby countries, a collapse in the world price of a country's main export, the election of politicians who do not understand macroeconomics—but it is far less likely that a series of fortunate accidents would allow a state to maintain economic stability in the face of diverse pressures. If some constellation of political characteristics helped avert the different threats that could have erupted in crises in Mexico in the 1950s and 1960s, then that constellation must have been a critical requisite of stability. If, after it eroded, the nation succumbed to a series of crises, then its loss is an important underlying cause of the crises, whatever contingent circumstances entered as well.

How did the Mexican state avert crises in the 1950s and 1960s? What did officials do to prevent the crises? Who proposed the policies? Who had political authority to enforce policies? The answer—surprisingly controversial, given the acknowledged power of Mexico's president—is that, time and again, he was at the head of the chain of command, he enforced the policies, though he usually accepted his finance secretary's advice. The president controlled the state so powerfully that he could require interior secretaries, labor secretaries, and other officials to carry out what the finance secretary said they must in order to avert crisis.

A FINANCE-BANKING ALLIANCE?

Simply telling the story of what happened in Mexican politics is rarely simple. Who actually had authority over economic policy before 1970? The answer is not obvious: formal institutions often appeared to work one way, while power might be really exercised in another way. There are two basic views:

- Finance independence. A fiscally conservative Finance Ministry, largely independent from the political realm—and in particular independent from the contest over presidential succession—controlled the economy. Such a politically independent agency, staffed by well-educated officials who enjoyed secure careers, had the capacity and incentive to maintain economic stability. This is much the way Asian success stories of economic management have been explained.
- Presidential authority. A president with the authority to set policy—and orchestrate state action to enforce it—defended the political system's long-term interests, high among them economic stability. Such an executive might well have the incentive to avert crises, as Mancur Olson, a political scientist who leans heavily on economic models, has suggested: "A secure autocrat has an encompassing interest in his domain that leads him to provide a peaceful order and other public goods."[3]

The theory of Finance independence is the majority view. It holds that the *políticos*, politicians, in the Interior Ministry, Labor Ministry, and party apparatus were responsible for maintaining political order—co-opting or, if necessary, repressing groups that caused problems—and were the only real contestants for the presidency.[4] In a separate arena, the *técnicos*, technical experts, in the Finance Ministry and Bank of Mexico managed the economy. The U.S. political scientist Miguel Ángel Centeno writes: "For all intents and purposes [the finance minister] had absolute control over the budget and general economic policy of the government. . . . [Finance] could even resist presidential efforts to curtail its autonomy."[5] The Mexican political scientist Miguel Basáñez goes so far as to say that "politicians were in charge of political problems; *técnicos* were in charge of economic and financial problems; and specialists [such as in the ministries of Education or Public Works] were in charge of general government services."[6]

Schematic as the idea seems—when have those in charge of political problems stayed away from the public purse? and when have investments in schools or infrastructure been managed by mere specialists?—it does have support from some former high Mexican officials. José Andrés de Oteyza, the leftist minister of State Industries under López Portillo, concurs that political and economic management were separate before 1970:

> The PRI never was a political party in the strict sense of the word; it was a political system that brought together distinct political forces and harmonized solutions among them. Under the umbrella of the PRI were currents of the center, center right, center left—not extremes, never fascists or communists, but a broad political compass—and that pluralism and its representation in the government allowed a *sui generis* form of democracy. I accept *sui generis*, but in the end it was democratic, plural, representative. It was why the system lasted for so many decades, for even though some express the opposite opinion, it never was a particularly authoritarian or repressive regime.
>
> In a country where neither the legislative nor the judicial branches had much weight at all, the real equilibrium of forces was determined at the heart of the executive power, in the president's cabinet. Within it were secretaries or ministers who represented different interests. To caricature the situation, the agriculture minister represented modern, mechanized agriculture, while the agrarian reform minister represented the poorest peasants. The industry minister obviously advocated for his industrial concerns, while there were representatives of intellectuals, academics, progressives. And the president managed this whole political contest, reserving the last word for himself.
>
> For decades, this contest was basically political, not spilling into economic management. That was delegated to the treasury secretary,

the secretary of finances, who had enormous force but really, really, never played a role in presidential succession. It was only the *políticos políticos* who could reach the presidency. There was an unwritten rule that to truly be a presidential candidate you had to have a certain electoral experience. All the presidents of the [early] era had it— Cárdenas, Alemán, Ruiz Cortines, López Mateos, Díaz Ordaz. They had been governors, senators, deputies. Finance had enormous economic power—uncontested economic power—but the contest for the presidency took place among the key political figures.

Manuel Suárez Mier, a former Bank of Mexico official at the other end of the Mexican political spectrum from de Oteyza, concurs that an unpoliticized Finance Ministry before 1970 was critical to economic stability:

There was a firewall between financial and political management. Political leaders trusted financial managers and left them fairly free; the *quid pro quo* was that they didn't have a political future. It was perceived that for economic success, you couldn't mingle the checkbook with political power.

This separation derived from the administration of Porfirio Díaz [before the Mexican Revolution]. His so-called *científicos* [the equivalent of *técnicos*] had a great deal of status and income, but no access to political power. After the Revolution, Adolfo de la Huerta was the last finance minister who aspired to be president. [His 1923 revolt was brutally quashed.] Look at President Lázaro Cárdenas—he was very leftist but throughout his administration maintained a conservative finance minister.

There are two rather different ways of understanding Finance independence. One sees it as based on an alliance with private Mexican banking and access to international lenders; the other sees it as simply based on elite norms and custom.

The idea of a banking–Finance Ministry alliance tries to explain not only the ministry's political independence in the 1950s and 1960s but also its loss of independence afterward. Politicians needed financing to cover budget deficits, the reasoning goes, so they had to borrow either from domestic banking or from abroad. Domestic banking was fiscally conservative and limited its loans. As long as foreign loans remained relatively scarce in the 1950s and 1960s, the only way *políticos* could borrow from abroad was through the Finance Ministry's connections to the World Bank, IMF, and other international lenders. Finance therefore

maintained leverage over the political arena. But after the oil shock in the early 1970s, when First World banks needed to lend out multibillion-dollar deposits from petroleum exporters and began courting Latin American nations as clients, Mexican politicians could borrow what they wanted without Finance Ministry assistance.[7] The *políticos* gained even greater access to their own funds and foreign loans after Mexico itself became a big petroleum exporter in the mid-1970s. (New oil fields were discovered a few years earlier.) Now the *políticos* really sidelined Finance.

Finance did maintain close ties with private banking. Antonio Ortiz Mena, the finance minister from 1958 through 1970 whose tenure is virtually synonymous with Mexico's stability during that era, notes:

> I maintained permanent contact both with individuals [in business] and with organized groups. My relationship with the Bankers Association of Mexico and the Mexican Association of Insurance Companies was most significant, as they had great economic importance of their own and exercised influence over other business groups as well.[8]

The close relationship between Finance and private bankers had been established before the Revolution. Then during the 1920s, Agustín Legorreta Sr., owner of the Banco Nacional de México (later Banamex), cemented a relationship between his family and Finance by helping settle foreign debts and secure new loans.[9]

Nevertheless, the theory that Finance maintained independence from the political arena through its alliance with private banking and access to foreign finance runs into problem after problem. Until 1936, the Bank of Mexico, which had the sole authority to create money, was a quasi-private institution with real independence from the government—so private banking could restrict politicians' ability to run deficits—but by 1938, the administration had subordinated the bank to its control, according to the respected Mexican economic historian Enrique Cárdenas.[10] From then through the mid-1990s, the government enjoyed legal and practical authority to write checks for expenditures on its Bank of Mexico accounts, no matter how much these expenditures might exceed revenue, according to such authoritative sources as Gustavo Romero Kolbeck, former director of the Bank of Mexico. At the end of each year, overdrafts were converted into government bonds.[11] Given politicians' access to pesos, it is hard to see how Finance could have parlayed an alliance with private banking into political independence.

Might Finance Ministry still have exercised leverage over politicians by controlling access to foreign loans and hard currency? From the 1930s through the 1950s, Finance could not have exerted any such leverage because no foreign loans were to be had: Mexico was in default. Politicians would therefore be expected to run large budget deficits, according to this theory. Indeed, Sylvia Maxfield, a proponent of it, says that during these decades, "Mexico followed a policy of loose money and high deficit spending."[12] Oddly, she has the facts wrong. Though monetary policy is debated, fiscal policy was anything but loose.[13] From 1934 through 1954, when Maxfield says the "inflationary system of deficit financing"[14] prevailed, government budget deficits averaged a mere 0.3 percent of GDP.[15]

Maxfield says that from the mid-1950s through the 1960s, when Mexico again had access to foreign loans, Finance "was finally able to impose its preference for tight monetary policy, with the assistance of foreign allies: international creditors."[16] It would have been at most a few years. The massive "floating" loans that came to light in 1964 occurred because Benito Coquet, the big-spending director of Social Security, went on a $200 million foreign borrowing spree in the early 1960s, which he concealed from the Finance Ministry.

Finally, the idea that loans from U.S. banks recycling petrodollars after 1970 allowed President Luis Echeverría to circumvent Finance and spend massively is not quite right, either. The Echeverría administration racked up its first big deficits beginning in late 1971, before the energy shock, hence before foreign banks could possibly have been recycling petrodollars. And even after the banks were pushing loans, 75 to 85 percent of the monetary expansion that contributed to inflation under Echeverría consisted of printing pesos domestically.[17] What changed in 1970 was that earlier presidents had not abused the long-standing political possibility of running large deficits, but Echeverría did abuse it.

ELITE NORMS OF FINANCE INDEPENDENCE?

Another argument is that the Finance Ministry's independence depended on elite norms respecting an economic arena distinct from the political arena. High economic officials of the 1950s and 1960s indeed thought of themselves as *técnicos*, as opposed to *políticos*. Finance Secretary Ortiz Mena speaks of his predecessor, Antonio Carrillo Flores, as "a *técnico*, not a *político*." Carrillo Flores comments in his diary: "I am convinced that it is difficult to understand 'the *políticos*.' The devil himself wouldn't tempt me to that side."[18] As early as the 1920s, when President Plutarco Elías Calles forged warring generals into a state, he deferred to conservative pre-Revolutionary finance experts.[19] President Lázaro Cárdenas, who ended Calles' behind-the-scenes reign in the 1930s, made his finance secretary arbiter in distributing public funds, and successors in that ministry continued to play the same role.[20]

A well-educated, well-paid, secure staff doubtless strengthened Finance. Mario Ramón Beteta, finance secretary under Echeverría, says, "Officials in Finance and the Bank of Mexico knew their business. If in any part of the government there was a true public sector career, it was there. We rose rung by rung—there were no subsecretaries just thirty years old—and we gained respect for knowing about economic matters." Rodrigo Gómez, director of the Bank of Mexico virtually throughout the 1950s and 1960s, would hire promising graduates and send them abroad to study further. On their return, he would place them in low-level jobs for a few years so they could learn how Mexico worked, as distinct from how foreign economic theory worked. They were paid generously and had good prospects for advancement in the bank or Finance Ministry.[21]

These financial areas of government, moreover, were considered clean. In *Distant Neighbors*, Alan Riding treats readers to a chapter full of corruption tales but notes that in "the Foreign Ministry, the Bank of Mexico, and parts of the Finance Ministry, officials enjoy a solid reputation for honesty and professionalism."[22] Luis Giménez Cacho, a steel industry entrepreneur, says that under President Miguel Alemán, whose administration from 1946 through 1952 was considered especially corrupt, if one received a public sector loan, one was expected to hand over a certain percentage of it in the form of a briefcase of hundred dollar bills. But the briefcase did *not* go to Bank of Mexico officials who competently assessed alternative projects and decided on loans. It went to three "buddies" of the president, who presumably distributed the contents through the political machine.

High Mexican officials saw Finance and the Bank of Mexico as a distinct arena of government for good reason. But for Finance to be politically independent means more than that. The finance secretary had to be able to act independently from the president, and he had to be excluded from the contest for presidential nomination. Was he?

Whether finance secretaries could really be presidential candidates is hotly debated by former officials. Finance Secretary Ortiz Mena denies

One of the strengths of the allied Finance Ministry and Bank of Mexico was their well-educated, well-paid, secure staff. Many were trained under Rodrigo Gómez, director of the Bank of Mexico from 1952 to 1970. However, neither the ministry nor the bank enjoyed autonomy from the president of Mexico.

that he was ever a presidential candidate. At the beginning of López Mateos' term in 1958, Ortiz Mena handed the president a letter renouncing presidential ambitions in exchange for full confidence in his economic management, and as the 1963 nomination contest approached, he assured Interior Secretary Gustavo Díaz Ordaz that he was not a rival.[23] But Ortiz Mena's advisors Victor Urquidi and Rafael Izquierdo insist that he was a candidate, and Romero Kolbeck, former Bank of Mexico director, concurs.[24] Urquidi and Izquierdo say, for example, that Ortiz Mena's 1962 Plan of Action, a comprehensive economic platform, presented as Mexico's response to President John F. Kennedy's Alliance for Progress, was in effect a campaign platform. Julio Rodolfo Moctezuma, director of public investments in the late 1960s and subsequent finance secretary, sees the letter to López Mateos as evidence that Ortiz Mena was not a candidate, but then adds: "You never could tell for sure. Ortiz Mena was such a clever politician, denying interest in the presidency could just have been a way of angling for it."

Ortiz Mena's predecessor in Finance, Carrillo Flores, records an intriguing discussion about his own possibilities for the presidency in his diary: "What an awful burden Finance can be!" he muttered to President Adolfo Ruiz Cortines. The president replied, "And you think this is such a lovely chair? I wouldn't recommend being a candidate for it." Replied Carrillo Flores, "I'd rather be dead." The president's reaction: "Oh, don't take every word I say so seriously. You know how I talk with you."[25]

Whether Ortiz Mena was really a presidential contender is unanswerable (Carrillo Flores is not considered to have been a potential candidate). No doubt each source, Ortiz Mena included, recalls the situation as he sees it, but there never was nor could there be a definitive list of presidential precandidates. Whatever the president was actually thinking, he had to persuade everyone that there were several powerful contenders so as to keep them and their *grupos* playing within the system, not splitting off to challenge it from the outside. Names of supposed precandidates, realistic or far-fetched, were leaked to the press or whispered among the political elite. The president sent supposed candidates to talk with the private sector or carry messages to former presidents as hints that they were in the game. Like Alfonso Corona del Rosal, a politically powerful governor of Mexico City, they would later deny that they were candidates even though everybody thought—and acted—as if they were. Then the president picked one. If the president had tricked a few into thinking they were contenders when they were in fact just "filling," he would take the secret to his grave because, having been forced to deceive close collaborators, he had no other choice.

As far as the political system went, a widespread *belief* that someone was a candidate was tantamount to being a candidate. If Ortiz Mena sought to assure Díaz Ordaz he was not a rival for the presidency, it was only because Díaz Ordaz believed he was a candidate. And one of the few things that Díaz Ordaz, that master operative of the Interior Ministry, has never been accused of is political innocence. Too many insiders saw Ortiz Mena as at least a real presidential possibility for Finance to have had true institutional independence.

Ortiz Mena's very letter renouncing his candidacy casts further doubts on the notion of Finance independence from the presidential succession. If such independence had been *institutionally* established, why write the letter? Rather, the letter seems like Ortiz Mena's personal effort to distance himself from presidential succession and thus build confidence in his advice, precisely because the norm did not sufficiently distance him.

Any debilities that the finance minister might have had as a presidential candidate were, at best, provisional. There was hesitancy in some quarters to make the minister the candidate, until one day— September 22, 1975, to be exact—Finance Minister José López Portillo was named and accepted as the presidential candidate. If some earlier norm had kept Finance at the margins of the arena where *políticos políticos*, as de Oteyza calls them, contested for the presidency, it was awfully tenuous.

Even if Finance did maintain some distance from political succession, would the president grant it "absolute control over the budget and general economic policy of the government," as Centeno says? There is no doubt that budget authority legally belonged to the president.[26] The annual budget had to be approved by the Chamber of Deputies, but it passed everything the president gave it. Further, during the course of the year, the executive regularly approved massive increases without even informing the chamber. For example, budget *increases* approved in 1965 were 106 percent of the original budget. Such increases fell principally under three rubrics: investment, public debt, and a catch-all called "additional expenditures" (*erogaciones adicionales*). This last category regularly exceeded its budgeted level by more than 100 percent, indeed, by 305 percent in 1970.[27]

Presidents did not delegate their ultimate budget authority to Finance. High economic officials from the 1950s or 1960s agree that presidents showed great deference to finance ministers' expertise, but not one of them said in interviews that Finance controlled economic policy independently.[28] Miguel de la Madrid, the subsequent president who began his career in the Bank of Mexico in 1960, says:

> I saw up close that presidents López Mateos and Díaz Ordaz placed complete confidence in their finance secretaries' technical management. But presidents also shared the same basic views as their finance secretaries—Antonio Ortiz Mena, and before him Antonio Carrillo Flores and Ramón Beteta and Don Manuel Suárez. The presidents established the political framework.

If the president decided not to listen to his finance ministry, no one was going to force him to. When President Echeverría fired his finance minister in 1973, infamously proclaiming that "the economy is managed from Los Pinos," the presidential office, de la Madrid doubts that it represented any real change in authority: "I think the economy had always been managed from Los Pinos, but in a different manner." Budgets were balanced or only slightly in deficit under President Cárdenas because, though a political leftist, he was a fiscal conservative, probably in reaction to runaway inflation during the Mexican Revolution,[29] when rival factions printed increasingly useless paper money.

In Ortiz Mena's book about economic policymaking under his stewardship, in every instance when he describes controlling excessive spending or curtailing other ministers' spending authority, he says he needed presidential backing.[30] Carrillo Flores' diary notes daily discussions with the president about expenditures. January 20, 1954: "Meeting with the president, long and cordial. . . . He approved the public-works projects, except for Communications." April 7, 1954: "Meeting last night in the presidential office with [Agriculture Secretary Gilberto] Flores Muñoz about the [financial resources he sought for two agricultural] banks. No decision reached, but as I left the president told me I should be 'more firm.'"

Fernando Solana, an official in the National Finance Bank and the Ministry of the Presidency in the 1960s, later holding several posts as cabinet secretary, suggests that, for example, when the navy secretary would ask President Ruiz Cortines for a million pesos, the president would say, "Of course! Just go see the finance secretary." Then he would pick up the telephone and tell Carrillo Flores, "The navy secretary is going to ask you for a million pesos. Don't give him anything."

THE PRESIDENT, DEVALUATION, AND STRIKES

Whenever events in the 1950s and 1960s threatened to provoke economic crisis or disrupt orderly economic policy, the president marshaled the political system's powerful response. Presidents respected finance ministers' advice, but when on occasion they rejected that advice, that was it for the advice.

President Ruiz Cortines faced the threat of crisis not long after entering office in 1952. The government had spent heavily before the election, when the Revolutionary general Miguel Henríquez Guzmán split from the ruling party to wage the last powerful independent presidential campaign until 1988. Probably more economically damaging was the boom-and-bust cycle produced by the Korean War.[31] From 1950 to 1951, Mexico's exports to supply the U.S. war build-up surged 40 percent, and its economy grew 18 percent. As the war ended and the United States entered recession, Mexico's exports dwindled, squeezing access to dollar reserves. At the same time, inflation hit 30 percent, and with a fixed exchange rate, the peso became overvalued. Extraordinary efforts to stop inflation and stabilize the economy failed. Banks were prohibited from lending out any new deposits whatsoever—to put it another way, the reserve requirement was set at 100 percent—and the government ran a budget surplus. Growth slowed to zero. Still, the Bank of Mexico kept losing reserves: $21 million in 1952, $42 million in 1953, and $43 million in the first several months of 1954, numbers that were worrisome then.[32]

From the moment he was appointed finance secretary in December 1952, Antonio Carrillo Flores told President Ruiz Cortines, with a sad feeling, that he thought devaluation would be necessary.[33] In the summer of 1953, he started talking in earnest with the president about it.[34] In February 1954, Ruiz Cortines agreed to raise tariffs 25 percent to reduce imports and conserve dollars, but still the Bank of Mexico kept losing reserves. Carrillo Flores' diary records daily movements. February 24: "Today we lost $1.6 million dollars"; February 26: "lost 1.2"; March 1: "still losing dollars"; March 2: "dollar tranquil"; April 9: "serious dollar problems"; April 10: "still bad"; April 11: "much better today"; April 14: "$10 million plundered." Carrillo Flores and Bank of Mexico Director Rodrigo Gómez wanted to devalue while a cushion of reserves remained.[35]

All involved knew that, no matter how successful in the long run, devaluation had serious political consequences. No one knew better than

Largely because Mexican exports surged at the beginning of the 1950s to supply the U.S. Korean War effort, then collapsed as the war wound down, Mexico began losing dollar reserves and faced imminent danger of crisis. Finance Minister Antonio Carrillo Flores warned of the danger and proposed an economic strategy to avert it. But it was President Adolfo Ruiz Cortines (above) who rallied the united force of the state to support this strategy. Photo reproduced with permission of the General Secretariat of the Organization of American States.

Interior Secretary Angel Carvajal, in charge of maintaining domestic political order. When he learned about the plans, he called Carrillo Flores: "He begged us to hold off the measure, he said the impact would be terrible," the finance minister notes in his diary.[36] Carrillo Flores was also deeply concerned. Shortly before the devaluation, he was playing golf with his friend Juan Sánchez Navarro, president of Grupo Modelo, a conglomerate that produces beers including Corona and a variety of industrial products. Sánchez Navarro recalls:

> Carrillo Flores played golf horribly that day. He always played badly, but this time his clumsiness was unbelievable. "Tonio, what's the matter?" I said. "No, nothing. I'm tired." He played right to the end. To raise his spirits, I invited him to a match where an extraordinary Mexican boxer, "the Rat" Macías, was playing against a black American. Macías' style was elegant, and he dominated opponents rapidly, but during the match Carrillo Flores seemed absent. The spectators loved the way the Mexican played, and by the eighth round, they began to scream, "Finish him off!" They were screaming, no? The Rat knocked him out, and Carrillo Flores didn't even notice. A week later the peso was devalued.[37]

On Easter Saturday, the beginning of a bank holiday, the president displayed "concern and sadness," recalls his public relations director, Humberto Romero Pérez:

> Ruiz Cortines asked me, "Humberto, how long will it take to assemble the radio and television press?" I imprudently remarked, "Señor president, it must be very important." He said, "Look, I'm not going to tell you why. Simply and without ado, how long will it take?" "Two hours," I said. When I had radio and TV journalists assembled, he said they should come in—I saw Carrillo Flores there—and the president said to me, "This is the hardest thing I have ever had to do in office." I kept wondering what it could be: there hadn't been any earthquakes, [the volcano] Popocateptl hadn't erupted, nothing. He was conscious how the consequences of a devaluation would impoverish people. Even if the situation may improve later, the poverty is serious. He said to me, "I am going to devalue the Mexican peso." But he said that after everyone was assembled, so I couldn't have committed an indiscretion.

Ruiz Cortines announced that, whereas 8.65 pesos had bought a dollar the day before, it would henceforth take 12.5.

Only the president could have marshaled broad-based government effort to successfully manage the devaluation. Unity across the political elite was crucial, as representatives of the president's office, Interior Ministry, Finance Ministry, Bank of Mexico, and the private sector agree.[38] And even if Finance exercised traditional leadership among the *técnicos*, no one has ever suggested that it controlled the *políticos*.

Secrecy had to be maintained before the devaluation. Besides the president, finance secretary, director of the Bank of Mexico, and interior secretary, those who knew about it ahead of time included the secretary of Industry and Commerce, the director of the National Development Bank, the director of the Public Works Bank, and Finance officials Raúl Ortiz Mena, Raúl Salinas Lozano, and Raúl Noriega.[39] Given the central role that Labor Secretary Adolfo López Mateos played in holding wages down, it seems inconceivable that Ruiz Cortines would have concealed the looming devaluation from him while informing the interior secretary. But complete secrecy was maintained. Sánchez Navarro did not find out why his friend the finance minister was so distressed until after the devaluation was publicly announced.

No doubt the image of seamless unity glosses over some internal discords. Victor Urquidi, then director of the Mexico City office of the U.N. Economic Commission for Latin America (ECLA), recalls that after the devaluation, Benito Coquet, the president's confidential secretary (later the big-spending Social Security director), called a secret meeting to seek advice. Having confirmed years later that the meeting was concealed from the finance secretary, Urquidi concludes, "Coquet's fear was that Carrillo Flores might be deceiving the president about what was going on." When there is only one real policymaker, deception is a principal means to affect policy.

But if there was less than unity of thought within the political elite, the unity of action was impressive. Political ministries immediately set about controlling the "three or four months of terrible crisis" that followed the devaluation, as Sánchez Navarro describes that tense period. Some 50,000 strike petitions—so fragmented was Mexican labor—kept Labor Secretary López Mateos living and sleeping in the ministry, hammering out salary accords.[40] He had been told by the financial authorities that he could increase salaries as much as 15 percent without provoking enough inflation to endanger economic stability; raises would have had to be almost 50 percent to restore the former dollar value of salaries. The labor secretary's political prospects depended on being seen as having official labor support, but he kept the average raise to 10 percent.[41] Interior Secretary Carvajal was deployed to calm the private sector—the dollar value of bank accounts had, of course, plummeted—as well as labor and *campesino* leaders.[42] His job was to make sure the devaluation would not produce political conflicts, says Romero Pérez: "He used political manipulation, political experience. Above all he attended to the state governors."

While demanding support from his secretaries, the president stood by them. Carrillo Flores was under enormous pressure. Pubic anger at the devaluation forced him for the first time ever to go around with a bodyguard; his father said he should be "ashamed."[43] The atmosphere when he addressed the bankers convention was icy.[44] The U.S. Treasury's attitude was "harsh and disagreeable," he noted in his diary. It refused to give Mexico a loan until after confidence had been restored.[45] Agustín Legorreta, president of the Banco Nacional de México, told Carrillo Flores that the talk in the street saw a cabinet shake-up as inevitable, and ex-president Alemán, playing golf with the finance secretary, said the government had "lost prestige" and needed "changes."[46] Rumors circulated that another devaluation had already occurred,[47] and over the course of three months reserves sank 50 percent.[48]

Four times the finance minister offered to resign.[49] But Ruiz Cortines would not hear of it. He finally told Carrillo Flores that if he resigned, "What will people say about *me?* 'That old *pendejo* [not polite Spanish], why didn't he fire him before?' If I thought you were not capable, I would have thrown you out earlier. Now don't come to me and say it's time to go."[50] By the end of 1954, reserves were returning, as Carrillo Flores notes in his diary. December 16: "we got 2½. [million] dollars"; December 18: "we got 1½." Mexico ended the year with $205 million in reserves, just clearing the magic $200 million Carrillo Flores had promised. The basis was set for sustained, stable growth.

The militant grassroots strike wave by railroad and telegraph workers, teachers, and other public sector unions that broke out as the 1958 presidential elections approached and continued into 1959 posed the next threat to economic stability. Nationwide social turmoil triggered capital flight, and wage demands could have loosed inflation. As always, Finance played an important role in averting crisis. For one thing, continuity in the ministry across administrations helped ensure expert management. Carrillo Flores had for some time effectively designated Ortiz Mena, his friend since school days,[51] to succeed him.[52] For example, when representing Mexico at the Finance Ministers of the Americas Conference in late 1954, he brought Ortiz Mena as an alternate delegate and, with financial flight still continuing, even told the U.S. delegation that if he were to leave, Ortiz Mena would take his place.[53] After López Mateos assumed office in December 1958, Ortiz Mena, surely working with Carrillo Flores, who had become ambassador to Washington,[54] secured a $90 million line of credit from the IMF and $100 million from the Export-Import Bank. On top of the Bank of Mexico's existing $356 bil-

Four times during the perilous months after the 1954 devaluation, Finance Minister Antonio Carrillo Flores (above) offered to resign. But President Ruiz Cortines would not have it. Unlike many later presidents, he stood by his finance minister, as he did his other ministers, despite enormous political pressures. Photo reproduced with permission of the General Secretariat of the Organization of American States.

lion in reserves and a $75 million stabilization fund,[55] such plentiful access to dollars helped financial authorities make the exchange rate stick.

However, these financial measures would not have worked had Presidents Ruiz Cortines and later López Mateos not organized a powerful front against the strikers. Here was a project that Finance would have lacked all authority to carry out, even if it had been politically independent. At a minimum, the secretaries of Labor, Interior, Industry and Commerce, and Communications and Public Works were deployed to end the strikes; military and police were mobilized nationwide. For example, the Industry and Commerce secretary announced to wives of railworkers that they would lose their government-supplied housing if the strikes continued.[56] The Communications and Public Works Ministry prevented workers from two railroads under its direct management from joining the strikers.[57] The authorities' methods were harsh: they bought off some workers with raises, fired many, evicted families from their houses, provoked violence, filled jails to overflowing, and locked up ringleaders for a decade. But it was a concerted effort to maintain economic stability. No government official provided support to the strikers.[58] The Mexican historian Enrique Krauze writes:

> The political system, in chorus, lined up behind the actions of the government. In the Lower House the deputies repudiated "the foreign elements which the union leadership supported. . . ." The judicial power maintained a prudent silence. Big business enthusiastically approved. The Church did not open its mouth but breathed easier after the blow had been delivered to the enemies of Christianity. Even *Siempre!*, the least dependent magazine among the "not so dependent" elements of the press, criticized the "unbelievable blindness" of [strike leader Demetrio] Vallejo.[59]

THE PRESIDENT AND HIS CABINET

Not only did the president marshal the entire political system's response to external threats, he also settled internal elite conflicts that could just as well have destroyed coherent macroeconomic management. When López Mateos entered office in December 1958, even as the powerful strike wave continued, a dangerous internal clash broke out among Finance, State Industries, and the Presidency (a newly created ministry distinct from the president's office) over budget authority. Finance's ultimate victory is often interpreted as demonstrating its political independence. Centeno writes that President López Mateos himself tried to limit its budget authority but "failed to control [its] power."[60] In fact, it was López Mateos who rescued the fiscally conservative Finance Ministry's primacy over other ministries on budget matters.

The administrative reorganization plan that caused this ruckus started as an attempt to solve problems that had cropped up under Ruiz Cortines. Finance Secretary Carrillo Flores had felt he lacked adequate information to set investment priorities for the public sector, so, in consultation with the president, he established the Investment Commission within Finance. It investigated and approved not only all federal government investment, as when the Education Ministry built schools or Hydraulic Resources built dams, but also state enterprise investment, as when Pemex drilled oil wells or the steel mill Altos Hornos constructed coke ovens. However—further evidence that Finance alone could not have managed the economy—officials would withhold information from the commission, so Carrillo Flores suggested that it be placed directly under the president, who could enforce cooperation.[61]

To address this problem, president-elect López Mateos asked Eduardo Bustamante, a former finance undersecretary, and Manuel Moreno Sánchez, a politician and lawyer, to draft an administrative reorganization. Adapting French ideas about planning and Italian ideas about control of state enterprises—in Mexico, these enterprises had been largely autonomous from the government—they proposed a new Ministry of Planning and Budget and a strengthened Ministry of State Industries.[62] Planning and Budget was intended to plan and budget current expenditures, as well as capital investment.[63]

Meanwhile, also at the president-elect's request, Antonio Ortiz Mena and his brother, Finance Undersecretary Raúl Ortiz Mena, developed a broad economic plan for the administration.[64] Julio Rodolfo Moctezuma, Raúl Ortiz Mena's private secretary at the time and later director of public investment and finance secretary, says that the plan laid out Mexico's most pressing problems clearly, organized data that had not been available in useful form, and projected development in different economic sectors for some years to come: "Probably no one at that time but Don Antonio [Ortiz Mena] had such a complete vision of the public sector. Everything that would be known as his program of Stabilizing Development was based precisely on that planning effort." On the other hand, Moctezuma says, Bustamante's administrative reorganization plan was "well done and well drafted."

There was just one problem here: to whom would the president delegate principal budget authority? Bustamante's proposal gave Planning and Budget that authority and strengthened State Industries not only because of his ideas about public sector management but also because he expected to be named secretary of an economic ministry other than Finance.[65] When the plan came to light, Ortiz Mena was alarmed.[66]

A cabinet dispute erupted, and, says Moctezuma, a "rather strange plan" emerged. The proposed Planning and Budget Ministry was renamed the Ministry of the Presidency and given general planning functions, unclear authority over spending, the responsibilities of the former Investment Commission, and some other roles. Rafael Izquierdo, economic advisor to Ortiz Mena, writes: "There was no way to reconcile Presidency's responsibility for the 'public spending program' with Finance's responsibility for 'the general expenditure budget.'"[67] The patched-together bill giving the same function to two different ministries, of course, sailed through the Chamber of Deputies. Bustamante was named secretary of State Industries, and Donato Miranda Fonseca, an experienced politician with no economic policy background, was named secretary of Presidency. This last appointment surely worked in Ortiz Mena's favor.

Ironically, the 1958–59 strike wave, far from eroding coherent budget management, as powerful populist demands are usually supposed to, turned out to be just the thing Ortiz Mena needed to persuade the president to concentrate budget management more than ever in his fiscally conservative Finance Ministry. He appealed to López Mateos, arguing that to split budget authority between ministries, as the law seemed to allow, would only cause excessive spending, inflation, another devaluation, erosion of real wages, and—a point that resonated with the new president from his old job as labor secretary—more strikes. Ortiz Mena handed over his famous letter renouncing presidential ambitions and asking for full confidence in his economic management. López Mateos agreed: "For me avoiding devaluation is a political problem; for you it is an economic problem."[68] The president ordered that each budget request by each ministry—item by item throughout the year—would now require a signature from Finance as well as his own.

Even day-to-day administration of budget requests required presidential support. Some secretaries tried to pressure Enrique Caamaño, the legendary scrooge who actually signed requests—his official title was undersecretary of Finance for expenditure—by securing the president's signature first. Again, Ortiz Mena went to López Mateos. The president agreed to require Finance's signature before he would consider a budget request.[69] President Gustavo Díaz Ordaz, on succeeding López Mateos, agreed to the same system.

One time the secretary of tourism slipped Díaz Ordaz a spending request along with other documents, and the president unknowingly signed it. On being presented with the document, Ortiz Mena reminded the secretary that it must first go to Señor Caamaño. As the unhappy tourism secretary was walking toward Caamaño's office, Ortiz Mena apprised his undersecretary of the situation. An hour later, the tourism secretary returned in an alarmed state: "I must tell you that Caamaño is going nuts. I presented him my petition, and he said it would be better to invest in the state of San Luis Potosí; it is necessary to convince the governor there to plant un-barbed cactus in an area where various sharp-eared extraterrestrials live." Caamaño had retained the budget request. When Ortiz Mena told President Díaz Ordaz, he burst into laughter and said Caamaño was a genius.[70]

In the early 1960s, it was runaway state enterprise spending that menaced economic stability: Bustamante's plan, based on Italian ideas about controlling those enterprises, evidently had not worked. Finance did approve transfers from the government to those enterprises, principally for investment projects. However, they enjoyed considerable autonomy, like the major businesses that they were, with their own income streams and ability to borrow abroad, as Social Security under Benito Coquet demonstrated. Pemex even began refusing to turn over gasoline taxes collected at the pump, and since some of these taxes were supposed to go directly to states, the federal government had to compensate the states even though it had not received the revenue in the first place.[71] Running from flagrant to surreptitious, state enterprise spending was massive enough to help inflate the entire economy and contribute to the danger of crisis in 1964.

Ortiz Mena did not use banking sector connections or invoke political tradition to control this spending; just after the new administration took office in December 1964, he went to the new president, Díaz Ordaz. The president agreed to enforce sharp public sector cuts to curtail inflation and avert the danger of a crisis. Ortiz Mena also pitched a plan to prevent state enterprises from going on another surreptitious spending spree. He suggested that they should deposit all their revenues and other receipts—notably from foreign loans—in Bank of Mexico accounts and should withdraw all expenditures from those accounts.[72] Given the Finance Ministry's alliance with the bank, this device would provide excellent supervision over Social Security, Pemex, electric utilities, steel mills, railroads, and the rest.[73] The president agreed.

In implementing the plan, Ortiz Mena added an embellishment. Once a year, without warning, in one of his regular meetings with each major state enterprise director, he would pull out the books. If the purpose of some expenditures had not been verified, he would remind the director about the embezzlement laws and ask for an accounting. Even Díaz Ordaz, the former Interior Ministry operative, called Ortiz Mena's scheme to ensure compliance "Machiavellian." The procedure was "simply realistic," Ortiz Mena said.[74]

Despite presidents' support for Finance, they never granted it independent budget authority: they could and did override it if they chose. For example, excessive spending approved by President López Mateos, along with massive surreptitious spending by Social Security and other state enterprises, contributed to the inflation that might have provoked a crisis in 1965. As early as 1963, Ortiz Mena warned that the public deficit was too large, but the president would not let him cut it. "In 1964 it was even more necessary to adjust public finances," Ortiz Mena writes. "Again I proposed that measure to President López Mateos, and again he rejected my proposal. He said that since it was the last year of his administration, it was extremely important to end things well."[75]

Gustavo Romero Kolbeck, director of public investment under López Mateos and later director of the Bank of Mexico, says that the president would allocate money for political reasons. The politically powerful Ministry of Water Resources might plead for an allocation to finish a dam a year early, before it had even built canals to irrigate fields, on the pretext that the dam could get washed away if rains came. Inaugurating a big dam would provide a political boost for Water Resources Secretary Alfredo del Mazo, a candidate for the presidential nomination.[76] If the president wanted to support del Mazo's campaign, he would approve the money, according to Romero Kolbeck. Finance retained budget authority to the extent that the president delegated it.

As for the other side of the budget, tax reform, it was inconceivable without presidential backing. In the late 1960s, Finance carefully planned a tax proposal to increase revenue, but it never went through. Even Ortiz Mena's economic advisor Victor Urquidi did not know quite why until the late 1990s, when Ortiz Mena explained: "I went to Díaz Ordaz and said, 'Here I have prepared my full, comprehensive, tax reform.' The president said to me: 'I have to deal with two big reforms, the labor law and taxes. I think you'll have to keep your tax reform for later.'"[77] That was the end of it.

Moctezuma, who rose through the ranks to finance secretary, says that the decision to devalue—but the same could be said of any major economic decision—was never quite transparent. "All of us"—he means other officials of the highest rank like himself—"can reconstruct little parts of the story, but only [the president] knows the complete history."

Economic stability could not have depended on Finance Ministry independence, not only because Finance repeatedly had to resort to the president to retain its budget authority and restrict that of other ministries, but also because its sphere of action, though broad, was still far too narrow to manage an entire economy and avert crises. Why should labor and interior ministers, those *políticos políticos*, risk political capital controlling strikes and pacifying governors, just to back up *técnicos* at Finance? Unless the finance minister controlled them, a notion no one has suggested, the idea is nonsensical.

The very concept of politically independent management over an entire economy seems exaggerated. An independent central bank might manage monetary policy, but how could the political arena somehow cede control over the whole spectrum of economic management to some separate technical sphere? What is politics without money? Authority for managing the economy rested with the president.

Mexican presidents wielded the authority to avert economic crisis in the 1950s and 1960s. But what gave them that authority in those decades, and why did they lose it in subsequent decades? To put it another way, aside from powers that the president had throughout the era of the PRI—aside from the legacy of concentrated rule under the Aztecs and Spain, the constitutional powers of the executive, the apparatus of party and corporatist sectors, and the threat of the secret police—what additional leverage might presidents have controlled before about 1970 and lost thereafter? What did the power consist of that allowed presidents in the 1950s and 1960s to marshal the whole panoply of state to make economic policies stick, take away the Ministry of the Presidency's budget oversight even if it existed on paper, require all ministries to solicit the signature of Finance's notorious Señor Caamaño on each spending request, and force state enterprises to make earnings and expenses transparent by passing them through that most rigorous of accountants, the Bank of Mexico? What critical requisite did the political system have so it did not need to abuse political expenditure to buy compliance?

Two unwritten rules of elite cooperation constituted the critical requisite, giving the president exceptional authority in the 1950s and 1960s. The first rule prohibited *grupos* from openly mobilizing their own members or, worse, mobilizing civil society to challenge the president. Any *grupo* that did so had to be destroyed because otherwise it could destroy the political system. This rule held almost throughout the period from 1929, when the PRI was founded under an earlier name (the National Revolutionary Party), until 2000, when the old political system collapsed. *Grupos* almost always obeyed; they very rarely mobilized openly. And those that dared to mobilize were indeed destroyed. The sole exception was the Democratic Current that split from the PRI in 1987 and ran Cuauhtémoc Cárdenas as its presidential candidate. And it did set the political machine on a course toward its destruction.

The second unwritten rule only obtained in full force during the 1950s and 1960s: as long as *grupos* did not openly challenge the president's authority, he promised them political survival in exchange. They were allowed to pitch proposals to the president, criticize alternatives, subtly support favored candidates, and impugn opponents—but only covertly, behind the screen hiding the political elite's inner sanctum, and in the end they had to accept the president's authority. As long as *grupos* did accept his authority during the 1950s and 1960s, the president was able to promise their political survival. This promise gave him the leverage to require ministers' cooperation, limit their reach, and curtail their spending. It was the coin more precious than the peso itself in buying loyalty.

These rules of elite cooperation are recognized by scholars such as Roderic Camp, Joy Langston, and Francisco Suárez Farías,[1] as well as by former officials. There were two means to control conflict under the old regime, says Jorge Gamboa de Buen, ex-director of Mexico City development: "One was the absolute power of the president. The incumbent president decided, and that was that. The other was that, as long as you behaved well, were loyal to the system, and maintained discipline, you were guaranteed a political post."

The story now turns to how the unwritten rules of elite cooperation were consolidated during the dangerous 1951–52 presidential succession and sustained through the 1950s and 1960s. The 1951–52 succession threatened to blow the PRI system apart, but at the last minute, negotiations within the political elite established the rules to solidify the regime. As long as those rules remained in force over the next two decades, the Mexican state worked, and worked well, however undemocratically.

CONSOLIDATING THE UNWRITTEN RULES

The unwritten rule assuring *grupos* political survival in return for eschewing societal mobilization was consolidated during the 1951–52 presidential succession. Miguel Alemán, president from 1946 to 1952, had marginalized two important and overlapping political currents: Revolutionary generals and the left. The portion of military men in national political office had declined from about 30 percent in the 1930s to 19 percent in the early 1940s, but Alemán slashed it to a mere 8 percent.[2] This was close to a bare minimum since military officers had to run the ministries of Defense and Navy. Alemán filled his administration with classmates from the Law Faculty of the National University, where it was said, "Here you study to be president."[3] He reversed agrarian policies of distributing large haciendas to peasants and fought the not-yet-supine labor movement. In 1948, when a labor coalition representing workers in railroad, petroleum, and electrical industries protested falling wages, Alemán threw his support behind a pliable rival leader, the infamous *El Charro*. Instigating baseless legal actions and seizing the union headquarters with the help of Federal Security police disguised as workers, *El Charro* broke the labor coalition. Under Alemán, real minimum wages fell by a third.[4]

But Alemán's great error was in trying to retain power beyond his constitutional term.[5] He proceeded with two strategies toward this end, more or less in parallel: getting himself reelected and establishing a dynasty by installing a crony as his successor. Both strategies posed the gravest political dangers. No reelection, one of the few powerful constitutional mandates, had been the cry of defiance against the nineteenth-century dictator Porfirio Díaz. Only the 1910 Revolution itself had finally ended his corruptly won, recurring terms in office. And for a president to establish a dynasty run by his favored *grupos* was tantamount to proclaiming the political demise of excluded *grupos*, in this case, Revolutionary generals and leftists. They would stop at nothing to prevent it.

The U.S. State Department and British Foreign Service recognized Alemán's self-aggrandizing propaganda as a reelection bid.[6] He bombarded the nation with publicity for "prolonging" his tenure; political entities ranging from a state governor to a labor federation publicly proposed the idea; the president of the PRI called for Mexico to be "Alemanized"; the official labor congress declared him "worker of the fatherland"; all state legislatures rendered homage to him.[7] Several generals—a political current likely to oppose him—were pressured to sign a statement agreeing to any constitutional amendment that might lengthen the presidential term or allowing reelection.[8]

Alemán's own finance secretary, Ramón Beteta, privately feared that if the Korean War should escalate into a U.S.-Russian confrontation, the Mexican right might use it as cover to extend Alemán's term in office and "take extreme measures against the left."[9] Abelardo Rodríguez, former president of Mexico from 1932 to 1934, spoke out against reelection, and when Alemán's private secretary sent intermediaries to ask General Lázaro Cárdenas, the most revered Mexican president of the twentieth century, what he thought of reelection, he said they were welcome to make his opinion public: "Only the false friends of president Alemán desire his reelection."[10] Finally, General Cándido Aguilar, Alemán's political mentor, warned the president against seeking reelection: "It's going to cost you your life."[11] The last Mexican president who had sought

President Miguel Alemán's (above) great error was in trying to get reelected or, failing that, to establish a dynasty, thus threatening to oust rival grupos forever from power. Among others, former President Lázaro Cárdenas forced him to back down. Scholars believe—and political elites believed—that Cárdenas, who had fought in the Mexican Revolution, threatened to take to the battlefield if Alemán did not recant. Photo reproduced with permission of the General Secretariat of the Organization of American States.

reelection, Alvaro Obregón, was assassinated the very day after he won the vote.

On further consideration, Alemán began leaning toward strategy number two. He would found a dynasty by installing as president his cousin, Fernando Casas Alemán.[12] Casas Alemán had practiced law with

him, served in political office under him, and, according to the historian Enrique Krauze, "owed everything to him."[13] By September 1951,
a month before the official party candidate was to be selected, the Unity
Group for Casas Alemán, the Group of a Million Workers, the Federation of University Affiliates and Workers (whoever exactly those instant
groups might have represented, quipped the historian Daniel Cosío Villegas), and numerous statewide organizations declared support for Casas Alemán.[14] Organizations beholden to the government did not lightly
come out for a candidate. Even *Newsweek* declared Casas Alemán the
president's choice.[15] He looked like the one.

But well before things reached this point, excluded military officers
and politicians on the left—the groups largely overlapped—had launched
a campaign against Alemán's strategies. Initially within the PRI, General
Miguel Henríquez Guzmán openly campaigned for the nomination, mobilizing labor unions and peasant groups. Many leaders of this campaign
had held high posts under Lázaro Cárdenas, such as director of agrarian
reform and secretary general of the National Peasants Federation.[16] They
protested the corruption of Alemán's "group of intimates"—the buddies
mentioned by the steel industry entrepreneur to whom loan recipients
delivered briefcases of hundred dollar U.S. bills—and demanded a democratic process for selecting the party's candidate.[17] When the leader of
the PRI warned that party members were prohibited from engaging in
electoral "propaganda," *henriquistas* countered that "the president of the
party does not have the authority to indicate the exact date when free
party members can voice their support."[18] So they said, but a good half
a year before the nomination, they knew they had no chance within the
PRI, broke off, and mounted an opposition campaign.

One individual, Lázaro Cárdenas, was critical to the outcome, doom-
ing the *henriquista* challenge but also blocking Alemán's dynastic ambitions. Cárdenas was Henríquez Guzmán's friend, and his wife and son
Cuauhtémoc Cárdenas (who would split from the PRI in 1987 to run
the next powerful opposition campaign) supported Henríquez Guzmán,
but the former president would not. He told his friend, "You only get to
national office by one of two routes: unanimous support of the people,
so clear that the government is forced to recognize the triumph, or government sympathy for the candidate."[19] Of course, it was inconceivable
that the "unanimous support of the people" could even have been recognized, if it existed, so controlled was the press.

At the same time, along with others of the ruling party's inner circle who feared Alemán's dynastic ambitions, Cárdenas used the external

henriquista challenge to force the president to back down. He threatened behind the scenes to join Henríquez Guzmán and even take to the battlefield unless Alemán relented.[20] Frank Brandenburg, an American political scientist who spent ten years interviewing Mexican political figures from that era, says that, along with ex-President Manuel Ávila Camacho, Cárdenas blocked Casas Alemán's nomination:

> Toppling [him] required the firm action of these two senior members of the inner circle. . . . Through a process of back-scratching and log-rolling that involved former presidents, military men, regional strongmen, and other individuals, a *modus vivendi* emerged. . . . [A]ll factions . . . would lend support to the candidacy of Adolfo Ruiz Cortines, a noncontroversial career civil servant.[21]

The acute Cosío Villegas, who moreover lived through those events, ridicules this story as having been told for years without evidence,[22] and indeed neither Krauze nor Brandenburg cites a source.[23] However, even Cosío Villegas concedes "the grave danger that Cárdenas and other public figures would take their opposition to the field of arms" to prevent Alemán's personal reelection.[24] Why would Alemán's attempt to appoint a lackey and found a dynasty not face much the same threat? Cárdenas' enormous prestige, his career as a Revolutionary general, his close relationship with Henríquez Guzmán, and the roster of military officers in the *henriquista* campaign posed a great peril to Alemán.

Even if the events did not occur quite as reported by Brandenburg (and they may have—despite the lack of a footnote, he was probably summarizing his extensive interviews), their functional equivalent did. Political elites understood that Alemán was forced to back down and compromise with other factions. This point is confirmed by Gustavo Carvajal, a subsequent president of the PRI whose father was interior secretary under Adolfo Ruiz Cortines, the president who finally succeeded Alemán. Casas Alemán generated powerful opposition within the political elite, Carvajal says:

> Ex-president Ávila Camacho, who had great force and moral authority with the political class, used a bit of strong arm behind the scenes, and ex-president Cárdenas was a figure of stability for the country. . . . The majority of cabinet secretaries said: "Ruiz Cortines is the man, the most institutional, the most respectful, the one who will not generate conflict." When the president opted for him, everyone supported him. . . .

The president had to make consultations. He didn't just say, "I'm going to pick my friend so-and-so." He consulted with power groups, ex-presidents, the private sector, the labor federation, the church, and so on. And from those consultations the candidate emerged.

Once the PRI had compromised on Ruiz Cortines, the united political machine defeated Henríquez Guzmán's presidential bid with legalistic maneuvers, electoral fraud, and bloodshed. His party was falsely accused of supporting a violent demonstration, and, officiously citing articles 29 and 41 of the electoral code (suitable articles could be found to justify almost anything), the Interior Ministry dissolved it. Olga Pellicer de Brody writes in the *History of the Mexican Revolution:* "From that time on, members of the political bureaucracy fully accepted that the unique manner of arriving at the cusp of power was to submit to whatever decision the incumbent president might make." [25]

In office, Ruiz Cortines reached out to individual *henriquistas,* echoing their criticisms of the Alemán administration as corrupt, launching a campaign against private sector "monopolizers" for driving up prices of necessities, and even fining some 16,000 firms for that infraction. Of critical importance for the political system, Pellicer de Brody notes, was that, once the renegade party was destroyed, "whichever [*henriquistas*] wanted to participate in exercising power and opted for reconciliation were permitted to obtain high positions in the administration almost immediately." [26] The portion of military men in national office rose from 8 percent under Alemán to 14 percent under Ruiz Cortines. [27]

Here were the unwritten rules: On the one hand, the president must not name a successor who would threaten any loyal *grupo;* he must promise all loyal *grupos* political survival. Violating this promise could cause elite schism, political breakdown, and mass violence. On the other hand, any *grupo* that openly mobilized to threaten the president's authority would be destroyed. This was the only viable system because Mexico had not yet reached the stage where elections were capable of resolving political disputes.

FROM ELITE COOPERATION TO STRUGGLE

The promise of political survival was the web that held Mexican politics together in the 1950s and 1960s. One important reason to believe that this promise played such a critical role is the timing. The relationship between state and society remained much the same throughout the decades after 1952 (change only began to affect the political system after 1988). The corporatist structure held, labor never posed a challenge (except briefly in 1958–59), and the official party crushed the opposition in elections. But the unwritten rules of elite cooperation within the heart of the state only held in full force during the 1950s and 1960s. The promise of political survival for *grupos* deteriorated rapidly after 1970.

Scholars who study *grupos* agree that the 1950s and 1960s were a period of unusual elite cooperation, when *grupos* had high and realistic expectations of survival. During these decades, the incoming president always appointed cabinet secretaries from competing *grupos*, assuring a place not only for appointees themselves but also for their followers[28]— until President Luis Echeverría disrupted the pattern in 1970.[29]

It would be almost impossible to gauge directly whether *grupos* enjoyed more stability in the 1950s and 1960s. Because of their fluidity and the secrecy surrounding them, it is hard enough to determine who belonged to a particular *grupo* at any moment, let alone to trace changes in their makeup over decades. Extensive interviews would be required, and many answers would conflict. As noted by Joy Langston, a political scientist who has done extensive interviews about *grupos:* "1. Everyone is in a group. 2. Most deny it vigorously. 3. Most have ties with other groups, whether competing or not, whose affiliation, however casual, is denied as well."[30]

A feasible alternative is to look at cabinet secretaries' career stability. As when Alfonso Corona del Rosal replaced Ernesto Uruchurtu in the governorship of Mexico City (one of the most important cabinet posts), if secretaries moved, a long train of officials under them normally followed.[31] For example, in a shake-up in 1979, López Portillo fired the secretaries of Planning and Budget, Interior, and Foreign Relations on a single day. That year turnover among high officials in the next three levels below secretary (subsecretaries, director generals, and directors) was 58 percent in Planning and Budget, 50 percent in Interior, and 45 percent in Foreign Relations (despite being the only area of government with something like a civil service). By comparison, turnover in Agriculture was 15 percent and in Presidency (then an office, not a ministry) was 19 percent.[32] If more cabinet secretaries' careers ended prematurely, their *grupos'* political hopes darkened.

Cabinet secretaries enjoyed unusual stability precisely during the 1950s and 1960s. One indication is the portion of secretaries replaced before the end of each administration (Graph 6.1). There was considerable instability before 1952, as Alemán replaced 35 percent of his

Graph 6.1: Percent of cabinet secretaries replaced

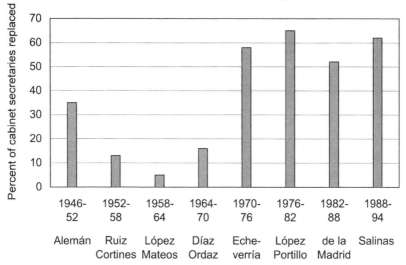

| | 1946-52 | 1952-58 | 1958-64 | 1964-70 | 1970-76 | 1976-82 | 1982-88 | 1988-94 |
| | Alemán | Ruiz Cortines | López Mateos | Díaz Ordaz | Eche-verría | López Portillo | de la Madrid | Salinas |

The 1950s and 1960s were an era of great stability for grupos—*an era when presidents promised them political survival in exchange for obedience—as gauged by turnover of cabinet secretaries. Turnover was relatively high under President Alemán before the unwritten rules of elite cooperation were consolidated. It fell to very low levels in the 1950s and 1960s, then surged after 1970 as the rules eroded.*

These graphs indicate the number of cabinet posts occupied by more than one secretary during each administration. Multiple replacements for a given cabinet post are not counted. (In the 1970s and 1980s, two, three, and even four different secretaries often rotated through a single post.) Data for 1946–82: Hernández Rodríguez 1992, 254. He does not provide this data for 1982–94, so turnover was calculated using his criteria (Hernández Rodríguez 1984, 21) and information on secretaries' careers from Camp 1995b, 904–940, and Aguayo 2000, 274–277.

original cabinet. Moreover, that figure understates the real threat to some *grupos* because it does not count his exclusion of leftists and military officers who were to lead the *henriquista* mutiny. Between 1952 and 1970, when all factions were included in cabinets—thus, instability would be better captured by data on replacement of secretaries—dismissals were minimal. Only about a tenth of the cabinet, from 5 to 16 percent to be precise, was replaced in each administration.

After 1970, dismissals surged. Practically two-thirds of each cabinet—58 percent under Echeverría (1970–76) and 65 percent under López Portillo (1976–82)—were replaced. Trying to avoid the infighting he had seen under López Portillo, de la Madrid (1982–88) set out to name a cabinet that, he hoped, would operate peacefully.[33] Nevertheless, he still ended up replacing 52 percent, and, as with Alemán, this figure misses the real threat to *grupos* because de la Madrid also excluded leftists, who fatally broke off in an opposition campaign in 1987. Salinas replaced 62 percent of his cabinet, often two, three, and even four times; he went through five attorney generals in six years. As he said, "In that tremendous battle [for political power], it is very difficult to think that whoever accedes to the responsibility of cabinet secretary at the start of an administration will still be in the same position by the middle or the end."[34] How different the 1950s and 1960s had been!

Contemporary officials were well aware of the unusual stability in the 1950s and 1960s and the instability later. For example, José Patrocinio González Blanco rose from director of public investment under López Mateos in the 1960s to interior secretary under Salinas in the 1990s. His father was labor minister from 1958 through 1970, and his father-in-law is Ortiz Mena. He says:

> Even though the Constitution talks of secretaries, [during the 1950s and 1960s] common usage and the newspapers referred to the labor minister, the finance minister. Under the López Mateos and Díaz Ordaz administrations, the labor secretary stayed on twelve years; the finance secretary was in office twelve years; and it appeared that the governor of Mexico City would do likewise, but he finally left because of a personal quarrel with the president. Interior enjoyed continuity, too, since the secretary ascended to being president. The idea was to provide continuity in areas of risk.

"Stability [among high officials] ended with Díaz Ordaz," says Luis Enrique Bracamontes, who served as undersecretary of public works from 1952 through 1964, then secretary of public works from 1970 through 1976. "Afterwards came instability, which continued in all administrations." Numerous other members of the political elite who served in different areas of government agree that the 1950s and 1960s were an era of unusual stability in office, and that instability surged after 1970—among them Mario Ramón Beteta, a Bank of Mexico official, finance secretary, and director of Pemex during the decades from the 1950s through the 1980s; and Humberto Romero Pérez, public relations director for President Ruiz Cortines and private secretary for President López Mateos.[35]

Javier Alejo believes that the big change occurred not under Echeverría in the early 1970s but under López Portillo in the late 1970s. He notes that many of Echeverría's replacements were caused by special circumstances such as illness. However, Alejo did not hold high office until 1970. Turnover in the 1950s and 1960s was practically zero if one takes special circumstances into account. Doing so would require investigating departures one by one, as an official story that someone left for health reasons was sometimes a cover-up. Thus, none of the data take special circumstance into account. It seems doubtful that officials got sick much more often after 1970 than before.

POLITICAL SUCCESSION AND ITS ECONOMIC CONSEQUENCES

It is clear enough why the promise of political survival should give presidents leverage to manage macroeconomic policy and curtail politically motivated spending or other dangerous economic gambles. Politicians divert spending to political uses to secure or retain power; spending is only a means to that goal.[36] The cooperative rules directly assured the goal of retaining power. Why spend surreptitiously?

Of course, no system is perfect; *grupos* could have more power or less; and there were occasional attempts to use the purse to grab more in the 1950s and 1960s, such as Benito Coquet's 1963 investment spree in Social Security. But if presidents found out what was going on, and if it went beyond what they had tacitly authorized, they meted out punishments. For example, when administrations changed in 1964, the four most important cabinet officials under López Mateos either stayed in the same office (the finance secretary, the labor secretary, the governor of Mexico City) or went on to become president (the interior secretary). Coquet's political career, however, ended.

Overall, in the 1950s and 1960s, the assurance of political survival for obeying the president was worth more than the uncertain chance of grabbing power by manipulating the public purse. Gustavo Carvajal notes that the way the system handled the 1951–52 presidential succession produced "great unity within the government. That is why the secret of the [1954] devaluation was kept with enormous caution." Humberto Romero Pérez, public relations director to Ruiz Cortines, likewise sees government unity as critical to the devaluation's success. Ernesto Fernández Hurtado, a bank of Mexico official since the late 1940s and its director from 1970 through 1976, says: "A clear, sustainable agreement with the government" was essential. He adds, "It was important that there was no Ministry of Planning and Budget"—no rival to the Finance Ministry, such as emerged after 1970. And when Finance Minister Carrillo Flores came under pressure to resign after the devaluation, the president stuck by him.

The 1958–59 strike wave also highlights how important the rules of elite cooperation were. Economic troubles that began boiling up even before the 1957 presidential nomination—falling wages in key industries and labor unrest among electric utility workers and Mexico City teachers[37]—would have favored a dissident political *grupo* that might have wanted to break off and launch an opposition campaign. The social context was comparable to those that helped Henríquez Guzmán launch his opposition campaign in 1951 and helped Cuauhtémoc Cárdenas launch his in 1987. But no one considered such a campaign. Not one *grupo* reached out to support the strikers, high officials agree.[38] On the contrary, ministries including Labor, Interior, Public Works and Communications, and Industry and Commerce sprang to end the strikes. The system closed ranks behind the president.[39] It was not the socioeconomic context, but the unwritten rules of elite cooperation, that blocked an external challenge.

The unwritten rules established a role for what, in the United States, is called the loyal opposition. But unlike in the United States, this role was not woven into a fabric of public and legally enforceable institutions. Observance of the rules depended crucially on the president of Mexico, the ruler atop the Aztec pyramid of power. Luis Echeverría, president from 1970 to 1976, took fateful aim at the loyal opposition. His efforts to marginalize opponents and entrench ideological and personal allies in power after his constitutional term struck a fatal blow against the rules of elite political cooperation.

Echeverría does not bear sole responsibility for undermining the unwritten rules because even if he had tried to sustain them, the climate of the early 1970s would have made his job difficult. Ideological "escalation," in the phrase of Albert O. Hirschman, a U.S. economist intimately familiar with Latin America, took hold across much of that region in the late 1960s.[1] Mexico, as always, was sui generis. Mexican political elites on the left did not move further left, nor did those on the right move further right; they maintained the same range of views from a pragmatic nineteenth-century liberalism to a pragmatic Marxism.[2] Rather, the essence of ideological escalation in Mexico was a growing belief that fundamental change might occur. An apocalyptic battle of ideas was supposed to be shaping up. Whoever won might win decisively, and whoever lost might lose decisively. As *grupos* feared that the stakes in winning or losing would increase, conflicts tended to escalate.

But ideological escalation just set the scene; Luis Echeverría staged the action. With a messianic obsession to right all the wrongs that had afflicted Mexico for five centuries and a genius for behind-the-scenes machination, he sought to install his like-minded *grupo* in power and establish a dynasty. Plutarco Elías Calles, first as president from 1924 to 1928 and then as strongman behind the scenes in the 1920s and early 1930s, had founded a dynasty, but President Lázaro Cárdenas had ended it. Three subsequent Mexican presidents are widely thought to have tried

Luis Echeverría, president of Mexico from 1970 to 1976, sought to entrench his ideological approach, marginalize opponents, and install personal allies in power after his constitutional term. He thereby struck a powerful blow against the old rules of elite political cooperation. Photo reproduced with permission of the General Secretariat of the Organization of American States.

the same, each time triggering drastic change. Miguel Alemán failed to build a dynasty as he prepared to leave office in 1951–52, and, in reaction, political elites forged the unwritten rules of cooperation. Carlos Salinas failed to build a dynasty as his term ended in 1993–94 and tore the ruling party apart. Luis Echeverría did a little better. Manipulating supporters, firing opponents, and spending as if he only cared how fast the presses could print pesos, he managed to install a like-minded, politically indebted successor as president: his boyhood friend José López Portillo. In the process, he loosed elite struggle and caused the 1976 crisis.

WHAT WENT WRONG?

The causes of change under Echeverría are disputed. Aside from blaming exhaustion of import substitution (that academic theory) or populist demands (those ephemeral movements), many Mexicans point to Echeverría's supposed efforts to restore political legitimacy. They say that he needed to restore legitimacy that the state had lost in 1968—and, as interior secretary, he had lost—when perhaps hundreds of demonstrators were massacred in anti-authoritarian protests at Tlatelolco Square. Others argue, as Echeverría himself proclaimed, that he ushered in change as the avatar of a new generation. Influenced by the 1960s, better educated, further left, and politically less experienced, this cohort of the political elite might have been different enough from its predecessors to change everything, and Echeverría was merely its conduit. These views deserve consideration.

The first question to answer is simply what it was about the Mexican polity that broke so decisively from the past. Three breaks from the norms of the 1950s and 1960s under Echeverría can be agreed on: massive spending increases and fiscal deficits, unprecedented dismissals and turnover of high officials, and conflictive and erratic policymaking. There is no prima facie reason why such changes had to be caused by elite politics; they could logically have been caused by underlying socioeconomic problems that also affected elite politics.

The massive spending increases and public sector deficits are impossible to miss in the Finance Ministry's budget data. The state's weight in the economy swelled from 20 percent of GDP during the 1960s to 30 percent of GDP under Echeverría, while budget deficits increased from a moderate 3 percent of GDP to a disastrous 10 percent of GDP.

During his term, officeholders began churning through posts, especially in the economic area. Ruiz Cortines and López Mateos had not changed a single secretary of an economic ministry during their administrations. Díaz Ordaz had changed one, promoting the state industries secretary, not an especially important post at the time (Finance had extended its sway over State Industries), to a more prominent position as governor of Mexico City.[3] But Echeverría went through three secretaries of Finance, two of Presidency, two of State Industries, two of Industry and Commerce, and three of Labor.

Political opponents agree that policymaking was unusually conflictive under Echeverría. Many saw an unparalleled rupture as "monetarists" led by Hugo Margáin in Finance, seeking to control the money supply, budget deficits, and inflation, battled "structuralists" led by Horacio Flores de la Peña in State Industries, seeking to solve what they saw as fundamental industrial problems.[4] "There had been conflicts between the left and right for a long time, but during the Echeverría administration, they became more radicalized and intense," says Javier Alejo, State Industries secretary after Flores de la Peña. Officials across the spectrum agree, from Fausto Zapata, an undersecretary of the Presidency who worked closely with Echeverría, to Miguel Mancera, a subdirector of the Bank of Mexico, which often opposed the president.[5] Mario Ramón Beteta, principal finance undersecretary and then finance secretary, says: "I had to have it out frequently with the president [to try to control spending], and not so much the president, because he and I had a good relationship, but with Flores de la Peña and his team. I had a very bad relationship with them; they were very irresponsible." According to Flores de la Peña, there was "constant, daily conflict over how to manage economic policy."

Different sides also saw policymaking as erratic. Not to mince words, the historian Enrique Krauze writes that "inconsistency, contradiction, and sheer unconsciousness reigned supreme."[6] Leopoldo Solís, centrist director of economic planning in the Presidency, describes how the incoming administration slashed investment 23 percent across the board to pursue an ill-advised anti-inflation effort promoted by the Finance Ministry, then when those cuts aggravated a slowdown already in the making, other ministries attacked Finance and raced to sink money in whatever projects they could put together, boosting investment more than 100 percent in two years.[7] Carlos Tello, a left-leaning official, describes the episode in strikingly similar terms: "To reverse its success in creating a recession, the public sector had to move full speed ahead with programs to improve employment and income distribution. Haste combined with inexperience, since many of the efforts were entirely new. . . . The resulting investments were sometimes inefficiently implemented and not productive."[8]

Economic policy was caught in a cycle of "brake and accelerate" throughout the administration, Tello emphasizes.[9] Expenditure grew less than 10 percent in 1971, 1974, and 1976 (within the 1960s norm), but surged more than 20 percent in 1972, 1973, and 1975 (see Table 4.3). Ground-level economic management was also erratic. For example, Victor Urquidi saw the Lázaro Cárdenas Steel Mill as useful, but the administration "built it at great speed with six or eight suppliers from different countries. I went to visit the plant when it was just beginning operations and was told, 'That's the British group; that's the German group—they don't like each other—and the French are down there.'"

A NEED TO RESTORE POLITICAL LEGITIMACY?

Many Mexican intellectuals say that Echeverría spent excessively to restore the political legitimacy lost at Tlatelolco.[10] This view is wrong but deserves consideration, in part to understand why so many who lived through those events have held it.

An "environment for a political and economic crisis" was brewing in the 1960s, according to the Mexican social scientists Roberto G. Newell and Luis Rubio, as the middle class acquired a higher standard of living, better education, and more democratic values. This socioeconomic progress increasingly alienated the middle class from the authoritarian state: "It became evident, through the explosion and later repression of the student movement in 1968, that the political system faced a dilemma of its own creation: it had organized and coalesced new social forces, but it had denied them access to institutions or representation."[11] When Echeverría came into office, he sought to "restrain the erosion of legitimacy" through aggressive spending that would provide "economic benefits for virtually everyone."[12]

One piece after another of this argument turns out to be fanciful. It is easy to imagine in retrospect more concerted demands in the wake of 1968 than actually existed. The fact that writers such as Octavio Paz, Carlos Fuentes, Elena Poniatowska, and Carlos Monsiváis later recounted the wrongs committed tends to obscure the extent to which public quiet was restored.[13] The 1968 Olympics proceeded in Mexico City as if nothing had happened.[14] Only one Mexican radio station, broadcasting in English, covered Tlatelolco.[15] And though the international press—mainly sportswriters there for the Olympics—reported much of the story, the Mexican press widely purveyed the version fed by the administration: foreigners and subversives were behind the protests; soldiers and demonstrators alike were shot; about twenty-five people sadly died.[16] Even the leftist press such as *Siempre!* lined up behind the government, blaming Tlatelolco on "foreign agents" who destabilize poor countries like

Mexico, driving them to "the protection of—or more properly, submission to—the government of the continental power."[17] (The United States can come in handy.)

All available polling data suggest that the state's legitimacy survived 1968 unblemished. Despite Mexicans' traditionally negative attitudes toward the corrupt lower levels of bureaucracy, a survey of every pertinent poll from the early 1960s through the late 1980s concludes that their enormous pride in national political institutions and the presidency served to "legitimize" the political regime.[18] A poll of low-income adults in Mexico City taken in 1970—thus after Tlatelolco had erupted and supposedly just when Echeverría needed to buy support—found that 59 percent approved the government's repression, 26 percent had no opinion, and only 15 percent opposed it. Nearly 80 percent agreed that the government was "good for the country," and only 8 percent considered it "bad for the country."[19] This is not the stuff of which legitimacy crises are made.

Most of organized Mexican society either explicitly supported the government in 1968—the case of big business and organized labor—or had nothing to do with it, the case of the peasantry. Asked whether unions and peasants were involved in the 1968 protests, Echeverría himself says, "No, no, that did not occur. Of course, there was a student explosion, but it was very concentrated in Mexico City and two or three other cities, not nationwide. The students did raise important social and political problems."

Nor did Tlatelolco drive subsequent business, labor, or peasant protest, such as it was. The private sector mounted the fiercest protest under Echeverría because it saw the president as too leftist, not because it cared about Tlatelolco. Like the "labor insurgency," peasant land invasions during the Echeverría administration were manipulated by the president himself.[20] Rafael Moreno Valle, a cabinet secretary under Díaz Ordaz, says that Echeverría's agrarian reform secretary, Augusto Gómez Villanueva, promoted those invasions: "And there were not only peasants but sometimes workers, tailors, vendors who went to see if they might get a little land." A rural guerrilla movement arose in the poor southern state of Guerrero, but it remained isolated from any base of mass support and limited compared with other Latin American movements.[21] The army crushed it.

Whatever exactly political legitimacy meant in Mexico (did it exist in 1961 when secret police killed supporters of Dr. Salvador Nava's campaign to be governor of San Luis Potosí?), the state did in some real sense lose legitimacy in 1968 in the eyes of many students and intellectuals, as well as much of the Mexico City middle class.[22] But none of them mounted an organized response that could have threatened the regime.

Student protests, surging before the 1970 election, were the most important continued expression of 1968, but placating them did not cost Echeverría a massive, 10 percent of GDP, public-spending increase; it cost him 1 percent of GDP. Victor Bravo, son of the education minister, notes that "in 1970 half of the universities were in full revolution, and it was my father's role to moderate them. He said to Echeverría what any cabinet secretary in his place would have: 'I will take charge of calming the movement, but you have to raise my budget.'" Echeverría increased the budget by 1 percent of GDP, a lot for schools and universities but hardly enough to cause economic crisis. A deadly student protest on Corpus Christi day, June 10, 1971, was sometimes blamed on conservatives in the government trying to humiliate Echeverría,[23] other times blamed on Echeverría trying to oust his conservative rival, Mexico City Governor Alfonso Martínez Domínguez,[24] but never blamed on mere grassroots demands. And there were no student demonstrations at all after 1973. Economic crises do not erupt years after the supposed provocation has evaporated.

For loss of political legitimacy to threaten the regime, it should have produced at least some expression at the polls. Not only did the PRI machine continue to flatten the opposition, but turnout in presidential elections increased steadily from 49 percent in 1958 to 69 percent in 1976.[25] In the 1973 midterm congressional elections, middle-class opposition to Echeverría's leftism outweighed any concerns about Tlatelolco, as the conservative National Action Party made substantial gains, winning 29 percent of urban votes.[26] Even when more organizations independent of the corporatist apparatus emerged in the 1980s, they concentrated on securing immediate demands for land, water, and housing, while avoiding the dangers of allying with opposition political parties.[27]

Echeverría himself says his policies derived not from political pressures to restore legitimacy but from his own long-held beliefs—he recalls a conference he helped organize as a student on "Critiques of the Mexican Revolution"—and from social problems he found during his electoral campaign as he traveled throughout Mexico, visiting the remotest villages by jeep. A map of his campaign that hangs in his house, as his former National University professor Daniel Cosío Villegas put it, looks like a military plan to occupy the nation.[28] Says Echeverría:

> I was a candidate a year after the events of 1968, and I didn't have any problem because of them. . . . That was the reality, and my political

campaign was practically without opposition. But I understood that the 1968 movement had raised many problems and demands emerging from the national situation, channeled through that neurological center of conscience and reflection, the universities and technical institutes. I traversed the country minutely [and saw that] higher education needed help; rural development demanded contact with peasant groups; and labor policy had to be a priority. . . . Political officials were shut up in their offices, never taking off their ties to go out.

Echeverría's spending was also timed wrong if it had been meant to buy political legitimacy. When new administrations try to shore up support, according to a systematic study of political spending across Latin America by Barry Ames, they boost their spending the *first* year they come into office, then let it taper off.[29] Spending in the first year of the Echeverría administration was too austere, even in the opinion of former finance officials.[30] The big spending surge, by 5 percent of GDP, which set the economy up for crisis, came in 1975, years after student protest had fallen quiet.

The administration's spending priorities were not well aimed to regain legitimacy, either. Politicians try to buy societal support by increasing social welfare, not building new steel mills, but Echeverría did the opposite.[31] Total social sector spending rose from 5 percent of GDP in the last year of the Díaz Ordaz administration to 8 percent of GDP in the last year of the Echeverría administration, that is, by 3 percent of GDP (Table 7.1). But employers' and employees' contributions to Social Security paid for one-third of that amount, so social sector spending from general public revenues and borrowing rose by 2 percent of GDP. Half of this was the 1 percent of GDP increase in education spending. The remaining 1 percent of GDP increase in social spending covered all state contributions to Social Security, the Labor Ministry, Health and Public Assistance, and quasi-public entities ranging from the National Commission for Free Textbooks (of course, government-approved) to Integral Family Development.[32] The big money went not to social welfare but to industrial development. State enterprises, which increased tenfold in number from 84 in 1970 to 845 in 1976,[33] accounted for more than half of the overall spending increase, or more than 5 percent of GDP through 1975, before falling back in the crisis year of 1976.[34] In addition to Pemex, these included, for example, electric generation, railroads, airlines, petrochemical plants, steel mills, and truck, bus, and railroad manufacturers.

Finally, in the face of powerful social pressures, the state might spend heavily to regain support, but why should such pressures disrupt internal

TABLE 7.1. SOCIAL SECTOR SPENDING, 1970–82 (PERCENT OF GDP)

	Total social sector spending	Social Security with employers' and employees' contributions	Employers' and employees' contributions to Social Security	Social sector without employers' and employees' contributions
Echeverría				
1970	4.8	2.2	1.7	3.1
1971	5.3	3.0	2.5	2.8
1972	6.3	3.2	2.7	3.6
1973	6.3	3.0	2.5	3.9
1974	6.7	3.5	2.9	3.8
1975	7.3	3.6	2.9	4.4
1976	8.1	3.6	3.0	5.0
Growth 1970–76	3.2	1.5	1.4	1.9
López Portillo				
1976	8.1	3.6	3.0	5.0
1977	7.8	3.3	2.5	5.3
1978	7.9	3.2	2.6	5.3
1979	8.4	3.1	2.5	5.9
1980	8.1	3.2	2.6	5.4
1981	9.2	3.0	2.5	6.6
1982	9.1	3.2	2.6	6.5
Growth 1976–82	1.1	-0.5	-0.4	1.5

Did Echeverría spend extravagantly to buy societal support? If so, he should have directed his spending to social welfare programs to benefit the middle and working class. He did just the opposite, directing resources to development programs such as the construction of new steel mills.

Social Security spending includes the program for private workers (IMSS) and government workers (ISSSTE). Total social sector spending and Social Security spending is from Salinas 1992, 173. Government transfers to Social Security are from Salinas 1992, 177. Employers' and employees' contributions are calculated as total Social Security spending minus transfers.

policymaking? Why should the coherent budget management of the 1950s and 1960s break up in conflict and inefficiency after 1970? Why should the dismissals of cabinet secretaries surge so dramatically under Echeverría? Social pressures could produce elite conflict if elites belonged to societal factions, but political *grupos* in Mexico did not. The powerful strike wave that threatened the 1958 presidential election elicited a unified, if brutal, government response. Why should much weaker grassroots pressures after 1970 cause incoherence and struggle within the state?

AN ELITE SPLIT OVER TLATELOLCO?

For doubts about political legitimacy to infect the state's internal operation, some mechanism would have to transmit them to the political elite. Mexico had nothing close to a free press or independent polls that could so much as provide evidence of declining legitimacy. If the story is just that Luis Echeverría perceived a loss of legitimacy—when, it bears repeating, concern about such a loss was not evident among business, organized labor, peasants, or middle-class voters turning to the conservative National Action Party—then the story is just about the president's personal belief. If loss of legitimacy was more than a figment of his imagination, if it was an external political fact requiring his action, it needed to be conveyed to him via some intermediate level of the pyramid of state.

A split in the political elite would be such an intermediate mechanism transforming an idea about loss of legitimacy into a fact that Echeverría had to address. If one faction of the political elite decisively rejected the authoritarianism bared at Tlatelolco, while another steadfastly defended the repression, the ensuing internal split could explain everything that happened under Echeverría. Indeed, the more logical accounts about loss of legitimacy assume such a split. Newell and Rubio argue that Tlatelolco "caused a split in the political family," that is, the political elite. The family was "very divided" about the government's repression at Tlatelolco and could not "compromise" on a successor to Díaz Ordaz in 1969, so the president had to make an "apparently unilateral decision."[35]

It was once thought that, with the children of many officials in the streets, the political elite did split over Tlatelolco. Moreover, this idea would seem to make sense, given the National University's historic role in shaping political elites and its prominence in the events of 1968. Not only were students and professors involved in the protests, but also the university was occupied by the military, and its rector, Javier Barros Sierra, openly broke with the president, leading mass protest marches and threatening to resign.

Yet the idea of a real elite split—anything that went beyond Barros Sierra himself—has lost credibility as the old Mexican regime has eroded and information about its workings has begun to emerge. After examining countless official archives long unavailable, the political scientist Sergio Aguayo concludes that in the wake of Tlatelolco "the 'revolutionary family' closed ranks behind the president." Even ex-president Lázaro Cárdenas, who was deeply troubled by Tlatelolco, publicly blamed it on "international and foreign elements" [36]—hence the similar line from the leftist press. As for professors, having taught politicians was one thing, influencing current policy was quite another. A study about intellectuals' relationship with the political system concludes that Tlatelolco only ended up isolating the National University: intellectuals "did not have much influence on the state in the aftermath of 1968." [37]

Officials from ministries across the spectrum of government agree that, tragic as the events of 1968 were, political elites supported the president. [38] Says Mario Ramón Beteta: "I don't mean to say that afterwards—I speak for myself—we were in agreement with what happened. I think we all lamented it, and none of us felt indifferent about it, but I think that Díaz Ordaz had the complete support of his government, including the principal cabinet secretaries." Least of all did Echeverría, interior minister in 1968, notice any dissent: "I didn't have a problem with people in the government who were dissidents. No, no, no, not that I remember. There was a realism about the issue." [39] Perhaps most telling is the testimony of Fernando Solana, at the time second in command to the National University rector, Javier Barros Sierra. He says that everyone in the political elite except Barros Sierra stuck by Díaz Ordaz.

Among former high officials interviewed, only three, Javier Alejo, Fausto Zapata, and Victor Urquidi, mention anything even resembling an elite split. Alejo, at the time a professor, not a high official, points to Emilio Martínez Manatou, the secretary of Presidency who was regarded as a soft-liner and had several intellectuals serving under him: "They transmitted the state of mind of the political class and the nation in general." Urquidi, at the time president of the Colegio de Mexico (his offices were machine-gunned by police in 1968), says there were individuals in government who "sympathized with the students and maybe protected them if they could" but no blocs of protest. He was

In 1968, President Gustavo Díaz Ordaz (above) used violent repression to end a string of anti-authoritarian protests. As interior secretary, Luis Echeverría was widely blamed for the ensuing massacre at Tlatelolco Square (though his actual role is disputed). Many Mexican intellectuals believe that the reason Echeverría spent extravagantly after becoming president was to buy back legitimacy for both the Mexican state and himself. He denies that this was so. As well, every survey of Mexican political opinion from the 1960s through the 1980s shows that the president and the Constitution retained enormously high approval. No drop whatsoever in approval is evident circa 1970. Photo reproduced with permission of the General Secretariat of the Organization of American States.

summoned by the supposed soft-liner Martínez Manatou, who, Urquidi recalls, "treated me as if my obligation were to keep a check on professors and students of the Colegio, as if I were responsible for what they did as citizens. I had never had such an unpleasant interview with a high government official before." Zapata, at the time a federal deputy from San Luis Potosí, agrees that, though Díaz Ordaz "lost moral authority," any protest within the government was "minimal and silent."

Further, the 1969 presidential succession did not work the way it should have if there had been a powerful elite split over Tlatelolco. If elites sympathetic to the protesters had had real clout, they should have persuaded Díaz Ordaz to nominate a soft-liner—or at least someone who was not uncompromising—as the PRI's presidential candidate. But the successful nominee, Luis Echeverría, was at the time universally regarded as a hard-liner.[40] The interior secretary, he ran the state's repressive apparatus in 1968, publishing innumerable diatribes supporting the president and condemning the students.[41] Díaz Ordaz, along with the rest of the political elite, believed he was choosing a successor close to his own thinking.[42] Later, when Echeverría "came out of the closet" as a leftist, as the former Bank of Mexico official Manuel Suárez Mier puts it, no one was more dumbfounded and angered than Díaz Ordaz.[43] The rupture between the two became bitter and extraordinarily public. The president even considered replacing Echeverría as the official candidate, saying to a confidante, "We're going to make this swine sick, and this time he's really going to be sick."[44]

Had some grupo opposed Díaz Ordaz over Tlatelolco, a consummate politician like Echeverría should have shored up his support by giving some members good posts when he became president. There was only one possible such grupo, under Martínez Manatou in Presidency (despite the way he pressured Urquidi). Far from rewarding its members, Echeverría demoted that grupo, even moving his old friend López Portillo, a member of it, to an unimportant undersecretariat of State Industries.[45] Two officials under Martínez Manatou who would subsequently become cabinet secretaries were marginalized: Julio Rodolfo Moctezuma was briefly made an advisor to Presidency, and Carlos Tello was named a subdirector general, the fourth level down. Two prominent economists in the grupo were left entirely out of government: Ifigenia Martínez, known for her work on income inequality, and Victor Flores Olea, known for his arguments about underlying structural problems. Pablo González Casanova, the well-known sociologist, became rector of National University for two years.

A NEW AND DIFFERENT GENERATION?

Another seemingly plausible but, in the end, incorrect idea is that a new generation of high officials, which many saw as having burst upon the scene in 1970, differed so radically from its predecessors that it inevitably transformed Mexican politics. High officials in the Echeverría administration were often seen as younger, more leftist, more technically educated, and less politically experienced than their predecessors.[46]

One must be careful about just what did and did not change about political elites under Echeverría. Informed impressions are remarkably at odds. Miguel Mancera, subsequent director of the Bank of Mexico, says "all the top bureaucracy continued almost as it had been. Ortiz Mena left, but the rest of the Finance *grupo* stayed."[47] Moreno Valle, who would likely notice change because he was close to Díaz Ordaz, says, "The secretaries, subsecretaries, and some department heads changed, but in general the bureaucracy was the same."[48] Yet Fausto Zapata, who rose to high office under Echeverría, believes that the Díaz Ordaz corps was marginalized, and changes among high officials were more decisive than they had been in the 1950s or 1960s. Much about Echeverría's administration can be explained by his "almost obsessive fixation not to repeat the errors Díaz Ordaz had committed," says Zapata. "Thus, one of the things Echeverría did was to keep out people he identified as too close to the former president." Emilio Carrillo Gamboa, who was director of Telmex under Echeverría, and whose father, Antonio Carrillo Flores, had been finance secretary and foreign secretary in the 1950s and 1960s, says that Echeverría shut out a whole generation of experienced officials, more decisively than the norm; differences were evident between the new and old generations' ways of thinking.[49]

A look at the sociological characteristics of the political elite reveals no distinct cohort rising through the ranks and assuming office in 1970; high officials under Echeverría were almost indistinguishable from their predecessors of the 1950s and 1960s. They were alike in socioeconomic origin (predominately from middle-class families of teachers, lawyers, and other professions) and educational level (the *licenciatura*), and the portion who had attended the National University was comparable (70.5 percent under Díaz Ordaz versus 68.1 percent under Echeverría).[50] More had *licenciaturas* in economics than in law—20 percent under Echeverría as opposed to 10 percent under Díaz Ordaz[51]—suggesting that on average they might have been more technocratic and leftist.[52] But this shift should not be overemphasized. Though the Economics Faculty was somewhat more leftist, many of its professors had held high government office, such as the self-proclaimed "heterodox Marxist" and finance undersecretary Jesús Silva Herzog.[53] Indeed, economics had been a division of the Law Faculty until 1935, when it split off.[54] The Law Faculty continued to teach political economy (neither department was what Americans think of as a law or an economics school), and they still reside side by side on the National University campus.

The sociological data do identify a "dramatic difference" in one emerging cohort of the political elite, but it was *not* the cohort that moved into high office in the 1970s under Echeverría. Rather, it was the cohort born after 1940 that moved into high office in the 1980s under de la Madrid.[55] Members of this cohort were the first who never knew Mexico's unstable post-Revolutionary era (the last armed revolt occurred in 1939), and they were influenced by the 1968 protests and Tlatelolco. They grew up in wealthier families than their predecessors, often attended private schools, and typically earned advanced economics degrees from U.S. universities.

Though the pool of candidates for high office in 1970 was just like that of its predecessors, the individuals Echeverría chose—and chose freely, as he himself emphasizes, sitting at his kitchen table, pencil in hand[56]—constituted an almost unknown cabinet of newcomers. He "invented them, fabricated them out of nothing as if it were a magic act," says Cosío Villegas. "One could barely point to two exceptions, [Mexico City Governor] Alfonso Martínez Domínguez, who had some political capital, and [Agrarian Reform Secretary] Augusto Gómez Villanueva, who had saved ten or fifteen cents. And remember the sad end that the first one met"—deposed six months later.[57] Mario Moya Palencia was catapulted, at age thirty-seven, from director of state cinematography to interior secretary, the highest political post after the president, and Emilio O. Rabasa was promoted from director of the Cinematographic Bank to foreign secretary. He had previously undertaken one diplomatic mission, Cosío Villegas notes: attending the Oscars.[58]

For all Echeverría's talk of a "generation of youths,"[59] his cabinet was a mere one year younger than Díaz Ordaz's, 49 instead of 50 on average (Table 7.2). But Echeverría's cabinet members had much less political experience. Secretaries' average length of public service when named to the cabinet had increased steadily from just under ten years under Alemán (he *had* ushered in sociological change, replacing a generation of military men with lawyers) to more than seventeen years under Díaz

TABLE 7.2. POLITICAL CAREERS OF CABINET SECRETARIES, 1952–82

	Average age when named cabinet secretary	Average number of years in government until named cabinet secretary
Miguel Alemán (1946–52)	44.6	9.8
Adolfo Ruiz Cortines (1952–58)	50.0	11.6
Adolfo López Mateos (1958–64)	51.7	15.0
Gustavo Díaz Ordaz (1964–70)	50.8	17.5
Luis Echeverría (1970–76)	49.8	11.2
José López Portillo (1976–82)	49.1	15.3

Did politics change so much under Echeverría not because of anything under his control but because a radically different generation of the political elite happened to be rising to power? His cabinet was unlike previous cabinets but mainly because, in his effort to oust the "emissaries of the past," he deliberately appointed secretaries with less political experience. Data: Hernández Rodríguez 1984, 37.

Ordaz, but then it fell abruptly to eleven years under Echeverría. The effect was more pronounced than the average numbers suggest because secretaries in more technical areas were often more experienced—Enrique Bracamontes, the public works secretary, had been in the public sector for twenty years and an undersecretary for twelve years—while top political appointees like Moya Palencia, if they did not quite pop out of the magician's hat, were newcomers. Although plenty of experienced candidates were available, Echeverría chose not to appoint them.

Roderic Camp discovered another anomaly among a broader group of some hundred-plus high officials under Echeverría, including undersecretaries, directors of major state enterprises, governors, some ambassadors, and Supreme Court justices. This group belonged to a younger generation than it should have according to the established norm:

A single generation has dominated each two successive presidential administrations in Mexico since 1935. . . . In 1970, however, this pattern was suddenly broken, and the impressionistic assumptions of most observers that President Echeverría was appointing young persons to high-level offices is borne out rather clearly in our data. Echeverría neglected his own generation [born in the 1920s] for the younger 1930 generation, selecting 50 (or 40 percent) of his collaborators from this group.[60]

As with his selection of a politically inexperienced cabinet, Echeverría's choice to sideline much of his own 1920s generation prematurely—one administration earlier than its members expected to retire from high office—seemed almost calculated to create tensions within the elite. But both of these anomalies resulted from the president's arbitrary decisions, not from any underlying sociological mandate. Indeed, in the next administration, López Portillo would bring the slighted generation back in an apparent attempt to restore the old balance.[61] But tensions, once triggered, are not so easy to reverse.

IDEOLOGICAL ESCALATION

The Echeverría administration broke with the past for two related reasons: the president's divisive choices, including those on matters that went well beyond his initial appointments, and a broader climate of ideological escalation. Hirschman saw ideological "escalation" in the increasingly tough challenges that Latin American economists, many of them his friends, posed for the state in the 1960s. In the 1940s and 1950s, a consensus embraced by the U.N. Economic Commission for Latin America and the World Bank had called on Latin American governments to promote industrialization, long-term planning, and economic integration of the continent. As if these goals were not enough, in the 1960s economists proclaimed that to get to the root of its economic troubles, Latin America also must overcome fundamental problems—maldistribution of wealth and "dependency" on the First World—that the region had faced since the Spaniards' arrival. These antagonistic goals—redistributing wealth threatened propertied classes and breaking dependency threatened First World governments and multinationals—"may well have contributed to that pervasive sense of being in a desperate predicament."[62] Hirschman argues that this pervasive sense promoted military coups in many South American nations.

One must be cautious about discovering ideological escalation in Mexico. Several knowledgeable interviewees expressed doubts that any such development occurred.[63] The broad range of economic views acceptable within the political elite had not changed significantly since the 1930s. A poll of political leaders taken just after the Echeverría administration ended showed them equally divided between those who thought that the state's role in the economy was sufficient and those who thought it should be expanded, but none reacted against the past by claiming that the state's role was excessive.[64] Further, Mexico's political elite was a tight-knit group, not split by the class-based antagonisms found across much of South America. Bank of Mexico Director Ernesto Fernández Hurtado, the principal advocate of fiscal restraint under Echeverría, and State Industries Secretary Horacio Flores de la Peña, the principal advocate of a larger state role in strengthening industry, knew one another from the National University classroom, and each in interviews spoke respectfully of the other. Such friendships moderated ideological conflict.[65] Hirschman argues that similar personal relationships among political elites allowed Colombia to avoid a military coup, despite the continent-wide ideological climate.[66]

Nevertheless, Mexican officials and scholars have described relations within the Echeverría administration as more combative than those in earlier administrations, and in specifically ideological terms. The broader climate of ideological escalation had certainly affected the Mexican intellectual climate. André Gunder Frank wrote *Latin America: Underdevelopment or Revolution*, one of the classic works on Third World "dependency," at the National University in the late 1960s. He argued that the metropolis (advanced capitalist nations such as the United States) extracted resources from the dependent periphery (poor nations such as Mexico): "The periphery . . . can develop only if it breaks out of the relation which has made and kept it underdeveloped, or if it can break up the system as a whole."[67] Victor Flores Olea, dean of the School of Political and Social Sciences at the National University, argued along similar lines.[68] And Pablo González Casanova, the most prominent critic of authoritarian Mexican politics, said that achieving real democracy would also require combating economic dependency.[69]

Some of Echeverría's highest appointees accepted these challenges to the economic and political order, impossible to achieve any time soon no matter how justified. State Industries Secretary Flores de la Peña, leader of the economic left, was far from the only one. Labor Secretary Porfirio Muñoz Ledo wanted to restructure the "exhausted" economic model and the corporatist political system.[70] Carlos Tello, a finance official (later planning and budget secretary), wrote: "Our people are conscious that their misery produces others' wealth. The accumulated rancor against political colonialism is now reborn against economic colonialism."[71]

Leopoldo Solís, chief economic advisor in Echeverría's Ministry of the Presidency, illustrates how thinking shifted in about 1970. In 1967, he debunked the idea that import substitution was exhausted and dismissed a book by the Harvard economist Raymond Vernon, *The Dilemma of Mexico's Development*, arguing that Mexico faced "inescapable obstacles" to continued growth. He said it was just another in a series of studies that "end by raising alarm about this or that problem impeding the country's economic development. Despite everything, development continues at a secular rate of 6 percent a year."[72] By 1973, Solís had turned around. Discussing economic development in a collection of readings about the Mexican economy, he said it is "accepted almost unanimously by national economists . . . that import substitution, as the key element of growth, can no longer continue." According to Solís, Mexico's economic model had to be restructured to keep income inequality from worsening. He favorably noted a selection arguing that Mexico's underdevelopment was "rooted precisely in political, social, and economic subordination imposed by colonial expansion."[73]

Here Tlatelolco, a powerful political symbol even if it produced no sustained social movements or splits within the political elite, may have crystallized more diffuse calls for change—the Vatican II Council announcing progressive Catholic doctrines, Marxist dependency theory, anti-Vietnam War protests, the Paris riots, Prague Spring. Cosío Villegas writes that fundamental criticisms of Mexico's development "did not just spread from some erudite essay, article, conference, or street gossip. Rather, the 1968 student rebellion gave them spectacular public standing."[74] Of course, not even university students march in the street protesting the import-substitution model of economic development, but the subsequent finance secretary David Ibarra insists that 1968 helped provoke "intellectual ferment" and "winds in favor of change."

Ideological escalation does not require some linear scale on which officials' views move simultaneously left and right, only that they should sense that some fundamental change is coming, however clearly or vaguely envisioned. All sides, whether for change or against it—and whatever exactly it might mean—can see the stakes rising because whoever controls change is likely to be in power for a long time to come, and whoever does not is likely to be left out. *Grupos* may begin to fear for their political survival, and a cooperative pact may begin to erode.

Conflictive and erratic policymaking, increasing turnover of high offi-cials as one faction struggles with another, and spending surges to carry out favored policies or build political support could result. Ideological es-calation is impossible to gauge but was surely a factor under Echeverría.

LUIS ECHEVERRÍA

Luis Echeverría used the immense authority of the Mexican presidency to engineer a decisive break from the past. He did so in three princi-pal ways. First, if Tlatelolco emitted a signal for change, already some-what muted by 1970, he amplified it in ways that exacerbated conflict within the political elite, as well as with the private sector. Second, his enormous ambitions for effecting change, combined with his enor-mous incapacity for coherent administration, or even for understand-ing that how government is administered matters, aggravated discord within his cabinet and eroded the rules of elite cooperation. Third, his Machiavellian efforts to concentrate power in his hands and install a politically dependent protégé in the presidency—López Portillo himself said, "truly, I did not have a *grupo*" [75]—loosed elite struggle, massive pub-lic spending, and economic crisis.

Echeverría was infected by his "megalomania to be a great Third World leader," as Mancera puts it; his "visions of himself as a new mes-siah for Mexico," as Urquidi puts it; his "monomania, and general mental disturbance," as Cosío Villegas puts it.[76] Judgments of him have been harsh, in good part because the results of his administration were poor, but his ambitions did focus on social goals. As described by Urquidi, Echeverría "thought of himself as a big, strong president of Mexico who was going to reduce poverty, improve social programs, everything. But he had no idea how to accomplish those goals." According to Fausto Zapata, undersecretary of information in Presidency, "Echeverría lived the six years of his administration with a continual sense of urgency. He had a kind of anxiety to advance by great strides, to correct in six years all the problems that had accumulated in 400, no? And added to that problem was his very vague notion about the economy."

Even if Mexican political elites were relatively unsusceptible to ideo-logical escalation, Echeverría's calls for change, time and again attacking the "emissaries of the past"—meaning political elites who had served in previous administrations—made them more susceptible. He proclaimed the urgent need for change without even explaining what change he wanted. Cosío Villegas:

Most [Mexicans who favored change] lacked any political or economic power, so their support for it could only be "diffuse," as political scientists say, latent but not active. More important, they did not even vaguely know what changes should be made, when, by whom, with what methods, or much less the benefits that they might legitimately expect. For his part, the presidential candidate spoke time after time about the need for change, but without defining either what it was or might be.[77]

Newell and Rubio say Echeverría's message was that failure to implement his new policies would mean "interrupting the orderly progress that the nation had enjoyed over the past four decades and opening the way for 'fascist' (authoritarian) regimes."[78]

Echeverría's supporters make it clear how crucial his own role was in propagating the message of change. Javier Alejo says, "I think Echeverría's great contribution was to have changed the national ideology because the president acted like a lay preacher, a preacher of social justice and education, a preacher who called for attending to peasants, for creating employment." Carlos Tello, like Alejo a qualified supporter of the president, notes that "in Mexico all socioeconomic reform, all important change of the development model, has depended on the state's initiation of a mass politics."[79] So it happened in 1970: "In reality, it was the state's own initiative (even if after the shock of 1968) that established the renovating discourse that has impregnated the whole Mexican social project."[80] Echeverría's name for the social project was "shared development," growth with redistribution.

If Echeverría's exhortations for amorphous change, almost calculated to provoke bureaucrats' fear, exacerbated conflict, so did his disorderly administration. It was bad luck that someone with no talent for managing a bureaucracy, yet who sought to change everything, should become the top bureaucrat.

To begin with, Echeverría seemed to need to do everything in excess—not only spend too fast, but even cut spending too fast. His initial bout of economic policymaking ironically suffered from this second excess. Julio Rodolfo Moctezuma, an economic advisor under Echeverría and a moderate fiscal conservative, says:

> At the end of 1970 [when Echeverría entered office], it was clear that public finances were out of adjustment. We—Finance, the Bank of Mexico, and Presidency—debated the matter and concluded that a little braking, not even braking, only a slower pace of increase, and a few

other measures, principally a well-justified increase in electricity rates and in petroleum-product prices, would have been sufficient. Those measures would have let us keep moving forward, and later we could have undertaken more serious projects. We communicated the plan to the president. And to all of our surprise, he considered it not only good, but too cautious. He said that we had to make a greater effort to cut back. At that point I left the government but I know that the government put on the brakes, and the result was called a period of economic "weakness," when all state investment was cut. That weakness was what in my opinion incubated the later inflation. Around October 1971 the president sensed pressures because of the lack of spending, and then, I think, took rushed investment measures, such as to prepare new agricultural land—but massively. Probably they were good projects, but they were too rushed, and the current of spending became very intense.

Once Echeverría decided that his caution had been excessive, critics and supporters alike agree, he turned around and spurred the race to invest in almost any project.[81]

When Echeverría had an idea, rather than implementing it through existing channels, he just added a new piece of bureaucracy. *Fideicomisos,* off-budget funds attached to public banks for ad hoc projects, mushroomed, says Labor Secretary Muñoz Ledo: "Echeverría hated administration per se because he had always held posts as a troubleshooter, posts getting rid of particular problems. His idea wasn't to reform the administration but to add a parallel one, as the whole world knows, to create new agencies." When Echeverría's successor López Portillo later made him ambassador to Australia, hoping to banish his ongoing machinations to the other side of the globe, Muñoz Ledo notes that everybody said, "It's so he can open a *fideicomiso* for the kangaroos."

Decision making in the 1950s and 1960s had been orderly, if hierarchical. Presidents had named cabinet secretaries with expertise in their areas, expected them to stay through the administration, given them latitude to carry out their responsibilities, and held them accountable for the results.[82] José Patrocinio González Blanco, who was director of public investment under López Mateos and whose father was labor secretary from 1958 through 1970, notes the important role of cabinet "ministers," as they were informally called:

They held their posts because of the president's confidence but also because of personal merit. They were persons whose dismissal would generate uncertainty and loss of confidence, just as their presence implied certainty and tranquility. It was neither easy to remove them nor necessary because they knew their responsibilities.

Virtually no cabinet meetings were called in that era,[83] says González Blanco, "precisely because the head of each area bore responsibility before the people and the president." The very architecture of the president's office reflected this delegation of responsibility, notes Moctezuma, director of public investments under Díaz Ordaz:

> The desk in the presidential office was ancient, and in front of it stood only one chair. There were other chairs around the room, but in front of that desk, only one. It was clear that one person was responsible to the president.

Echeverría turned this orderly system of decision making into ongoing chaos, says Moctezuma:

> When Echeverría came into office, he wanted to manage everything directly. He organized meetings, brought in many people to participate, and the sense of hierarchy was lost. There were meetings at all hours, going on at the same time in different rooms, and the president would pass from one to the other, proposing the most diverse topics for discussion. The problem was that everybody attended the meetings, the individual responsible for the area, others not responsible for it, and others who had made some incidental remark about it. They all gave their opinions, and decisions were diluted, or everybody was assigned tasks that bore no relation to each other. Everybody participated, everybody was together, but at the same time decisions were unclear. This change importantly affected government structure because the sense of authority that had existed was dispersed and lost. In great measure, officials' sense of responsibility for their functions disappeared.[84]

If groups never really made decisions, and things were left uncertain, then the one who decided was Echeverría, and other officials became interchangeable and dispensable. Muñoz Ledo, for example, went from undersecretary in Presidency, where he developed plans that were not adopted to solve the "twin exhaustion" of Mexico's political and economic models; to labor secretary, where he supported non-corporatist union currents, carrying out Echeverría's machinations against the labor boss Fidel Velázquez; to head of López Portillo's political campaign.

Echeverría fired many secretaries, moved others around rapidly, and agitated the bureaucracy by reaching much further down into it than any previous presidents had. Beteta says:

> Echeverría is a man of great social conscience; he was sincerely concerned about the misdistribution of wealth, he always fought to improve the life of peasants and the poor. . . . He never liked to do things just because that is how they had always been done. He wanted to be an innovator. Thus, if he thought a cabinet secretary was not adequately doing his job—at least as he saw it—he replaced him. And he did the same with subsecretaries and director generals, right down to the third rank.

Before Echeverría, not only had it been unusual for the president to reach down and fire officials at the third rank; it had been unusual for him to even talk to them.[85]

This incapacity for coherent administration went hand-in-hand with Echeverría's genius for political manipulation. He focused this genius especially on Finance. "Echeverría hated the finance secretaries," says Carrillo Gamboa. "He felt that they were kings that were always disputing the power of the president. So really what he wanted to do was squash the power of Finance." He appointed Flores de la Peña as state industries secretary in part for that purpose. From 1958 to 1970, as Finance Secretary Ortiz Mena had gained increasing control over state enterprises, Flores de la Peña, an official in State Industries, had been on the losing end. As director of the Commission to Control Decentralized State Enterprises, he had argued that those enterprises should be managed independently from the federal government. "He maintained a somewhat aggressive attitude toward Finance and the Bank of Mexico, and concretely toward Don Antonio [Ortiz Mena] and Don Rodrigo [Gómez]," says Moctezuma. "He had his aim fixed on them both."

By appointing Flores de la Peña state industries secretary, Echeverría assured conflict between him and Finance Secretary Margáin. Asked if the president could have forged a compromise between Finance and State Industries, Ortiz Mena replied, "Look, Echeverría used Flores de la Peña to propose projects in opposition to Margáin. I know that because Flores de la Peña said so to Margáin. He did things because, in fact, the president told him to." In short, Echeverría used the conflict between the ministries to more directly control decisions.

When Echeverría finally fired Margáin in 1973, it was to lay the groundwork for an even more devious machination. Margáin had drawn the line on budget deficits, saying there was no more money left to spend. The president infamously declared that "the economy is managed from Los Pinos," his own office, and said he would appoint a finance secretary who could find resources to spend. He appointed his boyhood friend López Portillo. José Andrés de Oteyza, who would later become state industries secretary, says that "when Echeverría named López Portillo in Finance, he was thinking about the presidential succession. Already he had López Portillo in mind."[86]

Replacing finance secretaries damaged the political system. Margáin's dismissal was the first time any finance secretary had been fired since the 1930s (except for Echeverría's own request that Ortiz Mena leave a few months early to make way for Margáin) and powerfully symbolized instability. But this was only one dimension of the damage. The heart of it was Echeverría's deliberate project, dangerously similar to Alemán's plan in 1951, to install a politically weak successor, beholden to him but lacking support within the political elite, so as to perpetuate his policies and retain some power beyond his term.[87]

Installing a politically weak successor in the presidency endangers elite cooperation by threatening the bulk of *grupos* who have been supporting a different candidate and have come to see their future as tied to his. There is no dispute that in 1975 Interior Minister Moya Palencia had widespread support and López Portillo did not.[88] Moreno Valle says that "the only powerful political current was Moya Palencia's," and informal polls conducted in the Ministry of Education showed Moya far ahead.[89] Echeverría himself said López Portillo won because he was the one with the fewest political attachments; his lack of political support was his supposed advantage.[90]

López Portillo's political weakness and ideological outlook, similar to that of Echeverría, made the president think his friend would share power with him. Says Rosa Luz Alegría, López Portillo's lover and a cabinet secretary in his administration, "López Portillo would take care of the glamour, the paraphernalia and ceremonies, and [Echeverría] would continue managing the inside threads of politics."[91] Echeverría signaled his intent to prolong his power in other ways. Toward the end of his term, he installed five cabinet secretaries as state governors and had another nominated for governor. Presidents often sought to install friendly governors, as they were the only politicians outside the central bureaucracy who mattered, but dispatching so many cabinet secretaries to governorships had no precedent in the 1950s and 1960s. Echeverría was trying to build a power base that would outlast his term.[92]

The other dangerous aspect of installing a politically weak successor was the machination it required. Jorge Castañeda writes in *The Inheritance*, his book on presidential succession, that Echeverría had to use "all the manipulation and art he had learned during a quarter-century at the heart of the Mexican political system to assure the success of an inexpert candidate lacking supporters of his own." [93] One of those manipulations was massive spending in 1975 to build support for the president and at least soften opposition to the finance minister through whose coffers the largesse passed. Total public sector spending excluding interest (which does not buy political support) increased 27 percent in real, inflation-adjusted terms, or 5 percent of GDP, in 1975 alone, the year López Portillo was nominated. In fact, if Social Security is excluded—its spending is largely distributed according to formulas—all major categories jumped 30 percent or more: federal government, state-owned enterprises, and revenue-sharing to states.[94] Spending of the Federal Electricity Commission, briefly López Portillo's domain before he became finance secretary—and thereupon very strangely put under the Finance Ministry's control—increased 65 percent, or by 1 percent of GDP.[95] Muñoz Ledo, as labor secretary, did not fail to notice López Portillo's generosity:

> Echeverría committed the worst possible mistake, the great historical error of Mexico, in naming the finance secretary as his successor—a man who didn't know anything about economics and had to hand out lots of money to be liked by the workers and the *campesinos*. He formed a Workers Bank and supported me [as labor secretary by raising wages]. But what did López Portillo do? He said to his boss: "Luis, you don't need to raise taxes. You don't need to reduce spending. The world is full of money. It's showering us with money."

Alejo believes that Echeverría made at least some attempt to slow the pace of López Portillo's spending:

> [Public Works Secretary] Luis Enrique Bracamontes and [Water Resources Secretary] Leandro Robirosa Wade were two of the most respected engineers in Mexico, great builders, extremely capable. They were close friends of the president since youth, like López Portillo—and capable of paving over the whole national territory if you let them! So on one occasion—I am sure of this—the president called together those two pharaohs [as they were called] and López Portillo, sat them down at the table with me and said, "Señor Finance Secretary, the director of the Bank of Mexico tells me that our expen-

ditures are spilling over. Señor Secretary, I order you to stop them. Stop them!" Then López Portillo said, "Señor, in fact, we are entering a real danger zone, as I have said various times." "Yes, Señor secretary, but I tell you to stop them. Stop them this very day!"

Perhaps, another cabinet secretary suggested, Echeverría told his friend López Portillo to stop the spending and winked behind Alejo's back, because even if the finance secretary surely oversaw or let pass plenty of spending, Echeverría himself was the biggest spender of them all. When he appointed Mario Ramón Beteta as the third finance secretary in the course of his administration—one who unlike López Portillo had worked his way up through Finance and learned its ethic— Echeverría said devaluation had to be avoided. Beteta recalls:

> I said to him, "In Mexico we are used to obeying the orders of the president of the Republic, and if you name me, I will accept the post, but I ask you for several hours—several hours!—to explain the situation. I think that we are already in danger of a devaluation, and there would have to be an important cut in public spending if we want to save the situation. And I will say to you, that you are not the type of person inclined to cut public spending." He gave me those hours, and I explained my viewpoint, but he didn't give it much importance, he didn't really think there could be a devaluation. He continued insisting on more spending. He had a part of the budget directly under him, at his discretion, providing resources for this and that, with an authentic social concern, without the slightest bit of corruption. But he kept spending in a disorderly way. When I learned about the spending, as finance secretary, I held it back. He knew I was going to, so he went around me, using his own resources in the presidential office.

The deluge of money benefited the president as well as López Portillo. He approached the end of his administration with "enormous political force," says Alejo, enough to pick practically anyone he wanted as his successor. Victor Bravo:

> Don Luis [Echeverría] was so strong at that time that he didn't even need the consensus of the National Executive Committee of the PRI. It was enough that one of the three corporate sectors should speak in support of the candidate and everyone else would say the same. Jesús Reyes Heroles was the president of the party, and he was the last one to learn [who the winning candidate would be]. There was no meeting of the executive committee, nothing.

Echeverría's massive overspending caused economic crisis, but it was not the worst damage. The way Echeverría threatened amorphous change amidst a climate of ideological escalation, installed a cabinet of unknowns, prematurely sidelined his own generation of the political elite, reduced a once orderly administrative process to chaos, dismissed cabinet secretaries and their *grupos* on all sides, and manipulated the system to install a vassal—or at least a protégé he hoped would be his vassal—mortally wounded the unwritten rules of elite cooperation. An internecine elite struggle emerged that no subsequent president would ever manage to control.

Increasingly after 1970, elite struggle permeated the heart of the Mexican state. Policy disputes merged into conflicts over political succession, succession conflicts grew more virulent, and—the defining characteristic of struggle—*grupos* came to fear for their very political survival. Luis Echeverría initially undermined the cooperative system and provoked struggle when, in his anxiety to bring about change, he intensified the broader Latin American climate of ideological escalation and, worse, sought to extend his grip on power beyond his constitutional term, relentlessly firing and replacing officials.

After Echeverría, elite struggle only worsened. Perhaps this progressive deterioration was not inevitable. The problem was partly individual presidents' obsessions and errors. President José López Portillo (1976–82) almost intentionally provoked cabinet conflict, relishing debates between "thesis" and "antithesis" so he could, as he put it, forge a "synthesis"—repeatedly dismissing losers, on both left and right, along the way. President Miguel de la Madrid (1982–88) cared more about imposing the free-market "Washington Consensus" on Mexico—not just moving toward a more liberal economy but forcing that move at any cost—than about the fracture of the political elite that, it became increasingly clear, his economic program was provoking. President Carlos Salinas (1988–94) manipulated everyone and everything in order to found a dynasty and, in his failure, tore the ruling party asunder.

But struggle was also cumulative, and, once provoked by Echeverría, struggle bred worse struggle. As officials saw that losers in policy debates and succession conflicts were ousted, they very reasonably feared being ousted and reached for increasingly dangerous expedients to win. To build tacit support for their presidential candidate, *grupos* surreptitiously deployed public spending, manipulated the economy, and deceived the president. The president ignored these transgressions because the more inflated the economy as the moment neared when he would "uncover" his successor, the less likely it was that the perilous succession struggle would tear the political system apart. Elites who feared they might lose the succession could not split from the party and mobilize an opposition because, in that political moment, all seemed well. As soon as the dauphin was named, all the party luminaries, especially the rivals who had lost, were obliged to congratulate him in the traditional *cargada*, or cavalry charge. Now, any *grupo* that split off would be a mere band of discontents facing a united front. The inflated economy might wind up in crisis—it always did—but, at least for the moment, the political system held.

THE GREAT ORGANIZER

Unlike Echeverría, who sought to shake up the political system, López Portillo sought in some real measure to restore order. When he took office in 1976, it looked as if he might relegate the acrimony of Echeverría's presidency to a disagreeable hiatus. Ex-presidents Miguel Alemán and Gustavo Díaz Ordaz welcomed the new president's inaugural address extending an olive branch to all sides. Where Echeverría had sidelined his own generation of the political elite, born in the 1920s, a generation that by conventional rights expected to move into power with him, and had favored a new generation of "youth" born in the 1930s, López Portillo brought the older generation back into office.[1] He also found room for his former rivals in the Echeverría administration: former Labor Secretary Porfirio Muñoz Ledo became education secretary; former Agrarian Reform Secretary Augusto Gómez Villanueva became leader of the Chamber of Deputies; and former Secretary of the Presidency Hugo Cervantes del Río became director general of the Federal Electricity Commission (the position that had launched López Portillo's meteoric rise). The new president reached out to diverse *grupos*, says Peter Smith in his study of the political elite, expressing "the continuity and harmony of postrevolutionary politics."[2]

López Portillo likewise mended bridges with business and the middle class; both had been infuriated by Echeverría's aggressive leftist rhetoric and economic debacle.[3] The private sector spokesman Juan Sánchez Navarro, head of the Grupo Modelo, welcomed the new president's inaugural address criticizing Echeverría and proposing "much more liberal positions with great success." López Portillo promised to stop printing money to cover deficits.[4] The administration signed an "Alliance for Production" with private sector groups, committing both sides to increased investment, and capital began returning to Mexico.[5]

President José López Portillo started out trying to repair the political system, as he saw it, after the incredible disorder of Echeverría. But he ended up presiding over political combat among half a dozen cabinet members, and their grupos, *for the presidency. This struggle caused the 1982 economic crisis. Photo: Dante Bucio.*

The president's conciliatory attitude extended as well to the left. An electoral reform four months into the administration legalized the Mexican Communist Party and Socialist Workers Party, introducing proportional representation to help opposition candidates get elected to the Chamber of Deputies.[6] Of course, the new rules posed no challenge to the PRI, but they did promise employment for dissenters. The left achieved real political influence through another channel: its representatives within the cabinet, particularly Carlos Tello as secretary of the powerful new Ministry of Planning and Budget and José Andrés de Oteyza as secretary of State Industries.

López Portillo was obsessed with order. He had focused on administrative reform as undersecretary of Presidency in the Díaz Ordaz administration.[7] Now he would put his theories to work, proclaiming that "a severe effort of organization, order, coordination, and planning must distinguish this term."[8] Julio Rodolfo Moctezuma, director of the PRI's research institute during the campaign, recalls, "We thought about public administration reform during numerous long meetings after the election. It preoccupied López Portillo; it was lodged in his mind. He wanted a great scheme of government, a matrix that would give him all the elements to manage."

This great organizer divided government into sectoral cabinets—for example, economic, agricultural, and national security cabinets—with a view to maintaining a vision for each unified sector. But since its establishment in 1976, "the economic cabinet has been where decisions were made," according to Fernando Solana, who held three cabinet secretary posts inside and outside that circle. "If you're not in the economic cabinet, you don't count," says Solana. "Other secretaries are the president's operatives. If you're a good operative, you can manage a ministry— Education or Environment. But if decisions don't come from the economic cabinet, they don't have power." The economic cabinet included the secretaries of Finance, Planning and Budget, State Industries, Commerce, Labor, and Interior (the last as the principal political ministry). Other members were the director general of the Bank of Mexico and Rafael Izquierdo, a López Portillo advisor who had also advised Finance Minister Antonio Ortiz Mena in the 1960s.[9] The new Ministry of Planning and Budget—a strengthened, renamed Ministry of the Presidency—was López Portillo's attempt to resolve once and for all the old ambiguities in the 1958 administrative reform giving Finance authority over spending but Presidency authority over planning and investment.[10] Planning and Budget was to do just what its name said: establish economic plans and supervise public sector budgets, both capital and current spending. Finance would just collect revenue. On paper, the scheme looked neat and workable.

Of course, the only real power even members of the economic cabinet had was persuasion. José Ramón López Portillo, the president's son and undersecretary of Planning and Budget, writes: "It was the exclusive prerogative of the president to decide on economic policy matters."[11] Miguel de la Madrid, Planning and Budget secretary after 1979, noted that the president liked to hear differences aired "so he could arrive at a synthesis." López Portillo envisioned himself, as he so often said, the "balance point of the scale," weighing contending views and discovering the equilibrium for the nation.

WAVES OF DISMISSALS

Dismissals resulting partly from tensions already injected into the political system by Echeverría and partly from López Portillo's formalistic administrative notions, untethered to the realities of Mexican politics, would undermine political equilibrium, instill *grupos* with fear of losing the presidential succession, and aggravate struggle.

The first wave of dismissals were the *echeverristas*, a group close to the former president. They had been appointed as a conciliatory gesture, but Echeverría began to use them to establish a rival power base—or, at least, so Interior Secretary Jesús Reyes Heroles persuaded López Portillo, providing evidence such as secretly recorded phone calls.[12] López Portillo solved the problem by purging them.[13] "The usual accusations and calumnies were trotted out" recalls Gómez Villanueva, who lost his post as president of the Chamber of Deputies and was dispatched as ambassador to Italy, while his protégé Félix Barra was charged with fraud.[14] Education Secretary Muñoz Ledo was soon expelled, as was Carlos Sansores Pérez, who had been named president of the PRI at Echeverría's behest.[15] The former president himself was trundled off as ambassador first to UNESCO in Paris, and then, to put him quite out of the way, to Australia. How serious Echeverría's plot to retain power may have been, and whether Gómez Villanueva or Muñoz Ledo had anything to do with it, remains uncertain because Reyes Heroles had long nourished an antagonism toward the lot of them (he had even fought with Echeverría over a girl in high school).[16] But one point was clear: López Portillo would follow Echeverría's example for resolving conflicts: if it was Reyes Heroles versus the *echeverristas*, one side had to go, and in 1977 that side was the *echeverristas*.

Meanwhile, economic policymaking erupted in a "feud among factions," says Manuel Suárez Mier, a former Bank of Mexico official.[17] First came the clash between Planning and Budget Secretary Tello and Julio Rodolfo Moctezuma, who had been named finance secretary. The usual story is that they clashed over the size of the budget deficit and need for state investment.[18] Moctezuma wanted to honor an IMF agreement signed after the 1976 crisis restricting public spending because inflation was still running high; Tello argued for abandoning the agreement and spending more to revive investment. López Portillo suggested splitting the difference between Tello's and Moctezuma's budget proposals, but Tello told him, "You promised me I would be secretary of the budget. Now you've set the line that I have to abide by Finance's commitments. That is not what you offered. I'm out." López Portillo tried to persuade him to stay: "If you go, I have to take Moctezuma out," his idea being to maintain the famous balance of the scale. "That's your problem," said Tello. He resigned, in effect forcing Moctezuma's ouster as well.[19]

The mutual knockout was not just a matter of policy disagreement. Neither official was blind to his opponent's thinking. Tello advocated what he called greater "economic independence" from the global economy and a stronger state role in directing industry and agriculture toward national purposes, for example, by producing basic rather than luxury goods, achieving self-sufficiency in food, and promoting critical capital equipment industries.[20] But Moctezuma hardly opposed industrial policies: as former director of Public Investments, the antecedent of the ministry that Tello now headed, he had overseen projects from steel mills to chemical plants, irrigation systems to schools. And Tello was hardly naïve about the danger of deficits. He insistently criticized Echeverría's spending as not supported by adequate revenue[21] and warned the current administration about that danger long before the crisis. Of the challenges it must "inescapably confront," he wrote, the first was "its own fiscal crisis, which will tend to widen to the extent that it stimulates the economy through public spending without substantive measures to finance that spending."[22]

Underneath the Tello-Moctezuma dispute, the roots of elite struggle were growing, in particular, the belief that one great faction stood to win all and its opponent to lose all. After leaving office, Tello, with Rolando Cordera, wrote *Mexico: The Dispute for the Nation*, depicting a contest between "nationalists" such as himself and "neoliberals," presumably including Moctezuma. (Tello has a tendency to talk abstractly and avoid naming names, so that it is not clear whether Moctezuma is supposed to be a card-carrying neoliberal, or if it is some ideal category that overlaps in certain respects with the real Moctezuma.) Further, Mexico had arrived at a "unique, strategic defining moment, which no one can escape." That is, fundamental change was coming, one way or another, and only its direction was up for dispute. In the face of inevitable change, opposing sides sought "to openly win social consensus and, above all, hegemony in state management."[23] Winning hegemony is not compatible with mutual survival. Losing factions could expect exile.

López Portillo's administrative thinking, formalistic and short on common sense, also set up the Tello-Moctezuma roulette. "López Portillo is a man of great culture and vision, and at the same time playful like a good intellectual," says Javier Alejo, who had worked closely with him under Echeverría. "So a nutty idea occurred to him." López Portillo had asked Tello to redesign the Finance Ministry, which would collect revenue, and Moctezuma to design Planning and Budget, which would spend it, but when the moment came to appoint secretaries, he switched them. "That strategy generated enormous conflict, one that López Portillo himself created," says Alejo. "He got in the middle of a screaming match and had to fire both." At the same time, he moved Commerce Secretary Fernando Solana to the Education Ministry. Thus, with the anti-*echeverrista* campaign still underway, López Portillo expelled three of the four principal economic secretaries (the fourth was de Oteyza[24] in State Industries).

Now another idea occurred to the president: instead of putting the more leftist official in Planning and Budget to spend money and the more conservative in Finance to collect it, the scale would stay in better balance if he inverted roles.[25] He named David Ibarra, a moderate leftist with long experience in the activist U.N. Economic Commission for Latin America, as finance secretary to collect money, and Ricardo García Sáinz, an economic conservative, as planning and budget secretary to spend it.[26] Horacio Flores de la Peña quipped that now the president had "put the nuns in the bordello and the whores in the convent."[27] The scheme made a certain sense, but the new planning and budget secretary proved incompetent.[28] López Portillo charged him, on appointment, with two key responsibilities: control spending and negotiate a Global Development Plan to harmonize economic policy. A year later, García Sáinz had produced no plan and, as Labor Secretary Pedro Ojeda says, "The spenders were eating him up." So on May 15, 1979, he was fired.

López Portillo made that day into a general political massacre, also dismissing the foreign secretary and Interior Secretary Reyes Heroles, who now suffered the same fate he had contrived for the *echeverristas.* According to *Latin American Political Report,* it was "one of the most dramatic political changes" since President Lázaro Cárdenas had exiled his predecessor, the strongman Plutarco Elías Calles, in 1936.[29] In 1979, the turnover of high-rank officials under the dismissed secretaries was three times greater than in other ministries.[30] Such high-profile expulsions could only aggravate realistic fears as to what losing the succession would mean, thereby increasing *grupos'* incentives to win at all costs.

Fear of expulsion even motivated an effort of the new secretary of Planning and Budget to build cooperation. The new secretary was Miguel de la Madrid, a moderate economic conservative who came from Finance. López Portillo told him, as he had García Sáinz: "You have two assignments. First, control spending, keep it in check. Second, get me my Global Development Plan."[31] "The Global Development Plan was President López Portillo's great dream," agrees de la Madrid.

"Neither Carlos Tello nor Ricardo García Sáinz had managed to fashion one. When they gave him drafts, he would say, 'But they aren't negotiated!' I think not negotiating was in good part why they failed. So I dedicated myself to negotiating with all the cabinet secretaries, principally Finance and State Industries—de Oteyza had enormous influence with López Portillo, no?—but I negotiated with each secretary."

De la Madrid presented the Global Development Plan in May 1980. According to José Ramón López Portillo—de la Madrid had been politic enough to name the president's son as one of his subsecretaries—the plan was "implemented" in 1981.[32] In fact, says Suárez Mier, "at the end of the presentation and the big brouhaha, it went into bureaucrats' desks."[33]

But having little affected policy does not mean that the plan had not succeeded. At the start, de la Madrid had told his team that if this work went well, it would open greater vistas to them, meaning the presidential candidacy, but "if it goes badly, we will be thrown out"[34]—as Tello and García Sáinz had been. The team worked to negotiate the Global Plan not only out of hope for success but also out of fear of failure.

POLITICAL STRUGGLE AND CAPITAL FLIGHT

The next major outbreak of elite political struggle—the economic cabinet's gambit to expel the ambitious Pemex director from politics—undermined private sector confidence, provoked capital flight, and contributed importantly to the 1982 crisis.

Like all debtor nations, Mexico faced an external economic shock as the U.S. Federal Reserve raised interest rates from 5 or 6 percent in the mid-1970s to 10 or 12 percent in 1979–80, then almost 15 percent in 1981.[35] But most economists, across a broad range of perspectives, see Mexico's principal problems in 1981–82 as internal.[36] Given its petroleum resources, Mexico did not have to wind up in a crisis, certainly nowhere near so bad a crisis. Between the period just before the crisis, 1979–81, and the period just after, 1982–84, the real purchasing power of Mexican exports increased 11 percent per year.[37] No other Latin American nation was remotely as fortunate—Brazil came closest with 4 percent annual export growth—and many suffered declines of 10 percent per year. Mexico's oil exports rose from $10.4 billion in 1980 to $14.6 billion in 1981, almost a 50 percent increase, and then to $16.5 billion in 1982.[38] They did not plummet until 1986, four years after the crisis. Some oil-importing nations, such as Korea and Thailand, that suffered severe shocks were nevertheless able to avoid crisis.[39]

The biggest immediate trigger of Mexico's crisis was capital flight, reaching $12 billion in 1981 alone, three times the trade deficit.[40] The reason was not panic spilling over from other nations: Mexico's crisis was the first. Rather, the government prompted capital flight by running massive deficits, postponing devaluation even though the finance minister and Bank of Mexico director repeatedly urged it, and irrationally demanding that its petroleum customers pay more than the going world price, a performance that cost it not only a billion dollars but, worse, private sector confidence.

Struggle over presidential succession prompted these bad policies. Pemex Director Jorge Díaz Serrano, a friend of the president, was so flagrantly angling for the nomination that, even if the economic cabinet might have been in a dispute for the nation, it was united in wanting Díaz Serrano's scalp. It saw his extravagant spending as promoting waste and corruption,[41] in addition, of course, to providing resources for his presidential ambitions. He was importing machinery that, with a more moderate rate of expansion, could perfectly well have been made in Mexico; he even imported the Pemex office tower in Mexico City, module by module, from the United States.[42] He disdained calling required meetings of Pemex's administrative council—including José Andrés de Oteyza (council president), Miguel de la Madrid, David Ibarra, and Commerce Secretary Jorge de la Vega Domínguez—instead asking the president personally to approve key decisions. These same officials just happened to be Díaz Serrano's rivals for the presidency—except for de Oteyza, ineligible because his parents were Spanish.[43] "We were fighting with him all day long," says de Oteyza.[44]

A dip in world oil prices in May 1981 gave Díaz Serrano's rivals their chance. As usual without consultation, he got López Portillo's approval[45] and announced that Mexico would lower its oil prices $4 a barrel. De Oteyza relates the upshot:

> Díaz Serrano was seen as a serious presidential contender, so everyone wanted to get rid of him. When he took the step of lowering petroleum prices without notifying us—any of us—we were going to cut his head off. The dispute was not over prices, but over the way he made the decision without consultation. I went to protest it to the president, so he called a meeting and said, "Okay, we're going to debate the matter." When the economic cabinet had gathered, I put a newspaper in front of the president that said, "Mexico Reduces Oil Prices $4 Dollars" and banged on the table: "What's the point of the meeting if

the prices are already lowered?" The president was extremely angry, but, actually, I think López Portillo was the one who really wanted to knock Díaz Serrano out of the game. Díaz Serrano was very pro-Yankee, a big friend of [then Vice President George] Bush, and I don't think López Portillo ever liked the Americans. So the president cut off his head with the pretext that he hadn't submitted a major decision to the administrative council or the economic cabinet.

Again the environment of struggle thus furthered struggle: the president and cabinet seemed to accept that if a bid for power went awry, the penalty was exile. The only remedy for Díaz Serrano's hubris that anyone conceived of was to "cut off his head."

Having dispatched Díaz Serrano on June 3, 1981,[46] the cabinet raised oil prices $2 a barrel as justification. In an address to Congress, de Oteyza warned Mexico's clients that "a barrel lost by them today, may be lost forever."[47] At the upcoming North-South Conference, President López Portillo prepared to sing the praises of primary products and rail at the "monsters of the north."[48] Many of Mexico's oil customers did not understand why they should pay more than going world prices, so Mexico lost revenue estimated at between one billion and several billion dollars.[49]

The monetary loss was the least of the problem. By August, Mexico lowered its price and regained sales, and, as mentioned, in the end, total oil export revenue rose from about $10 billion in 1980 to nearly $15 billion in 1981. The real cost of the oil price fiasco was the private sector's conclusion that chaos prevailed in the economic cabinet. Says Miguel Mancera, at the time subdirector of the Bank of Mexico and later its director:

> A far more serious problem [than the price of petroleum] was the government's total lack of realism. It seemed to think it could sell at whatever price it wanted. But how could it sell at $37 dollars a barrel if others were selling at $35? The public said, "This government is *loco*. This is the way to the abyss." I think that was the turning point. A rapid deterioration began, despite the fact that the situation should have been readily salvageable. Petroleum exports were increasing rapidly, and if the prices weren't $37 dollars, well, they still were plenty high at $35. If there had been a little common sense, a little moderation in public spending, perhaps the 1982 crisis wouldn't have occurred.

Officials, business managers, and economists alike saw June 1981, when Díaz Serrano was fired, as the moment of disaster. Planning and

Pemex Director Jorge Díaz Serrano, thought to be a powerful candidate for the ruling party's presidential nomination, unilaterally lowered oil prices without calling the legally required meeting of the state-owned firm's administrative council. The rest of the economic cabinet—most of the members sat on the administrative council—grabbed the chance to "cut his head off" politically, says José Andrés de Oteyza (above). Oteyza, the secretary of state industries, was not himself a candidate; he was constitutionally precluded from the presidency because his parents were Spanish. Photo: Archivo General de la Nación, Fondo Hermanos Mayo.

Budget Undersecretary José Ramón López Portillo, on the left, says, "Relative optimism prevailed into mid 1981. . . . The private sector forecast it would be a very positive year." But after the oil price fiasco, "suddenly, the universal impression of success . . . was shattered."[50] As Ernesto Zedillo, a conservative Bank of Mexico official and subsequent president of Mexico, writes, "The possibility of an exchange-rage devaluation still looked somewhat academic just before the 'oil price affair.' Such a possibility became an open threat by mid-June, however, leading to a tremendous capital flight."[51] Though good business relations had kept capital in Mexico—some was even repatriated in 1980[52]—in June 1981, capital flight "assumed tremendous proportions," says one well-regarded economist.[53] It became "rampant" says another.[54]

Mexican policymakers are often excused[55]—and excuse themselves[56]—as having made an understandable error, supposing with everyone else that oil prices would continue rising. De la Madrid says, "We were all wrong, but so was the rest of the world."[57] The argument is disingenuous. The rest of the world was *not* wrong in the same way that the Mexican economic cabinet was wrong. True, many energy experts predicted that oil prices would keep rising, but it is one thing to err in a medium-range prediction, quite another to demand that customers pay more than the going price today. Indeed, the problem was precisely that the rest of the world considered that the economic cabinet was not only wrong but so wrong as to be "*loco.*"

POLITICAL STRUGGLE AND PUBLIC SPENDING

Just because the economic cabinet opposed Díaz Serrano's massive spending does not mean that other members would not spend and disguise spending to win the presidency. A major cause of Mexico's 1982 crisis, on top of the oil price affair, was that the budget deficit went out of control, from a troublesome 7 percent of GDP in 1980 to a catastrophic 14 percent of GDP in 1981.[58] This rising deficit, along with the oil price fiasco, is why economists concur that Mexico's economic situation remained salvageable through 1980 but that crisis became inevitable in 1981.[59] As Francisco Gil Díaz, a subsequent finance secretary of Mexico, writes, "Everything fell apart in 1981."[60]

The deficit resulted not from declining revenue, which was constant as a portion of GDP, but from expenditures increasing by 6 or 7 percent of GDP.[61] This spending drove a foreign borrowing spree.[62] The symbol of Mexico City—the image movie directors flash to establish setting—is the Angel of Independence, standing over Paseo de la Reforma. In 1981, Angel Gurría, director of external borrowing in Finance, dubbed himself the "Angel of Dependency," as he trotted from one First World bank to another, borrowing $20 billion.[63] Mexico's external debt, 31 percent of GDP and considered reasonable in 1980,[64] increased to 39 percent of GDP in 1981.[65] Worse, short-term debt, which must be continually renewed to avoid economic crisis, mushroomed from a comfortable $1.5 billion at the end of 1980—a month of oil exports—to a perilous $10.8 billion by the end of 1981.[66]

The economic cabinet did not suffer from some grave misconception about how economies work. No one, left, right, or center, disagreed in principle that the deficit was serious and had to be controlled.[67] When he appointed de la Madrid, López Portillo had told him to contain spending. The 1981 budget theoretically allowed no increases even to compensate for inflation, running at almost 30 percent,[68] an injunction that should have meant big real cuts. The president insisted that the budget should be "strictly observed" and follow the established timetable.[69] Translation: *grupos* should not cram all their spending into the early part of the year to build political support for the presidential nomination in September. In June, López Portillo decreed an across-the-board 4 percent cut—though now 4 percent below increases he had already approved.[70]

Despite these proclamations, fears swirling around the contest for presidential nomination boosted spending dramatically in 1981. López Portillo personally approved large expenditures on the run.[71] As a down payment on the nomination, Planning and Budget let public enterprises spend half their entire allotments by the end of the first quarter.[72] Even de la Madrid's supporters concede that he bears substantial responsibility for the spending. Suárez Mier says: "De la Madrid wanted to be president, so from June 1981 until his nomination in September, he sort of kept his mouth shut. And he was in a sense right because if he had been too critical, the nomination would have gone to Ibarra or Tello," both of whom, Suárez believes, would have been worse in the long run.[73] In short, though one could spend exorbitantly and lose, as Díaz Serrano demonstrated, no one was going to win without spending. José Ramón López Portillo says that "the political race, in a 'political year,' and the resulting anxiety among all [*grupos*] to avoid affecting their respective clienteles" fueled excessive spending.[74]

The deficit was originally planned to be the peso equivalent of $17 billion, and as late as August—relying on pre–oil fiasco data from April, even though July data were available—Planning and Budget estimated

Even though President José López Portillo had told Planning and Budget Secretary Miguel de la Madrid (above) to contain spending, and the 1981 budget called for substantial cuts, de la Madrid let the budget mushroom out of control. Otherwise, nearly all sources say, he would not have won the presidential nomination. Photo: Dante Bucio.

it had only inched up to $20 billion.[75] Planning and Budget's statistical director, one Carlos Salinas,[76] well knew that highlighting loss of spending control would do no good for his boss's presidential ambitions or his own career. Only forty-five days later, after the nomination, his estimate suddenly jumped to $31 billion. Now, José Ramón López Portillo notes,

Planning and Budget turned around and "insisted on budget control," recommending "a drastic cut in expenditure."[77] But it was too late: by the end of the year, the deficit had more than doubled to $35 billion.

Economic secretaries obscured the data because they feared that confrontations with the president or with each other would get them ousted; they would meet the fate that had befallen too many secretaries before them. De Oteyza says:

> After June 1981, four months before the decision about the presidential candidate, there were many economic cabinet meetings in which we discussed what to do. Petroleum income kept falling, we kept contracting short-term debt, and the deficit kept rising. But clear economic information was never available, because everyone was playing with their cards face down. On a little piece of paper de la Madrid would say the deficit was one thing, Ibarra would say another. On a little piece of paper! Where did the figures come from? Nobody wanted to say. Nobody wanted to get into another conflict because they had seen what happened to Tello and Moctezuma, what had happened to Díaz Serrano. Nobody wanted to create conflict with the president just when he was going to select the candidate. De la Madrid said he was going to cut spending 4 percent, but really he wasn't cutting it because if he had his political possibilities would have been affected. Ibarra didn't stop contracting debt to feed the spending because if he had failed to obtain resources, his candidacy could have been affected. The decision was made, Miguel de la Madrid was chosen, and we finished that year with an enormous deficit, a barbaric deficit, great pressure and great capital flight.

López Portillo says point-blank that he was deceived by the data.[78] His son notes that "at one point the president felt he was without anyone he could trust; those around him used or concealed information and distorted analysis in order to . . . protect their political prospects."[79] To be sure, even under the best of circumstances, generating accurate, timely information on public spending was extremely difficult. It came in under different rubrics, spanning different time periods, and intended for different purposes from Planning and Budget, State Industries, Finance, the Bank of Mexico, and other sources. As finance secretary, sitting at his desk surrounded by data, Moctezuma would sometimes be unable to tell what it all meant.[80] But interagency cooperation had produced better data in the 1950s and 1960s. By the time of the López Portillo administration, even traditional allies such as Finance and the Bank of Mexico were quarreling over data.[81] In short, conflict produced conflicting information about spending as well as spending itself. López Portillo, the ex-finance secretary who had bought his presidential nomination with a 27 percent, or 5 percent of GDP, real public spending increase in 1975, and had silenced Bank of Mexico budget data by banging his fist on the table, should not have been surprised.

IDEOLOGICAL POLARIZATION?

There is a view that ideological polarization caused the crisis. It is certainly true that continual and powerful conflicts erupted over economic policy. But the usual history of those conflicts—the supposed pitched battle between Keynesian expansionists and cautious monetarists—is not quite right and, most important, the crisis was not caused by any victory of leftist big spenders over fiscal conservatives.

Newell and Rubio contend that conflict between "radically opposed and mutually exclusive philosophical differences" divided the López Portillo administration.[82] The right advocated freer markets, "an open economy with a pragmatically defined role for foreign investment, indirect government intervention in the economy when necessary, . . . and fiscal conservatism." The left advocated "a closed economy with strong limits to foreign investment, direct government intervention, . . . and a rapid growth of subsidies, government spending, and government-owned corporations."[83] Principal leftist ministries were Planning and Budget under Tello and State Industries under de Oteyza, they say; rightist ministries were Finance under Moctezuma, and the Bank of Mexico under Gustavo Romero Kolbeck.[84] The leftists won during the transition years of 1978–79; then "the years of populism," 1980–82, brought crisis.[85] Miguel Mancera, a high Bank of Mexico official who would later become its director, agrees that "there was one group led by Ibarra and Romero Kolbeck, and another—more or less the rest—led by de Oteyza. The financial group advocated a certain budget moderation, a spending level that would be less overwhelming; the others thought those were just monetarist ideas. And de Oteyza and company won the battle."

Despite economic disagreements in López Portillo's cabinet, it is impossible to draw a meaningful ideological divide with left-leaning activists in State Industries and in Planning and Budget on the one side, and right-leaning monetarists in the Finance Ministry and in the Bank of Mexico on the other. From the start, neither Tello in Planning and Budget nor Moctezuma in Finance were such neat ideological packages as often portrayed. Tello saw the real danger that excessive deficits would destabilize the economy, and Moctezuma had dedicated much of his career to planning state investment and continued to consider it important to economic progress.[86] And any meaningful line that may have existed disappeared when López Portillo's 1977 reshuffle of Finance and Planning and Budget put "the nuns in the bordello and the whores in the convent."

The story about leftists winning an ideological struggle really breaks down when it comes to explaining the crisis: institutional interests proved stronger than ideology. Though Finance Secretary Ibarra was a center-leftist,[87] who had spent fifteen years at the *dirigiste* U.N. Economic Commission for Latin America and, in an intense cabinet debate, opposed Mexico's locking in less protectionist policies by entering the General Agreement on Tariffs and Trade (GATT),[88] he repeatedly and insistently warned the president to cut spending. Not only does Ibarra himself say he warned about cutting spending, but also the leftist de Oteyza, the conservative Jesús Silva Herzog (later finance secretary), and the centrist Ojeda.[89] No doubt Ibarra is a wise economist, but, as well, his institutional interests prompted fiscal conservatism: the more the public sector spent, the greater the pressure on Finance to obtain loans.

Conversely, Planning and Budget Secretary de la Madrid, a center-rightist who had worked for twenty years in Finance and the Bank of Mexico and had supported joining GATT, turned out to be the biggest spender of all. José Ramón López Portillo, who later became estranged from his ex-boss, says that de la Madrid "proved to be flexible enough to . . . disguise his own economic position in order not to endanger his political future."[90] Labeling de la Madrid thus becomes thorny for the ideological divide story: Newell and Rubio skirt the matter by not assigning him to a camp; Teichman calls him "quasi-populist"; Centeno puts him "in the middle."[91] What does ideological polarization mean if the most powerful economic official was "in the middle"?

The problem is that ideological labels may not match political interests. "De la Madrid thought the way we did," says Bank of Mexico Director Romero Kolbeck, "but he had an interest in the presidency."[92] And his entire *grupo* shared that interest. He had brought them from Finance and the Bank of Mexico, both with a tradition of fiscal conservatism, but their interests drove them toward spending and overlooking others' spending. Surely de la Madrid did not take it on himself alone to provide bad fiscal data. He may not even have received good figures—top

Runaway deficits that contributed to the 1982 crisis were not orchestrated by an ir-responsible left. Finance Secretary David Ibarra (above), on the moderate left, kept warning about excessive expenditure, while Planning and Budget Secretary de la Madrid, on the moderate right, kept countenancing it. What mattered was institu-tional interests: Ibarra had to raise revenue; de la Madrid oversaw spending it. Photo: Dante Bucio.

Planning and Budget officials were far more interested in the presidency than in statistical accuracy—but neither did he insist on them. Contention for the presidency was a *grupo* effort.

WHERE THE MONEY WENT

Just who spent the money? De la Madrid on the right and de Oteyza on the left propose the same answer. Both say they advocated that spending be cut, but it occurred in areas they could not control: agriculture, Pemex, and Mexico City.[93] De la Madrid: "President López Portillo, in all good faith, authorized that spending on the march, and when we learned about it, it was too late to stop." De Oteyza: "All the principal economic cabinet secretaries shared the consensus that we had to control the spending of Pemex, Mexico City, agriculture, and several other branches. There wasn't debate on this matter." The answer is partly true, partly convenient, and, in any case, compatible with the nomination contest having been the problem.

With his eye on the presidential nomination, Díaz Serrano boosted Pemex spending 36 per cent, or 1.3 percent of GDP, in 1981, but how much blame he deserves for the deficit could be debated.[94] The government collected massive revenues from Pemex that never went into the oil company's coffers. When gasoline cost 6 pesos per liter, 1.25 went to Pemex and 4.75 to the government; some 70 percent of petroleum export revenues went straight to the government.[95] Julio Rodolfo Moctezuma, the former finance minister who was appointed to replace Díaz Serrano in Pemex, says that the government did not leave the company adequate resources to invest. "Though Pemex contracted a lot of debt," he says, "the truth is that it was just channeled though Pemex to the public sector. It was a way for the government to borrow." Including the taxes it paid to the federal government, Pemex ran a surplus of 4.1 percent of GDP in 1981, though that surplus had fallen sharply from 6.3 percent of GDP in 1980.[96]

Like Díaz Serrano, Carlos Hank González, governor of Mexico City, was a profligate, close friend of the president—he even bought imported police cars when perfectly good cars were made in Mexico[97]—who increased spending 30 percent in 1981, after large increases in preceding years. But that total increase was still only 0.3 percent of GDP. There were bigger culprits.

So-called agriculture spending meant just about everybody. The Mexican Food System, a plan to achieve self-sufficiency in food, embraced not only the Agriculture Ministry, concerned with commercial agribusiness, and Agrarian Reform, concerned with peasant farming, but also the national food distribution firm CONASUPO, under Commerce; major state enterprises such as the fertilizer producer FERTIMEX, under State Industries; agricultural banks such as BANRURAL, under Finance but influenced by Agrarian Reform—indeed almost a third of all the 966 public enterprises that existed.[98]

At first, the Mexican Food System had had its well-placed enemies. When López Portillo presented it to his cabinet as a fait accompli on March 18, 1980, just as the presidential succession contest was heating up, he felt it necessary to emphasize, "We must make a team effort, leaving behind . . . bureaucratic fiefdoms."[99] Food self-sufficiency meant a pro-peasant strategy because corn, beans, and other basic grains are predominantly grown by peasants. Of course, Javier García Paniagua, the agrarian reform minister and presidential contender, could embrace the program. Finance Secretary Ibarra, another presidential contender, and State Industries Secretary de Oteyza saw the goal of food self-sufficiency as important. Agriculture Secretary Francisco Merino Rábago opposed it because he was close to agribusiness, as did Miguel de la Madrid, of course another presidential contender, because he saw the Mexican Food System as effectively rivaling his Global Development Plan.[100]

López Portillo's solution to this struggle among presidential contenders was to buy compliance by expanding the food "system" into a "vast influx of resources" for all sides, except the actual peasants who grew the food crops, notes Jonathan Fox in his book on the program.[101] National accounts are not organized under rubrics that tell which presidential contender spent how much, but the category of "food spending" went from 8.2 percent of GDP in 1979 to 10.8 percent in 1981[102]—half of the total public spending increase that contributed to the crisis. Actually, neither the Agrarian Reform nor Agriculture ministries accounted for much of the money; it was everywhere else. The food distribution firm CONASUPO, under Commerce Secretary and presidential contender Jorge de la Vega Domínguez, increased spending 55 percent, or 0.6 percent of GDP, in 1981, after a hefty increase in 1980. Government subsidies to BANRURAL, the largest agricultural bank, nominally under Finance Secretary and presidential contender David Ibarra but closely allied to Agrarian Reform Secretary and presidential contender García Paniagua,[103] increased 37 percent. García Paniagua also managed to double the number of peasant families receiving land in 1980, and double it again to 93,000 in 1981.[104] After distributing land, the government had to pay the former owners.

De Oteyza was not exactly a miser. Even after the oil price affair, he kept demanding "more dollars for investment" in State Industries, says Bank of Mexico Director Romero Kolbeck.[105] The spending of the principal industrial firms dear to him, such as producers of fertilizers, paper, and steel, grew 27 percent in 1981, after large increases in 1979 and 1980. However, the increase was not so large in absolute terms: 0.2 percent of GDP in 1981, or a third of CONASUPO's growth. The spending of all of the enterprises overseen by de Oteyza, including in the huge electric utilities, increased 0.3 percent of GDP in 1981.

Presidential contender de la Madrid was ultimately responsible for controlling all spending.[106] To the extent that he let de Oteyza invest, it was in good part because de Oteyza, though ideologically further left, supported his presidential bid.[107] Political alliances ran stronger than ideological affinities. De la Madrid doubtless also gained support by letting federal government investment, a flexible area under his control, grow 26 percent in 1981. And the total size of government investment growth—0.8 percent of GDP—was several times the spending increase of de Oteyza's state enterprises.

Finance Secretary Ibarra, de la Madrid's rival, might have spent in two big-growth areas if he was serious about building support for his presidential nomination: revenue-sharing with states and development bank lending.[108] In 1981, the first grew 37 percent in real terms, or 0.6 percent of GDP; the second grew 26 percent in real terms, or a massive 2.3 percent of GDP. Although outside the fiscal budget, development bank lending can increase the money supply and contribute to inflation, and its growth was more than that of the Pemex and Mexico City budgets combined. Possibly, Ibarra's fiscal conservatism applied mainly to areas under Planning and Budget control.

Presidential contender Jorge de la Vega Domínguez was hardly left far behind. His ministry, Commerce, did not spend much in absolute terms, even if its budget grew 20 percent in 1981, but, as mentioned, the food distribution firm CONASUPO under Commerce massively increased its spending, accounting for a large growth in 1981, 0.6 percent of GDP. Further, de la Vega's political ally, Education Secretary Fernando Solana, managed to raise his spending 23 percent, or 0.5 percent of GDP.

The only presidential contender who did not spend much in absolute terms was Pedro Ojeda. Though his Labor Ministry enjoyed an extraordinary 110 percent increase in 1981, it was not even 0.1 percent of GDP. Lending by INFONAVIT, the state program to provide home mortgages for workers, actually fell by a miniscule portion of GDP.

THE MOTIVE OF STRUGGLE

A contest for power caused politically motivated spending, but to what extent was it just ambition to win, which presumably always existed and always will, and to what extent was it specifically elite struggle, that is, increasing fear that losers would be banished? Many remarks point to that fear: de la Madrid's warning his team that if their work went badly "we will be thrown out"; José Ramón López Portillo's view that de la Madrid disguised his real fiscal conservatism "in order not to endanger his political future"; de Oteyza's description of how presidential contenders hid data, avoided conflict, and spent because "they had seen what happened to Tello and Moctezuma, what had happened to Díaz Serrano"; and Tello's vision of an Armageddon between neoliberals and nationalists.

Fear of political exile is hard to gauge, but the prominent and frequent expulsion of high officials and their *grupos* should well have provoked it. Major expulsions before the nomination included the *echeverristas*; Tello and Moctezuma; García Sáinz and the May 15, 1979, political massacre; and Díaz Serrano. And as if to confirm the pattern, afterward Ibarra and Romero Kolbeck were fired for little apparent reason other than having been too insistently right. Then when de la Madrid entered the presidency, he validated everyone's fears by expelling losers wholesale. Pedro Ojeda was the only former cabinet secretary left—in the Ministry of Fisheries, not exactly a top policymaking spot.

Fear of losing power is also the most plausible motive for the extraordinarily intense conflict that, all sources agree, beset the López Portillo cabinet. A *grupo* has two motives to attack rivals—ambition to advance its members' careers and fear that rivals will end its members' careers—but fear is the more powerful. Many officials might have contentedly remained directors, director generals, or subsecretaries rather than engage in high-stakes struggle, but fear obliged them to take the offensive before opponents preempted them. This is the very problem that drives Thomas Hobbes' state of nature. Self-interest, he argues, motivates all people to protect their security. Only a few desire to grab more power than their security requires, but the rest are afraid of those few. People who "otherwise would be glad to be at ease within modest bounds" are forced to "increase their power," attacking just to protect themselves. Such aggression is "necessary to a man's conservation," therefore it ought to be "allowed."[109] Prominent and frequent exile of losers pushed elite competition closer to such a Hobbesian state of nature.

A conceivable military threat from Agrarian Reform Secretary Javier García Paniagua suggests how deeply fear had eroded old norms. He had been head of the Federal Security Directorate, the secret police; his father had been defense secretary; and the current defense secretary supported his candidacy. As the nomination approached, Interior Minister Enrique Olivares Santana carefully took Porfirio Muñoz Ledo to a spot where possible eavesdropping devices could not hear them and said, "I wouldn't want the defense secretary to present himself before the president one day and say, 'We want the candidate to be Javier.'"[110] Muñoz Ledo told the president about worries that García Paniagua might invoke military force, and he believes he confirmed the president's decision to preempt trouble by unexpectedly announcing the nomination a month earlier than usual.

The president's fear that the political succession mechanism might break down amidst struggle also contributed to his refusal to devalue the peso in time. In October 1980, businessmen led by Banamex President Agustín Legorreta tried to convince him that economic stability depended on devaluing the peso before it crashed.[111] Finance Secretary Ibarra had urged devaluation since 1977,[112] and Bank of Mexico Director Romero Kolbeck had urged it since early 1981.[113] Other members of the economic cabinet favored a more or less gradual devaluation, but kept quiet.[114] The rumor that de Oteyza privately opposed devaluation and urged the president to impose capital controls[115] is wrong. De Oteyza says he supported a gradual, controlled devaluation and not capital controls.[116] Because he freely agrees that he supported the radical measure of bank nationalization, why should he cover up supporting the moderate policy of capital controls, used, for example, by several European countries, Colombia, and Brazil? In any event, he says, during the nomination contest, the economic cabinet did not discuss devaluation because "nobody wanted to engage in such polemics; a devaluation could have hurt candidates' chances."

The one who opposed devaluation was the president.[117] When Romero Kolbeck persisted in advising devaluation, López Portillo said, "We are not going to, and if you keep on this way, I will not give you any more appointments."[118] The president opposed devaluation partially on general political grounds, saying that "the president who devalues is devalued." But, as Ojeda notes, he especially did not want to devalue before the nomination. On this critical point the president's son agrees: López Portillo "feared that a devaluation would jeopardize the process of succession in power." Amid such a tense succession, the last thing a president would want to do is devalue, curb spending, increase taxes, or take any other measure that would produce an immediate economic shock and threaten the political system. The economy just had to endure.

After Miguel de la Madrid was named the party's candidate, political tension subsided, and López Portillo did devalue 40 percent in February 1982 [119]—six months before the election. During the election year, real public sector spending (excluding interest) was slashed 8 percent. López Portillo decreed a 30 percent wage increase in March to propitiate the official union apparatus, an important cog in the electoral machinery that disliked the technocratic presidential candidate Miguel de la Madrid.[120] In any event, real wages rose less than 1 percent for the year, and the minimum wage fell 11 percent.[121]

The crisis broke in August. López Portillo had gone through four secretaries of Planning and Budget, three secretaries of Finance, and three directors of the Bank of Mexico—in each case (considering Presidency as the predecessor of Planning and Budget), more individuals than had occupied those posts throughout the period from 1952 through 1970. Pedro Ojeda says, "Each of us did our job very well, and the result was very bad."

Much as José López Portillo began his term by trying to heal the enormous acrimony Luis Echeverría had left behind, so Miguel de la Madrid initially sought to restore a lost political and economic order, as he saw it. The two presidents took opposite tacks, so one might have supposed that one approach or the other would have worked. But they just failed in opposite ways, unwittingly showing how obdurate elite struggle can be.

López Portillo had incorporated all factions in his cabinet—left and right, *político* and *técnico*—and found himself mired in destructive conflicts. De la Madrid interpreted those conflicts as having been caused by ideological battles:

> I saw polarization: on one side expansionists, Keynesians, supposed progressives; on the other, finance officials, conservatives, monetarists. The lesson I learned was that we wasted time trying to resolve disagreements and arguments. Though the president said he liked the dialectical process of confronting thesis and antithesis to derive a synthesis, I don't think it worked. The synthesis was neither the one nor the other but halfway measures. So, in fact, I wanted a homogeneous cabinet, in basic agreement, even if there were debates about implementation.

If de la Madrid had been right that the real problem was ideological polarization, his appointment of a homogeneous cabinet should have brought peace. But the problem was elite struggle—the idea that you must wipe opponents out, or they will wipe you out, regardless of ideology—so it just continued. The more winning *grupos* exiled opponents, the more everyone believed that winning required exiling opponents. As well, de la Madrid, like López Portillo, cared more about an abstract fixation than the old unwritten rules. De la Madrid's fixation was not the dialectic of synthesis and antithesis but liberalizing the economy—and not just doing so gradually, but imposing a categorical free-market formula. The result was a decisive fracture of the political elite that would never be repaired and would further the regime's demise.

THE DUEL TO BE ECONOMIC CZAR

There was an aura of restoration to the de la Madrid presidency. The president's principal collaborators had begun their careers in what they saw as a golden age under Antonio Ortiz Mena in Finance and Rodrigo Gómez in the Bank of Mexico, and all had won his confidence through long-term relationships with him in the financial sector of government.[1] The inner circle included Jesús Silva Herzog in Finance, Carlos Salinas in Planning and Budget, Francisco Labastida in State Industries, Bernardo Sepúlveda in Foreign Relations, Ramón Aguirre as governor of Mexico City, and Francisco Rojas as comptroller, a new position designed to symbolize the administration's announced motto of honesty.[2]

Political restoration always involves an element of innovation, and whereas the original Ortiz Mena-Gómez *grupo* had been confined to the financial sector (Finance, the Bank of Mexico, and related banks and funds), de la Madrid deployed descendents of this *grupo* in ministries and agencies across the state. "Even the agriculture minister was from the Bank of Mexico," says José Andrés de Oteyza. "Finance and the Bank of Mexico took power and never let it go." Though on average, 32 percent of cabinet officials since the 1950s had come from the financial sector, under de la Madrid that percentage almost doubled to 59 percent.[3] In his study of the cabinet, Rogelio Hernández Rodríguez argues that this group believed that the Echeverría and López Portillo administrations' bungling had been the "principal cause" of Mexico's major political and economic problems.[4]

Within the restoration, cabinet struggle nevertheless erupted. The first combat was between Finance Secretary Jesús Silva Herzog and Planning and Budget Secretary Carlos Salinas. The issue was not ideology—there was hardly any ideological difference—but power: who would become the economic czar, who would secure the presidential nomination, and who would be ousted. It was "the same old story," reflects Silva Herzog.[5] Again Planning and Budget would win by using expenditures to build political support. Again Finance would lose by insisting that excessive expenditures were being hidden.

The economic context in which the same old political story played out could hardly have been more different from that of the López Portillo administration. Then the economy was growing faster even than in the 1950s and 1960s, and measures to avert crisis were clear: hold public expenditure down to some halfway sensible level, devalue the peso

By the mid-1980s, elite struggle had become entrenched, and it had nothing to do with ideology. Though their economic views hardly differed, Finance Secretary Jesús Silva Herzog and Planning and Budget Secretary Carlos Salinas (above) fought a political duel to determine who would become the economic czar and who would be ousted. Salinas won. Photo: Arturo López.

moderately, and do not try to charge more for petroleum than everybody else in the world.

Under de la Madrid, the economy was in ruins, and there may have been no good way to fix it, let alone any clear understanding how to. The president and his *técnicos* with advanced degrees from U.S. universities thought that the usual IMF shock therapy—slashing budget deficits, drastically devaluing the peso, driving down wages—would solve Mexico's economic problems. Eager to be star performers, they devalued 50 percent on taking office and slashed public sector deficits to IMF targets.[6] The IMF said inflation would fall from 100 percent to 55 percent, but it stayed at 80 percent; the IMF said the economy would experience zero growth, but it shrank 4 percent.[7] Real wages plunged more than 20 percent.[8] The economy just would not obey economists' promised targets. Perhaps the fundamental problem was that, throughout the administration, Mexico was forced to make net payments to First World creditors averaging 6 percent of GDP per year.[9] Those payments meant slashing investment by 6 percent of GDP. Growth collapsed.

Silva Herzog initially seemed to be in a stronger political position than Salinas. A long-time friend and contemporary of de la Madrid, Silva Herzog belonged to the generation of the 1930s that should have, by all political rights, dominated this and the next administration, while Salinas belonged to the generation of the 1940s, too young to assume the presidency until the mid-1990s. Furthermore, Finance played in the limelight, renegotiating Mexico's foreign debt in the wake of the crisis, but Planning and Budget was assigned the shadowy role of enforcing draconian spending cuts amid a deep recession.

But when political succession, indeed political survival, depends on the good graces of "the unique office-holder," as de la Madrid himself had categorized the Mexican president, there is such a thing as too much limelight. It was not an advantage when *Euromoney* declared the globe-trotting Silva Herzog "finance minister of the year."[10] Jorge Castañeda notes in *The Inheritance*, "Every foreign magazine cover where Silva Herzog appeared represented a blow, slight at first, sharp at the end, to Miguel de la Madrid's ego."[11]

Back home, Salinas played the president's loyal operative.[12] He had assumed this role under de la Madrid during the López Portillo administration, negotiating the famous Global Development Plan, a political coup even if it landed in bureaucrats' trash cans, and hiding unwelcome fiscal data. And, even amidst recession, he was clever enough to deploy judicious spending to win political elites' support.[13] The international airports sprouting around Mexico in towns like Piedras Negras that Silva Herzog got wind of were only one example.

Salinas managed to cast blame for budget cuts on his opponent, while Silva Herzog, bristling with economic correctness, seemed insensible to the effects that budget cuts had on the programs concerned—or on his standing in the eyes of the president. He recalls an altercation eerily like several in the Echeverría administration.[14] He was arguing in a cabinet meeting that Agriculture had to cut spending, while the agriculture secretary, backed by Salinas, pressed for more resources. De la Madrid finally sided with Agriculture, pointing at his finance secretary and ordering him to find the resources: "And if you can't find them, invent them." Silva Herzog felt it necessary to declare, "Señor president, I will follow your instructions. But I want it to be set down that the finance secretary is in complete disagreement with the president of the republic about this matter." De la Madrid banged his fist on the table and ended the meeting.

One night toward the end of 1985, Salinas sent Silva Herzog the proposed 1986 budget.[15] Both were to sign it in the president's office at ten o'clock the next morning. Silva Herzog saw that Programming and Budget had badly underestimated necessary spending in a number of categories, he says. For example, the budget projected the interest payments of one large state-owned enterprise at 4 million pesos, when in fact they were known to be 44 million.[16] Silva Herzog picked up the phone: "Carlos, I'm not going to sign the budget." Salinas went directly to his office, at eleven o'clock at night, and they finally agreed they would sign the next morning but would explain their disagreements to the president and resolve them in January. Of course, nothing was ever resolved. "In other words, the budget was overspent from the start," says Silva Herzog.

Evidently Silva Herzog's budget concerns had some merit. Mexico kept missing the IMF targets. It had agreed to hold the budget deficit to 3.5 percent of GDP in 1985, but it swelled to 9.6 percent of GDP. So the IMF suspended financing, and the peso crashed again. Then in 1986, oil prices collapsed, and this time they really collapsed, plunging from $25 a barrel to $12. Total petroleum exports fell by $8.5 billion in a single year—a quarter of public sector revenue, half of export revenue—and inflation shot back up to more than 100 percent. Again the economy shrank 4 percent.[17]

Amidst this dismal scenario, the economic cabinet continually argued about the source of the problems, the size of the deficit, and what to do.[18] Silva Herzog estimated that the fall in petroleum prices would reduce revenues by $6 billion in 1986. He proposed to cut public spending by $2 billion, secure $2 billion in foreign loans, and let the deficit rise by $2 billion.[19] Salinas famously proclaimed that spending had been cut "to the bone" and said the deficit was not so serious.[20] If Finance would do its job of securing foreign loans to tide over the emergency, Mexico could achieve 3 or 4 percent growth in 1986 and 1987[21]—coincidentally, just when the next presidential candidate would be selected. Silva Herzog saw "deliberate deception" in Salinas' budget figures.

Francisco Labastida, secretary of State Industries under de la Madrid and the PRI's presidential candidate in 2000, concurs with Silva Herzog.[22] "He was right; the financial problem was worse than Salinas was saying. Salinas was really manipulating the theory of expectations: you have to say inflation is 30 percent, even if the figures would indicate 60 percent, in order to influence economic agents' behavior." In an administration of *técnicos* with advanced economics degrees, economists' terms of art—"rational expectations"—had became political weapons. The only problem was that if the theory of rational expectations is actually correct, it says that economic actors cannot be fooled; they should see through invented projections. In fact, they did see through them, Labastida says: "Both the figures that were announced and the policies that were adopted lost credibility."

The president kept trying to persuade Salinas and Silva Herzog to work out their differences. They played tennis on weekends, but tennis was not going to resolve a power struggle, Salinas telling his rival to borrow more, Silva Herzog telling his rival to spend less.[23] The conflict reached the point of no return: somebody was going to be exiled from de la Madrid's attempted restoration of political and economic harmony.

Silva Herzog was more experienced, more independent, even more of a rival to de la Madrid, notes Victor Urquidi, then president of the Colegio de Mexico. Silva Herzog himself acknowledges that he was "disrespectful" toward the president, insisting, "If you can't control Salinas' spending, it is going to be useless."[24] And, as David Ibarra might have warned him, harassing the president about another cabinet secretary's spending was no way to win at palace politics. Silva Herzog resigned in mid-1986. "Of course," he admits, "if I hadn't resigned, the next day the president would have fired me."

The president appointed Gustavo Petricioli, a capable "negotiator," as de la Madrid puts it, to be finance secretary. Petricioli was a "mild person who would go along with things," says Urquidi. Petricioli was "intelligent, but saw that the president was leaning toward Salinas and became, in effect, undersecretary of Planning and Budget," says Silva Herzog. A year before de la Madrid would nominate his successor to the presidency, Salinas had won the first stage. He was economic czar.[25]

SPLITTING FINANCE IN HALF

It seems odd that de la Madrid had set up the Salinas-Silva Herzog duel by preserving López Portillo's division of functions: Planning and Budget spent, while Finance raised revenue. Many who looked back to the Ortiz Mena era as a golden age, when Finance was preeminent, held that splitting it in half had been a recipe for economic disaster.[26] Indeed, Miguel de la Madrid himself held this view. In 1976, before López Portillo took office, he and Finance Secretary Mario Ramón Beteta had prepared a white paper opposing the establishment of Planning and Budget. They had urged the incoming president to leave Finance in charge of revenue and expenditure, de la Madrid says: "But López Portillo had made his mind up."

Why, when he became president, did de la Madrid not take his own advice and reconstitute the old Finance Ministry? The tradition of its preeminence was long-standing. The separation had lasted one mere term, and it had proven a disaster. Nor was administrative reform some matter of great patriotic fervor such that reversing it might cause a political explosion. Presidents always redesigned their cabinets to signal that they would set a new course. Why not this time? Furthermore, to what extent was the Finance–Planning and Budget split, rather than broader elite struggle, the cause of Mexico's crises?

A sort of sorcerer's apprentice story could be posited here: The Mexican miracle of the 1950s and 1960s depended on presidents' deference to a coherent Finance Ministry, allied with the Bank of Mexico. But as that financial bureaucracy came to control an increasingly large and complex public economic sector, it threatened to become a superministry, a rival even to presidential power. Echeverría, López Portillo, and de la Madrid, however dissimilar in other ways, came to fear that Finance would undermine their authority. So in an attempt to weaken the apprentice who had gone out of control, they broke the ministry in half, and left it in half.

In part, the sorcerer's apprentice story seems to make sense. The Finance Ministry under Ortiz Mena did insinuate itself into practically every social and economic question, via its array of development banks and funds. As just one example, the national development bank, Nafinsa, created in 1934, invested in more than five hundred private or mixed-ownership firms such as the major cement manufacturer Cementos de Guadalajara; owned majority shares in state enterprises such as Altos Hornos (steel) and Guanos y Fertilizantes (fertilizers); and engineered takeovers of multinational subsidiaries such as electric utilities and sulfur mines.[27] In those takeovers Nafinsa did not balk at lining up $100 million lines of credit abroad, assembling banking syndicates from New York to Hong Kong, and putting up straw men to hide its identity.[28] And Nafinsa ran a good business: electric generation growth nearly doubled after it wrested control from several multinationals,[29] and Mexico's sulfur output rose to second in the world after it took over foreign-owned mines.[30]

Nafinsa was the single biggest bank under Finance in the 1950s and 1960s, but there were many others, such as the Banco Nacional Agropecuario for agribusiness, the Banco Nacional de Crédito Ejidal for peasant farming, Banobras for infrastructure and housing, and the Banco Nacional de Comercio Exterior for export industries. And then there were the *fideicomisos*, or development funds. When a bank made a loan for a project, a *fideicomiso*, attached to the Bank of Mexico or Nafinsa, would guarantee it, purchase it from the bank, and provide technical assistance. For example, FIRA provided crop credits, FOGAIN promoted medium and small industry, FOMEX assisted export firms, FOVI financed housing for the middle and working class, and INFRATUR developed tourist centers such as Cancun and Ixtapa.[31]

"Ortiz Mena was a powerful finance minister," says Horacio Flores de la Peña, who as an official in State Industries in the 1960s waged a rearguard action against Ortiz Mena for control over state-owned enterprises.[32] He "wanted to manage the whole economy; he had an unlimited thirst for power." Echeverría appointed Flores de la Peña as state industries secretary so he could move his battle against Finance to the front lines.

López Portillo institutionalized Echeverría's strategy. Earlier, as undersecretary of Presidency under Díaz Ordaz—the same ministry that he would elevate to Planning and Budget—he had conceived a jealousy toward Finance. "The guy who discovered that there were 870 *fideicomisos* in the Bank of Mexico is named López Portillo," says Porfirio Muñoz Ledo, his successor in the same subsecretariat of Presidency. "He found that the government's right wing, which kept complaining about the growth of the bureaucratic apparatus, had created its own bureaucratic apparatus, the *fideicomisos*. The only thing he wanted to do was get those *fideicomisos* out of the Bank of Mexico. He created Planning and Budget, and he moved the *fideicomisos* to their respective sectors," that is, putting them under related ministries such as Tourism, Agriculture, or Public Works. De Oteyza, one of López Portillo's closest advisors, concurs: In the Ortiz Mena era, "a *fideicomiso* would be created precisely to make an end run around budget restrictions and other agencies; it was what would really manage sectoral matters. And all those *fideicomisos* were under the finance secretary. That is why Finance had such enormous power. Ortiz Mena had it, Margáin maintained it under Echeverría, and so did López Portillo himself" as finance minister. So when he became president, according to de Oteyza, López Portillo said, "I am going to break up that ministry; it's too powerful; I don't like it." And he split it in half.[33]

Surely Echeverría and López Portillo did want to weaken the finance sector bureaucracy, but the sorcerer's apprentice story does not apply to the de la Madrid and Salinas administrations. To begin with, this kind of metaphor works better to describe changing relationships between public and private sectors. At first, the state nourishes domestic firms through protectionism and subsidies, but over time, as firms grow into robust producers, their sheer economic might tips the balance of power against the state. One reason this kind of story does not work well within the Mexican state is that presidents in the 1970s and 1980s could, and repeatedly did, fire finance secretaries and key members of their *grupos*. To recall de la Madrid's remark once more, all cabinet secretaries and directors of state enterprises were mere "auxiliary collaborators dependent on the unique office-holder, the president."[34]

The notion that presidents feared any comprehensive economic ministry is also contradicted by the fact that de la Madrid effectively reestablished just such a ministry in 1986. By firing Silva Herzog and installing Petricioli in Finance as Salinas' operative ("undersecretary of Planning and Budget"), de la Madrid simply placed the principal economic responsibility in a different ministry. After Salinas himself became president, he eliminated Planning and Budget and restored Finance to its former eminence. President Ernesto Zedillo left Planning and Budget in the grave. Moreover, if presidents feared that an economic superagency might deceive them, they should have realized that a twin agency rivalry would also deceive them, as López Portillo discovered.

Nor did the Finance–Planning and Budget split have anything to do with three of the four crises that Mexico succumbed to after 1970.

Echeverría had one economic supersecretary, namely Echeverría, who, along with his protégé López Portillo in the Finance Ministry, steered the nation toward crisis. Divided economic authority, between Ibarra's Finance and de la Madrid's Planning and Budget, was a factor in the 1982 crisis. However, de la Madrid made Salinas economic czar in 1986, in good time to start inflating the financial bubble that would contribute to the 1987 crisis. And after Salinas restored Finance to its former eminence under Pedro Aspe in 1992, the two of them proceeded to overvalue the peso on the way to the 1994 crisis.[35]

So why did de la Madrid not reincorporate Planning and Budget with Finance on entering office in 1982? The most logical reason would be to avoid upsetting the balance among competing *grupos*. Already in the 1970s, and even more so in the ongoing recession of the 1980s, the ministers who managed the economy were becoming the most politically prominent, and Silva Herzog was a powerful figure. If de la Madrid had brought Planning and Budget under his control, Silva Herzog says, "it would have been clear who his successor was. But in Mexican politics, there must always be weights and counterweights."

One preeminent competitor for the presidency, without adequate counterweights, would damage the mechanism of political succession. Even if a president had a successor in mind, he had to fabricate rivals— *relleno*, or filling, they were called—to sustain the hopes of other *grupos* and keep them playing within the system for their favorites' nomination, not breaking off to threaten the ruling party from without. In 1987, after Silva Herzog's elimination, the real candidates were widely considered to be Carlos Salinas, State Industries Secretary Alfredo del Mazo, and Interior Secretary Manuel Bartlett, yet de la Madrid held a sort of mock primary debate among these and three more candidates, for good measure. He declared all had done well, and then picked Salinas, who undoubtedly had been the only real candidate in his mind. But he needed to keep everyone hoping until the official nomination.

Making Salinas the economic czar in 1986 was dangerous, but not as dangerous as it would have been to install Silva Herzog in that role in 1982. In 1986, Salinas still lacked Silva Herzog's stature; he was not seen as a sure bet for the presidency. Francisco Labastida, who had been in de la Madrid's cabinet but moved to the governorship of Sinaloa, says: "I think that even when Salinas actually became the candidate, it was a surprise for many." Indeed, on October 4, 1987, when Carlos Salinas de Gortari, to use his full name, was nominated, Alfredo del Mazo committed the horrible blunder of publicly congratulating the wrong candidate:

Attorney General Sergio García, one of the *relleno* crew. Del Mazo had heard that García had won from a seemingly reliable source, but that source, having ascertained that "SG" was the winner, had thought the initials stood for "Sergio García" instead of "Salinas de Gortari."[36]

FRACTURING THE PARTY

The Salinas–Silva Herzog duel was only the beginning. For much the same reasons that struggle had worsened under López Portillo, it now led to a decisive fracture of the ruling party. First, struggle tends to feed on itself, and second, the president cared more about an abstract political project than about honoring the unwritten rule that promised all *grupos* survival.

De la Madrid's project was economic liberalization: lowering trade barriers and introducing freer markets. But he might have moved Mexico from import substitution toward a more liberal economic regime without provoking elite fracture had he not insisted on transforming economic policy categorically and abruptly, along the lines of what came to be called the "Washington Consensus." By imposing an unpopular Carlos Salinas as his successor to ensure unconditional economic transformation, he broke the rules of elite cooperation. Not only did he leave the so-called Democratic Current—a group of old-guard politicians on the economic left—no option but to split off and run an opposition campaign, but he also alienated resentful factions that remained within the PRI.

This story of elite fracture begins when de la Madrid appointed a government run by former Finance and Bank of Mexico officials. In completely shutting out Echeverría's and López Portillo's allies, he broke the unwritten rule that no major *grupo* should be excluded.[37] Even those cabinet secretaries who did not come from the financial sector, such as Interior Secretary Manuel Bartlett, were de la Madrid's close collaborators.[38] Only four lacked personal ties with him, and they were in posts of secondary importance such as Fisheries, occupied by Pedro Ojeda. Plotting out the careers of cabinet secretaries over decades, Rogelio Hernández Rodríguez concludes that not since Miguel Alemán—the president who had almost driven opposing factions to the battlefield—had the cabinet been so closely identified with the president or so completely determined by personal friendship.[39]

Even more startling than de la Madrid's takeover of the central administration was his takeover of the party apparatus and state governorships.[40] Presidential nominees would install one—and only one—close associate in the National Executive Committee of the PRI during their electoral campaigns, but de la Madrid unprecedentedly filled almost the whole committee with close allies, largely the same individuals he later appointed cabinet secretaries. Adolfo Lugo Verduzco, the party president de la Madrid named in 1982 after the election, had had no prior electoral or party experience, a rarity for that post, and, worse, was under orders to favor politicians like those in the president's inner circle. De la Madrid only introduced subtle changes in the legislature—it was the U.N. General Assembly of the Mexican state, all chatter and no power—but his appointment of officials with central administration careers to twenty-three of twenty-six governorships, including four secretaries and four subsecretaries from his cabinet, produced a systemic shock.[41] Electoral and party posts traditionally constituted their own sphere to reward the leaders in the PRI sectors—labor, peasant, and "popular"—who handled societal pressures that might boil up and made sure the party won overwhelming electoral victories. De la Madrid shut them out from the best jobs they could aspire to.

After Salinas defeated Silva Herzog, prospects further dimmed for political elites outside de la Madrid's circle. If Salinas became president, they could expect to be out for good, not just for political but also for generational reasons. Those who would split off to form the Democratic Current—notably Cuauhtémoc Cárdenas, governor of Michoacán and son of the much-loved president Lázaro Cárdenas, and Porfirio Muñoz Ledo, cabinet secretary under Echeverría and López Portillo—not only were on the left but also belonged to the generation of the 1930s. Longstanding tradition dictated that presidents of a given generation should dominate two successive administrations and make appointments predominately from their age cohort, with whom they had established the closest networking ties, to the hundred or so highest offices.[42] Thus, the generation born in the teens dominated the administration of both López Mateos, born 1910, and Díaz Ordaz, born 1911. As mentioned, Echeverría, born 1922, broke the rule (as he broke so many) and favored the younger 1930s generation in filling many posts, but López Portillo, born in 1920, restored the 1920s generation to high office.[43] De la Madrid, born in 1934, favored his 1930s generation (Salinas was an exception).[44] Silva Herzog, born in 1935, would likely honor tradition and reappoint members from that generation again. Salinas, born in 1948, would install his peers and end the 1930s generation's hopes forever: there would be no second chance.

Denying a political cohort its expected time in high office might always provoke instability, but especially in this case. The sharpest generational divide among Mexican elites, in social background, educational attainment, and historical outlook, falls between those born before and after 1940.[45] One quarter of Mexican elites born before 1940 (now including public sector, private sector, church, and military) came from the working class, but practically none born after 1940 did. Elites born after 1940 were dominated by natives of Mexico City rather than the provinces, and, unlike their predecessors, always had university degrees, half of them Ph.D.s. The older generation had seen the political system end decades of terrible violence—the last serious military revolt and the bloody Cristero religious rebellion against anti-clerical laws were not over until 1930—and establish an age of order and progress. The younger generation had watched that order and progress disintegrate in Tlatelolco, economic crises, and conflictive politics.[46] High government officials born before 1940 were importantly shaped by ideals transmitted through the National University. Those born after 1940 increasingly attended private Mexican universities and received advanced degrees in the United States, typically in economics.[47] Ideology is fungible, but leaders of the Democratic Current, born predominately in the 1930s, were the generation of state-led development, while Salinas' allies, born in the 1940s and mostly after 1945, would be the generation of the Washington Consensus. It was the sociological divide between generations that gave ideological differences traction.

Those who would form the Democratic Current broke the unwritten rules because they had no choice. As de la Madrid proceeded to marginalize them—a tactic they explicitly saw as violating elite political norms[48]—their only plausible strategy for retaining influence was to retaliate. Cuauhtémoc Cárdenas, Porfirio Muñoz Ledo, and Rodolfo González Guevara, the ambassador to Spain, began holding informal chats.[49] At first, they sought only some influence within the PRI.[50] But after Salinas won primacy in the economic cabinet, ousting Silva Herzog on June 17, 1986, and threatening the older generation's hopes for the next administration, they began to raise the stakes. Only a few weeks later, they held their first larger meeting, at the house of Ifigenia Martínez, a prominent left-leaning economist, in the fashionable Mexico City neighborhood of Coyoacán.

In July 1986, Gonzalo Martínez Corbalá, senator from San Luis Potosí, invited fifteen or twenty potential Democratic Current members to what would prove a fateful dinner. The ostensible purpose was to discuss policy proposals,[51] but things turned far more serious than many had expected. August Gómez Villanueva, agrarian reform minister under Echeverría, recalls his uneasy feelings:

> The meeting was called to talk about the political situation and how we might organize a group in the party to be sure the leadership did not stray from the Mexican Revolution's historical project. . . . [But] there were two tendencies at the dinner. One was saying, let's run Cuauhtémoc Cárdenas as the party's presidential candidate and then negotiate. I was opposed. Other people had spontaneously come, and it seemed disloyal to commit them to something they had not been previously informed about. A dinner should not be manipulated into a meeting to make political decisions—decisions that seemed to me to go dangerously far, because they amounted to initiating a schismatic process within the heart of the party. I even said, clearly, that I was concerned that whatever happened would get out: "I want to make it clear that we are not conspiring against President de la Madrid, who is Muñoz Ledo's and my personal friend, nor are we forming a coalition that could play a schismatic role within the heart of the party." Such a process would only play into the hands of [the conservative] National Action Party and right-wing forces in the United States—as in fact did happen.

There can have been no one there who did not know the unwritten rules. Political currents could try to build support for a presidential contender in any number of discreet ways, from networking with friends of friends to strategically disbursing public works funds, but they must not establish a formal power base, sign up supporters, and openly defy the president. Such a challenge could lead to a genuine primary or a schism. But the party never admitted primaries; when one PRI president in the mid-1960s had tried to institute primaries even for unimportant municipal offices, he had lost his job and died in a suspicious plane crash. Indeed, the unwritten rules about not organizing an open schism turned out to be written. The PRI leadership told the Democratic Current in no uncertain terms that it was welcome to join an established sector such as the Mexican Workers Federation or the National Peasants Federation—had it done so, it would have been smothered—but party statutes prohibited creating any new formal institution.[52]

When Porfirio Muñoz Ledo leaked news of the dinner at Martínez Corbalá's house to the newspaper *Unomásuno*, his claim that he was merely

The moment Cuauhtémoc Cárdenas, governor of Michoacán, and Porfirio Muñoz Ledo, a former cabinet secretary, initiated group discussions about forming a Democratic Current within the ruling party, former Agrarian Reform Secretary Augusto Gómez Villanueva (above) recognized it for what it became: a fatal schism. Photo: Dante Bucio.

seeking to clarify the group's unsubversive nature and democratize the party[53] was surely disingenuous. As a former president of the PRI's National Executive Committee, he perfectly well knew that nothing could be more subversive than organizing a pressure group within the party.

At that moment, says Gómez Villanueva, he and Muñoz Ledo had reached a divide: "From this point on, our lives in the battle. I respect your decision, but it is not my path." The allusion is surely to the Revolution, when those who parted ways did meet in battle. But Muñoz Ledo's leak was a necessary step to see how the message would be received and to seek supporters for a potentially overt power base.

A few newspaper stories were not yet the point of no return. Party President Adolfo Lugo Verduzco said the PRI leadership "welcomed" the initiative and would meet with Muñoz Ledo.[54] But only failed negotiations, missed phone calls, and public recriminations followed. De la Madrid left matters in the hands of two PRI presidents, first Lugo Verduzco, then Jorge de la Vega Domínguez. "They tried to negotiate," de la Madrid says. "They each met fifteen or twenty times with the Democratic Current; they had infinite patience. Porfirio and Cuauhtémoc persevered in their project." The leaders of the Current thought they tried negotiating, too. When de la Vega was installed as a new party president, they were the first to congratulate him.[55] De la Madrid authorized Gómez Villanueva as a messenger of truce between himself and the Current, but Gómez Villanueva's phone messages never got past the president's private secretary, Emilio Gamboa.[56]

Failed negotiations and missed communications merely obscured the fact that de la Madrid would only offer the Democratic Current two options: surrender or revolt. He made this point clear on March 4, 1987, after convoking what was billed as a "unity" assembly of the PRI. "And then we discovered that the idea was to expel part of the party," says de Oteyza, not a member of the Democratic Current. On de la Madrid's orders—not even the National Executive Committee had discussed the matter[57]—de la Vega Domínguez refreshed everyone's memory about the party's prohibition against subgroups other than the established sectors. He closed the ceremonies by saying:

> From this great Assembly, we say to all those who from here on do not wish to respect the will of the immense majority of [PRI members], that they resign from our party and seek affiliation in other political organizations. . . . In the PRI there is no room for fifth columns nor for Trojan horses.[58]

The leaders of the Democratic Current still hung on within the PRI, hoping against hope, but when Salinas was in fact nominated on October 4, 1987, they revolted.

The upshot was the PRI's worst political crisis since 1952—in fact, the worst ever, since the schism would never be repaired. It had arisen from within the elite. Civil society was discontented, to be sure, after years of zero growth and falling wages, but it played no role in organizing the Democratic Current. Only after Salinas had been nominated, after the Democratic Current had seceded from the PRI to form an opposition party—the Democratic Front—and months after the campaign had set out to mobilize support did civil society begin to join, and then reluctantly.[59] Groups seeking housing, utilities, or other concrete benefits did not want to alienate the political machine that might provide for them.

The PRI may actually have won the 1988 election, but its massive fraud profoundly damaged the political system. The story of election day merits a brief retelling.[60] Interior agreed to let representatives of the conservative National Action Party (*Partido Acción Nacional*, PAN) and the Democratic Front monitor the election returns, but their terminals, only indirectly linked to the central computer, were fed doctored numbers that showed votes from "good" districts where the PRI was winning and held back votes from "bad" districts. The ruse failed because a PAN technician had discovered the setup ahead of time and had figured out how to hack into the central computer. On election night, as votes from "good" districts started appearing on the oppositions' screens, he hacked into it. Now the real figures showed the Democratic Front winning by a landslide in Mexico City. No surprise—the capital, where results came in first, was its stronghold—but the PRI had perpetrated an appalling deception. The technician was forcibly yanked from his chair, and on orders from the interior secretary, opposition parties' screens went blank. The PRI said the "system" had crashed. As metaphor, it could hardly have been more apt. When the computers, if not the political system, came back on line, to no one's surprise they indicated that the PRI had won.

The fracture with the Democratic Current had not resulted from an inevitable need to restructure the economy; de la Madrid could have avoided fracture by moving Mexico toward freer markets more gradually, probably more successfully. True, de la Madrid says—and there is no reason to disbelieve his sincerity—that he chose Salinas because he "guaranteed the continuation of my economic policies." A number of scholars concur. Joy Langston says the president closed off the highest ranks of the elite because he was "forced to impose a new economic model." [61]

With hindsight—admittedly, a great advantage over de la Madrid's position in 1987—it is clear that more or less the same free-market restructuring would have occurred a little sooner or a little later, as it did across Latin America, no matter which candidate had been chosen. A more moderate pace might well have benefited Mexico, particularly if the government had done more to help smaller firms prepare for foreign competition and had privatized banks more carefully. Poor regulation and bankers' inexperience in the headlong rush to privatize caused the banking system's collapse, cost Mexican taxpayers $100 billion to fix, and contributed importantly to the 1994 crisis. But the key point here is that, at a minimum, slower economic liberalization would not have been worse than cataclysmic liberalization, and the principal candidates other than Salinas—namely, Interior Secretary Manuel Bartlett or State Industries Secretary Alfredo del Mazo—would have liberalized the economy anyway. Francisco Labastida, who as a member of the economic cabinet had supported Salinas' basic economic program, says Mexico "would have done better" with either of these other candidates:

> At least Alfredo [del Mazo], whose thinking I know better, would have promoted economic modernization, perhaps more gradually, with more negotiation and less of a shock—and I think he could have negotiated better with the Democratic Current—but I insist that all of us in the economic cabinet believed in economic opening.

Neither Bartlett nor del Mazo would have provoked anything like the fear of exile that Salinas did among leaders of the Democratic Current. Even de la Madrid says, "They almost told me they would accept any candidate but Salinas" [62]—despite the grave danger of telling the president point-blank that one opposed any candidate. The Democratic Current did not even form until just after Silva Herzog's firing made a Salinas presidential candidacy likely. The other candidates left more possibilities open to the Current. Bartlett, born in 1936, belonged to their same generation and had been Cárdenas' friend in youth.[63] Del Mazo, born in 1943, fell on the other side of the 1940 generational divide but was close enough, in the approximate world of politics, to pose less of a threat than the decisively younger Salinas, born in 1948. Moreover, leaders of the Democratic Current had no personal conflicts with del

Cuauhtémoc Cárdenas (above) and the rest of the Democratic Current told de la Madrid almost point-blank that there was one candidate they would reject: Carlos Salinas. The issue was only partly ideological. Belonging to a younger generation that by all traditions should not yet reach the pinnacle of political power, Salinas could be expected to forever end their political prospects within the party. When de la Madrid chose Salinas anyway, they had no choice but to break off and run an opposition campaign. The political system never recovered. Photo: Dante Bucio.

Mazo, as some had with Salinas, and del Mazo's support from the labor sector and López Portillo gave him a profile closer to theirs.[64]

The political system could have survived economic restructuring per se. It was the way de la Madrid injected restructuring into the system, catalyzing elite struggle, that proved explosive. For the Democratic Current, the Washington Consensus was not just an objectionable ideology; it was an ideology incarnate in Salinas' *grupo* of Ph.D.s from U.S. universities—Salinas himself (Harvard), Pedro Aspe (MIT), Jaime Serra (Yale), Ernesto Zedillo (Yale), José Cordoba (Stanford)—that constituted a decisive threat to their political survival. The very sociological divide between the post-1940 generation of Mexican politicians and its predecessors that now seems so sharp might not have been had del Mazo or Bartlett—National University graduates who had studied abroad, but in England and France, not in the United States—been nominated for the presidency.

STRUGGLE AND THE 1987 CRISIS

Mexico's 1987 economic crisis was not caused solely by political struggle for the nomination. Too many other factors contributed, such as the
massive debt burden left since 1982, understandable errors in managing
an extraordinarily difficult economic situation, and the October 1987
U.S. stock market crash. But like successful candidates before him, Salinas inflated the economy to win support. He helped set the economy up
for crisis and ensured that the crisis would be worse than it had to be.

If the Democratic Current was Salinas' most vocal opposition—and it
bears recalling that it remained at least nominally within the PRI during
the party's nomination process—many others liked him no better but
kept their mouths shut. Though de la Madrid says Salinas had the political skill to "build his candidacy," gaining the widest support among cabinet secretaries, state governors, party leaders, businessmen, and workers,
almost no other informed observers agree. In his book on presidential
succession, Castañeda says that Salinas carried too many "drawbacks,
hostilities, and outright deficiencies to be imposed without cost."[65] José
Ramón López Portillo says that old guard *políticos*, the bureaucracy, and
official labor opposed him.[66] Francisco Labastida agrees. Victor Bravo,
advisor to del Mazo, says, "The political class obviously wasn't with Salinas." Party operatives demonstrated their antipathy toward the PRI's
candidate in their deliberately lackluster campaign management.[67] For
example, at one supposed Salinas rally, the crowd hurled orange peels
and stones at him, shouting "Cárdenas! Cárdenas!"[68]

Salinas' strategy for winning support went well beyond spending
money to build airports in towns like Piedras Negras. His technocrats'
vaunted economic management skills were his political capital. "They
know how to do it" was the refrain.[69]

The first step in demonstrating that Salinas' *grupo* "knew how to do
it," initiated even before Silva Herzog resigned, was to seek large new
loans from the United States. Washington was recognizing the gravity
of the Third World debt crisis and pushing banks to extend lending under the Baker Plan, promoted by Treasury Secretary James Baker. Mexico wheedled its way into becoming the pilot case [70] by, on the one hand,
insinuating that it might default, Silva Herzog's role, while, on the other
hand, parlaying expertise learned in U.S. university economics depart-
ments to its advantage, Salinas' role. Silva Herzog hinted that Mexico
might take a hard line on debt, for example, mentioning in a speech in
London that it had to place its responsibility to its people above that to

its creditors. He also started moving Bank of Mexico deposits from the U.S. Federal Reserve to Switzerland, implying that Mexico wanted to keep them from being frozen should it default. In fact, the economic cabinet had no intention of defaulting—it was too concerned about the harm that creditors would inflict—but the threat was part of the negotiation.[71] It apparently worked: Federal Reserve Chairman Paul Volcker later testified before Congress that Mexican default would have had a "domino effect."[72]

At the same time, the Salinas team talked up the idea in Washington that the inflation-adjusted, or "operational," government deficit should count, rather than the deficit as usually calculated, namely the simple difference between expenditure and revenue.[73] The operational deficit is smaller, implies more success at paying off debt, and strengthens the case for more lending. It is also a legitimate idea, accepted by some critics of de la Madrid's economic policies.[74] The gist is that when inflation is high—it was in the 100 percent range—the huge interest payments on domestic public debt (in pesos) actually include a substantial portion of principal because inflation rapidly erodes the *real* value of the remaining principal. The operational deficit properly counts this effect. The argument worked: Salinas parlayed technical expertise into a political tool. His team ultimately landed a generous $12.5 billion package from the IMF, World Bank, and private banks,[75] five times more than Silva Herzog had even sought.[76]

With an infusion of funds from Washington, Salinas had his chance to make the economy go. Only days after being installed as economy czar, he initiated his new, more expansionist "Plan of Promotion and Growth," encouraging investment by making more credit available.[77] Development bank lending rose massively, from 22 percent of GDP in 1985 to 33 percent of GDP in 1987.[78] That kind of bank credit, as well as buying political support, can increase the money supply, cause inflation, and set the economy up for crisis—and it was not visible in the government budget.

Public sector spending itself, excluding interest, remained about flat in 1987, but that performance was still far better than average for the administration, especially in the areas most useful for building political support.[79] Revenue sharing with states rose 8 percent in real terms: outside the central administration, governors were the only important politicians in Mexico. Though privatizing state-owned firms was one of de la Madrid's goals and would be one of Salinas' accomplishments, in 1987 investment in them rose by 2.5 percent of GDP, the only year during the administration when it did not contract. Federal government investment fell 6 percent, but it was the smallest decline during the administration.

Salinas further launched his candidacy and aggravated the coming economic crisis by helping send the Bolsa, the Mexican securities exchange, skyrocketing. In 1986, the Bolsa index shot up 320 percent, or 220 percent in real terms.[80] From January through September 1987, it shot up another 630 percent, or 530 percent in real terms, a larger absolute increase than in its previous ninety-three years of existence.[81] This was hardly just small print for the financial pages. Brokerage houses opened on plazas of principal cities from Ciudad Juárez along the U.S. border to Mérida in the Yucatán, as little investors jumped into the market, their numbers swelling from 186,000 in 1986 to 374,000 in September 1987.[82] Housewives started investment societies, dubbed *vacas*, or milk cows, to buy packages of securities.[83] Capital that had fled the country after the 1982 crisis began to return.[84] It was an impressive display for winning support and disarming opposition as the nomination approached. The point was, as Silva Herzog puts it, breaking into English, "We made it, we made it again."

Finance Secretary Gustavo Petricioli, whose previous job had been director of the commission overseeing the Bolsa, was now manipulating the Bolsa and reporting daily to Salinas about its operations, according to an official in a position to know, speaking off the record: "The idea was to support Salinas' candidacy by maintaining the appearance that everything was a success, everything was a bonanza." Del Mazo has also stated that Salinas manipulated the Bolsa.[85] Victor Urquidi, an economist with decades of knowledge about the Mexican government and economy, but no direct evidence about operations on the Bolsa, also believes Petricioli was bidding up securities prices to support Salinas' candidacy.

The Mexican political scientist Miguel Basáñez begins the story of government manipulation of the Bolsa in 1982.[86] De la Madrid had opposed López Portillo's bank nationalization, and when he took office, he paid bank owners handsome compensation. He then reprivatized ancillary businesses owned by the banks, notably brokerage houses, largely by selling them back to former bank owners. The next step was to strengthen these brokerage houses. The government moved away from its traditional borrowing method, requiring banks to lend to the Bank of Mexico at low interest rates, and instead increasingly sold bonds, principally the type known as Cetes, at higher interest rates—and thus at greater cost to the public sector—through brokerage houses. The government further weakened the banks by paying low interest rates on deposits. As the volume of bank deposits and hence loanable funds sank, private businesses increasingly issued bonds on the Bolsa for their financing needs. The administration thus made the Bolsa into a parallel banking system, owned by much the same individuals who had once owned the actual banks.

Cetes accounted for about half the value of all securities traded on the Bolsa,[87] so the government could help maintain the market's momentum through its own bond sales.[88] In addition, by slowing the depreciation of the peso, the Bank of Mexico brought back capital that had fled in 1981 and 1982, and a substantial portion of that capital began spilling into stocks rather than bonds. The $12 billion IMF loan package, partial recovery of oil prices to $16 a barrel[89] (obviously just good luck), business optimism fueled by the privatization and deregulation of the brokerage houses, and a cheering financial press all helped push up stock prices. But financial markets operate largely on appearance, and the "environment of euphoria" that the Salinas team sold the public, as Labastida puts it, made no small contribution. Salinas kept reporting that inflation was lower than in truth it was. The soaring Bolsa, says Labastida, "was largely provoked by expectations that did not correspond to reality." To make sure things kept moving along, Urquidi believes but without direct evidence, the Salinas team "must have put a lot of government money into buying stocks." In the words of one interviewee, off the record: "yet again the struggle for power had contaminated the economy."

Salinas was nominated as the official candidate on October 4, 1987. The Bolsa rose for a couple more days on the news, then started its long, dizzy descent, losing 14 percent by October 16.[90] On October 19, the New York Stock Exchange sank 23 percent, sending shock waves around the world. But the market that fell the furthest anywhere, by far, was the Mexican Bolsa.[91] From October 1987 to January 1988, it lost three-quarters of its value in nominal terms, not even counting the additional erosion caused by inflation, then running at more than 100 percent. As investors and speculators rushed to minimize losses by dumping their pesos for dollars, they put pressure on the Bank of Mexico's reserves. On November 18, 1987, in its familiar phrase, the bank "withdrew from the foreign-exchange market." The next peso crisis had struck.[92]

Chapter 10	THE INEVITABILITY
	OF ELITE POLITICS

The distinguished Argentine political scientist Guillermo O'Donnell noted in 2001 that among the fifteen Latin American scholars writing on politics whom he considered most influential, only two had degrees in political science and one in history; the rest were sociologists. And the founders of modern Latin American social science a generation earlier had all been sociologists.[1] The idea that socioeconomic pressures determine politics, not surprisingly, became the default.

This intellectual default is hardly unique to Latin America. Even in the case of the Soviet Union, the conventional thinking was that, beneath the veil of the authoritarian state, political succession somehow operated like democratic elections, as factions vied for mass support. Only as the Soviet system was crumbling did the political scientist Philip G. Roeder dispute this idea. He argued that general secretaries seeking to consolidate power shifted spending *not* into areas such as housing to build mass support, but into areas such as the military to court factions of the political elite.[2]

Even the way political scientists think about state autonomy has, ironically, assumed away elite politics at the heart of the state: they look at how political elites might operate autonomously from society but very little at how they might resolve debates among themselves. In his influential study on this subject,[3] Peter Evans depicts the autonomous state as a seamless whole, an elite corps of officials independent from the business class, educated together at a prestigious university and promoted on merit within a civil service system. But how does such a homogeneous group decide divisive issues? Is it supposed to be evident which individuals at the very top have more "merit" and should be accorded the ultimate word? Evans does not say.

An interesting example of this thinking applied to Mexico is Miguel Angel Centeno's *Democracy within Reason.* Centeno is almost alone in examining how Mexican *grupos* actually affected policy. He agrees with the argument of *Palace Politics* that, beginning in 1970, losing *gru-*

pos were increasingly excluded from top posts, until, in 1988, "the extended 'Revolutionary Family' was reduced to a nucleus surrounding the president"—Carlos Salinas.[4] Centeno argues persuasively that it was the emergence of this "powerful, cohesive, and homogeneous elite" under Salinas that allowed the Mexican state to turn the economy around overnight, from *dirigiste* to free-market.[5] Neither foreign nor domestic business can have been the cause because they did not even ask for such sudden change. President Miguel de la Madrid dropped tariffs to less than half the level requested to enter the General Agreement on Tariffs and Trade (GATT), predecessor of the World Trade Organization.[6] Where it sought a maximum tariff of 50 percent, he cut the maximum to 20 percent and lowered many tariffs to 10 percent or 5 percent. The private sector spokesman Gilberto Borja Navarrete of Grupo ICA, a Mexican conglomerate that benefited enormously under free trade, says that Mexico would have done better economically to lower its protectionism more gradually.

However, Centeno's static snapshot of the Salinas *grupo* at the height of its power, so dominant that it could order the leviathan of state to about face, misses any politics continuing within that leviathan. Or more precisely, he observes some of that politics—noting that by 1992 the Salinas *grupo* had begun to split into factions vying for presidential succession[7]—but misses the importance of his observation. It does not fit into his argument because radical economic restructuring, once effected, soon becomes entrenched. It creates powerful economic interests to defend it, and in this case the restructuring was written into the North American Free Trade Agreement. But Centeno's picture of Mexican politics remains incomplete. He says almost nothing about important kinds of policymaking that are revisited daily. No momentary decision can secure economic stability once and for all; the threat of economic crisis is perpetual. In an ongoing matter such as this, relations among competing groups within the political elite are central.

Recognizing that the Mexican state was not a unitary leviathan, but rather let competing factions into its very heart, leads to two central conclusions. The first is that conflict among such factions over political succession posed the gravest threat to its stability. This conflict did not inevitably cause crises, any more than electoral competition in democracies inevitably does, but it nevertheless remained the gravest threat the state faced. The second central conclusion is that the state could better control internal conflict when elites maintained a cooperative system and contending factions expected to survive in the long term, win or lose any particular contest. When losing factions expected exile, struggle overwhelmed the state.

Did elite political cooperation in Mexico have to turn to struggle in about 1970? Or was its emergence in that era essentially an accident, a result of the mere fact that Echeverría, regarded by Díaz Ordaz and the rest of the political elite as a system man, turned out to be just the opposite? Given the confines of the old Mexican political system, did elite cooperation have to turn to struggle at some point or other? If struggle emerged, could cooperation have been restored? More broadly, does elite politics matter when elections determine political succession or, at least, social demands on the state are stronger? And what kind of politics might better sustain cooperation? Consider these questions in the context of a few critical moments in both authoritarian and democratic states.

MEXICO 1994

The crisis that erupted in December 1994 was Mexico's worst, at least since the 1930s, twice as bad as 1982 by some measures.[8] True, the recovery was less drawn-out than after 1982, but mainly thanks to international assistance. In 1995, the Clinton administration and IMF provided a $50 billion loan package that stopped panic and allowed Mexico to resume growth. After 1982, the Reagan administration and the IMF forced Mexico to pay First World banks roughly 6 percent of its GDP per year[9]—nearly the entire margin of growth available to the economy—until they finally provided a $15 billion loan package in late 1986 and early 1987.

In 1994, elections were no longer quite so irrelevant as they had been, but it was still struggle within the political elite that drove the economy toward crisis. Carlos Salinas wanted to build a dynasty or else to get reelected, diverse currents agree. José Patrocinio González Blanco, interior secretary under Salinas, says the president wanted reelection. Of course, it required changing the Constitution, but, says González Blanco, "how easy it was!" Salinas had reversed the state's distant relationship with the Catholic church—before his administration, priests had not even been allowed to vote—and gutted Article 27 of the Constitution, the basis of land reform and symbol of the Revolution. "Why couldn't the Constitution be revised so that a man that all Mexico loved could remain in office?" González Blanco asks. "The only problem is that in Mexico presidents who are reelected are assassinated." Victor Urquidi, who had known "Carlitos" Salinas since youth, says, "I think he knew he couldn't be reelected, but with all the money he and his brother were accumulating [his brother, Raúl Salinas, was subsequently jailed for "illegal enrichment," among other crimes] and the influence they had, he wanted to be the power behind the throne, as Calles was after his presidency."

Salinas used two ways to buy support for his dynastic ambitions: an innovative approach to orchestrating political spending and the usual approach to overvaluing the peso. Under the watchful eyes of Washington, he and his technocrats ingeniously controlled the fiscal deficit while enlisting private banks to boost Mexicans' spending power. When his administration had privatized the banks in 1990 and 1991, it protected them from foreign competition but left them virtually free from regulation, reserve requirements, or interest rate controls.[10] The businessmen who bought the banks, much the same individuals who had owned them before bank nationalization in 1982, knew they were getting a good deal and paid for it, often three or more times the supposed book value.[11] Despite a stagnant economy, growing only 3 percent per year[12] and practically not at all *per capita*, the bankers increased bank credit at the "phenomenal" rate of some 35 percent per year, in real terms, according to Sergio Ghigliazza, director of the Center of Latin American Monetary Studies. Consumer loans from banks fueled the so-called "home appliance boom" and bought middle class support. And since Mexican industrial groups typically maintain close ties with particular banks, and the banks were making handsome profits, the privatization also bought business support.

A key aspect of the privatization was intended to strengthen Salinas' control over the PRI. He used the $12 billion received from bank sales[13] to fund Solidarity, his much-touted anti-poverty program. With some seventy thousand offices throughout Mexico dispensing favors,[14] Solidarity was designed as a new political machine that would displace the party's traditional apparatus.[15] It would weaken the old-fashioned currents within the PRI that had opposed Salinas from the start.

The problem with this strategy was the banks' overzealousness and inexperience. Their portion of bad loans rose from 1.3 percent of their portfolios at the beginning of the Salinas administration to 8.3 in September 1994 (before the crisis made their situation much worse).[16] Though dangerous financial flight began in 1994, Bank of Mexico Director Miguel Mancera says he was afraid to raise interest rates to keep capital in Mexico because doing so would have forced more borrowers to default, putting the banking system at grave risk. Economists agree that the banks' weakness was a principal cause of the 1994 crisis.[17]

Remarkably like statist administrations as they approached presidential succession, Salinas' *técnicos* also inflated the economy by encouraging massive foreign borrowing, 6 to 7 percent of GDP per year for three years running, almost all speculative finance.[18] By 1993, they had overvalued the peso 25 to 40 percent by a range of estimates, about the same amount as in 1981.[19] Victor Urquidi, a close observer of Mexican economic policy since he had joined that nation's Bretton Woods delegation in 1944, considered the $20 billion trade deficits a stark sign of overvaluation.[20] Overvaluation was evident even at the supermarket, notes Ghigliazza: "Housewives were saying, 'How is it possible that stores are selling Perrier and Evian water cheaper than [the Mexican brand] Tehuacán? How can it cost less to take the kids to Orlando than to Cancun?'"

Salinas' cabinet overvalued the peso partly through naiveté. International finance was euphoric about his economic program. Economists were asking if it was time to consider Mexico an industrialized rather than developing nation, Steven Greenhouse reported in the *New York Times*,[21] and right through the fall of 1994, IMF reports on Mexico continued to be glowing.[22] Treasury Undersecretary Lawrence H. Summers, a macroeconomist who probably knew better (but treasury undersecretaries have to be financial cheerleaders), lauded Mexico in late 1993: "Countries that do things right will be rewarded with rapid capital inflows. Those that do things wrong are punished."[23] This over-optimism naturally affected Mexican policymakers. As an independent member of the Bank of Mexico board, Urquidi warned other members about overvaluation to no avail:

> They'd stare me and say, "You don't understand economics. All this trade deficit is because we have capital inflows." I said, "Yes, but I distinguish between foreign direct investment, which is fine"—a lot of it was really going into office buildings and the like, though a lot of it was going into manufacturing—"and short-term money, which is not a guarantee of anything." They said: "Don't you know that the money going into the stock exchange is very favorable because Mexicans take that money and put up new investments." I said, "Give me one example." And I never got it. Serious people in the bank were telling me those things.

Still, Salinas' economic cabinet was not quite so naïve as the financial pages of U.S. newspapers. It surely took note when Rudiger Dornbusch

of MIT, the finance minister's former professor of international economics, warned about overvaluation as early as 1992.[24] Salinas himself
notes that economic cabinet members discussed the large trade deficits
on September 10 and September 28, 1992, as well as during many of their
forty-five other meetings through that year and 1993.[25] The safer option
was to devalue, making exports cheaper and imports more expensive so
as to close the trade deficit, but as always, costlier imports would tend to
raise prices throughout the economy, spoiling Salinas' hope of driving
inflation down to First World levels.[26] The economic historian Enrique
Cárdenas says that "the risk was clear" of not devaluing. Inflows of financial capital were not likely to last too much longer, as Salinas' private
secretary, José Córdoba, admitted to the 1993 Mexican Stock Market
Convention,[27] and if they stopped, the peso might crash. The decision
was nevertheless to take the risk.

Salinas knew as well as his predecessors that a strong peso would
make a strong president and help him found a dynasty. As early as 1991,
when Mexico was already borrowing 5 percent of GDP per year, so the
economy was looking better than it was actually doing, a chant could be
heard at pro-government rallies: "*Uno, dos, tres, Salinas otra vez.*" ("One,
two, three, Salinas another time.")[28] Substantial devaluation, Salinas
later wrote, "would have meant the loss of confidence in Mexican economic policies."[29] Or, as López Portillo had put it: "A president who
devalues is devalued."

Salinas' dynastic ambitions, violating the now weakened rules of elite
cooperation, also directly aggravated an elite struggle that drove the
economy further toward crisis. In general terms, it was same the old
problem. Among presidential hopefuls, whoever gained Salinas' favor
could expect to stay in power for years to come, and whoever did not
gain his favor (or, alternatively, did not manage to destroy him politically) could expect to be out of power for years to come.

Salinas' plan was to install Luis Donaldo Colosio, manager of his
political-machine-cum-anti-poverty-program Solidarity, as a pliable
successor. Jorge Gamboa de Buen, an official close to Colosio's rival,
Mexico City Governor Manuel Camacho Solís, says that this plan was
hatched by Salinas' inner circle, including his brother Raúl, his private
secretary José Córdoba, and Emilio Gamboa, de la Madrid's private secretary who had helped Salinas win the PRI candidacy in 1987:

> They convinced Salinas to chose Colosio [as his successor] because
> they thought they could control him, while Camacho they could not

have. They told [Salinas], "Donaldo [Colosio] is your little brother, your creation; he is going to be loyal and faithful." They even got it through to him—when I was told this I thought it was a lie, but it was true—they said: "Look, you're going to run the World Trade Organization with some help from your buddies the gringos, and when you return, Donaldo is going to change the Constitution and you will be the first president of the twenty-first century at age 52. You will end up the best president in the history of Mexico; you're going to complete your economic project." It sounded logical, so they convinced him.

"They built everything to last, incredibly powerful, founded on international alliances," says Camacho Solís. "The strange thing is what actually happened."

Elite struggle makes strange things happen: such strange things during 1994 that neither historians nor the courts are ever likely to get to the bottom of them. Did Salinas' political enemies provoke a rebellion in the southern Mexican state of Chiapas on January 1, 1994, the very day his crowning accomplishment, the North American Free Trade Agreement, came into force, to destroy his economic project and his hand-picked candidate? Salinas says so.[30] Did Salinas then change directions, scheming to oust Colosio from the candidacy and substitute Camacho Solís instead, as Colosio's allies have charged?[31] Or did the *"nomenklatura,"* Salinas' term for retrograde factions of the PRI, plot to undermine Colosio's campaign and assassinate him on March 23, 1994, to destroy Salinas, as he maintains?[32]

In any case, elite struggle exploded more brutally than ever; political elites themselves saw it as sinking into mutual assassination. When asked to gauge the level of struggle in 1994 from 1 to 10, Raúl Salinas Lozano, father of Carlos Salinas and a high economic official in the 1950s and 1960s, said, "Now we're talking seriously" and put it at 9. Alfonso Corona del Rosal, who had only kind words for Luis Echeverría after Echeverría had bested him for the presidency and ended his political career, wrote in 1995: "Our people have not forgotten [Salinas'] authoritarianism, his recurring deceptions, and his self-worship. If he should appear in a public place, he would probably be attacked."[33] The political scientist Joy Langston said that past contests for the nomination had been "neither so bloody nor so open"; only recently had PRI politicians "publicly menaced their fallen companions with witch hunts."[34] In late 2000, when an attorney general's report on the Colosio assassination came out, the

Carlos Salinas wanted to build a political dynasty. Many political elites thought he chose Luis Donaldo Colosio (above) as the party's presidential candidate because he believed he could manipulate Colosio. Whether it would have been so or not, Colosio was assassinated. Salinas blamed the crime on his political enemies, the "nomenklatura," as he called them. Photo: Arturo López.

respected weekly *Proceso* featured elite political struggle on the cover for three weeks running: The War I, The War II, and The War III.

Even if political struggle did not cause the political shocks of 1994, as many claim, it blew them into major crises. Chiapas involved a mere handful of protestors—protesters rather than rebels because they had only one weapon that was not a joke: public support via the media and Internet.[35] By contrast, the railworkers, teachers, and other public sector unions that struck across Mexico in 1958 were twenty thousand strong and announced their cause by bringing the national transportation system to a halt. Of course, there were many differences, but a key one was that in 1958 no political elites supported the strikers; in 1994 important political elites did. Camacho Solís, the powerful politician who had lost the presidential nomination only days earlier, warned Salinas that he would personally take to the streets if the government tried to put the revolt down. The crisis, even if it was a spontaneous eruption in a poor region, struck at the heart of the state.

In agreeing to Camacho Solís' demand to be appointed a volunteer "commissioner of peace" to negotiate in Chiapas, Salinas only recast the crisis. This move installed Camacho Solís at the center of public attention and, simultaneously, ensured his continuing eligibility to run for president in that summer's elections: the Constitution required presidential candidates to resign from the government six months before elections. Salinas then ousted Colosio allies from the all-important positions as interior minister and attorney general, substituting Camacho Solís allies.[36] As Colosio's presidential campaign sank from sight, his *grupo* turned furious, not only with Camacho Solís but with Salinas.[37] One Colosio collaborator, for example, charges that Camacho Solís was "a willing accomplice of all those led by Salinas who orchestrated a premeditated strategy to obstruct Colosio's campaign." Ernesto Zedillo, Colosio's campaign manager at that time, says that he feared Camacho Solís would take advantage of his appointment as Chiapas negotiator "for his own personal political ambitions."[38]

Any assassination is a political crisis, but the death of Colosio detonated terrible struggles. As Salinas himself puts it, "The political offensive to gain control over the nomination did not even wait for the burial. The struggle for power erupted within the PRI."[39] Camacho Solís was accused of complicity in the assassination, and when Colosio's wife refused to exonerate him, she put him out of the running. More serious, the *nomenklatura* refused to give Salinas the needed time and leeway to choose

When rebellion erupted denouncing the oppression of indigenous peoples in the southern state of Chiapas—more a powerful political protest than any military threat—Manuel Camacho Solís (above), who had lost the presidential nomination, threatened to take to the streets to support it. No cabinet secretary in the 1950s and 1960s would have dreamed of hazarding such a schism. Salinas may have named Camacho Solís commissioner of the peace to prevent it. Opponents accused Camacho Solís of using that prominent post to try to reclaim the nomination after all. Photo: Arturo López.

a replacement candidate from his cabinet. The six-month time limit for resigning from government in order to run as a candidate had expired. The PRI had enough votes in the legislature and state governments to amend the Constitution, as it had hundreds of times before, or, more appropriately, simply pass a law postponing that one election, but legislators led by Echeverría's old ally Augusto Gómez Villanueva, aka the *nomenklatura*, made it known that they would block any such change. Their candidate was PRI President Fernando Ortiz Arana, not in the cabinet and therefore eligible. As one billion dollars a day fled Mexico, Salinas chose Ernesto Zedillo, a former programming and budget secretary who had by chance resigned to run Colosio's campaign and was therefore eligible.

Pedro Aspe now drew on all the connections he had forged with U.S. mutual fund managers during six years as finance secretary, and the Clinton administration extended a $6 billion line of credit. From a high of about $30 billion, Mexico's reserves sank to about $17 billion but there they held. Under the circumstances, it was an amazing performance.

The elections went without a hitch. For all the erosion the authoritarian state had suffered, power was still not in play.[40] If the PRI did not win by fair means, it would deploy all the foul ones at its disposal against a fragmented opposition. The Democratic Front, assembled from a faction of the PRI in 1988, had managed to ignite mass protest then only through an extraordinary set of circumstances: six years of zero growth, plummeting wages, a stock market crash, an economic crisis, and technocrats' broken promises. Its hasty foundation and lack of internal democracy—indeed, near lack of any internal order at all—weakened its medium-term efforts to convert itself into a viable political party, the Party of the Democratic Revolution, *Partido de la Revolución Democrática* (PRD).[41] And the more conservative National Action Party, *Partido Acción Nacional* (PAN) showed no appetite to disrupt its covert alliance with the Salinas faction. No sooner did its candidate, Diego Fernández de Cevallos, rout both Ernesto Zedillo and PRD candidate Cuauhtémoc Cárdenas in a 1994 debate than he mysteriously stopped campaigning.[42] Ernesto Zedillo won by a landslide, more than 20 percent of the vote.

And then, just after calm appeared to have returned to Mexico, economic crisis exploded, largely because of still-seething elite political struggle. It cannot be confidently determined how to allot blame for Mexico's 1994 crisis among the overvalued peso, the politicized bank privatization, the shocks produced by the Chiapas uprising and Colosio assassination, and a botched attempt to devalue the peso 15 percent on December 20. But they all had a component of elite struggle to them.

The "errors of December" were the immediate trigger of crisis. One of the cardinal points about crises is that just because one was disastrous does not mean it had to happen. As economists say, an economy can settle at different equilibriums; some are not so terrible and others are indeed terrible. The 1994 Mexico crisis surpassed anyone's worst fears because of the way a planned devaluation was botched.[43] González Blanco, a friend of Salinas' finance minister Pedro Aspe, who had left office in November, puts it this way:

> Cardinal [Juan Jesús] Posadas was killed [in Guadalajara in 1993], the Chiapas conflict exploded, Colosio was shot, [PRI Secretary General José Francisco] Ruiz Massieu was assassinated, and nothing terrible happened to this fragile economy. Zedillo won with 17 million votes,

nobody contested the triumph, there was national and international rejoicing. And then came the economic problems. It was an error in the way the economy was managed.

The Chilean economist Sebastian Edwards, who had warned for two years that the peso was overvalued, says that the crash was so unexpectedly severe because of "the almost complete loss of confidence in Mexico, its institutions, and its leaders."[44]

The precipitating issue was that the new administration acted in an "inexperienced and confused" manner, according to Nora Lustig, a Mexican economist. Investors felt deceived because only days earlier the administration had promised not to devalue, and then when it did devalue, it made no attempt to explain itself.[45] According to Gamboa de Buen, also a friend of Aspe's:[46]

> When capital movements started, the Americans tried to get in touch with [Zedillo's new finance secretary] Jaime Serra, and they couldn't find him. Nobody knew what was happening. The U.S. treasury secretary called up Pedro Aspe and asked him, "What is going on?" Aspe said, "I don't know—I'm not finance secretary any more—call Serra." "I already called him; he says he'll get back. What is going on?" "I don't have the slightest idea." That is the way all the money fled.

Mexican Finance authorities had apparently not made contact with the U.S. Treasury before the devaluation.[47] They announced it without having set out any program to underpin the economy. The administration did not even wait for Friday to devalue, when it would have had a weekend to calm markets. Investors pulled $5 billion out in two days.[48]

Aspe had offered to stay on as finance secretary long enough to take responsibility for stabilizing an economy that, he himself admitted, was stuck together with pins. But, he reportedly said, "Why did they have to pull the pins out?"[49] Antonio Sánchez Díaz, then president of the Mexican Employers' Federation, says that if Aspe had been allowed to stay, "as all of us hoped and expected," things would have worked out much better: "I don't say he would have avoided the crisis, but I do say it would have been milder, less drastic. . . . [Serra] did not have the experience, contacts, or imagination of Aspe."

The reason Aspe did not stay is that his political enemy Zedillo—whose Ministry of Planning and Budget had been dissolved into Aspe's Finance Ministry—fired him.[50] That much was perhaps understandable, but it was not understandable that Zedillo cleaned out virtually the en-

*In late 1994, the Mexican economy was in precarious condition. It was perhaps un-
derstandable for President Ernesto Zedillo (above) to replace the experienced Finance
Secretary Pedro Aspe, a political enemy. But it was a grave error to virtually clean out
the top ranks of the ministry under Aspe, including all the subsecretaries at the second
level, 90 percent of the director generals at the third level, and many more. Lacking
any institutional memory, Finance Ministry bungled an attempted devaluation and
badly worsened the ensuing economic crisis. By many gauges, it was the deepest since at
least the 1930s. Photo: Arturo López.*

tire Finance Ministry as well, including all subsecretaries below Aspe, 90 percent of the director generals at the third level, 79 area directors, and 176 subdirectors.[51] In so doing, Zedillo wiped out all institutional memory just when it was most needed to handle devaluation. For no apparent reason other than to obliterate Aspe's *grupo*, he had broken a tradition predating the Mexican Revolution of maintaining continuity in Finance, a tradition that even President Vicente Fox of the opposition PAN restored after winning the July 2000 election. It was a striking contrast to 1964, when President Gustavo Díaz Ordaz had reappointed his presidential rival, Finance Secretary Ortiz Mena, along with the rest of his Finance team, to successfully tame a precarious economic situation.[52]

STABILITY IN COLOMBIA AND BOLIVIA

Other authors have suggested that economic stability depends on something like Mexico's elite cooperation in the decades before 1970, and economic crises may be caused by something like the elite struggle that erupted after 1970. These are scattered accounts, however, that have not been forged into a broader line of thinking. One interesting account is Albert O. Hirschman's response to the literature on (one of those political science mouthfuls) "bureaucratic authoritarianism."[53] That literature sees exhaustion of import substitution as having caused the military overthrow of Latin American democracies in the 1960s and 1970s. The resulting regimes are called bureaucratic-authoritarian because modern military bureaucracies, rather than individual strongmen, managed the governments.

The argument about bureaucratic authoritarianism is particularly well articulated by Robert R. Kaufman.[54] He concedes that military officers never specifically saw import substitution as exhausted; they had probably never even heard of it. Rather, as industrial exhaustion choked growth, he argues, it put impossible pressures on democratically elected governments. Though squeezed by declining growth, they could not abandon their political base—domestic firms and workers in import substitution industries—so they granted these core constituents ever larger subsidies and social welfare programs. As a result, they borrowed and spent their way to economic crises and political chaos, whereupon the military stepped in to fix things. Although this literature seeks to explain the military coups, it must also necessarily explain the powerful economic crises that preceded and triggered them. If something else had caused the crises, that thing would also have been an important cause of the coups.

Hirschman, an economist, doubts that import substitution was blocked or that it could have caused the military dictatorships that swept Brazil in 1964, Chile in 1973, and Argentina in 1976. Moreover, he argues, if important substitution had been blocked, why would it not also have caused a coup in Colombia, which was at roughly the same stage of economic development? He sees a common problem across Latin America in ideological "escalation," the climate that, *Palace Politics* argues, Echeverría also faced in Mexico. Vociferous intellectuals and economists on the left challenged the state to achieve increasingly impossible goals—ending "dependency" on the First World, which dated from the moment the conquistadors landed, and severe income inequality, which predated even the conquistadors—and business interests reacted ferociously. Colombia escaped, Hirschman contends, because the tight-knit character of its political elites muted such escalation. As elsewhere, they were split between defenders of business and the "entrepreneurial function," on the one hand, and defenders of workers and the "reform function," on the other. But they were able to rescue "limited pluralism" (one would hardly call Colombia in those days a democracy) because, unlike their counterparts in Brazil, Chile, or Argentina, they all belonged to one durable "oligarchy":

> Communication between the two groups was often strained, but was never quite cut off, in part because of personal relationships and in part because, after a while, it became obvious that the reformers . . . were by no means revolutionaries, but were acting in the best interests of their brethren.[55]

Oddly for an economist (perhaps because he was writing in 1979 before Latin America's devastating crises of the 1980s), Hirschman does not ask whether this working relationship between political elites also underpinned Colombia's successful macroeconomic management. But for most of the twentieth century, that nation enjoyed unusual economic stability. Alone among the major Latin American nations, it avoided debt crisis during the "lost decade" of the 1980s.[56]

One usual explanation for Colombia's stability, as for Mexico's stability in the 1950s and 1960s, is an independent finance ministry. For example, the Colombian economist Miguel Urrutia argues that after widespread violence ended in 1958, all administrations appointed a technocrat or industrialist as finance minister and gave him "virtually total power in the areas of monetary, fiscal, and exchange policy. These areas have therefore been isolated from day-to-day politics."[57] Urrutia makes an unconvincing attempt to suggest why what he calls a "clientelistic state"—with a trickle-down system of distributing money through the ranks to build support—should cede such a fabulous resource as the finance ministry to a mere technocrat.

Elite cooperation seems a better explanation of Colombia's stability. In 1946, an ongoing civil war took a turn for the worse, and as peasants allied with the Liberals fought other peasants allied with the Conservatives, largely over land, some two hundred thousand people were killed. An entire generation came to consider pervasive violence, *la violencia* captured in some of Gabriel García Marquez's writings, just life as usual. Finally, in 1957 and 1958, leaders of the two main parties met secretly, initially in Spain,[58] to work out a power-sharing pact termed the "National Front." The presidency would alternate between them every four years; they would evenly divide high administrative posts and the legislature; and no other party could even participate in elections. Spelled out in a formal declaration and approved by plebiscite, the pact formally lasted until 1974, but even after its demise, the Constitution required that whichever party lost the presidency should retain "adequate and equitable participation" in the executive branch.[59] Such a promise of political survival would give both sides a sufficient interest in the regime's long-term stability to put technocrats in charge of the finance ministry. By the 1980s, violence was back in the form of guerrillas, drug traffickers, and death squads roaming the countryside, but the fact that Colombia still avoided debt crisis only underscores the importance for economic policy of elite consensus, as opposed to general social peace. As violent external threats began to overwhelm the state in the 1990s—in effect, new elites outside the pact established themselves—they finally did erode the long record of economic stability.

In 1985, a newly elected administration in Bolivia forged a similar elite pact, indeed based on this understanding of Colombia's success, to end one of the worst hyperinflations ever. With inflation more than 10,000 percent, and calculated to have risen to 60,000 percent in summer 1985,[60] it would have been impossible to fix the foreign exchange rate, so in some sense there was an ongoing currency crash, but the principal problem was seen as inflation. At those dizzying rates, the price of a loaf of bread rises continually; when a customer walks in, the shop owner calls the bakery to check the price of the hour.

President Víctor Paz Estenssoro sought to impose his "New Economic Policy," a standard package of cutting public sector employment, reducing fiscal deficits (they had reached an unbelievable 23 percent of

GDP), and freezing wages. He could call a state of siege to block the Bolivian Labor Central, as always, poised to challenge austerity measures, but he could not maintain the state of siege without congressional support, and his party, the Nationalist Revolutionary Movement, lacked a majority in Congress.

Paz Estenssoro solved his political problem by forging elite cooperation. His pact with the principal opposition party, General Hugo Banzer's Nationalist Democratic Action, bought legislative support for the economic plan through patronage—public sector jobs—and, in a secret addendum, pledged to back Banzer as president in the next election. The idea was to rotate the presidency between the parties, in short, to guarantee political survival in exchange for presidential supremacy over policy during each president's term. This "Pact for Democracy" did effectively neutralize Congress—a majority now voted as it was told—and allowed Paz Estenssoro to install a "super-minister" of planning to manage the economy relatively unfettered. Eduardo A. Gamarra argues in an essay that this pact, a smaller-scale version of the pact between Colombian Liberals and Conservatives, "was key to ensuring the continuity" of the economic plan.[61] Paz Estenssoro brought inflation down to 15 percent, and though growth remained stagnant—2 to 3 percent per year by the late 1980s—at least it was better than the shrinking economy of the early 1980s. Later, the principal party of the left was brought into the pact in exchange for an electoral reform engineered, or so the parties hoped, to give the three of them an oligopoly on political power.[62]

The pact fell apart in 1989. The Nationalist Revolutionary Movement candidate, the former super-minister of planning, broke it by launching an American-style negative campaign.[63] (So much, yet again, for the notion that successful finance ministers need political independence.) He did not get a majority, so, in accordance with the Constitution, it fell to the Congress to designate the president. No one was willing to cooperate with the Nationalist Revolutionary Movement, but having seen how well the pact had worked in the past, the other two parties forged a new and renamed pact. It too had its problems, but the principle was clear: elite cooperation was an effective way to govern the economy.

ARGENTINA 2001

The crisis that erupted in Argentina in 2001 shows how elite struggle can undermine economic stability even in a consolidated democracy. And despite the infamous spectacle of running through five presidents

in a couple of weeks, Argentina's democracy proved that it was consolidated—precisely because it held throughout the crisis. When the
Argentine president resigns, as Fernando de la Rúa was forced to on
December 20, 2001, the Constitution gives Congress an essentially par-
liamentary power to bargain over a replacement. For all the apparent
disorder, marathon bargaining resolved the political crisis in accordance
with established laws and procedures.[64] No one, least of all the military, so much as suggested the possibility of military intervention. Yet,
even in such a democratic context, elite political struggle—first within
the Peronist (more properly Justicialist) Party when Carlos Menem was
president in the late 1990s, then within the Alianza, an alliance of parties that captured the presidency from October 1999 through December 2001—was an important cause of the economic crisis.

Argentina's economic crisis rivaled that of Indonesia for the worst
that has befallen a nation since the Great Depression. The peso plummeted something like 75 percent against the dollar, economic output
sank to its level of almost a decade earlier, the banking system collapsed,
official unemployment rose to 22 percent, and in just the first six months
of 2002, 1.5 million people fell below the poverty line.[65]

The crisis had important economic causes unrelated to proximate
political events.[66] Argentina's so-called currency board, not a board at
all but a mechanism for fixing the peso one-to-one against the dollar,
was undoubtedly a bad idea, particularly given that the nation's principal trading partners are Brazil and the European Union. From the
start, it should have been apparent that if the dollar became overvalued
compared with the Brazilian *real* and the euro, as was bound to happen
sometime, the Argentine peso would become overvalued too, as it did.
Especially after the crisis and devaluation of the *real* in late 1998 and
early 1999, Argentina's exports became uncompetitive in Brazil, eroding
its access to foreign reserves. The dollarization of the Argentine banking
system—many borrowers took out loans denominated in dollars—made
the crisis far worse because it left borrowers owing several times as many
pesos after the crash as they had before. Of course, they could not pay,
so the banking system collapsed. On top of these economic problems,
the IMF's and U.S. Treasury's brutal treatment of Argentina, in sharp
contrast to support for Mexico after 1994, produced far worse damage
than was necessary.

Javier Corrales, a political scientist, nevertheless argues persuasively
that a condition he calls the "state without a party"—political struggle between the president and factions of his own party—contributed

importantly to Argentina's economic crisis.[67] The state-without-a-party problem in Argentina began with Carlos Menem, president from 1989 through 1995. He secured a constitutional reform in 1994 allowing presidential reelection for a second term, was reelected, and served again from 1995 through 1999. About mid-term he succumbed to the Latin American *caudillo*, or strongman, mentality (or it always was his mentality) and began seeking an unconstitutional third term. He planned to win support from his own party and exert enough pressure on the Supreme Court to declare that his first term did not count as one of the two permitted by the new Constitution. But, aside from being opposed by 80 percent of the electorate, his gambit threatened the political futures of powerful Peronist governors, notably Eduardo Duhalde of the Province of Buenos Aires. The result was an intra-party power contest, not just over who would be the next presidential candidate, but also over the fundamental rules for ascending to power.

This power contest "unleashed a spending race between the president and the leading Peronist governors," according to Corrales.[68] In particular, Duhalde pushed the important Buenos Aires deficit from 7 percent of revenues in 1997 to 25 percent of revenues in 1999. Economic officials recommended increasing taxes, decreasing expenditures, and using funds from privatization to pay off the rising debt, but neither Menem nor the governors would, Corrales concludes:

> The only recourse left to economic officials was to increase the already high levels of debt and to delay payments to public-sector suppliers. This only served to restore the "credibility deficit" that had plagued the state in the 1980s. Once again, the government was in the business of cheating private agents. . . . When the aftershocks of the Russian financial crisis hit Argentina in mid-1998, the "concern" of skeptical business leaders turned into panic.[69]

A doubt about this argument is that overall Argentine fiscal deficits in 1997 and 1998, as the Menem-Peronist contest proceeded, were fairly modest. Without interest on the debt—it had been principally incurred to carry out a social security privatization and bank restructuring supported by the IMF[70]—Corrales' own data show that Argentina was running a small fiscal surplus.[71] Including interest, the deficit both years was 2.1 percent of GDP, hardly a level usually considered dangerous.[72]

Argentina's bigger problem must have been the state's "credibility deficit." As with Mexico's 1981 oil price fiasco, that kind of deficit can well contribute to a crisis. If business leaders responded to the state's delaying payments and cheating them, vocal disputes between economic and political officials, and power struggles between Menem and the governors, their fear alone, combined with the Russian crisis, could well trigger an investment strike. It did. Between the July 1998 Russian crisis and mid-1999, industrial production fell almost 20 percent, nearly to its 1993 level.[73] A deep recession set the stage for the crisis that would arrive in 2001, as if in slow-motion enactment of now destined events.

Part of Corrales' explanation of the final 2001 crisis seems doubtful: the idea that the Alianza that won the 1999 presidential election suffered from economic illiteracy.[74] An old patriarch, Raúl Alfonsín, ran one of the parties in the alliance; grassroots organizers, rather than experienced administrators, ran the other. The Alianza's congressional delegation lacked "technical experts," says Corrales: only 3 percent were economists, compared with 12 percent of Menem's Peronists. The Alianza therefore supposedly failed to understand the gravity of the fiscal deficits and prevented President de la Rúa from balancing the budget. But economist-politicians are hardly proof against dangerous economic policies: witness de la Madrid and Salinas. Besides, it is far from clear that Argentina's deficits, less than 4 percent of GDP including interest in 2000, were so terrible.[75] Paul Krugman, hardly short on technical expertise himself, argues that they were not.

Corrales' more persuasive argument centers on the way de la Rúa alienated the political alliance that had backed him. The Alianza was cobbled together in 1996 between the Radical Civic Union, an established party that had done badly in the 1995 elections, and Frepaso (Front for a Country in Solidarity), an ad hoc party of socialists, human rights leaders, and renegade Peronists that had done surprisingly well in 1995 but recognized its long-term weakness. De la Rúa, the Radical party's presidential candidate, won the primary within the Alianza against Frepaso's candidate, and when he took office in October 1999, he gave Frepaso only two second-class cabinet posts. He even shut out much of his own party, instead appointing advisors who lacked political experience.[76] De la Rúa therefore put himself at odds with his own coalition from the start.

The interest rates demanded by foreign lenders rose in parallel with the political struggle between de la Rúa and his own coalition. As conflict heated up between de la Rúa and Vice President Carlos Álvarez in fall 2000, and the vice president resigned, Argentina's country-risk rating, and thus the interest rates it had to pay, began to climb.[77] By spring 2001, as two economics ministers in two weeks were hounded out by

Alianza opponents,[78] Argentina was forced to pay 12 percent interest.[79] The budget deficit was only 3.6 percent of GDP in 2000, hardly disaster level, but the increase since 1998 had been *entirely* due to interest payments.[80] When U.S. officials made it clear that they would not bail out Argentina, economic crisis was unavoidable.

The collapse of de la Rúa's administration in December 2001 provided an extraordinary *ex post* gauge of the internal struggle that had caused it. When de la Rúa asked the Peronist opposition to form a unity coalition, it rejected the offer. Fearing a possible breakdown of democracy itself, the political scientist Hector E. Schamis asked a Peronist official why. The answer was that even congressional leaders of the president's own party had refused to take part in any government he might lead.[81] Fernando de la Rúa fell as he had ruled, concludes Schamis, "at odds with his own party."

WHY ELITE POLITICS MATTERS

No broad historical circumstances dictated that cooperation among Mexican political elites had to erode in the early 1970s. It was an accident that Luis Echeverría turned out not to be the political system man everybody thought, but a firebrand who attacked the unwritten rules. In choosing Echeverría as his successor, Gustavo Díaz Ordaz just made a mistake. True, the ideological escalation spreading across Latin America made elite cooperation harder to sustain, but Colombia managed to do so, and Mexico could have. Perhaps sustaining elite cooperation would have been worse in the long run, prolonging the transition to democracy, or perhaps it would have supported economic growth and even facilitated the transition. We will never know. But it could have lasted much longer.

Could elite political cooperation have continued indefinitely in Mexico? It is extremely doubtful. The president's enormous authority in office—one of the two unwritten rules—itself provided the mechanism to disrupt the other unwritten rule, the promise that all *grupos* would survive. Of course, the president knew that choosing the wrong successor—one who would close off the political future for opposing currents of the PRI—could destroy the regime, but he never knew quite where the line was. And there was no external judge to keep him within it. He pushed as far as he thought safe, and if he pushed too far to perpetuate his ideological beliefs or establish a dynasty, the evidence would be the irreparable damage he caused. Harmed political elites would see that he had violated the unwritten rules, as the Democratic Current saw when de la Madrid guaranteed its political demise within PRI, but they had no lever to stop him in advance. Their only resort, after he had acted, was to carry out the always implicit threat of schism.

Elite political cooperation is certainly not inimical to democracy. Michael Burton, Richard Gunther, and John Higley have argued in a series of articles that "elite settlement"—rules for ascending to political power that assure survival for all principal factions, even if they lose particular succession contests—is the requisite of a consolidated democracy.[82] Their argument oversteps somewhat. Elite settlement in their sense provides a basis more for stability than for democracy. For example, they specifically say that Mexico after 1950 enjoyed the requisite elite consensus,[83] just as *Palace Politics* has argued, but it certainly was not a democracy. Indeed, Mexico arguably became a democracy only after political elites, by tearing that consensus to shreds, destroyed the old authoritarian regime.

A more persuasive idea is that a consolidated democracy serves as a sort of external judge—the external judge did not exist to constrain presidents under the old Mexican system—capable of sustaining political cooperation. Barry R. Weingast makes essentially this argument. The idea is that citizens see some basic set of governing rules, written or unwritten, as guaranteeing their *own* vital long-run interests—for example, protecting them against violation of their human rights or confiscation of their property. And they must be willing to defend the rules, even at the cost of giving up a short-run advantage.[84]

For example, President Franklin Delano Roosevelt's attempt to pack the Supreme Court in 1937 to support his policies died because even many of his supporters rejected the plan as an illegitimate constitutional violation.[85] Argentine democracy survived in 2001, despite worse economic pressures than those that had toppled many an earlier regime, not because of political elites' restraint—Carlos Menem resorted to the same *caudillo* tactics as ever—but because Argentine society, including the military, now stood united against constitutional usurpation. In effect, Argentina had developed what an earlier generation of political scientists called "civic culture."

But civic culture does not replace elite politics. They play different though important roles. Fundamental support for democracy—a plebiscite so powerful that it need not even be held—cannot similarly restrain day-to-day policy. People take to the streets to denounce authoritarianism, not macroeconomic errors (except perhaps after a crisis strikes). The broad consensus that rescued Argentina's democracy could not prevent elite political struggle from corrupting the economy. Even atop a sound political edifice, elite struggle can emerge, destroying all coherent policymaking without necessarily destroying the regime. Of course, elite cooperation does not guarantee economic stability—nothing does, because crises have many possible causes, ranging from external shocks to mere error—but elite struggle does come close to guaranteeing crisis.

Mexican fiscal data are widely taken from Instituto Nacional de Estadística Geografía e Informática (National Institute of Statistics, Geography, and Informatics). INEGI's *Estadísticas Históricas de México* (*Historical Statistics of Mexico*) uses the best and most basic source, the Finance Ministry's *Cuenta de la Hacienda Pública Federal* (*Federal Budget*), published in yearly volumes and not available outside of the Finance Ministry's own libraries. For example, Cárdenas 1994, Table A.25, and Cárdenas 1996, Table 1.7, use *Estadísticas Históricas*.

Unfortunately, the way *Estadísticas Históricas*—and many other secondary sources—present fiscal data poses serious problems. For one thing, *Estadísticas Históricas* data prior to 1980 often treat borrowing as part of revenue and include it in data on revenue (see INEGI 1994, Table 17.6, pages 760–761; also Graphics 17.6a and 17.6b). Obviously, if borrowing is included in revenue, there is no such thing as a deficit or surplus (except to the extent that the government over-borrows or under-borrows in any year). This problem can be corrected easily: *Estadísticas Históricas* gives the amount of borrowing, so one can net it out to obtain real revenue, as I have done.

The other major problem—found in much Mexican fiscal data from secondary sources as well as *Estadísticas Históricas* and rarely identified—is harder to correct: amortization is included as well as interest in debt payments. Amortization is not real spending. For example, suppose a government raises $100 billion in revenue and spends $105 billion by borrowing $5 billion. Its total spending is obviously $105 billion. Now suppose everything is the same but the government has $15 billion worth of short-term debt to pay off and renew during the course of the year (many Mexican government 28-day bonds must be constantly paid off and renewed). Now the government still raises $100 billion in revenue and spends $105 billion, but it borrows $20 billion and amortizes, or pays off, $15 billion worth of principal. Its real spending is still obviously $105 billion, but if amortization is included, the data indicate that it spends $120 billion. Typically, on the order of 15 percent of Mexican government spending, even during the 1960s, actually was amortization of debt, and the portion varied considerably from year to year. Budget data that include amortization, properly called "*gasto bruto*," or gross spending, but often not properly labeled, is therefore erratic and very problematic. Amortization is also often included in state enterprise spending, where it can be particularly hard to detect or weed out.

The best long-term series of fiscal data, going back to 1965, excluding amortization, and properly called "*gasto neto*," or net spending, is found in the appendices to the Carlos Salinas *Informes de Gobierno*. Unfortunately, the Zedillo administration did not continue that long-term data series. In other series, fiscal data from the *situación financiera*, financial condition, of the federal government, Mexico City, and state enterprises typically exclude amortization, or indicate it and net it out, but unfortunately this type of data usually only gives current spending and the capital-spending *deficit*, not total spending. And the *situación financiera* is not provided at all in *Estadísticas Históricas*.

Unless one goes to the Finance Ministry for data before 1965, one is therefore stuck with *Estadísticas Históricas* and other equally problematic sources such as Nacional Financiera, *Economía Mexicana en Cifras* (*Mexican Economy in Figures*), where amortization is not indicated and so cannot be netted out. Izquierdo 1995, Tables VII.4 and VII.5, does give amortization figures separately for the years he covers, 1959–70. He was an important economic advisor to the Finance Ministry during much of that period and thus a reliable source. INEGI, *Información sobre gasto público, 1970–1980* (*Information on Public Spending, 1970–1980*), Table 1.6, p. 5, also details amortization as a portion of public sector spending for the decade of the 1970s. Correcting data from *Estadísticas Históricas* by netting out amortization given by either of these sources gives essentially the same figures as the Salinas *Informes* for 1965 on.

I have always deducted borrowing from revenue figures, but because I do not have data on amortization before 1959, I have left it in total spending, as everyone else does. Thus, data on total spending and the total deficit for the period before 1959 should be treated with more than the usual suspicion.

Spending *excluding* debt service—thus excluding both amortization and interest—is reliable, as far as I know. Spending growth can therefore be calculated from it with reasonable confidence, and it is a good indicator of deficits (but of course lower than the total deficit would be).

Izquierdo's figure for total debt payments in 1965 is incorrect because of a clerical error. His amortization figure for this year is correct, as it checks with Salinas 1992, *Cuarto Informe*. Thus, where I cite him, I keep his amortization figure and correct his total debt figure for this year, using INEGI, *Estadísticas Históricas de México* 1994, Table 17.10.

I used a regression to capture how the Mexican political cycle affected public spending as distinct from economic factors. The regression is based on Barry Ames' model in his study of public spending across Latin America,[1] but it omits factors irrelevant to Mexico, such as military coups and changes of the political party in power, and it is modified to accord more closely with how Mexican officials say the expenditure process unfolded.

In Ames' model, current public spending is assumed to depend on last year's public spending, the growth (or decline) of current GDP (providing domestic resources to spend), the growth (or decline) of last year's foreign reserves (providing external resources to spend), and whether it is a pre-election, election, or post-election year.

Why should public spending depend on current GDP growth?[2] There is no automatic mechanism that feeds higher GDP into higher public spending. Rather, economic performance provides a signal to policymakers, but with a lag. (In advanced nations, "automatic stabilizers," such as unemployment insurance, may even boost public spending when GDP growth slows.) For example, though the presidential economic advisor Leopoldo Solís believed that Mexico was in recession in early 1971, hence that cutting investment to curb inflation was ill-advised, hard data were not available until late in the year. Only in 1972 did the government respond when it "became clear that the economic slump was far more severe than anyone had imagined."[3]

Independent variables affecting spending in year t are:

Spndg(t−1)	Public sector spending in the previous year
ChngGDP(t−1)	Percent GDP growth (or decline) in the previous year
ChngRsrvs(t−1)	Percent growth (or decline) in foreign reserves in the previous year
Y_1	1 in the first post-election year of each administration, otherwise 0
Y_5	1 in the fifth pre-election year of each administration, otherwise 0
Y_6	1 in the sixth election year of each administration, otherwise 0

The regression model, with the b_i coefficients to be determined by the regression, is:

Spndg(t) = b_0 + b_1Spndg(t−1) + b_2ChngGDP(t−1)Spndg(t−1) + b_3 ChngRsrvs(t−1)Spndg(t−1) + b_4Y_1Spndg(t−1) + b_5Y_5Spndg(t−1) + b_6Y_6Spndg(t−1)

Since public spending rose by almost a factor of ten over the period, the independent variables ChngGDP(t−1), ChngRsrvs(t−1), Y_1, Y_5, and Y_6 cannot be treated as affecting spending by some absolute quantity of pesos but rather by some *portion* of the previous year's spending; their effect on current spending results from multiplying them by the previous year's spending. In the principal regression, the coefficients are estimated based on data from 1960, when complete public sector spending first becomes available, through 1988.

Though Ames found significant increases in electoral year spending across Latin America, they did not occur in Mexico. In election years spending *decreased* 12.7 percent. In pre-election years spending *increased* 11.6 percent. Though Ames found that spending dropped in post-election years across Latin America, there was no such pattern in Mexico. The change in spending in the post-election year is not statistically significant.

Because this is an autoregression, the OLS method estimates coefficients that are biased but consistent—as sample size increases, the bias disappears—and is generally adopted as the most appropriate method.[4] A problem arises if

COEFFICIENT ESTIMATES

	Coefficients	Standard error	t statistic	Significance
Constant	14.47	8.54	1.69	0.1049
Spndg(t−1)	0.899	0.037	24.29	0.000000
ChngGDP(t−1)	0.0156	0.0033	4.77	0.000104
ChngRsrvs(t−1)	0.000968	0.000294	3.30	0.00345
Y_1	0.0038	0.0503	0.08	0.9406
Y_5	0.116	0.036	3.22	0.0041
Y_6	−0.127	0.033	−3.79	0.0011

MODEL SUMMARY

R Square	Adjusted R square	Durbin-Watson statistic
0.986	0.982	1.819

the errors are autocorrelated, i.e., if there is a systematic correlation between the error for one period and the error for the next. The Durbin-Watson statistic for the regression (1.82) indicates lack of autocorrelation but is inappropriate; the Durbin m test is the right one.[5] In this test, the OLS residuals are regressed on the lagged OLS residuals and the original regressors; an F test is then used to check whether the coefficients of the lagged residuals are significantly different from o. If so, there is systematic correlation between residuals and lagged residuals, i.e., autocorrelation. These coefficients were not significantly different from o: the F statistic was 0.186, yielding a probably p = 0.671 that they were no different from o.

How closely do these results depend on the particular model used? Not at all: a variety of alternative models, including one duplicating Ames' approach, using current GDP growth instead of that of the previous year, yield the same results, though with lower levels of confidence.[6] An alternative model, regressing the change in spending on the change in the previous year's GDP growth, change in the previous year's reserves, and Y_1, Y_5, and Y_6—thus avoiding autoregression—produced essentially the same results, with a Y_5 (pre-electoral year) increase of 8 percent and a Y_6 (electoral year) decrease of 9 percent, both significant. Regressing change in spending over dummies for the six years of each administration, that is, not controlling for contributions of economic factors, again shows a large and significant fifth-year increase.

Extending the time period through 1994, when electoral competition was more of a factor, weakens the results without changing them. Extending it back to 1948 does change them. Public sector spending is not available before 1960, so only government spending can be tested. The significant increase in pre-electoral spending remains, but not a significant decrease in election year spending. Spending was heavy in the election years 1952, when Henríquez Guzmán ran his powerful opposition campaign, and 1958, when there was a massive strike wave.

NOTES

INTRODUCTION

1. The Mexican public and political scientists widely recognized this interdiction. See, for example, Cosío Villegas 1975, 10–11; Camp 1976, 62; Newell and Rubio 1984, 267.

2. Some ministries changed names several times, so to avoid confusing readers, I have picked a generic English name and stuck with it throughout the book. Finance was always *Hacienda y Crédito Público;* the Bank of Mexico always *Banco de México;* Presidency was *Presidencia;* Planning and Budget, transformed in 1976 from what had been Presidency (here I do change names because the function changed importantly) was *Programación y Presupuesto;* Industry and Commerce was *Economía* (1952–58), *Industria y Comercio* (1958–76), *Comercio* (1976–82), and *Comercio y Fomento Industrial* (1982–94); State Industries was *Bienes Nacionales* (1952–58), *Patrimonio Nacional* (1958–76), *Patrimonio y Fomento Industrial* (1976–82), *Energía, Minas e Industria Paraestatal* (1982–94); Interior was always *Gobernación;* Labor was always *Trabajo y Previsión Social.*

3. I included all individuals considered to have been precandidates by at least two of the following sources: Camp 1995b or 1976, Cosío Villegas 1975, Castañeda 1999, Langston 1997a.

4. Julio Rodolfo Moctezuma has died since talking with me. The finance secretary I did not interview was José López Portillo, subsequently president. His son's account of economic policymaking during the period (López Portillo Romano 1994) traces his point of view in detail.

5. *La herencia: Arqueología de la sucesión presidencial en México.* The English version is a truncation.

CHAPTER ONE

1. Silva Herzog said this in 2000. Whenever I cite an individual without giving a written source, the citation is from my interview with that individual. Dates and locations of interviews are listed at the back of the book.

2. Ortiz Mena 1998, 114, 151.

3. I sometimes adopt the common convention of using public spending as shorthand for public spending *without* comparable public revenue. Spending per se is not a problem, but rather massive budget deficits.

4. Aguayo 2000, 199.

5. On Mexican banks' foreign borrowing, see Cárdenas 1996, 189; Sachs 1998, 249.

6. The peso's exchange rate, if defined in the usual way as the number of pesos per dollar, rises when the value of the currency falls. But to avoid this counterintuitive way of speaking, I follow some economists who adopt the opposite definition, making the peso's exchange rate the number of U.S. cents per peso, and speak of the exchange rate as falling when the value of the local currency falls.

7. Esquivel and Larraín 1998, 10–11.

8. Obstfeld 1996.

9. Sachs 1998, 249–250.

10. Vernon 1963, 122, including on the $200 million of capital flight.

11. Eatwell and Taylor 1998b, 4.

12. Radelet and Sachs 1998, 2.

13. Eichengreen 1999, 145.

14. Eichengreen 1999, Eatwell and Taylor 2000.

15. Eichengreen 1999, 1.

16. Eatwell and Taylor 1998a, 1.

17. Rodrik 1999, 78.

18. Eichengreen 1999, 138.

19. I am implicitly assuming here that the velocity at which money changes hands is constant. It often is not. But there is little disagreement that massive monetary creation can lead to inflation and crises.

20. Cárdenas 1996, 194.

21. For example, Eichengreen 1999, 143–169; Radelet and Sachs 1998; and Krugman 1998 evaluate how well competing theories apply to the Asia crisis. Eichengreen and Wyplosz 1993 do the same for the European monetary system crisis of 1992. Taylor 1988, 75–143; Kahler 1985, 358–359; and Golub 1991 do the same for the 1980s wave of developing nations' crises.

22. IMF staff 1998, 18–19.

23. There have also been a few efforts to unravel how the politics of financial deregulation can lead to economic crises. An excellent example is Kessler 1998 on Mexico's 1994 crisis.

24. Rodrik 1999, 84. Similarly Frankel 1998 and Lee 1998. The following quote is from Rodrik 1999, 92.

25. Huntington 1968 helped launch this idea. See also O'Donnell 1973; Skidmore 1977; Goldthorpe 1978, 202; Lindberg 1985, 45; Kaufman 1985, 489.

26. Haggard 1985, 510.

27. Katzenstein 1985, 95.

28. Schmitter 1981, 323.

29. Stepan 1978 is one of the best accounts of state corporatism.

30. Haggard and Kaufman 1992b, 293.

31. Haggard 1990, 134–136; Amsden 1989, 101–105.

32. Authors who specifically attribute macroeconomic stability to state autonomy include Nelson 1990a, 21; Nelson 1990b, 341; Haggard and Kaufman 1989, 269–270; and Remmer 1993, 402.

33. Haggard and Kaufman 1992b, 271.

34. The usual explanation (Maxfield 1990, 72) is that the long border with the United States made capital controls impossible to enforce. I find this idea implausible—even in the nineteenth century, major capital flight took the form of transfers between banks, not bandits running briefcases of hundred dollar bills across the Rio Grande—but I am not sure of the real reason why Mexico allowed free financial flows. Perhaps it had to do with the powerful Mexican banking sector's ability to survive the Revolution and shape financial legislation. In any event, the only post-revolutionary attempt to enforce exchange controls was abandoned in the 1930s.

35. Reynolds 1977, Solís 1981, Boltvinik and Hernández Laos 1981, Newell and Rubio 1984, Zedillo 1985, Buffie 1990, Bazdresch and Levy 1991, Maddison 1992, Cárdenas 1996, and Heath 1999 all point predominately or exclusively to internal causes. Lustig 1998, 19, says that the U.S. recession of the early 1970s, eroding Mexican exports to the United States, contributed to the 1976 crisis. She cites a consensus of economists across the ideological spectrum who see Mexico's 1982 crisis as caused by domestic problems (1998, 26). The "fiscal crisis of the state" argument taken up by Fitzgerald 1978, which blames crises on an alliance of international and large national capital, will be discussed in Chapter 3.

36. Fishlow 1990.

37. Díaz Alejandro 1987, 21.

38. Buffie 1990, 442; Lustig 1998, 21—see Chapter 8. See Cárdenas 1996, 142, on Mexican oil export revenues.

39. *The Economist*, September 4, 1982, 48.

40. Haggard and Kaufman 1992b, 288.

41. The literature includes, for example, work by Roderic Camp, Peter Smith, Rogelio Hernández Rodríguez, Joy Langston, Francisco Suárez Farías, Miguel Angel Centeno, and other authors discussed in Chapter 3.

42. Hernández Rodríguez 1984, 101. Langston 1998, 19, notes that politicians she interviewed generally talk about *grupos políticos* rather than *camarillas*, though she uses the latter term.

CHAPTER TWO

1. Knight 1990, 87, as well as on labor insurgency.

2. Paz 1985, 241–242, 245–246.

3. Hernández Rodríguez 1992, 242. Pablo González Casanova's *Democracy in Mexico* (1970, originally published 1965) is a comprehensive and powerful account of the centralized system. Lawson 2000, 268–269, summarizes features of the old regime and provides a list of references. Bailey 1988, 31; Cornelius and Craig 1991, 23–26; Ortiz Salinas 1988, 14–18; Bruhn 1997, 33*ff.*; Luna 1988, 252; Suárez Farías 1988, 308; and Hernández Rodríguez 1984, 8–10 are just a few authors who succinctly describe the principal political features of presidential control over a hegemonic party and official corporatist organizations.

4. Rubin 1996, 85.

5. Fox 1994, 151–152, 158.

6. Paz 1985, 315–316.

7. Cornelius and Craig 1991, 14.

8. Almond and Verba 1965, 310–311; Craig and Cornelius 1989, 353–354, 375–376.

9. Stepan 1978, 96.

10. Camp 1984a, 134.

11. Camp 1984a, 42.

12. González Casanova 1970, 68–69.

13. González Casanova 1970, 11.

14. Cornelius and Craig 1991, 31.

15. Ortiz Salinas 1988, 15–16.

16. Cornelius and Craig 1991, 33.

17. Quoted in Ortiz Salinas 1988, 14.

18. Quoted in Ortiz Salinas 1988, 16.

19. Camp 1993, 142.

20. Cosío Villegas 1975, 101.

21. Cornelius and Craig 1991, 25, 60–61.

22. González Casanova 1970, 20; Cornelius and Craig 1991, 31.

23. Cornelius and Craig 1991, 33; González Casanova 1970, 24.

24. Bravo.

25. Cornelius and Craig 1991, 31; Lawson 2000, 283.

26. Dillon 2000, A-3; Aguayo 2000, 285.

27. Dillon 2000, A-3.

28. Collier and Collier 1991, 578.

29. González Casanova 1970, 41, 50; Cornelius and Craig 1991, 56. González Casanova says the military had de facto political power and could bargain independently with political rulers, but most authors do not see it as having more clout than any other part of the bureaucracy.

30. Cornelius 1975, 143, 146, 159–160.

31. Statements that the state effectively controlled corporatist sectors include Stepan 1978, 61–66; Cornelius and Craig 1991, 85–92; Collier and Collier 1991, 574; Camp 1993, 121–125; Middlebrook 1991, 9, and 1995, 27; Smith 1979, 54; Newell and Rubio 1984, 272; and Frank 1969, 314.

32. Collier and Collier 1991, 571.

33. Knight 1991, 274–277.
34. Bizberg 1990, 321.
35. Stepan 1978, 61; Knight 1991, 257–258.
36. Stepan 1978, 61.
37. Middlebrook 1991, 9.
38. Middlebrook 1995, 267.
39. Camp 1993, 122.
40. Pérez Arce 1990, 110.
41. Middlebrook 1991, 4, on the makeup of boards. Stepan 1978, 65, on firing participants.
42. Middlebrook 1995, 265–266, 269.
43. Pérez Arce 1990, 109.
44. Hernández Rodríguez 1992, 244–247.
45. Cornelius and Craig 1991, 33.
46. Camacho Solís.
47. Cornelius and Craig 1991, 90.
48. Collier and Collier 1991, 582; Cornelius and Craig 1991, 85; Smith 1979, 53–54.
49. Gamboa.
50. Suárez Mier. His source is the person who was on Díaz Ordaz's left.
51. Lawson 2002, 31, 33, 35.
52. Krauze 1997, 687.
53. Lawson 2002, 30, 46.
54. Camp 2002, 113, 250.
55. Camp 1984a, 153.
56. Camp 1995a, 100.
57. Camp 1984a, 121, and chapter 6.
58. Camp 1984a, 100.
59. Camp 1980, 78, 197.
60. Camp 1980, 94.
61. Camp 1980, 169, 178.
62. Camp 2002, 12.
63. Smith 1979, 213.
64. Smith 1979, 197.
65. Camp 1990, 85, 90.
66. Ramos 1962, 64, quoted in Camp 1980, 15.
67. Craig and Cornelius 1989, 372.
68. Camp 1990, 88.
69. Grindle 1977, 49.
70. Langston 1995, 255.
71. Langston, 1995, 256.
72. Langston 1995, 257–258.
73. Langston 1995, 256; Centeno 1994, 146; Camp 1993, 103.
74. Camp 1995b, 710.

75. Corona del Rosal 1995, 160.

76. The remainder of this paragraph is from Corona del Rosal 1995, 160–163.

77. Langston 1995, 265, 268.

78. Grindle 1977, 39.

79. Grindle 1977, 62, footnote 5.

80. Langston 1998, 23.

81. Grindle 1977, 40, 50.

82. Camp 1990, 106.

83. Langston 1995, 255; Camp 1976, 63–64.

84. Corona del Rosal 1995, 278.

85. Langston 1994, 18, footnote 42.

86. Hernández Rodríguez 1984, 42.

87. Smith 1979, 186.

88. Camp 1980, 204.

89. Hernández Rodríguez 1992, 244.

90. Cosío Villegas 1975, 12.

91. Cosío Villegas 1975, 12.

92. The rest of this paragraph is from Cosío Villegas 1975, 10–11.

93. Langston 1997a, 8; Cornelius and Craig 1991, 37; Urquidi and Bracamontes.

94. Aguayo 1998, 207–208, citing court testimony.

95. Aguayo 1998, 208–213.

96. Langston 1998, 28–29.

97. Camp 1976, 73; Langston 1995, 249; Grindle 1977, 52; Cornelius and Craig 1991, 37; Newell and Rubio 1984, 71; Suárez Farías 1988, 316. Castañeda 1999, from beginning to end, is about covert conflict among *grupos* for the presidency.

98. Castañeda 1999, 185.

99. Grindle 1977. She never identifies de la Vega Domínguez by name, only as director of the food distribution firm, but he held that position from 1971 to 1976 when she was doing her research.

100. Quoted in Castañeda 1999, 159–160.

101. De la Madrid, Bracamontes.

102. Bracamontes, particularly on López Mateos and Díaz Ordaz as popular, López Portillo as unpopular.

103. Bravo.

104. Camp 1976, 82.

105. Bracamontes, Alejo, but this was not a secret.

106. Corona del Rosal 1995, 141.

107. Corona del Rosal 1995, 141–142.

108. Corona del Rosal 1995, 142

109. Corona del Rosal 1995, 143.

110. Langston 1997a, 8.

CHAPTER THREE

1. Hirschman 1985, 54, notes this view without supporting it.

2. Krugman 1998, 1.

3. Frankel 1998.

4. Suárez Mier.

5. A prominent early work, published in 1970, was Ian M. D. Little, Tibor Scitovsky, and Maurice Scott, *Industry and Trade in Some Developing Countries.*

6. Reynolds 1977, 998. The history mentioned is *The Mexican Economy: Twentieth-Century Structure and Growth*, New Haven: Yale University Press, 1970.

7. *El Financiero*, December 15, 1996, 68.

8. A prominent work was Andre Gunder Frank's *Latin America: Underdevelopment or Revolution?*, written at the National University of Mexico and published in 1969.

9. Fitzgerald 1978.

10. Cardoso and Faletto 1979, 204.

11. Golub 1991 summarizes structural arguments about Latin American crises. Lustig 1998, 17, notes that Mexico's economic crises are widely attributed to industrial exhaustion, but she disagrees. On the left, Tello 1979, 205–206, says that Mexico's economic problems from 1970–76 resulted from structural problems, while Hector Guillén Romo 1984, 13, contends that the nation's "financial and monetary problems [were] only a manifestation of the crisis of the model of accumulation; in no way should they be considered the cause of this crisis." Boltvinik and Hernández Laos 1981, 482, and Casar et al. 1990, 9, make interesting arguments about industrial problems, which they say caused economic crises. Though Kaufman 1979 principally argues that industrial problems caused Latin American military coups, he also provides a particularly good account of how they could have caused the preceding economic crises.

12. Cárdenas 1996, 19, provides a succinct statement, but the idea runs through his books published in 1994 and 1996 covering Mexican macroeconomic policy from 1929 to 1994.

13. For example, Smith 1991, 325–327; Collier and Collier 1991, 602; Basáñez 1996, 160; Lawson 2000, 272; Bruhn 1997, 62–63; Basave 1996, 39.

14. Hirschman 1979, 69. Hirschman is not one of those critics; he just notes when the criticism emerged.

15. I largely paraphrase Kaufman 1979, one of the best accounts of the exhaustion of import substitution. He is actually explaining military coups in South America (following O'Donnell 1973), but argues that industrial problems, unresolved by politicians, caused economic crises, and the military stepped in to fix things.

16. Deepak Lal and Hla Myint, "Foreword," in Maddison 1992, vii.

17. Rodrik 1999, 77.

18. Esquivel and Larraín 1998, 17–20.

19. Rodrik 1999, 76–78. It is corroborated by Rodrik that Argentina and Colombia both had high levels of protection, as well as that Argentina succumbed to and Colombia avoided the 1982 wave of crises.

20. Villarreal 1977, 71.

21. Vernon 1963, 116–117.

22. Ros 1994, 172.

23. Ros 1994, 174. Maddison 1992, 180, reports a broadly similar pattern of "implicit protection," the difference between world and domestic prices.

24. Banco Nacional de Comercio Exterior 1971 discusses these policies.

25. Ros 1994, 172–173, 174. Maddison 1992, 180, reports a broadly similar pattern of implicit protection.

26. My argument broadly parallels Ros 1994.

27. Bennett and Sharpe 1985.

28. All total-factor productivity figures are from Hernández Laos and Velasco Arregui 1990, 662.

29. Shapiro and Taylor 1990, 863–865.

30. Deepak Lal and Hla Myint, "Foreword," in Maddison 1992, vii.

31. Casar et al. 1990, 36, table 2.3.

32. Mancera.

33. Moreno and Ros 1994, 135.

34. See Graph 3.1 for sources for manufacturing trade deficits.

35. Cárdenas 1996, 213.

36. Krugman 1990.

37. Structural problems in the banking sector are the exception, but such problems were not an issue in Mexico until 1994.

38. Cárdenas 1996, 214. The Spanish word is *atonía*.

39. Buffie 1990, 413–414.

40. Moctezuma.

41. Maddison 1992, 159.

42. Villarreal 1990, 312.

43. Export figures in current dollars from *United Nations Statistical Yearbook*, various years.

44. Maddison 1992, 4.

45. Ortiz Mena; Izquierdo 1995, 19.

46. Ortiz Mena confirms López Mateos' statement, and Izquierdo concurs.

47. Maxfield 1990, 88–93.

48. Cárdenas 1996, 96; Maxfield 1990, 88–93.

49. Flores de la Peña.

50. Solís 1981, 74.

51. Solís 1981, 74.

52. Solís 1981, 76.

53. Maxfield 1990, 92. Alejo, Izquierdo, and Suárez Mier concur about the private sector's position, but, unlike Solís, do not say the Bank of Mexico made the argument.

54. Alejo.

55. Solís 1981, 75–76

56. Maxfield 1990, 92.

57. Maxfield 1990, 88–93.

58. Solís 1981, 72.

59. Solís 1981, 93.

60. Solís 1981, 84, 100.

61. Maxfield 1990, Solís 1981, Buffie 1990.

62. Alejo.

63. Villarreal 1977, 97, 107.

64. Alejo, Suárez Mier.

65. Buffie 1990, 419, 422.

66. Ibarra.

67. Moreno and Ros 1994, 128, 141.

68. The following sources were used in this calculation: for 1953–58 government spending data are from INEGI 1994, Table 17.10, revenue from Table 17.6. For 1959–70 government spending is from Izquierdo 1995, Table VII.5, revenue from Table VII.8. All these data come originally from the same source: the budget (*Cuenta de la Hacienda Pública Federal*) exercised during each year as reported by the Finance Ministry (Secretaría de Hacienda y Crédito Publico, SHCP). GDP is from INEGI 1994, Table 8.1.

69. Gil Díaz 1984, 341.

70. Ortiz Mena 1998, 289.

71. Quoted in Solís 1981, 82.

72. The quote is from Tello 1979, 123.

73. Buffie 1990, 422–423.

74. Gil Díaz 1984, 341, gives 2.76 percent of GDP (which I round in the text) as the average current-account deficit, without adjusting for inflation, for 1960–70. His slightly lower figure for current-account deficits adjusted for inflation would be more favorable to my argument. Average current-account deficits for 1958–70 given by Buffie 1990, 399, of only 1.9 percent of GDP, would also be more favorable to my argument.

75. Basáñez 1996, 153; likewise Tello 1979, 11.

76. Bracamontes, de la Vega Domínguez, Mancera, Moreno Valle, Romero Kolbeck, and Moctezuma agree, not only that they saw the economy as doing well but also that the general view did as well.

77. Tello 1979, 11.

78. Paz 1985, 230.

CHAPTER FOUR

1. Pellicer de Brody and Reyna 1978. I mention Reyna alone in the text because he wrote the section on the 1958–59 strike wave. Except where noted to the contrary, the account of the 1958–59 strikes is his but is consistent with other histories such as Smith 1991, Krauze 1997, and Bizberg 1990.

2. Carr 1991, 133.

3. The raise was to be applied across the board, regardless of railworkers' differing pay levels. Reyna, in Pellicer de Brody and Reyna 1978, 175, says that the average railworker's wage was 916 monthly in 1957.

4. Krauze 1997, 635–636, 663.

5. Ortiz Mena.

6. Collier and Collier 1991, 601.

7. Buffie 1990, 409, 412.

8. Tello 1979, 43.

9. Pérez Arce 1990, 110, 111.

10. Except where noted to the contrary, this account is from Bizberg 1990, 304–325. It is essentially consistent with others such as Pérez Arce 1990, 109–113; Hellman 1983, 244–246; Middlebrook 1995, 222–225; and Carrillo Gamboa interview.

11. Hellman 1983, 242, and Schmidt 1991, 78, concur.

12. Bizberg 1990, 314; Pérez Arce 1990, 112; Franco G. S. 1991, 114.

13. Pérez Arce 1990, 113.

14. Middlebrook 1995, 166.

15. Cordera and Tello 1981a, 72.

16. Buffie 1990, 434. Bizberg 1984, 168, likewise shows real declines throughout the López Portillo administration, in both manufacturing and minimum wages, except for a roughly 2 percent increase in 1981.

17. Bizberg 1984, 181. Middlebrook 1995, 165, shows a sharp increase in strikes from 108 in 1981 to 675 in 1982. These would have responded to rather than caused at least the first crisis (uncontrolled devaluation) in January 1982. But Bizberg 1984, 180, says the overwhelming majority were one-day strikes at local radio stations; otherwise, strike activity fell in 1982. He calculates that the number of person-days lost per 1,000 workers peaked in 1980, fell to only 16 percent of that level in 1981, then rose to 50 percent of that level in 1982 (1984, 183).

18. Middlebrook 1995, 257.

19. Middlebrook 1991, 12.

20. Middlebrook 1995, 265.

21. Haggard and Kaufman, 1989, 272; Nelson 1990a, 23; Nelson 1990b, 340; Heath 1999, 10–11.

22. Haggard and Kaufman 1992a, 31.

23. Haggard and Kaufman 1992b, 290.

24. Ames 1987, 1.

25. Ames 1987, 27, footnote 12. Ames' regression does not determine a percentage by which spending increased. Remmer 1993 finds little evidence of an electoral cycle in Latin America from 1982 through 1991. The reason is that this was the disastrous decade following the 1982 crises: "By the time elections approached, Latin governments in the 1980s were often less master than the victim of the economy" (405). Her data is not relevant to Mexico from 1970 through 1982, when there were plentiful resources.

26. Aguayo 2000, 242.

27. González Casanova 1970, 124.

28. Aguayo 2000, 242.

29. All sources concur; see Chapter 9.

30. Ames 1987, 33.

31. Cited in Smith 1979, 274–275.

32. Ortiz Mena, Urquidi, and Izquierdo.

33. The account of these events is from Ortiz Mena, Izquierdo, and Urquidi (Finance); Romero Kolbeck (Bank of Mexico); and Moctezuma (Presidency). Some facts are taken from some interviews, some facts from others, but the stories are consistent.

34. Urquidi.

35. Izquierdo 1995, 131.

36. I translated the increase in Social Security spending to dollars at the going exchange rate of 12.5, then divided by accumulated foreign debt in 1962 from Ortiz Mena 1998, 148.

37. Ortiz Mena 1998, 145.

38. Moctezuma.

39. Ortiz Mena mentioned that Díaz Ordaz was already concerned about rivals for the presidency in the third year of the administration.

40. Chapter 8 details this account.

41. López Portillo Romano 1994, 147.

42. López Portillo Romano 1994, 168.

43. Suárez Mier (a supporter), de Oteyza, López Portillo Romano 1994, 169; Castañeda 1999, 397–398.

44. Credit issued by development banks (*banca de desarrollo*) is from Salinas 1994 (*Sexto Informe de Gobierno: Anexo*), 116. GDP in current pesos is from Cardenas 1996, Table A.4, 214–215.

45. Basáñez 1996, 254.

46. Chapter 9 details these events.

47. Basave 1996, 154.

48. Fernández Hurtado.

49. Hernández Rodríguez 1992, 262; Langston, 1997b, 3. Chapters 6 and 9 detail these elite rebellions.

50. Castañeda 1999, 317.

51. Castañeda 1999, 407.
52. Castañeda 1999, 168.

CHAPTER FIVE

1. Economists' models at least attempt to explain both periods of crisis and periods of stability, a method political scientists should adopt. Some, such as Haggard and Kaufman, do.

2. According to the most complete data that Gerardo Esquivel and Felipe Larraín at the Harvard Institute for International Development were able to obtain (Esquivel and Larraín 1998). Developed nations averaged 1.7 crises each, and countries that moved from developing to developed during the period averaged 2.8 crises each. Developing nations have more crises in part because they borrow more from abroad, precisely to develop. When they do borrow, unlike the United States, they cannot issue bonds in their own currency but rather in dollars or other hard currency, for which their central banks cannot act as lender of last resort. Developing countries also undoubtedly have more crises because of their relative political instability.

3. Olson 1993, 567. Olson states his claim almost as a political theorem. I only propose it as a political possibility.

4. Centeno 1994, 77–78.

5. Centeno 1994, 78–79.

6. Basáñez 1996, 66.

7. Maxfield 1990; Centeno 1994, 83. The argument about the source of Finance–banking strength comes from Maxfield, but she uses it to explain the state's ability to promote investment, not its ability to sustain economic stability.

8. Ortiz Mena 1998, 83–84.

9. Maxfield 1990, 41.

10. Cárdenas 1993, 680.

11. Ghigliazza concurs. Córdoba (1994, 253) notes that the Bank of Mexico only achieved "full autonomy" via a constitutional amendment passed in 1993, though the extent of even that autonomy has been debated.

12. Maxfield 1990, 76.

13. Cárdenas 1993, 675. Cárdenas argues that government monetary policy was conservative, but private banks, the public, and external shocks contributed to occasionally expansionary growth.

14. Maxfield 1990, 76.

15. Cárdenas 1994, Table A.25.

16. Maxfield 1990, 16; see also 83*ff.*

17. I am referring to the expansion of the monetary base. Source: Cárdenas 1996, Table III.3, 99.

18. Entry for March 16, 1954. The diary for 1954, minus some personal references, was provided by Carrillo Flores' son, Emilio Carrillo Gamboa.

19. Maxfield 1990, 39–40.

20. Camp 1993, 134.

21. Beteta.

22. Riding 1989, 121

23. Ortiz Mena. José Patrocinio González Blanco, director of public investments under López Mateos, subsequently interior minister and Ortiz Mena's son-in-law, concurs that Ortiz Mena was not a candidate.

24. David Ibarra and Jesús Silva Herzog, both former finance secretaries, say Ortiz Mena was a real presidential candidate in 1970, but Manuel Suárez Mier, a former Bank of Mexico official, does not think so.

25. Carrillo Flores diary for 1954, February 23.

26. Ortiz Salinas 1988, 10–12.

27. Izquierdo 1995, 62.

28. Ortiz Mena, Urquidi, Izquierdo, Moctezuma, Fernández Hurtado, Beteta. Suárez Mier and de Oteyza, from a later generation, did not see firsthand how the system worked in the 1950s or 1960s.

29. Cárdenas 1993, 689.

30. Ortiz Mena 1998, 97, 99, 142, 168, and 169–172.

31. One view has been that excessive spending was the problem (Ortiz Mena), but Cárdenas argues persuasively that it was the Korean War boom-and-bust cycle. My account of the economics of the episode is from him (Cárdenas 1996, 44–47). In any event, the cause of the problem does not matter to my point that the president provided the authority to control it.

32. Cárdenas 1994, Table A.21, for 1952 and 1953; Alemán Velasco 1997, 247, for early 1954.

33. Carrillo Gamboa.

34. Carrillo Flores diary.

35. Carrillo Flores diary. Also Carrillo Gamboa, Fernández Hurtado, Ortiz Mena.

36. April 14, 1954, entry.

37. Sánchez Navarro said the next day, but Carrillo Flores' diary shows that the boxing match was Saturday April 10 and the devaluation was Saturday April 17, so I revised the quote.

38. Interviews with Romero Pérez; Gustavo Carvajal (son of the interior minister and subsequent president of PRI); Carrillo Gamboa (finance secretary's son); Fernández Hurtado (Bank of Mexico); Sánchez Navarro.

39. Carrillo Flores diary; Ortiz Mena 1998, 36–37.

40. Romero Pérez.

41. Carrillo Gamboa, both on financial authorities' approving 15 percent raises and on López Mateos' keeping average raises to 10 percent.

42. Gustavo Carvajal.
43. Carrillo Gamboa.
44. Carrillo Flores diary, April 26, 1954.
45. Carrillo Flores diary, September 15, December 16, 1954.
46. Carrillo Flores diary, December 15 and 18, 1954.
47. Carrillo Gamboa.
48. Ortiz Mena 1998, 37.
49. Carrillo Flores diary, November 1, 1954.
50. Carrillo Gamboa.
51. Ortiz Mena.
52. Carrillo Gamboa.
53. Ortiz Mena 1998, 38.
54. I do not have direct evidence that they worked together but infer it.
55. Ortiz Mena 1998, 86–87.
56. Salinas Lozano.
57. Bracamontes.
58. Salinas Lozano, González Blanco, Carrillo Gamboa.
59. Krauze 1997, 638.
60. Centeno 1994, 80.
61. Moctezuma, Romero Kolbeck.
62. Moctezuma. This ministry was the Secretaría de Bienes Nacionales before 1958, the Secretaría de Patrimonio Nacional after 1958 (Ortiz Mena 1998, 46), and later changed its name several more times. To avoid complications, I have called it State Industries throughout—it managed state industries.
63. Carrillo Castro 1981, 494.
64. Ortiz Mena 1998, 40–45; Moctezuma.
65. Ortiz Mena 1998, 46; Romero Kolbeck and Izquierdo on Bustamante's political ambitions. José Patrocinio González Blanco, who was subdirector of public investments in Presidency from 1960–61 and director from 1961–64—and is, moreover, Antonio Ortiz Mena's son-in-law—but was chancellor in the London embassy when these events took place, says that Bustamante designed a strong Finance Ministry because he thought he would be finance minister. This is the only account I heard that conflicts with the history laid out in the text. I find it doubtful, not only because Ortiz Mena, Izquierdo, and Romero Kolbeck disagree, but also because Antonio Carrillo Gamboa, Carrillo Flores' son, is so confident that Ortiz Mena was the principal, if not exclusive, candidate to succeed Carrillo Flores.
66. Ortiz Mena 1998, 47; Moctezuma.
67. Izquierdo 1995, 46.
68. Ortiz Mena. His book is consistent with his interview but offers fewer details.
69. Ortiz Mena 1998, 168.
70. Ortiz Mena 1998, 168–169, and Ortiz Mena interview.

71. Ortiz Mena 1998, 170–171.

72. Ortiz Mena 1998, 99, 172—on both curtailing spending immediately and the longer-term plan.

73. There are data on all public sector spending, including state enterprises, after 1965 precisely because of this new system.

74. Ortiz Mena 1998, 173

75. Ortiz Mena 1998, 97.

76. Camp 1995b, 196, corroborates that del Mazo was a friend of the president and precandidate.

77. Ortiz Mena 1998, 163, corroborates this account.

CHAPTER SIX

1. Camp 1980, 17, and 1976, 62; Langston, 1995, 247; 1997a, 8; and 1997b, 27; Suárez Farías 1988, 306.

2. Camp 1995a, 49, 126.

3. Krauze 1997, 586.

4. Middlebrook 1995, 140, 214.

5. Servín 2001, 119–127; 204–208.

6. Servín 2001, 122.

7. Cosío Villegas 1975, 118–119.

8. Cárdenas 1973, 399–400.

9. Cárdenas 1973, 417.

10. Cárdenas 1973, 440. Raúl Salinas Lozano, a high official in the 1950s and 1960s and father of Carlos Salinas, says Cárdenas forced Alemán to back down by threatening to run himself.

11. Krauze 1997, 559.

12. Smith 1991, 345.

13. Krauze 1997, 559.

14. Cosío Villegas 1975, 114.

15. Krauze 1997, 559.

16. Cosío Villegas 1975, 127.

17. Pellicer de Brody and Reyna 1978, 46–47.

18. Pellicer de Brody and Reyna 1978, 47.

19. Cárdenas 1973, 452.

20. Krauze 1997, 559–560.

21. Brandenburg 1964, 106–107.

22. Cosío Villegas 1975, 16.

23. Suárez Farías (1988, 317) and Camp (1976, 52–53) tell the same story, but Suárez Farías does not cite a source either, and Camp cites Brandenburg. Nor does Cárdenas himself say anything in his diary (1973) about participating in the episode.

24. Cosío Villegas 1975, 120.

25. Pellicer de Brody and Reyna 1978, 60.

26. Pellicer de Brody and Reyna 1978, 20, 56. Likewise Langston 1997b, 23, citing additional sources.

27. Camp 1995a, 126.

28. Camp 1976, 57–58; Smith 1979, 51; Suárez Farías 1988, 306; Langston 1997a, 8.

29. Centeno 1994, 153; Schmidt 1991, 154; Cosío Villegas 1974, 20–21.

30. Langston 1994, 5.

31. Hernández Rodríguez 1987, 21.

32. Bailey 1988, 78. Bailey also includes turnover in Defense, where the secretary did not change—it was 24 percent—but notes that the figure is inflated, as a number of the changes are the same individuals shifting positions in the ministry. Also, Defense was its own area, outside the normal political circuit.

33. De la Madrid. Also de la Madrid interview in Castañeda 1999.

34. Castañeda 1999, 239–240.

35. Likewise Ortiz Mena, Carrillo Gamboa, and Suárez Mier.

36. Ames 1987, 1.

37. Carr 1991, 133.

38. Salinas Lozano, González Blanco, Carrillo Gamboa.

39. Krauze 1997, 638.

CHAPTER SEVEN

1. Hirschman 1979, 85. He saw ideological escalation as explaining military coups that struck Latin American nations in the 1960s and 1970s. He is also at least implicitly explaining the economic crises that almost always triggered those coups.

2. Camp 1995a, 100, and Camp 1984a, 121, and Chapter 6.

3. Finance Minister Ortiz Mena was replaced in the last six months of the Díaz Ordaz administration, but only at the behest of president-elect Echeverría. About the same time, Rodrigo Gómez, director of the Bank of Mexico throughout the 1950s and 1960s, died and was replaced.

4. Basáñez 1996, 83. Likewise Luna 1983, 457; Tello 1979, 91–92; López Portillo Romano 1994, 96–97.

5. Moctezuma and Suárez Mier concur; Zapata specifically speaks of conflict as ideological.

6. Krauze 1997, 748.

7. Solís 1981, 47–48, 64, 67–68.

8. Tello 1979, 78.

9. Tello 1979, 81, 87–89, 109. De Oteyza, also on the left, agrees that policy-

making turned conflictive and erratic under Echeverría. Solana calls it "badly managed" and "highly unproductive."

10. Newell and Rubio 1984; Bazdresch and Levy 1991, 237, 252.

11. Newell and Rubio 1984, 109–110, 111.

12. Newell and Rubio 1984, 122.

13. Hellman 1983, 184.

14. Aguayo 1998, 265.

15. Krauze 1997, 726.

16. Aguayo 1998, 262, 268.

17. Aguayo 1998, 271–272.

18. Craig and Cornelius 1989, 354.

19. Craig and Cornelius 1989, 354, 377, 393, footnote 159.

20. Schmidt 1991, 98–102; Riding 1989, 186–187.

21. Collier and Collier 1991, 607; Carr 1991, 136.

22. Zapata particularly emphasizes this point.

23. Hellman 1983, 204.

24. Krauze 1997, 752.

25. Smith 1979, 55.

26. Newell and Rubio 1984, 198.

27. Cornelius and Craig 1991, 58. As discussed in Chapter 9, these opposition groups joined the Cuauhtémoc Cárdenas campaign in 1988 only late and cautiously (Bruhn 1997, 112–113).

28. The analogy is from Cosío Villegas; Echeverría showed me the map before I interviewed him.

29. Ames 1987, 26–28.

30. Moctezuma, Urquidi (a Finance advisor); and Solís 1981.

31. Newell and Rubio 1984, 137.

32. Public Works, a large budget, was also included in social sector spending and should not have been: by the 1990s when the data from which I took Table 7.1 were compiled, Public Works had evolved into Urban Development and Ecology and was properly classified as social sector spending, but under Echeverría it built infrastructure. Its secretary, Enrique Bracamontes, was nicknamed "Rapamontes," or mountain-leveler.

33. Cornelius and Craig 1991, 110. Smith 1979, 281, says they increased from 86 to 740.

34. Calculated from the same data set, Salinas 1992 (*Cuarto Informe de Gobierno: Anexo*), as used for Table 4.3.

35. Newell and Rubio 1984, 124.

36. Aguayo 1998, 150, 270, 271.

37. Camp 1985, 209.

38. Beteta, Fernández Hurtado, and Carrillo Gamboa for Finance and the Bank of Mexico; Moreno Valle and de la Vega Domínguez for the more politically oriented ministries.

39. Likewise Ibarra, in the U.N. Economic Commission for Latin America at the time ("the government itself closed ranks behind the president, for good reasons or bad"), and Bracamontes, who was out of government but had been an undersecretary for twelve years and would be public works secretary under Echeverría.

40. Newell and Rubio 1984, 123–124; Carrillo Gamboa. Aguayo 1998, 303, persuasively argues that Echeverría's actual role in Tlatelolco was much more marginal than once thought. This reassessment does not affect the argument in the text: at the time he was widely *seen* as a hard-liner.

41. Aguayo 1998, 161.

42. Moreno Valle, Carrillo Gamboa.

43. Bracamontes, Beteta, Zapata.

44. Castañeda 1999, 347.

45. Muñoz Ledo on the unimportance of the undersecretariat. López Portillo's subsequent rise to the presidency began later.

46. Echeverría, Ortiz Mena, Urquidi, Carrillo Gamboa, Izquierdo, Beteta; Smith 1979, 281.

47. Alejo, finance undersecretary and state industries secretary under Echeverría, emphasizes the same point.

48. Moctezuma, director of public investment under Díaz Ordaz and finance secretary under López Portillo, does not think there was unusual change, or at least doubts that whatever change occurred mattered much.

49. Beteta agrees. He considers himself an *echeverrista*, an Echeverría supporter, though he was in Finance.

50. Camp, 1980, 78.

51. Smith 1979, 91.

52. On the more leftist bent of the Economics Faculty: Camp 1984a, 58; Beteta concurs at least for the 1970s.

53. Camp 1984a, 121.

54. Camp 1980, 160.

55. Camp 2002, 235, on the "dramatic difference" in elites born after 1940; 239, on their attending private universities and earning U.S. economics degrees; 240, on post-1940 political elites' wealthier background.

56. Castañeda 1999, 71.

57. Cosío Villegas 1975, 39.

58. Cosío Villegas 1974, 22–24.

59. Cosío Villegas 1974, 20.

60. Camp 1980, 50.

61. Camp 1980, 50.

62. Hirschman 1979, 84–86.

63. Urquidi, Bracamontes, Flores de la Peña.

64. Camp 1984a, 147.

65. Camp 1980, 208.

66. Hirschman 1979, 95.

67. Frank 1969, 354.

68. Flores Olea 1972, 471.

69. González Casanova 1970, 147.

70. Muñoz Ledo. Ibarra, Mexico City director of ECLA and an advisor in important administration economic debates, saw the economic model of the 1950s and 1960s as deteriorating.

71. Tello 1979, 53.

72. Solís 1967, 86.

73. Solís 1973, 449–450.

74. Cosío Villegas 1974, 50.

75. Castañeda 1999, 116.

76. Quoted by Krauze 1997, 747. Ortiz Mena saw Echeverría as a demagogue. Guillermo Barnes says he "wanted power and wanted to move things left."

77. Cosío Villegas 1974, 16–17.

78. Newell and Rubio 1984, 130.

79. Cordera and Tello 1981b, 68.

80. Cordera and Tello 1981a, 56. Basáñez 1996, 155, says that satisfaction with the successes of the 1950s and 1960s dominated public discourse until the Echeverría campaign challenged it.

81. Solís 1981, 67–68; Tello 1979, 78.

82. Bracamontes, Romero Pérez, González Blanco.

83. Rafael Izquierdo 1995, 47, confirms the lack of cabinet meetings.

84. Likewise Urquidi, Barnes, and Muñoz Ledo comment on the mass or incoherent meetings that accomplished little.

85. Beteta.

86. Bank of Mexico Director Ernesto Fernández Hurtado, an official at the opposite end of the political spectrum from de Oteyza, agrees that López Portillo's ascent to Finance was in preparation for the presidency. Zapata agrees that Echeverría was thinking that López Portillo would be his successor when he appointed him finance secretary but does not think that is why he fired Margáin. Flores de la Peña notes that Echeverría had specifically requested that he appoint López Portillo as a subsecretary in State Industries at the beginning of the administration so he could learn about economic problems. He thinks that even then Echeverría was thinking of his friend as a possible presidential successor.

87. Camp 1984b, 591. Smith 1991, 373, and Bailey 1988, 38, agree that Echeverría chose López Portillo because he lacked political support and would be the easiest candidate to control.

88. Camp 1976, 54–55, footnote 10, says Moya had stronger support from *grupos;* Rosa Luz Alegría, quoted in Castañeda 1999, 368, says López Portillo had no *grupo;* Smith 1979, 288 says the same; Bracamontes thinks Moya "possibly had most support." No source suggests a contradictory account.

89. Castañeda 1999, 362.

90. Smith 1991, 373.
91. Castaneda 1999, 371–372.
92. Smith 1979, 282.
93. Castañeda 1999, 352.
94. Calculated from the same data as used for Table 4.3, Salinas 1992 (*Cuarto Informe de Gobierno: Anexo*).
95. Federal Electricity Commission (CFE) spending from Salinas 1992 (*Cuarto Informe, clasificación sectoral*), 172–177. Echeverría himself says he put the CFE under Finance (Castañeda 1999, 82), surely to promote his candidate; it was under State Industries in other administrations.

CHAPTER EIGHT

1. Camp 1980, 50.
2. Smith 1979, 303.
3. Newell and Rubio 1984, 201; Teichman 1988, 114.
4. Buffie 1990, 431.
5. Newell and Rubio 1984, 205; Smith 1979, 312.
6. Newell and Rubio 1984, 206; Aguayo 2000, 243.
7. Muñoz Ledo.
8. Carrillo Castro 1981, 503.
9. De Oteyza and Ojeda gave the same list, but Ojeda forgot Izquierdo. López Portillo Romano (1994, 92) gives the same list but omits Interior.
10. Carrillo Castro 1981, 508.
11. López Portillo Romano 1994, 89. His full name is José Ramón López Portillo Romano. In the text, I omit the matronymic Romano and refer to him as José Ramón López Portillo, the name he usually goes by. Moctezuma, Tello, and Solana concur that the president made the final decisions.
12. Castañeda 1999, 380–382.
13. Langston 1995, 269.
14. Gómez Villanueva.
15. Castañeda 1999, 381.
16. Castañeda 1999, 117, 119.
17. Likewise Alejo, de Oteyza, Moctezuma, and de la Madrid.
18. Bailey 1988, 45.
19. The quotes in this paragraph are from Emilio Carrillo Gamboa. He is a friend of Carlos Tello and was director general of Teléfonos de México (Telmex). De la Madrid said that López Portillo fired both secretaries precisely to maintain the balance point of the scale (*la fiel de la balanza*).
20. Cordera and Tello 1981a, 59–66.
21. Tello 1979, 37, 56–57, 61, 199–202.

22. Cordera and Tello 1981a, 115; similarly Cordera and Tello 1981b, 60, from a November 1980 talk.

23. Cordera and Tello 1981a, 9, 14.

24. He is referred to as Oteyza or de Oteyza. I have used just de Oteyza to avoid confusion.

25. López Portillo Romano 1994, 124; de Oteyza.

26. García Sáinz is considered an economic conservative by all sources. On Ibarra, see the section, "Ideological polarization."

27. Muñoz Ledo.

28. Ojeda, Alejo, Suárez Mier; Grayson 1984, 173.

29. Quoted in Grayson 1984, 173.

30. Bailey 1988, 78.

31. Ojeda.

32. López Portillo Romano 1994, 153.

33. Likewise Romero Kolbeck.

34. Castañeda 1999, 165.

35. *Economic Report of the President*, 1995, Table B 72. The interest rates refer to commercial paper, but the increases are about the same in all categories.

36. Lustig 1998, 26, 233. She cites economists including Guillermo Ortiz, Carlos Bazdresch, and Rudiger Dornbusch (conservative to mainstream), as well as Jaime Ros and Lance Taylor (progressive).

37. Díaz Alejandro 1987, 21, on this sentence and the next.

38. Cárdenas 1996, 142.

39. Rodrik 1999, 78.

40. Lustig 1998, 23; similarly Buffie 1990, 441.

41. De Oteyza and de la Madrid; Castañeda 1999, 187–188; Teichman 1988, 106–107.

42. De Oteyza.

43. It is sometimes said that one parent was Spanish, but both were (de Oteyza).

44. Likewise de la Madrid and López Portillo quoted in Castañeda 1999, 126.

45. There is some question whether López Portillo approved. Ojeda says he did, as does Bailey 1988, 51–52, and Grayson 1984, 177, infers that he did. López Portillo himself claims he only approved the increase pending a discussion in the economic cabinet (López Portillo Romano 1994, 161).

46. Teichman 1988, 108.

47. Grayson 1984, 177.

48. Castañeda 1999, 126.

49. Grayson 1984, 178; Teichman 1988, 108.

50. López Portillo Romano 1994, 158, 161. De Oteyza, also on the left, concurred that the oil pricing episode was when the economic situation became "really grave."

51. Zedillo 1985, 313. Romero Kolbeck; Teichman 1988, 113–114; and Bazdresch and Levy 1991, 249, 251, also consider the oil price episode a critical turning point.

52. Lustig 1998, 23.

53. Buffie 1990, 442.

54. Lustig 1998, 27.

55. Lustig 1998, 21.

56. De Oteyza, Ojeda interviews.

57. López Portillo Romano 1994, 163–164.

58. Lustig 1998, 22; Buffie 1990, 435; Zedillo 1985, 311. A better way to calculate deficits in an inflationary economy shows an even larger jump. Inflation erodes the principal remaining on public debt (higher interest payments implicitly pay that principal). An adjustment taking this phenomenon into account thus shows the state as paying off its debt faster than unadjusted figures given in the text. By the adjusted method, the real public sector deficit was 3.7 percent in 1980, not a grave problem, and 13.76 percent in 1981—disaster level (Gil Díaz 1984, Table A-5).

59. Lustig 1998, 24; Zedillo 1985, 313; Buffie 1990, 446.

60. Gil Díaz 1984, 351.

61. Zedillo 1985, 313; Buffie 1990, 442.

62. Buffie 1990, 437; Zedillo 1985, 310.

63. Suárez Mier.

64. Zedillo 1985, 306, 308; Lustig 1998, 21.

65. Zedillo 1985, 306; Buffie 1990, 440, shows a smaller increase.

66. Zedillo 1985, 314.

67. De la Madrid, Ibarra, de Oteyza, Ojeda. López Portillo from López Portillo Romano 1994, 160.

68. Zedillo 1985, 312; Buffie 1990, 442.

69. López Portillo Romano 1994, 160.

70. Zedillo 1985, 313; Buffie 1990, 442; López Portillo Romano 1994, 165. Ojeda says that after the oil price fiasco the president gave instructions that budgets should be cut 10 percent. Romero Kolbeck doubts there was any agreement to cut spending: "I wish there had been."

71. Zedillo 1985, 312; de la Madrid and de Oteyza.

72. López Portillo Romano 1994, 169.

73. Ibarra quoted in Castañeda 1999, 407; Guillermo Barnes, a former Finance official; Manuel Camacho Solís; José Ramón López Portillo Romano 1994, 147; and Grayson 1984, 174, all agree that de la Madrid spent to build support for the nomination.

74. López Portillo Romano 1994, 160.

75. August budget estimate (490 billion pesos) and post-nomination budget estimates (767 billion pesos) are from López Portillo Romano 1994, 168–169; original planned level (415 billion pesos) and final result (865 billion pesos) are

from Zedillo 1985, 313. Exchange rate is from International Monetary Fund, *International Financial Statistics Yearbook 2000*, 698.

76. Castañeda 1999, 400–401.

77. López Portillo Romano 1994, 167.

78. Castañeda 1999, 142.

79. López Portillo Romano 1994, 145.

80. Moctezuma.

81. Ghigliazza.

82. Newell and Rubio 1984, 208.

83. Nobody seems to agree on terms. Newell and Rubio 1984 use the loaded (not to mention awkward) "liberal-rationalists" and "nationalist-populists" (it is good to be rational, bad to be populist); others use other expressions. Leftist versus rightist are the simplest terms I can find; none of the terms that have been used are very accurate anyway.

84. Newell and Rubio 1984, 207, 209, 224.

85. Newell and Rubio 1984, 215, 220. Centeno 1994, 187–189, and Teichman 1988, 94–95, 102, line up roughly the same opposing teams. Centeno says that "those who favored unlimited production and the expansion of the state's role in the economy dominated"; with falling oil prices and rising interest rates, the economy "went into a tailspin" (1994, 189). Teichman does not see ideological struggle as having caused the crisis (1988, 127).

86. Moctezuma expressed these views in his interview.

87. Thus de Oteyza and Alejo characterize him; I agree based on having interviewed him and read much by him. José Ramón López Portillo, who read the notes of all economic cabinet meetings during his father's presidency, says Ibarra "championed economic nationalism and moderate state-led growth" (1994, 146).

88. Basáñez 1996, 180.

89. Likewise López Portillo Romano 1994, 150, and Castañeda 1999, 391–392. There is debate as to whether Ibarra's presidential ambitions were serious: Mancera is quite certain they were; Camacho Solís more doubtful.

90. López Portillo Romano 1994, 147.

91. Newell and Rubio 1984; Teichman 1988, 102; Centeno 1994, 187.

92. Similarly Camacho Solís.

93. Likewise Ojeda and Gustavo Carvajal, president of the PRI.

94. Schlefer 2003, 143, Table 7.1, attempts to break down all presidential pre-candidates' spending. Unfortunately, the results are intricate and not too useful, in part because an accounting change in 1980 makes it impossible to calculate growth of many ministries' spending for that crucial year. Major transfers to enterprises associated with those ministries had been lumped under a single category of *erogaciones adicionales*, additional spending. In 1980, they were allocated to the individual ministries. Sources of spending data used in this section, except as otherwise noted, are as follows: spending of all ministries is from

Salinas 1992, 168–169. Spending for major industrial firms under State Indus-tries—Fertimex (fertilizers), Concarril (railroad cars), Pipsa (paper), Azucar (sugar), Dina (trucks and buses), and several steel mills—is from Salinas 1992, 176. Spending of CONASUPO (a firm that purchased basic food crops and dis-tributed basic foods) is from Salinas 1992, 175. Federal government investment is from Salinas 1992, 168. Development bank credit is from Salinas 1994, 116. Lending by INFONAVIT (mortgages for workers) is from Salinas 1994, 437. BANRURAL's total financing is from de la Madrid 1986, 941. BANRURAL's subsidies are from Salinas 1992, 172. Land distributed, in thousands of hec-tares, is from Salinas 1994, 191. Mexico City (Federal District) spending is from Salinas 1992, 193.

95. Moctezuma.

96. Buffie 1990, 436.

97. De Oteyza.

98. Fox 1992, 89–90.

99. Fox 1992, 70.

100. Fox 1992, 72, 78.

101. Fox 1992, 122–123.

102. Fox 1992, 123, footnote 82.

103. Two high economic officials, off the record, on the tie between BANRURAL and García Paniagua.

104. Fox 1992, 68.

105. Miguel Mancera, who became Bank of Mexico director in 1982, says that "de Oteyza and company" won the spending battle.

106. Planning and Budget officially controlled parastatal as well as govern-ment spending. Ibarra, Ojeda, and others concur that, this time, what was on paper was the way things worked.

107. De la Madrid, quoted in Castañeda 1999, 187.

108. Off-the-record statements from two high economic officials.

109. These quotes are from Thomas Hobbes, *Leviathan*, Chapter 13, "Of the Natural Condition of Mankind, as concerning their Felicity, and Misery."

110. This episode is from Castañeda 1999, 406.

111. López Portillo Romano 1994, 171–173.

112. Ibarra. All other sources, including Ojeda interview and López Portillo Romano 1994, 171–173, concur that he recommended devaluation, though with-out giving a specific date.

113. Romero Kolbeck. Mancera and López Portillo Romano 1994, 171–173, concur, again without giving a specific date.

114. José Ramón López Portillo says that de la Madrid and Ojeda favored a faster "crawling peg," or gradual devaluation (López Portillo Romano 1994, 171–173). De la Madrid agrees that he supported this approach but says that the exchange rate was not discussed in the economic cabinet.

115. López Portillo Romano 1994, 171–173. The rumor is credited, for ex-

ample, in Ros 1987, 80–81, though he claims no direct knowledge about the matter.

116. He adds that Carlos Tello, still a presidential adviser, and Jorge Espinoza de los Reyes, director of the National Development Bank (Nafinsa), did recommend capital controls, though neither was in the economic cabinet at the time.

117. Mancera notes that the Bank of Mexico was not, and as of 2000 was still not, independent of the president in setting the exchange rate.

118. Romero Kolbeck.

119. Buffie 1990, 433.

120. Bailey 1988, 182.

121. The nominal annual wage index deflated by the consumer price index, both from IMF, *International Financial Statistics* CD, give 0.8 percent real growth for 1982. Minimum wage in Mexico City is from INEGI 1994, Table 5.2.1, deflated by the cost of living for workers in Mexico City, ibid., Table 19.11.

CHAPTER NINE

1. Hernández Rodríguez 1987, 34–35.

2. The list of de la Madrid's inner circle from Finance sector origins is from Hernández Rodríguez 1987, 36. For reasons I do not understand, Hernández Rodríguez does not include Silva Herzog, but his career had paralleled de la Madrid's in Finance, and they were longtime friends (de la Madrid interview).

3. Hernández Rodríguez 1987, 15. López Portillo Romano (1994, 225) says that thirteen of eighteen secretaries came from the financial sector.

4. Hernández Rodríguez 1987, 35.

5. I was unable to interview Carlos Salinas, as he was outside Mexico while I was there, except for a brief and disastrous sweep to promote a book, ending in his hasty retreat.

6. Lustig 1998, 29, 35. I am defining the exchange rate as dollars per peso; thus, a 50 percent devaluation means that one peso is worth half as much U.S. currency. Using the usual (but somewhat confusing) definition of pesos per dollar, as Lustig does, makes the devaluation 100 percent.

7. Lustig 1998, 35.

8. Lustig 1998, 40.

9. Lustig 1998, 55.

10. Castañeda 1999, 417.

11. Castañeda 1999, 416.

12. López Portillo Romano 1994, 297–298.

13. Lustig 1998, 36, confirms that Mexico relaxed fiscal controls. Urquidi (interview) and Castañeda (1999, 417–418) agree, along with others cited later in this chapter, that Salinas inflated spending to win support.

14. This account is from Castañeda 1999, 420.

15. This account is from Silva Herzog. Castañeda relates a slightly different version of it.

16. The figure was actually 4 billion and 44 billion old pesos, the equivalent of 4 million and 44 million new pesos. I translated it into new pesos so as not to give a wildly exaggerated sense of the magnitude.

17. Lustig 1998, 39–40.

18. Labastida.

19. Silva Herzog.

20. Silva Herzog, Labastida, Castañeda 1999, 418–420.

21. López Portillo Romano 1994, 298.

22. López Portillo Romano (1994, 233), citing the president's notes, says: "De la Madrid confirmed that one of his main disappointments and at times even causes for despair was the frequent lack of reliable and timely information and analysis."

23. Silva Herzog.

24. Urquidi supplied this quote.

25. Bravo says Salinas became the "secretary of the whole economy."

26. Suárez Mier.

27. Ortiz Mena 1998, 130–131, 191–205, 207.

28. Ortiz Mena 1998, 200–201.

29. Ortiz Mena 1998, 216.

30. Corona del Rosal 1995, 156.

31. Ortiz Mena 1998, 134–135.

32. Moctezuma on Flores de la Pena's conflict with Finance over control of state-owned firms.

33. López Portillo Romano 1994, 123, confirms the transfer of *fideicomisos* to administrative sectors, without saying why.

34. Quoted in Ortiz Salinas 1988, 14.

35. Taking 1989, the first full year of Salinas' presidency, as a base, the peso was overvalued by 14 percent in 1991, 25 percent in 1992, and 33 percent in 1993 (Cárdenas 1996, 213, Table A.3).

36. Castañeda 1999, 437–438.

37. This is the consensus. Langston (1997b, 30) says that only one member of Echeverría's or López Portillo's factions secured a cabinet post—Pedro Ojeda. A few others such as Jesús Reyes Heroles in Education were at least debatably in one of those factions, but all sources agree with the general conclusion, for example, López Portillo Romano 1994, 201, and Castañeda, 1999, 148–149.

38. Hernández Rodríguez (1987) does an especially persuasive job of articulating the view that de la Madrid drew his cabinet from friends and close associates in Finance and the Bank of Mexico, but it is the consensus, for example, shared by Bailey, 1988, 57, and Langston 1997b, 29.

39. Hernández Rodríguez 1987, 36, 37.

40. Hernández Rodríguez 1987, 253.

41. Hernández Rodríguez 1992, 258–259, 260.

42. Camp 1995a, 50. Adolfo Ruiz Cortines was a technical exception who nevertheless followed the spirit of the rule. Appointed as a compromise candidate after Alemán (born 1900) had tried to succeed himself or appoint his peer Casas Alemán (born 1905), Ruiz Cortines was older (born 1890) but continued to favor the Alemán generation that, according to the normal course of things, should have been favored (Camp 1995a, 50).

43. Camp 1980, 50.

44. He probably favored the generation of the 1930s, but I only have data that he favored the broader generation of the 1920s and 1930s (Camp 1995a, 45). In any event, he favored those born before 1940.

45. Camp 2002, 235.

46. Camp 2002, 236–237, 250.

47. Camp 2002, 239.

48. Bruhn 1997, 86.

49. Bruhn 1997, 325–326.

50. Bruhn 1997, 76.

51. Bruhn 1997, 326.

52. Bruhn 1997, 92.

53. Bruhn 1997, 88, states this claim without calling it disingenuous.

54. Bruhn 1997, 89.

55. Gómez Villanueva.

56. Gómez Villanueva.

57. Bruhn 1997, 97.

58. Bruhn 1997, 97.

59. Bruhn 1997, 113.

60. Castañeda 1999, 449–450.

61. Langston 1997b, 28; likewise Hernández Rodríguez 1992, 252.

62. De la Madrid makes a similar though slightly less explicit statement in Castañeda 1999, 162–163.

63. Castañeda 1999, 427.

64. Labastida says that, unlike Salinas, del Mazo did not have personal conflicts with the Current. Bravo and Castañeda, 1999, 425, both note del Mazo's closeness to López Portillo and his support from labor.

65. Castañeda 1999, 436.

66. López Portillo Romano 1994, 348.

67. Bruhn 1997, 122–122; Hernández Rodríguez 1992, 263; Langston 1997b, 24.

68. Bruhn 1997, 130.

69. *El Financiero*, December 15, 1996, 69.

70. Lustig 1998, 46, notes that it was the pilot case.

71. Silva Herzog.

72. López Portillo Romano 1994, 305.

73. Lustig 1998, 44; Castañeda 1999, 420–421.

74. Ros 1987, 86.

75. Lustig 1998, 46–47.

76. Silva Herzog says he sought to borrow $2 billion; Castañeda (1999, 418) says the Finance team under him thought it could not obtain more than $3 billion. López Portillo Romano (1994, 316) mentions a loan package to the Salinas team of $14.4 billion, though much was not available until mid-April 1987—still in time to help with the nomination.

77. Cárdenas 1996, 146.

78. Credit issued by development banks is from Salinas 1994 (*Sexto Informe de Gobierno: Anexo*), 116. GDP in current pesos is from Cardenas 1996, 214–215.

79. Two former high economic officials agreed in off-the-record comments that development bank lending, revenue sharing with states, and public investment are areas where Salinas might have spent to build support, if he sought to so do. Revenue sharing (*participaciones*), federal government investment, and state-enterprise investment are all from Salinas 1992 (*Cuarto informe de Gobierno: Anexo*), 168.

80. Basáñez 1996, 253, gives the Bolsa index numbers. All inflation corrections calculated from quarterly CPI, from International Monetary Fund, *International Financial Statistics* CD.

81. Basáñez 1996, 254.

82. Basáñez 1996, 254. López Portillo Romano (1994, 334) says 520,000 in 1987.

83. Silva Herzog.

84. Basáñez 1996, 257; Cárdenas 1996, 147.

85. Castañeda 1999, 436. As well, an economic cabinet member—speaking off the record, possibly the same source as mine—told Castañeda that Salinas manipulated the Bolsa.

86. The account of turning brokerage houses into a parallel banking system is from Basáñez 1996, 254–257.

87. At the end of 1987 (I cannot find figures for September when the market was at its height), the total value of securities traded on the Bolsa was 55.6 million new pesos, while the value of Cetes was 28.0 million new pesos (Salinas 1994, 124).

88. Basáñez 1996, 256–257, on this paragraph except as otherwise noted.

89. Cárdenas 1996, 147.

90. Basave Kunhardt 1996, 154, 155.

91. Basave Kunhardt 1996, 154.

92. At the time, Mexico had a controlled exchange rate for major industrial imports (to hold down their cost to domestic firms) and a free exchange rate for most other purposes. On November 18, 1987, the Bank of Mexico withdrew from the foreign-exchange market. Both controlled and free exchange rates fell (gauged in pesos per dollars), becoming effectively indistinguishable and deter-

mined by speculation. The consumer price index hit an annual inflation rate of 159 percent. However, the Bank of Mexico let the peso go before allowing its foreign reserves to be depleted; it ended the year with $13.7 billion (Cárdenas 1996, 147–148).

Particularly because the Bank of Mexico did not let its reserves be depleted, there could be some dispute as to whether 1987 was a crisis. Also, Miguel Mancera, director of the Bank of Mexico, points out that the controlled exchange rate was devalued partly to compensate for the process of slashing trade barriers from 1985 through December 1987, after Mexico's entry into GATT. Although the devaluation increased the price of imports, the drastic cut in tariff levels reduced their price, so he says that the controlled exchange rate devaluation had little or no overall inflationary effect.

However, Mexicans always speak of 1987 as a crisis—de la Madrid agrees Mexico was forced to devalue—and in political terms it was seen as a crisis during the 1988 presidential campaign, when a real opposition emerged. Jonathan Heath (1999) gauges Mexico's crises since 1970 by creating a sort of Richter scale of pressures on the economy, a composite index combining the fall in the exchange rate, the inflation rate, and the loss of foreign reserves. By this gauge, the 1987 crisis fell into Heath's most extreme category, "severe," substantially worse than 1976 but not as bad as 1982 or 1994 (1999, 4–7).

CHAPTER TEN

1. O'Donnell 2001, 809.
2. Roeder 1985.
3. Evans 1995.
4. Centeno 1994, 153, 166.
5. Centeno 1994, 171.
6. Urquidi.
7. Centeno 1994, 170.
8. Heath 1999, 7.
9. Lustig 1998, 55.
10. Kessler 1998.
11. Lustig 1998, 162.
12. Cárdenas 1996, Table A.4, 214–215, for real GDP.
13. Lustig 1998, 162.
14. Centeno 1994, 67.
15. Dresser 1991.
16. Lustig 1998, 164.
17. Lustig 1998, 163–167; Velasco and Cabezas 1998, 153.
18. Lustig 1998, 144–145, gives the current account deficit as 7.4 percent of GDP in 1992, 5.8 percent in 1993, and 7.1 percent in 1994. A calculation based

on Cárdenas 1996, Table A.8, gives 74 percent of capital inflows for 1992–94 as financial investment. Ros 1995 says that current account deficits were comparable in 1993 to what they had been before earlier crises.

19. Many economists agree about this overvaluation: Dornbusch and Werner 1994; Ros 1995; Velasco and Cabezas 1998, 139; Eichengreen and Fishlow 1998, 50. Cárdenas 1996, Table A-3, estimates a comparable range for the peso's real exchange rate in 1981 and in 1993.

20. In 1992 and 1993, trade deficits were $21 and $19 billion dollars, excluding the export-oriented *maquiladora* plants, not an integral part of Mexican industry. The trade deficit including them was $16 billion in 1992 and $8 billion in 1993. The current account deficits were $24 billion in 1992 and $23 billion in 1993. All data are from the Bank of Mexico.

21. *New York Times*, December 17, 1993, D-1.

22. Edwards 1997, 100–101; Salinas 2000, 1,073.

23. *New York Times*, December 17, 1993, D-1.

24. Edwards 1997, 107.

25. Salinas 2000, 1,093–1,094.

26. Cárdenas 1996, 184–185.

27. Cárdenas 1996, 185.

28. Centeno 1994, 3.

29. Salinas 2000, 1,092–1,093.

30. Salinas 2000, 862.

31. Castañeda 1999, 490.

32. *Proceso*, October 22, 2000, 20. Other informed sources, including Urquidi and Gamboa de Buen, believe this story is essentially correct.

33. Corona del Rosal 1995, 290–291.

34. Langston 1995, 276.

35. Among others, Smith 1997, 40, argues that Chiapas itself was not a serious threat.

36. Castañeda 1999, 488–489.

37. *Proceso*, October 22, 2000, 16–20; Castañeda 1999, 488–498.

38. Both quotes are from *Proceso*, October 22, 2000, 17–18.

39. Salinas 2000, 884–885.

40. Castañeda 1999, 456; Smith 1997, 43; Camacho Solís.

41. Bruhn 1997.

42. Smith 1997, 43.

43. Lustig 1998, 167; Edwards 1997, 118.

44. Edwards 1997, 118.

45. Lustig 1998, 168.

46. Aspe has a policy of not commenting on the 1994 crisis.

47. Edwards 1997, 117.

48. Lustig 1998, 162.

49. *Proceso*, October 15, 2000, 31, quotes Antonio Sánchez Díaz on this and the following citation.

50. González Blanco and Gamboa de Buen; *Proceso*, October 15, 2000.

51. Salinas 2000, 1,114.

52. Izquierdo 1995, 47.

53. Hirschman 1979.

54. Kaufman 1979.

55. Hirschman 1979, 95.

56. Stallings 1990, 156–159.

57. Urrutia 1991, 384.

58. Field and Higley 1985, 27.

59. Kline 1990, 240–242.

60. Gamarra 1994, 104 and footnote 1.

61. Gamarra 1994, 107.

62. Gamarra 1994, 109.

63. Gamarra 1994, 110.

64. Schamis 2002, 90.

65. Corrales 2002, 2p.

66. My account of the economics of the Argentine crisis comes largely from Paul Krugman's talk on the Argentine crisis at the University of Texas, April 22, 2002. He emphasizes the importance of external shocks and circumstantial events; he does not believe that the fiscal deficit was big enough to explain it. Aside from finding Krugman persuasive, I follow his account because it is the most *difficult* one to square with internal political causes. If most other economic stories, such as that of the IMF, that place more emphasis on fiscal deficits are correct, they leave more room for domestic political causes, strengthening the argument I lay out, following Corrales (2002) and Schamis (2002).

67. Corrales 2002.

68. Corrales 2002, 33.

69. Corrales 2002, 34.

70. Schamis 2002, 84–85.

71. Corrales 2001, 21.

72. The deficit data come from Corrales 2001, 21. Krugman says the deficit was not enough to cause crisis.

73. Corrales 2001, 20.

74. Corrales speaks of "nonadaptation" (2002, 34–35), but the meaning seems to be economic illiteracy.

75. The deficit figure itself is from Corrales 2001, 21, taken from IMF data.

76. Schamis 2002, 86–87.

77. Schamis 2002, 85, 87.

78. Corrales 2002, 35.

79. Schamis 2002, 85.

80. Corrales 2001, 21.

81. Schamis 2002, 85.

82. Burton, Gunther, and Higley 1992; Field, Higley, and Burton 1990. They also say that "elite convergence," a slower motion version of elite settlement, can achieve the same goals.

83. Field and Higley 1985, 19.

84. Weingast 1997, 260.

85. Weingast 1997, 254.

APPENDIX B

1. Ames 1987.

2. Ames uses the change in reserves from the previous year but current GDP. Instead of expressing the change in reserves as a percentage, he sets a dummy equal to 1 if reserves increase 50 percent or more and another equal to 1 if they fall 50 percent or more. The 50 percent mark does not capture the Mexican situation well; for example, during the late 1970s when resources were pouring in from abroad, reserves rose 35 or 40 percent a year for several years in a row. I could have used 30 percent instead of 50 percent as a cutoff, but it seemed less arbitrary to use the numerical percentage of change in reserves. The point is not to predict how reserves affected spending but only to control for them.

3. Solís 1981, 62.

4. Kennedy 1992, 140–141

5. Kennedy 1992, 257.

6. This replication, however, still expressed the change of reserves in percent rather than via dummy variables.

INTERVIEW LIST

This list includes public officials, as well as a few private sector and labor leaders. Academics who were interviewed are generally included only if they were also high officials or had firsthand access to information about policymaking.

Abedrop, Carlos (president of Banco Atlántico), August 14, 1997, Mexico City.

Alejo, Francisco Javier (secretary of State Industries, 1975–76), October 11, 2000, Mexico City.

Barnes, Guillermo (subsecretary for administration, or *oficial mayor*, and other posts in Finance; leader of PRI delegation from Mexico City in late 1990s), March 23, 2000, Mexico City.

Bassols, Angel (academic; father was secretary of Interior and opposition party leader), October 23, 2000, Mexico City.

Bazdresch, Carlos (economist known for work on economic crises), April 17, 2000, Mexico City.

Beteta, Mario Ramón (economic posts beginning in 1960, subsecretary and secretary of Finance, 1970–76), October 12, 16, and 24; November 16, 2000, Mexico City.

Borja Navarrete, Gilberto (president of Grupo ICA), April 7, 1997, Mexico City.

Bracamontes, Luis Enrique (subsecretary of Public Works, 1952–64; secretary of Public Works, 1970–76), October 18, 2000, Mexico City.

Bravo, Victor (advisor to Alfredo del Mazo, 1987 presidential precandidate; father was education secretary, 1970–76), December 7, 2000, Mexico City.

Camacho Solís, Manuel (economic posts, 1972–88; political advisor to Carlos Salinas; head of Federal District, 1988–93; presidential precandidate), December 5, 2000, Mexico City.

Cárdenas, Enrique (economist known for macroeconomic history of Mexico), April 14, 2000, Puebla.

Carrera, Eduardo (executive secretary, CIHAC, construction industry group), February 3, 1997, Mexico City.

Carrillo Gamboa, Emilio (Telmex official, 1960–75; director of Telmex, 1975–87; father was finance minister 1952–58), August 15, 2000, Mexico City.

Carvajal Moreno, Gustavo (president of National Executive Committee of PRI, 1979–81; father was interior secretary, 1952–58), November 17, 2000, Mexico City.

Chávez Presa, Jorge (head of budget control in Finance in 1990s; economist in Bank of Mexico in 1980s), August 25, 2000, Mexico City.

Corona del Rosal, Alfonso (politician since the 1940s; governor of Mexico City, 1967–70; presidential precandidate 1969), March 31, 2000, Mexico City.

De la Madrid, Miguel (Bank of Mexico and Finance, 1960–79; secretary of Planning and Budget 1979–82; president of Mexico, 1982–88), November 10, 2000, Mexico City.

De la Vega Domínguez, Jorge (commerce secretary 1977–82; presidential precandidate 1981; president of PRI 1986–88), December 12, 2000, Mexico City.

De Oteyza, José Andrés (economic posts since 1965; secretary of State Industries, 1976–82), August 15, 2000, Mexico City.

Echeverría Álvarez, Luis (subsecretary and secretary of Interior 1958–70; president of Mexico, 1970–76), December 16 and 19, 2000, Mexico City.

Fernández Hurtado, Ernesto (Bank of Mexico, 1948–70; director of Bank of Mexico, 1970–76), October 27, 2000, Mexico City.

Flores de la Peña, Horacio (economic official, 1959–70; director of Economics Faculty, National Autonomous University of Mexico; secretary of State Industries, 1970–75), December 6, 2000, Mexico City.

Gamboa de Buen, Jorge (urban development director of Mexico City, 1988–94), August 9, 2000, Mexico City.

Ghigliazza, Sergio (Bank of Mexico official since 1960s, assistant director, 1985–90; director, Center of Latin American Monetary Studies), October 20, 2000, Mexico City.

Giménez Cacho, Luis (industrialist, steel industry, beginning in 1940s), February 3, 1997, Cuernavaca.

Gómez Villanueva, Augusto (secretary of Agrarian Reform, 1970–75; presidential precandidate), December 18, 2000, Mexico City.

González Blanco Garrido, José Patrocinio (subdirector and director of Public Investment, 1960–64; interior secretary, 1992–94; father was labor secretary, 1958–70; father-in-law was finance secretary, 1958–70), November 20, 2000, Mexico City.

Gout, Gonzalo (construction industry entrepreneur, beginning in 1950s; vice president, CONCAMIN, industry federation, 1960s) February 25, 1997, Mexico City.

Ibarra, David (U.N. Economic Commission for Latin America official 1958–73; finance secretary 1977–82), August 28, 1997, May 2, 2000, Mexico City.

Izquierdo, Rafael (advisor to finance secretary, 1964–70; advisor to President, 1976–82), May 12, 2000, Mexico City.

Labastida Ochoa, Francisco (state industries secretary, 1982–86; governor of Sinaloa; interior secretary, 1998–99; presidential candidate 2000), December 7, 2000, Mexico City.

Luján, Berta (leader of independent union, the Authentic Labor Front), August 26, 1997, Mexico City.

Mancera Aguayo, Miguel (economic official since 1957; director general of Bank of Mexico, 1982–96), August 24, 2000, Mexico City.

Martínez, Ifigenia (economic official in 1960s and 1970s; opposition party leader, *Partido de la Revolución Democrática;* academic), September 4, 1997, Mexico City.

Moctezuma, Julio Rodolfo (economic official since 1959; finance secretary, 1976–77), May 19, 2000, Mexico City.

Moreno Toscano, Alejandra (secretary general of Social Development, Mexico City, 1988–94; father was prominent politician, 1940s to 1960s), November 9, 2000, Mexico City.

Moreno Valle, Rafael (secretary of health, 1964–68; close friend of President Gustavo Díaz Ordaz), October 17, 2000, Mexico City.

Muñoz Ledo, Porfirio (labor secretary, 1972–75; close to President Luis Echeverría; education secretary, 1976–77; opposition party leader 1987 through 1990s), November 24, 2000, Mexico City.

Ojeda Paullada, Pedro (attorney general, 1971–76; labor secretary, 1976–81; presidential precandidate), November 14, 2000, Mexico City.

Ortiz Mena, Antonio (director of Social Security, 1952–58; finance secretary 1958–70; president of Inter-American Development Bank, 1971–88), May 16, 2000, Cuernavaca.

Rey Romay, Benito (director of National Finance Bank, 1970–81; academic), January 30, 1997, Mexico City.

Romero Kolbeck, Gustavo (economic posts since 1944; director of Bank of Mexico, 1976–82), November 21, 2000, Mexico City.

Romero Pérez, Humberto (public relations director for President Adolfo Ruiz Cortines, 1953–58; private secretary for President Adolfo López Mateos, 1958–64; journalist), November 15, 2000, Mexico City.

Salinas Lozano, Raúl (economic posts since 1946; secretary of Industry and Commerce, 1958–64; father of President Carlos Salinas), July 11, 2000, Acapulco.

Sánchez Navarro, Juan (director general of Grupo Modelo; private sector spokesman), August 11, 1997, Mexico City.

Silva Herzog, Jesús (economic posts since 1956; finance secretary, 1982–86), November 9, 2000, Mexico City.

Solana, Fernando (secretary general of National Autonomous University of Mexico, 1966–70; secretary of three ministries—Industry and Commerce, Education, and Foreign Relations—during the years 1976–94), August 15, 2000, Mexico City.

Suárez Mier, Manuel (Bank of Mexico official since 1960s; academic), March 24, 2000, Mexico City.

Tello, Carlos (economic posts since 1959; secretary of Planning and Budget, 1976–77; director general of Bank of Mexico, 1982; advisor to President José López Portillo), September 2, 1997, Mexico City.

Urquidi, Victor (economic posts since 1940s; director of the United Nations Economic Commission for Latin America's Mexico City office in 1950s; advisor to finance secretary, 1958–64; president, Colegio de Mexico, 1966–85), May 4, 5, and 15, 2000, Mexico City.

Zapata Loredo, Fausto (subsecretary of presidency, close to President Luis Echeverría, 1970–76; journalist), December 13, 2000, Mexico City.

BIBLIOGRAPHY

Aguayo Quezada, Sergio, ed. 2000. *El almanaque mexicano*. Mexico City: Editorial Grijalbo and Hechos Confiables.

———. 1998. *1968: Los archivos de la violencia*. Mexico City: Grijalbo.

Alemán Velasco, Miguel. 1997. *No siembro para mi: Biografía de Adolfo Ruiz Cortines*. Mexico City: Editorial Diana.

Almond, Gabriel A., and Sidney Verba. 1965. *The Civic Culture: Political Attitudes and Democracy in Five Nations*. Boston: Little, Brown.

Ames, Barry. 1987. *Political Survival: Politicians and Public Policy in Latin America*. Berkeley: University of California Press.

Amsden, Alice H. 1989. *Asia's Next Giant: South Korea and Late Industrialization*. Oxford: Oxford University Press.

Bailey, John J. 1988. *Governing Mexico: The Statecraft of Crisis Management*. New York: Macmillan.

Banco de México. *Indicadores del Sector Externo* (periodical). Mexico City.

Banco Nacional de Comercio Exterior. 1971. *México: La política económica del nuevo gobierno*. Mexico City.

Basáñez, Miguel. 1996. *La Lucha por la hegemonía en México: 1968–1990*, tenth edition. Mexico City: Siglo Veintiuno Editores.

Basave Kunhardt, Jorge. 1996. *Los grupos de capital financiero en México (1974–1995)*. Mexico City: Instituto de Investigaciones Económicas, Universidad Nacional Autónoma de México.

Bazdresch, Carlos, and Santiago Levy. 1991. "Populism and Economic Policy in Mexico, 1970–1982." In *The Macroeconomics of Populism in Latin America*, edited by Rudiger Dornbusch and Sebastian Edwards. Chicago: University of Chicago Press.

Bennett, Douglas C., and Kenneth E. Sharpe. 1985. *Transnational Corporations Versus the State: The Political Economy of the Mexican Auto Industry*. Princeton: Princeton University Press.

Bizberg, Ilán. 1990. *Estado y sindicalismo en México*. Mexico City: El Colegio de México.

———. 1984. "Política laboral y acción sindical en México (1976–1982)." *Foro Internacional* 25(2): 166–189 (Oct.–Dec.).

Boltvinik, Julio, and Enrique Hernández Laos. 1981. "Origen de la Crisis Industrial: El Agotamiento del Modelo de Sustitución de Importaciones. Un Análisis Preliminar." In *Desarrollo y crisis de la economía Mexicana: Ensayos de interpretación histórica*, edited by Rolando Cordera. Mexico City: Fondo de Cultura Económica.

Brandenburg, Frank. 1964. *The Making of Modern Mexico*. Englewood Cliffs: Prentice-Hall.

Bruhn, Kathleen. 1997. *Taking on Goliath: The Emergence of a New Left Party and the Struggle for Democracy in Mexico*. University Park: Pennsylvania State University Press.

Buffie, Edward F. 1990. "Economic Policy and Foreign Debt in Mexico." In *Developing Country Debt and Economic Performance*, vol. 2, edited by Jeffrey D. Sachs. Chicago: University of Chicago Press.

Burton, Michael, Richard Gunther, and John Higley. 1992. "Introduction: Elite Transformations and Democratic Regimes." In *Elites and Democratic Consolidation in Latin America and Southern Europe*, edited by John Higley and Richard Gunther. Cambridge: Cambridge University Press.

Burton, Michael G., and John Higley. 1987. "Invitation to Elite Theory: The Basic Contentions Reconsidered." In *Power Elites and Organizations*, edited by G. William Domhoff and Thomas R. Dye. Newbury Park, Calif.: Sage Publications.

Camp, Roderic Ai. 2002. *Mexico's Mandarins: Crafting a Power Elite for the 21st Century*. Berkeley: University of California Press.

———. 1995a. *Political Recruitment across Two Centuries: Mexico, 1884–1991*. Austin: University of Texas Press.

———. 1995b. *Mexican Political Biographies: 1935–1993*, third edition. Austin: University of Texas Press.

———. 1993. *Politics in Mexico*. New York: Oxford University Press.

———. 1990. "Camarillas in Mexican Politics: The Case of the Salinas Cabinet." *Mexican Studies/Estudios Mexicanos* 6(1): 85–107 (winter).

———. 1985. *Intellectuals and the State in Twentieth-Century Mexico*. Austin: University of Texas Press.

———. 1984a. *The Making of a Government: Political Leaders in Modern Mexico*. Tucson: University of Arizona Press.

———. 1984b. "Mexican Presidential Candidates: Changes and Portents for the Future." *Polity* 16(4): 588–605 (summer).

———. 1980. *Mexico's Leaders: Their Education and Recruitment*. Tucson: University of Arizona Press.

———. 1976. "El Sistema Mexicano y las Decisiones Sobre el Personal Político." *Foro Internacional* 17(1): 51–83 (July–Sept.)

Cárdenas, Enrique. 1996. *La política económica en México, 1950–1994*. Mexico City: Colegio de México and Fondo de Cultura Económica.

———. 1994. *La hacienda pública y la política económica, 1929–1958*. Mexico City: Colegio de México and Fondo de Cultura Económica.

———. 1993. "La política económica en la época de Cárdenas." *El Trimestre Económico* 60(3): 675–697 (July–Sept.)

Cárdenas, Lázaro. 1973. *Obras. I-Apuntes 1941–1956*, vol. 2. Mexico City: UNAM.

Cardoso, Fernando Henrique, and Faletto, Enzo. 1979. *Dependency and Development in Latin America*, translated by Marjory Mattingly Urquidi. Berkeley: University of California Press.

Carr, Barry. 1991. "Labor and the Political Left in Mexico." In *Unions, Workers, and the State in Mexico*, edited by Kevin J. Middlebrook. San Diego: Center for U.S.-Mexican Studies.

Carrillo Castro, Alejandro. 1981. "El sistema nacional de planeación, las nuevas estructuras administrativas y procesos institucionales que lo conforman." In Secretaría de Programación y Presupuesto, *Aspectos jurídicos de la planeación en México*. Mexico City: Editorial Porrúa.

Carrillo Flores, Antonio. 1954. Diary. Provided by his son, Emilio Carrillo Gamboa. Mexico City.

Casar, José I., Carlos Márquez Padilla, Susana Marván, Gonzalo Rodríguez G., and Jaime Ros. 1990. *La organización industrial en México*. Mexico City: Siglo Veintiuno.

Castañeda, Jorge G. 1999. *La herencia: Arqueología de la sucesión presidencial en México*. Mexico City: Aguilar, Altea, Taurus, Alfaguara.

Centeno, Miguel Ángel. 1994. *Democracy within Reason: Technocratic Revolution in Mexico*. University Park: Pennsylvania State University Press.

Collier, Ruth Berins, and David Collier. 1991. *Shaping the Political Arena: Critical Junctures, the Labor Movement, and Regime Dynamics in Latin America*. Princeton: Princeton University Press.

Cordera, Rolando, and Carlos Tello. 1981a. *México: La disputa por la nación*. Mexico City: Siglo Veintiuno.

———. 1981b. "Perspectivas y opciones de la sociedad mexicana." In *Las relaciones México Estados Unidos*, edited by Carlos Tello and Clark Reynolds, Lecturas 43. Mexico City: Fondo de Cultura Económica.

Córdoba, José. 1994. "Mexico." In *The Political Economy of Policy Reform*, edited by John Williamson. Washington: Institute for International Economics.

Cornelius, Wayne A., and Ann L. Craig. 1991. *The Mexican Political System in Transition*. Monograph Series, 35. San Diego: Center for U.S.-Mexican Studies.

Cornelius, Wayne A. 1975. *Politics and the Migrant Poor in México City*. Stanford: Stanford University Press.

Corona del Rosal, Alfonso. 1995. *Mis memorias políticas*. Mexico City: Grijalbo.

Corrales, Javier. 2002. "The Politics of Argentina's Meltdown." *World Policy Journal* 19:3 (fall).

———. 2001. "The Political Causes of Argentina's Recession." Washington: Woodrow Wilson Center.

Cosío Villegas, Daniel. 1975. *La sucesión presidencial.* Mexico City: Cuadernos de Joaquín Mortiz.

———. 1974. *El estilo personal de gobernar.* Mexico City: Cuadernos de Joaquín Mortiz.

Craig, Ann L., and Wayne A. Cornelius. 1989. "Political Culture in Mexico: Continuities and Revisionist Interpretations." In *The Civic Culture Revisited,* edited by Gabriel A. Almond and Sidney Verba. Newbury Park, Calif.: Sage.

De la Madrid Hurtado, Miguel. 1986. *Cuarto informe de gobierno. Estadístico,* vol. 12. Mexico City: Presidencia de la República.

Díaz Alejandro, Carlos. 1987. "Some Aspects of the Development Crisis in Latin America." In *Latin American Debt and the Adjustment Crisis,* edited by Rosemary Thorp and Laurence Whitehead. Pittsburgh: University of Pittsburgh Press.

Dillon, Sam. 2000. "Mexico's Chief Justice Strives to Oil a Creaking System." *New York Times,* A-3 (March 10).

Dornbusch, Rudiger, and Alejandro Werner. 1994. "Mexico: Stabilization, Reform, and No Growth." Brookings Papers on Economic Activity, no. 1. Washington: Brookings Institution.

Dornbusch, Rudiger, and Sebastian Edwards. 1991. "The Macroeconomics of Populism." In *The Macroeconomics of Populism in Latin America,* edited by Rudiger Dornbusch and Sebastian Edwards. Chicago: University of Chicago Press.

Dresser, Denise. 1991. *Neopopulist Solutions to Neoliberal Problems.* La Jolla, Calif.: Center for U.S.-Mexican Studies.

Eatwell, John, and Lance Taylor. 2000. *Global Finance at Risk: The Case for International Regulation.* New York: New Press.

———. 1998a. "The Performance of Liberalized Capital Markets." Working paper no. 8, CEPA Working Paper Series III. New York: Center for Economic Policy Analysis, New School for Social Research. September.

———. 1998b. "International Capital Markets and the Future of Economic Policy." Working paper no. 9, CEPA Working Paper Series III. New York: Center for Economic Policy Analysis, New School for Social Research. September.

Economic Report of the President. 1995. Washington: U.S. Government Printing Office.

Economist, The. Weekly periodical. London.

Edwards, Sebastian. 1997. "Bad Luck or Bad Policies? An Economic Analysis of the Crisis." In *Mexico 1994: Anatomy of an Emerging-Market Crash,* edited by Sebastian Edwards and Moisés Naím. Washington: Carnegie Endowment for International Peace.

Eichengreen, Barry. 1999. *Toward a New International Financial Architec-*

ture: A Practical Post-Asia Agenda. Washington: Institute for International Economics.

Eichengreen, Barry, and Albert Fishlow. 1998. "Contending with Capital Flows: What Is Different about the 1990s?" In *Capital Flows and Financial Crises*, edited by Miles Kahler. Ithaca: Cornell University Press.

Eichengreen, Barry, and Charles Wyplosz. 1993. "The Unstable EMS." *Brookings Papers on Economic Activity* 1: 51–143. Washington: Brookings Institution.

Esquivel, Gerardo, and Felipe Larraín B. 1998. "Explaining Currency Crises." Cambridge: Harvard Institute for International Development. June.

Evans, Peter. 1995. *Embedded Autonomy: States and Industrial Transformation*. Princeton: Princeton University Press.

Field, Lowell G., John Higley, and Michael G. Burton. 1990. "A New Elite Framework for Political Sociology." Revue Européene des Sciences Sociales. 28(88): 148–182.

Field, Lowell G., and John Higley. 1985. *Research in Politics and Society*. 1:1–44.

Financiero, El. Newspaper. Mexico City.

Fishlow, Albert. 1990. "The Latin American State." *Journal of Economic Perspectives* 4(3): 61–74 (summer).

Fitzgerald, E. V. K. 1978. "The Fiscal Crisis of the Latin American State." In *Taxation and Economic Development*, edited by J. F. J. Toyo. London: Frank Cass.

Flores Olea, Víctor. 1972. "Poder, legitimidad y política en México." In *El perfil de México en 1980*, vol. 3, by Jorge Martínez Ríos and nineteen other authors, including Víctor Flores Olea. Mexico City: Siglo Veintiuno.

Foweraker, Joe. 1990. "Popular Movements and Political Change in Mexico." In *Popular Movements and Political Change in Mexico*, edited by Joe Foweraker and Ann L. Craig. Boulder: Lynne Rienner.

———. 1989. "Popular Movements and the Transformation of the System." In *Mexico's Alternative Political Futures*, edited by Wayne A. Cornelius, Judith Gentleman, and Peter H. Smith. Monograph Series, 30. San Diego: Center for U.S. Mexican Studies.

Fox, Jonathan. 1994. "The Difficult Transition from Clientelism to Citizenship: Lessons from Mexico." *World Politics* 46 (2):151–184.

———. 1992. *The Politics of Food in Mexico: State Power and Social Mobilization*. Ithaca: Cornell University Press.

Franco G. S., and J. Fernando. 1991. "Labor Law and the Labor Movement in Mexico." In *Unions, Workers, and the State in Mexico*, edited by Kevin J. Middlebrook. San Diego: Center for U.S.-Mexican Studies.

Frank, Andre Gunder. 1969. *Latin America: Underdevelopment or Revolution*. New York: Monthly Review Press.

Frankel, Jeffrey A. 1998. "The Asian Model, the Miracle, the Crisis and the Fund," talk delivered at the U.S. International Trade Commission (April 16).

Gamarra, Eduardo A. 1994. "Crafting Political Support for Stabilization: Political Pacts and the New Economic Policy in Bolivia." In *Democracy, Markets, and Structural Reform in Contemporary Latin America: Argentina, Bolivia, Brazil, Chile, and Mexico*, edited by William C. Smith, Carlos H. Acuña, and Eduardo A. Gamarra. New Brunswick, N.J.: Transaction Publishers.

Gil Díaz, Francisco. 1984. "Mexico's Path from Stability to Inflation." In *World Economic Growth*, edited by Arnold C. Harberger. San Francisco: ICS Press.

Goldthorpe, John H. 1978. "The Current Inflation: Towards a Sociological Account." In *The Political Economy of Inflation*, edited by Fred Hirsch and John H. Goldthorpe. Cambridge: Harvard University Press.

Golub, Stephen S. 1991. "The Political Economy of the Latin American Debt Crisis." *Latin American Research Review* 26(1): 175–215.

González Casanova, Pablo. 1970. *Democracy in Mexico*, second edition, translated by Danielle Salti. New York: Oxford University Press.

Grayson, George W. 1984. *The United States and Mexico: Patterns of Influence.* New York: Praeger.

Grindle, Marilee S. 1977. "Patrons and Clients in the Bureaucracy: Career Networks in Mexico." *Latin American Research Review* 12(1): 37–66.

Guillén Romo, Héctor. 1984. *Orígenes de la crisis en México: Inflación y endeudamiento externo (1940–1982).* Mexico City: Ediciones Era.

Haggard, Stephan. 1990. *Pathways from the Periphery: The Politics of Growth in the Newly Industrializing Countries.* Ithaca: Cornell University Press.

———. 1985. "The Politics of Adjustment: Lessons from the IMF's Extended Fund Facility." *International Organization* 39(3): 505–534.

Haggard, Stephan, Jean-Dominique Lafay, and Christian Morrison. 1995. *The Political Feasibility of Adjustment in Developing Countries.* Paris: OECD.

Haggard, Stephan, and Robert R. Kaufman. 1992a. "Introduction." In *The Politics of Economic Adjustment: International Constraints, Distributive Conflicts, and the State*, edited by Stephan Haggard and Robert R. Kaufman. Princeton: Princeton University Press.

———. 1992b. "The Political Economy of Inflation and Stabilization in Middle Income Countries." In *The Politics of Economic Adjustment: International Constraints, Distributive Conflicts, and the State*, edited by Stephan Haggard and Robert R. Kaufman. Princeton: Princeton University Press.

———. 1989. "The Politics of Stabilization and Structural Adjustment." In *Developing Country Debt and the World Economy*, edited by Jeffrey D. Sachs. Chicago: University of Chicago Press.

Heath, Jonathan. 1999. *Mexico and the Sexenio Curse: Presidential Successions and Economic Crises in Modern Mexico.* Washington: CSIS Press.

Hellman, Judith. 1983. *Mexico in Crisis*, second edition. New York: Holmes & Meier.

Hernández Laos, Enrique, and Edur Velasco Arregui. 1990. "Productividad y

Competitividad de las Manufacturas Mexicanas, 1960–1985." *Comercio Exterior* 40:7 (July).

Hernández Rodríguez, Rogelio. 1992. "La División de la Élite Política Mexicana." In *Lecturas 73: México: Auge, crisis y ajuste: Volumen I: Los tiempos de cambio, 1982–1988*, edited by Carlos Bazdresch, Nisso Bucay, Soledad Loaeza, and Nora Lustig. Mexico City: Fondo de Cultura Económica.

———. 1987. "Los hombres del presidente de la Madrid," *Foro Internacional* 28(1): 5–38 (July–Sept.).

———. 1984. *Formación y trayectoria de los secretarios de estado en México, 1946–1982.* Thesis. Mexico City: Facultad Latinoamericana de Ciencias Sociales.

Hirschman, Albert O. 1985. "Reflections on the Latin American Experience." In *The Politics of Inflation and Economic Stagnation: Theoretical Approaches and International Case Studies*, edited by Leon N. Lindberg and Charles S. Maier. Washington: Brookings Institution.

———. 1979. "The Turn to Authoritarianism in Latin America and the Search for Its Economic Determinants." In *The New Authoritarianism in Latin America*, edited by David Collier. Princeton: Princeton University Press.

Huntington, Samuel P. 1968. *Political Order in Changing Societies.* New Haven: Yale University Press.

Instituto Nacional de Estadística, Geografía e Informática (INEGI). 1996. *Anuario estadístico de los Estados Unidos Mexicanos: Edición 1995.* Aguascalientes.

———. 1994. *Estadísticas históricas de México*, 2 vols. Aguascalientes.

———. 1993. *Anuario estadístico de los Estados Unidos Mexicanos: Edición 1992.* Aguascalientes.

International Monetary Fund. 2002. *International Financial Statistics.* CD

———. 2000. *International Financial Statistics Yearbook 2000.*

———. 1998. "The Asian Crisis: Causes and Cures." *Finance and Development* 35:2 (June).

Izquierdo, Rafael. 1995. *Política Hacendaria del Desarrollo Estabilizador, 1958–70.* Mexico City: Fondo de Cultura Económica.

Johnson, Chalmers. 1986. "The Nonsocialist NICs: East Asia." *International Organization* 40(2): 557–565.

Kahler, Miles. 1985. "Politics and International Debt: Explaining the Crisis." *International Organization* 39(3): 357–382.

Katzenstein, Peter J. 1985. *Small States in World Markets: Industrial Policy in Europe.* Ithaca: Cornell University Press.

Kaufman, Robert R. 1985. "Democratic and Authoritarian Responses to the Debt Issue: Argentina, Brazil, Mexico." *International Organization* 39(3): 473–503.

———. 1979. "Industrial Change and Authoritarian Rule in Latin America: A Concrete Review of the Bureaucratic-Authoritarian Model." In *The New Authoritarianism in Latin America*, edited by David Collier. Princeton: Princeton University Press.

Kennedy, Peter. 1992. *A Guide to Econometrics*, third edition. Cambridge: MIT Press.

Kessler, Timothy P. 1998. "Political Capital: Mexican Financial Policy under Salinas." *World Politics* 51 (October): 36–66.

Kindleberger, Charles P. 1989. *Manias, Panics, and Crashes: A History of Financial Crises*, revised edition. New York: Basic Books.

———. 1986. *The World in Depression: 1929–1939*, revised edition. Berkeley: University of California Press.

Kissinger, Henry. 1999. *Years of Renewal*. New York: Simon & Schuster.

Kline, Harvey F. 1990. "Colombia: The Struggle Between Traditional 'Stability' and New Visions." In *Latin American Politics and Development*, edited by Howard J. Wiarda and Harvey F. Kline. Boulder: Westview Press.

Knight, Alan. 1991. "The Rise and Fall of Cardenismo, c. 1930–c. 1946." In *Mexico Since Independence*, edited by Leslie Bethell. Cambridge: Cambridge University Press.

———. 1990. "Historical Continuities in Social Movements." In *Popular Movements and Political Change in Mexico*, edited by Joe Foweraker and Ann L. Craig. Boulder: Lynne Rienner.

Krauze, Enrique. 1997. *Mexico: Biography of Power. A History of Modern Mexico, 1810–1996*, translated by Hank Heifetz. New York: HarperCollins Publishers.

Krugman, Paul R. 2002. "Argentina: What Happened? What Now?" Talk given at conference on "The Argentine Crisis: Past, Present and Future" at the Argentine Studies Center at the University of Texas at Austin. (April 22.) www.lanic.utexas.edu/project/etext/llilas/cpa/spring02/argcrisis/

———. 1998. "What Happened to Asia?" MIT Economics Department (January.). http://web.mit.edu/krugman/www/DISINTER.html (Cited October 1, 2002).

———. 1990. "The Narrow Moving Band, the Dutch Disease, and the Competitive Consequences of Mrs. Thatcher: Notes on Trade in the Presence of Dynamic Scale Economies." In *Rethinking International Trade*, edited by Paul R. Krugman. Cambridge: MIT Press.

———. 1979. "A Model of Balance of Payments Crises." *Journal of Money, Credit, and Banking* 11: 311–325.

Langston, Joy. 1998. "The *Camarillas*: A Theoretical and Comparative Examination of Why They Exist and Why They Take the Specific Form They Do." Working Paper 12. Mexico City: CIDE.

———. 1997a. "The Role of the Political Groups in the Succession Process." Working Paper 19. Mexico City: CIDE.

———. 1997b. "Three Exits from the Mexican Institutional Revolutionary Party: Internal Ruptures and Political Stability," Working Paper 11. Mexico City: CIDE.

———. 1995. "Sobrevivir y prosperar: Una búsqueda de las causas de las facciones políticas intrarrégimen en México." *Política y Gobierno* 2(2): 243–277.

———. 1994. "An Empirical View of the Political Groups in Mexico: The *Camarillas*." Working Paper 15. Mexico City: CIDE.

Lawson, Chappell H. 2002. *Building the Fourth Estate: Democratization and the Rise of a Free Press in Mexico*. Berkeley: University of California Press.

———. 2000. "Mexico's Unfinished Transition: Democratization and Authoritarian Enclaves in Mexico." *Mexican Studies/Estudios Mexicanos* 16(2): 267–287 (summer).

Lee, Martin, 1998. "Testing Asian Values." *New York Times* (January 28).

Lindberg, Leon N. 1985. "Models of the Inflation-Disinflation Process." In *The Politics of Inflation and Economic Stagnation: Theoretical Approaches and International Case Studies*, edited by Leon N. Lindberg and Charles S. Maier. Washington: Brookings Institution.

Little, Ian M. D., Tibor Scitovsky, and Maurice Scott. 1970. *Industry and Trade in Some Developing Countries: A Comparative Study*. London: Oxford University Press.

López Portillo, José. 1982. *Sexto informe de gobierno: Sector comercio*. Mexico City: Presidencia de la República.

———. 1978. *Segundo informe de gobierno: Anexo histórico estadístico*, vol. 3. Mexico City: Presidencia de la República.

López Portillo Romano, José Ramón. 1994. *Economic Thought and Economic Policy-making in Contemporary Mexico: International and Domestic Components*. D.Phil. thesis, Oxford University.

Luna, Matilda. 1988. "La administración estatal y el régimen político." *Revista Mexicana de Sociología* 50(3): 247–268 (July–Sept.).

———. 1983. "Las transformaciones del régimen político mexicano en la década de 1970." *Revista Mexicana de Sociología* 45(2): 453–472 (April–June).

Lustig, Nora. 1998. *Mexico: The Remaking of an Economy*. Washington: Brookings Institution Press.

MacIntyre, Andrew. 1999. "Political Institutions and the Economic Crisis in Thailand and Indonesia." In *The Politics of the Asian Economic Crisis*, edited by T. J. Pempel. Ithaca: Cornell University Press.

Maddison, Angus, and Associates. 1992. *The Political Economy of Poverty, Equity, and Growth: Brazil and Mexico. A World Bank Comparative Study*. Oxford: Oxford University Press.

Maxfield, Sylvia. 1990. *Governing Capital: International Finance and Mexican Politics*. Ithaca: Cornell University Press.

Middlebrook, Kevin J. 1995. *The Paradox of Revolution: Labor, the State, and Authoritarianism in Mexico*. Baltimore: Johns Hopkins University Press.

———. 1991. "State-Labor Relations in Mexico: the Changing Economic and Political Context." In *Unions, Workers, and the State in Mexico*, edited by Kevin J. Middlebrook. San Diego: Center for U.S.-Mexican Studies.

Moreno, Juan Carlos, and Jaime Ros. 1994. "Market Reform and the Changing Role of the State in Mexico: A Historical Perspective." In *The State, Markets, and Development: Beyond the Neoclassical Dichotomy*, edited by Amitava Krishna Dutt, Kwan S. Kim, and Ajit Singh. Brookfield, Vt.: Edward Elgar.

Nacional Financiera. 1995. *La economía mexicana en cifras 1995*, fourteenth edition. Mexico City.

———. 1990. *La economía mexicana en cifras 1990*, eleventh edition. Mexico City.

Nelson, Joan M. 1990a. "Introduction: The Politics of Economic Adjustment in Developing Nations." In *Economic Crisis and Policy Choice: The Politics of Adjustment in the Third World*, edited by Joan M. Nelson. Princeton: Princeton University Press.

———. 1990b. "Conclusions." In *Economic Crisis and Policy Choice: The Politics of Adjustment in the Third World*, edited by Joan M. Nelson. Princeton: Princeton University Press.

New York Times, The. Newspaper. New York.

Newell, Roberto G., and Luis Rubio F. 1984. *Mexico's Dilemma: The Political Origins of Economic Crisis*. Boulder: Westview Press.

Obstfeld, Maurice. 1996. "Models of Currency Crises with Self-fulfilling Features." *European Economic Review* 40: 1,037–1,047.

O'Donnell, Guillermo A. 2001. "Latin America." *PS: Political Science and Politics* 34(4): 809–811 (December).

———. 1973. *Modernization and Bureaucratic Authoritarianism: Studies in South American Politics*. Berkeley: Institute of International Studies, University of California.

O'Donnell, Guillermo, and Philippe C. Schmitter. 1986. *Transitions from Authoritarian Rule: Tentative Conclusions about Uncertain Democracies*. Baltimore: Johns Hopkins University Press.

Olson, Mancur. 1993. "Dictatorship, Democracy, and Development." *American Political Science Review* 87(3): 567–576.

Ortiz Mena, Antonio. 1998. *El desarrollo estabilizador: Reflexiones sobre una época*. Mexico City: Fondo de Cultura Económica.

Ortiz Salinas, Antonio. 1988. *Régimen político y toma de decisiones*. Mexico City: Privately published.

Paz, Octavio. 1985. *The Labyrinth of Solitude, The Other Mexico, and Other Essays*. New York: Grove Press.

Pellicer de Brody, Olga, and José Luis Reyna. 1978. *Historia de la Revolución Mexicana, 1952–1960, Vol. 22: El afianzamiento de la estabilidad política*. Mexico City: Colegio de México.

Pérez Arce, Francisco. 1990. "The Enduring Union Struggle for Legality and Democracy." In *Popular Movements and Political Change in Mexico*, edited by Joe Foweraker and Ann L. Craig. Boulder: Lynne Rienner.

Proceso. Weekly periodical. Mexico City.

Radelet, Steven, and Jeffrey Sachs. 1998. "The East Asian Financial Crisis: Diagnosis, Remedies, Prospects." Cambridge: Harvard Institute for International Development (April 20).

Ramos, Samuel. 1962. *Profile of Man and Culture in Mexico*. Austin: University of Texas Press.

Remmer, Karen L. 1993. "The Political Economy of Elections in Latin America, 1980–1991." *American Political Science Review* 87(2): 393–407.

Reynolds, Clark W. 1977. "Por qué el 'desarrollo estabilizador' de México fue en realidad desestabilizador." *El Trimestre Económico* 44(4), no. 176: 997–1,023.

Riding, Alan. 1989. *Distant Neighbors: A Portrait of the Mexicans*. New York: Vintage Books/Random House.

Rodrik, Dani. 1999. *The New Global Economy and Developing Countries: Making Openness Work*. Baltimore: Johns Hopkins University Press.

Roeder, Philip G. 1985. "Do New Soviet Leaders Really Make a Difference? Rethinking the 'Succession Connection.'" *American Political Science Review* 79(4): 958–976.

Ros, Jaime. 1995. "La crisis mexicana: Causas, perspectivas, lecciones." *Nexos* (May 1).

———. 1994. "Mexico's Trade and Industrialization Experience Since 1960." In *Trade Policy and Industrialization in Turbulent Times*, edited by G. K. Helleiner. London: Routledge.

———. 1987. "Mexico from the Oil Boom to the Debt Crisis: An Analysis of Policy Responses to External Shocks, 1978–85." In *Latin American Debt and the Adjustment Crisis*, edited by Rosemary Thorp and Laurence Whitehead. Pittsburgh: University of Pittsburgh Press.

Ros, Jaime, and Alejandro Vázquez Enríquez. 1980. "Industrialización y comercio exterior, 1950–77." *Economía Mexicana* (CIDE) 2: 27–47.

Rubin, Jeffrey W. 1996. "Decentering the Regime: Culture and Regional Politics in Mexico." *Latin American Research Review* 31(3): 85–126.

Sachs, Jeffrey D. 1998. "Alternative Approaches to Financial Crises in Emerging Markets." In *Capital Flows and Financial Crises*, edited by Miles Kahler. Ithaca: Cornell University Press.

Salinas de Gortari, Carlos. 2000. *México: Un paso difícil a la modernidad*. Barcelona: Plaza & Janés.

———. 1994. *Sexto informe de gobierno: Anexo*. Mexico City: Presidencia de la República.

———. 1992. *Cuarto informe de gobierno: Anexo*. Mexico City: Presidencia de la República.

Schamis, Hector E. 2002. "Argentina: Crisis and Democratic Consolidation." *Journal of Democracy* 13(2): 81–94 (April).

Schlefer, Jonathan. 2003. *Fractured Elites: The Politics of Economic Crisis in Mexico*. Ph.D. thesis. Cambridge: MIT.

Schmidt, Samuel. 1991. *The Deterioration of the Mexican Presidency: The Years of Luis Echeverría.* Tucson: University of Arizona Press.

Schmitter, Philippe C. 1981. "Interest Intermediation and Regime Governability in Contemporary Western Europe and North America." In *Organizing Interests in Western Europe*, edited by Suzanne Berger. Cambridge: Cambridge University Press.

Secretaría de Hacienda y Crédito Público (SHCP). 1982. *Estadísticas Hacendarias del Sector Público 1965–1982.* Mexico City.

Servín, Elsa. 2001. *Ruptura y oposición: El movimiento henriquista, 1945–1954.* Mexico City: Cal y Arena.

Shapiro, Helen, and Lance Taylor. 1990. "The State and Industrial Strategy." *World Development* 18(6): 861–878.

Skidmore, Thomas E. 1977. "The Politics of Economic Stabilization in Postwar Latin America." In *Authoritarianism and Corporatism in Latin America*, edited by James M. Malloy. Pittsburgh: University of Pittsburgh Press.

Skocpol, Theda. 1979. *States and Social Revolutions: A Comparative Analysis of France, Russia, and China.* Cambridge: Cambridge University Press.

Smith, Peter H. 1997. "Political Dimensions of the Peso Crisis." In *Mexico 1994: Anatomy of an Emerging-Market Crash*, edited by Sebastian Edwards and Moisés Naím. Washington: Carnegie Endowment for International Peace.

———. 1991. "Mexico since 1946: Dynamics of an authoritarian regime." In *Mexico Since Independence*, edited by Leslie Bethell. Cambridge: Cambridge University Press.

———. 1979. *Labyrinths of Power: Political Recruitment in Twentieth-Century Mexico.* Princeton: Princeton University Press.

Solís M., Leopoldo. 1981. *Economic Policy Reform in Mexico: A Case Study for Developing Countries.* New York: Pergamon Press.

———. 1973. "El desarrollo económico: Introducción." In *La economía mexicana: II: Política y desarrollo*, edited by Leopoldo Solís M. Mexico City: Fondo de Cultura Económica.

———. 1967. "Hacia un análisis general a largo plazo del desarrollo económico de México." *Demografía y Economía* (Colegio de México) 1(1): 40–91.

Soros, George. 1997. "The Capitalist Threat." *Atlantic Monthly.* February: 45–58.

Stallings, Barbara. 1990. "Politics and Economic Crisis: A Comparative Study of Chile, Peru, and Colombia." In *Economic Crisis and Policy Choice: The Politics of Adjustment in the Third World*, edited by Joan M. Nelson. Princeton: Princeton University Press.

Stepan, Alfred. 1978. *The State and Society: Peru in Comparative Perspective.* Princeton: Princeton University Press.

Stevenson, Linda S., and Mitchell A. Seligson. 1996. "Fading Memories of the Revolution: Is Stability Eroding in Mexico?" In *Polling for Democracy: Pub-*

lic Opinion and Political Liberalization in Mexico, edited by Roderic Ai Camp. Wilmington: Scholarly Resources.

Suárez Farías, Francisco. 1988. "La élite política." *Revista Mexicana de Sociología* 50(3): 295–321 (July–Sept.).

Taylor, Lance. 1988. *Varieties of Stabilization Experience: Towards Sensible Macroeconomics in the Third World*. Oxford: Clarendon Press.

Teichman, Judith A. 1988. *Policymaking in Mexico: From Boom to Crisis*. Boston: Allen & Unwin.

Tello, Carlos. 1979. *La politica económica en Mexico, 1970–1976*, second edition. Mexico City: Siglo Veintiuno.

United Nations. *Statistical Yearbook* (annual). New York.

Urrutia, Miguel. 1991. "On the Absence of Economic Populism in Colombia." In *The Macroeconomics of Populism in Latin America*, edited by Rudiger Dornbusch and Sebastian Edwards. Chicago: University of Chicago Press.

Velasco, Andrés, and Pablo Cabezas. 1998. "Alternative Responses to Capital Inflows: A Tale of Two Countries." In *Capital Flows and Financial Crises*, edited by Miles Kahler. Ithaca: Cornell University Press.

Vernon, Raymond. 1963. *The Dilemma of Mexico's Development: The Roles of the Private and Public Sectors*. Cambridge: Harvard University Press.

Villarreal, René. 1990. "The Latin American Strategy of Import Substitution: Failure or Paradigm for the Region?" In *Manufacturing Miracles: Paths of Industrialization in Latin America and East Asia*, edited by Gary Gereffi and Donald L. Wyman. Princeton: Princeton University Press.

———. 1977. "The Policy of Import-Substituting Industrialization, 1929–1975." In *Authoritarianism in Mexico*, edited by José Luis Reyna and Richard S. Weinert. Philadelphia: Institute for the Study of Human Issues.

Weingast, Barry R. 1997. "The Political Foundations of Democracy and the Rule of Law," *American Political Science Review* 91(2): 245–263 (June).

Weintraub, Sidney. 2001. "Recent Latin American Financial Crises: How Much Systemic, How Much Policy." Paper presented at conference on "Current Policy Dilemmas in Latin America's Foreign Economic Relations." Fletcher School of Law and Diplomacy, November 1–2.

Williamson, John, and Stephan Haggard. 1994. "The Political Conditions for Economic Reform." In *The Political Economy of Policy Reform*, edited by John Williamson. Washington: Institute for International Economics.

Wolf, Charles, Jr. 1998. "Too Much Government Control." *Wall Street Journal*, February 4.

Zedillo Ponce de León, Ernesto. 1985. "The Mexican External Debt: The Last Decade." In *Politics and Economics of External Debt Crisis: The Latin American Experience*, edited by Miguel S. Wionczek. Boulder: Westview Press.

Note: Italic page numbers refer to photographs, graphs, and tables.

agriculture, 41, 55, 175–176
Alejo, Javier: and Echeverría, 126–127, 132, 149, 155; and López Portillo, 126, 162–163; and tax reform, 68, 69, 70–71; and Tlatelolco Square massacre, 139
Alemán, Miguel: cabinet secretary replacements, 124–125, 126, 143, 191; and Lázaro Cárdenas, 119, 121–122, 247nn10, 23; and Carrillo Flores, 109; and corruption, 100; Echeverría compared to, 153; and López Portillo, 158; photograph of, *120;* political career of, *144;* and political expertise, 97; and presidential succession, 53, 118–121, 123, 130, 247n10
Ames, Barry, 85, 136, 229, 230, 231, 243n25, 264n2
Argentina: democracy in, 225; economic crisis in, 13, 14, 221–224, 263nn66, 72; and elite struggle, 220–221, 226; and military dictatorship, 19, 218; and protectionism, 59, 240n19; strikes in, 38; and value of currency, 24, *24,* 221
Asia: crisis of late 1990s, 18, 21, 22, 55; East Asia, 14, 18; economic management in, 95

Aspe, Pedro, 190, 199, 213, 214, 215, 217
auscultación, 51–52, 54
authoritarian states, 12, 22–23, 133

Bailey, John J., 248n32
Baker, James, 200
Bank of Mexico: autonomy of, 98, 244n11; and devaluation, 105, 109, 165; and exchange rate, 20, 203, 260–261n92; and interview process, 4, 6, 7; and López Portillo, 91; and overvaluation, 208; and pegged exchange rate, 20; and public spending, 171; reserves of, 203, 214, 261n92; and return of capital, 203; and state borrowing from, 68; and tax reform, 69; technical experts in, 96, 100
Barnes, Guillermo, 3
Bartlett, Manuel, 190, 191, 198, 199
Basáñez, Miguel, 96, 202
Beteta, Mario Ramón: and Echeverría, 100, 132, 152, 155, 250n49; as finance secretary, 100, 104, 119, 126; and Planning and Budget Ministry, 187; on Tlatelolco Square massacre, 139
Bizberg, Ilán, 242n16
Bolivia, 219–220
Bolsa, 202–203, 260nn85, 87
Boltvinik, Julio, 239n11
Borja Navarrete, Gilberto, 62, 205

Bracamontes, Luis Enrique, 50, 126, 144, 154, 250n39

Brandenburg, Frank, 47, 122, 247n23

Bravo, Victor, 36–37, 48, 135, 155, 200

Brazil: and Argentina, 221; and capital controls, 179; economic crisis in, 13, 14; and export growth, 164; and military dictatorship, 19, 218; strikes in, 38; union activity in, 78; and value of currency, 24, 24

Bretton Woods system, 19, 23, 24

business interests: business elites, 42–43; and Echeverría, 70, 71, 74, 134, 158; and economic policies, 205; and López Portillo, 74, 158; and Pact of 1958, 67; and presidential power, 37; and Salinas, 203; subsidies for, 57, 59, 67–68

Bustamante, Eduardo, 112, 113, 114, 246n65

Caamaño, Enrique, 113–114, 117

Calles, Plutarco Elías, 34, 100, 129, 163, 207

Camacho Solís, Manuel, 11, 209, 210, 212, 213

camarillas, 29, 235n42. See also grupos; political elites

Camp, Roderic, 3, 7, 34, 41–43, 46, 118, 144–145, 247n23

capital controls, 67–68, 179, 257n116

capital flight: and Echeverría, 74; and economic crises, 19; and economic crisis of 1982, 165, 202, 203; and economic crisis of 1994, 207–208, 215; and free financial flows, 24, 235n34; and grassroots strike wave, 109; and López Portillo, 164, 171; and tax reform, 68, 69, 70

Cárdenas, Cuauhtémoc: and Democratic Current, 117, 192, 193; and election of 1994, 214; opposition campaign of, 49, 53, 84, 92, 117, 121, 128, 194, 249n27; photograph of, 199

Cárdenas, Enrique, 57–58, 98, 209, 227, 239n12, 244n13, 245n31

Cárdenas, Lázaro: and Alemán, 119, 121–122, 247nn10, 23; and Calles, 129, 163; and elite cooperation, 10; and expropriation of foreign oil companies, 33; finance minister of, 97, 100; as fiscal conservative, 104; labor and agrarian reforms of, 33, 37–38; and Lombardo, 81; photograph of, 39; and political expertise, 97; on Tlatelolco Square massacre, 139

Cardoso, Fernando Henrique, 57

Carrillo Flores, Antonio: and devaluation, 25, 105–109, 128, 245n37; diary of, 7; and Ortiz Mena, 109; photograph of, 110; and reorganization of Finance Ministry, 111–112; and Ruiz Cortines, 102, 104; as technical expert, 99–100, 104

Carrillo Gamboa, Emilio, 7, 83, 142, 152, 196, 209

Carvajal, Ángel, 7, 106, 108

Carvajal, Gustavo, 92, 122–123, 127

Casas Alemán, Fernando, 120–121, 122, 259n42

Castañeda, Jorge, 7, 29, 154, 184, 200, 260n76

Catholic Church, 37, 42, 52, 111, 206

Centeno, Miguel Ángel, 29, 43, 96, 103, 111, 173, 204–205, 255n85

central banks, 17, 18, 23. See also Bank of Mexico

Cervantes del Río, Hugo, 158

charros, 38–39, 79, 81, 83

Chiapas uprising, 210, 212, 214

Chile, 22, 78, 218

Clinton administration, 206, 213

Colombia: avoidance of economic
crises, 59, 60, 240n19; avoidance of
military coup, 146, 218; and capital
controls, 179; political elites in,
218, 220, 224; and protectionism,
59, 240n19
Colosio, Luis Donaldo, 209–210, *211*,
212, 214
confianza, 43–44
Constitution of 1917, 33, 35, 36, 206,
213
Coquet, Benito, 87–88, 99, 108, 114,
127
Córdoba, José, 199, 209, 244n11
Cornelius, Wayne A., 32–33
Corona de Rosal, Alfonso: and
campaigning for political position,
49; and governorship of Mexico
City, 124; and *grupos*, 44–45, 46;
photograph of, *45*; and presidential
succession, 53–54, 102; published
account of, 7; and Salinas, 210
corporatist structure: and labor, 77,
81, 83, 124; and Muñoz Ledo, 146;
and presidential power, 37–40;
and PRI, 27, 31, 32, 37–40, 41, 84;
separation from political elite, 47;
and social conflict management,
22–23
Corrales, Javier, 221–223, 263nn72, 74
Cosío Villegas, Daniel, 47–48, 121,
122, 135, 143, 147, 148–149
Craig, Ann L., 32–33
currency: and economic crises, 16–18.
See also devaluation; exchange rate;
Mexican peso; overvaluation of
peso

de confianza, 43
de la Madrid, Miguel: and cabinet
secretaries, 125, 126, 181, 182,
187, 189, 191–192, 257n5, 258n38;
and cause of economic crises, 57;

and decline in strikes, 84; and
Democratic Current, 41, 196, 197,
198, 225; and devaluation, 184,
256n114, 257n6; and Díaz Serrano, 165; and dismissals, 178, 189;
economic policies of, 181–182,
184, 187, 190, 191, 197–199, 201,
202–203, 205; election of, 27; and
elite struggle, 181, 182, 199; and
Finance Ministry, 104, 187; *grupo*
of, 44, 173, 175, 178, 182, 189,
191–192; and López Portillo, 44,
52, 160, 163–164, 168, 169, 191;
photograph of, *170;* and political
elite, 143, 157, 250n55; and presidential nomination, 169, 173, 175,
176, 177, 180; and presidential
power, 35, 187; and presidential
succession, 48, 51–53, 89, 93, 184,
187, 190, 191, 197, 200; and PRI
apparatus, 191–192; and public
spending, 89, 91, 169, 173, 175,
176, 177; and restoration of order,
181, 182, 186, 187
de la Rúa, Fernando, 221, 223, 224
de la Vega Domínguez, Jorge, 45, 165,
176, 177, 196, 238n99
del Mazo, Alfredo, 115, 190–191,
198–199, 202
democracies: consolidated democracy,
225–226; role of political elites in,
10, 12, 15, 225; and social conflict
management, 22; survey of political culture in, 33–34
Democratic Current, 41, 117,
191–194, 196–199, 200, 225
Democratic Front, 27, 29, 197, 214
Democratic Tendency, 81, 83
de Oteyza, José Andrés: and de la
Madrid, 182; and devaluation, 179;
and Díaz Serrano, 165–166; on
Echeverría, 248–249n9; and López
Portillo, 153, 159, 164, 171, 172,

173, 175, 176, 177, 189; on PRI, 34–35; on separation of political and economic management, 96–97, 103

devaluation: and Carrillo Flores, 25, 105–109, 128, 245n37; and de la Madrid, 184, 256n114, 257n6; and economic crisis of 1982, 165; and economic crisis of 1994, 17, 214, 215, 217; and economic growth, 17, 25; and López Portillo, 179–180, 209; and Ruiz Cortines, 107–108, 109, 127; and Salinas, 209, 214, 215

developing nations: and economic crises, 19, 94, 244n2; and lenders of last resort, 17

Díaz, Porfirio, 97, 119

Díaz Ordaz, Gustavo: and cabinet secretaries, 126, 131, 143–144, 192; and Chávez Sánchez, 40; and Finance Ministry, 104, 113, 114; and labor, 83; and López Portillo, 158; and media control, 40; and Moreno Valle, 7; and Ortiz Mena, 9, 102, 103, 114, 217; photograph of, *45, 140;* political career of, *144;* and political expertise, 97; presidential nomination of, 50, 52, 53–54, 238n102; and presidential rivals, 243n39; and presidential succession, 141, 142, 206, 224; and public spending, 88, 89, 136; and Tlatelolco Square massacre, 8, 81, 138, 139, 141; and Uruchurtu, 44

Díaz Serrano, Jorge, 51, 165–166, *167,* 168–169, 171, 175, 178, 253n45

distributive conflicts, 21–23, 26

Dornbusch, Rudiger, 76, 208–209

Duhalde, Eduardo, 222

Durbin-Watson statistic, *230,* 231

Eastern Bloc, fall of, 22

Echeverría, Luis: as ambassador to Australia, 150, 161; and business interests, 70, 71, 74, 134, 158; and cabinet secretary replacements, 125, 126–127, 131–132, 138, 143–145, 150, 152, 153, 155–157; and calls for change, 148–150, 156, 157; decision making of, 151–152; and de la Madrid, 191; and economic growth, 66; economic policies of, 71, 74, 132–133, 148, 149–150, 182, 190; and elite struggle, 10, 124, 129, 131, 146, 148, 152, 156, 157, 160, 206, 224; and Finance Ministry, 104, 142, 152, 188; and foreign loans, 99; and González Guevera, 46; and *grupos,* 129–131, 141, 153, 156; and ideological escalation, 129, 145–148, 156, 157, 218; interview with, 4, 5, 7; and labor, 27, 81, 83, 134, 138; and new generation, 131, 142–145, 158, 192; and Pact of 1958, 68, 71, 74; photograph of, *82, 130;* policymaking of, 131, 132, 138; political career of, *144;* and political legitimacy, 131, 133–136, 138; and political manipulation, 152–154, 156; and presidential power, 36, 124, 153, 157, 161, 187; and presidential succession, 52, 83, 131, 148, 153–154, 157–158, 215nn86, 87, 252n95; and public spending, 74, 75, 89, 91, 99, 131, 132–133, 135, 136, 138, 154–156, 162; and tax reform, 68, 69, 70, 71; and Tlatelolco Square massacre, 81, 131, 133, 135–136, 141, 148

Economic Commission for Latin America (ECLA), 58, 108, 145, 173

economic crises: causes of, 55, 94, 187, 189–190, 217, 226, 244n1; Colombia's avoidance of, 59, 60, 240n19; and developing nations, 19, 94, 244n2; and elite struggle,

14, 15, 187, 217, 221, 226; and external economic shocks, 20–21, 26; factors in, 16–17; Heath's gauge of, 261n92; and macroeconomic policies, 19–20, 66, 67–71, 74, 76; mechanics of, 17–21; and money supply, 19–20, 59, 234n19; political causes of, 15, 18, 21–23, 244n2; and political cohorts, 193; and political spending, 13; and presidential power, 105, 117, 245n31; and structural industrial problems, 21, 55, 57, 66, 76, 239n11; threat of, 205

economic crisis of 1976: causes of, 25, 27, 55, 235n35; and Echeverría, 131, 156, 190; and exhaustion of import substitution, 59–60, 62–67; and Pact of 1958, 68; and protectionism and government subsidies, 57

economic crisis of 1982: and capital flight, 165, 202, 203; domestic causes of, 164, 190, 235n35; and economic growth, 206; and exhaustion of import substitution, 59–60, 62–67; and ideological polarization, 172–173, 175; and López Portillo, 164, 180, 190; and "lost decade" of 1980s, 1, 14; and oil revenues, 19, 25–26, 164; and Pact of 1958, 68; and public sector deficits, 168; and structural industrial failure, 55

economic crisis of 1987, 190, 200, 261n92

economic crisis of 1994: and devaluation, 17, 214, 215, 217; and elite struggle, 206, 214; and global financial speculation, 1; and IMF, 206, 221; and inflation, 15, 16; and macroeconomic policies, 26; and overvaluation of peso, 15, 214, 215; and weakness of banks, 208

economic growth: and cooperation among political elites, 5; and de la Madrid, 184, 185, 186; and devaluation, 17, 25; and economic crises, 182; and economic crisis of 1994, 206; and grassroots strike wave, 77; and import substitution, 60, 61; and labor insurgency of 1970s, 79, 81; and oil revenues, 66–67, 74; and overspending, 58, 66; and perfect dictatorship, 1; real growth of manufactured exports, 62, 63, 64; real manufacturing growth, 61

economic stability: and Bretton Woods system, 23, 24; in Colombia, 218–219; and devaluation, 179; and economic policies, 205; and elite cooperation, 13, 14, 15, 94, 109, 111, 217, 219–220, 226; and Finance Ministry, 95–96, 97, 109, 115–116; and international financial architecture, 23; and Ortiz Mena, 98; perceptions of, 75, 241n76; and presidential power, 95, 116, 117; and public spending, 14; and Ruiz Cortines, 105, 109; sustaining of, 22, 94

Education Ministry, 88, 96

Edwards, Sebastian, 215

Eichengreen, Barry, 19

El Barzón, 16, *16*

elite politics. See *grupos;* political elite

Elizondo, Eduardo Angel, 36

Espinoza de los Reyes, Jorge, 257n116

Esquivel, Gerardo, 244n2

European Union, 221

Evans, Peter, 204

exchange rate: and Bank of Mexico, 20, 203, 260–261n92; defined, 234n6; and devaluation, 257n6; and economic crises, 16–17, 66; and financial panic, 17, 18; pegged exchange rate, 20 external economic shocks, 20–21, 23, 26

Federal Electricity Commission, 81, 154, 252n95
Federal Security Directorate, 36, 179
Fernández de Cevallos, Diego, 214
Fernández Hurtado, Ernesto, 4, 24, 91, 127–128, 146, 251n86
fideicomisos, 88, 150, 188–189
Finance Ministry: and access to foreign loans, 99; alliance with banking, 97–98, 187, 188; and Coquet, 87; and de la Madrid, 104, 187; and Echeverría, 104, 142, 152, 188; and economic stability, 95–96, 97, 109, 115–116; and interview process, 4, 6; lack of independent budget authority, 115; and López Portillo, 188–189, 190; maintaining continuity in, 217; and Mexican fiscal data, 228; and Ortiz Mena, 55, 67, 98, 104, 109, 113, 114, 115, 142, 187–188, 189, 217, 248n3; and presidential succession, 103; and protectionism, 62; and public investment cuts, 66; and public spending, 86, 131, 171; reorganization of, 111–112; and tax reform, 70; technical experts vs. politicians in, 8–9, 96, 97, 99–100, 102–104, 107, 110–111, 116
financial panic, 17, 18, 20
First World dependency, 145
Fitzgerald, E. V. K., 57, 235n35
Flores de la Peña, Horacio: and Echeverría, 152, 251n86; and industrial problems, 132, 146; interview with, 4; and López Portillo, 163; and Ortiz Mena, 188; and tax reform, 68
Flores Muñoz, Gilberto, 50, 104
Flores Olea, Victor, 141, 146

foreign loans: and de la Madrid, 184, 186; and economic crisis of 1994, 16; and floating loans, 88–89, 99; and López Portillo, 168–169; politicians' access to, 97–99; and public budget deficits, 68; and Salinas, 200–201, 208
Fox, Jonathan, 32, 176
Fox, Vicente, 2–3, 35, 217
France, 24, 41
Frankel, Jeffrey A., 55
free-market view: and de la Madrid, 157, 181, 191, 197–198; and exhaustion of import substitution, 58; and López Portillo, 172; and protectionism, 63; of structural economic problems, 55, 57, 58, 60

Galván, Rafael, 81, 83
Gamarra, Eduardo A., 220
Gamboa de Buen, Jorge, 46, 118, 209, 215
García Paniagua, Javier, 176–177, 179
García Sáinz, Ricardo, 163, 164, 178, 253n26
GDP. *See* gross domestic product (GDP)
General Agreement on Tariffs and Trade (GATT), 64, 173, 205, 261n92
Ghigliazza, Sergio, 64, 91–92, 207, 208
Gil Díaz, Francisco, 71, 75, 168, 241n74
Giménez Cacho, Luis, 62, 100
Global Development Plan, 163–164, 176, 184
gold standard, 19
Golub, Stephen S., 239n11
Gómez, Rodrigo, 100, *101*, 105, 152, 182, 248n3
Gómez Villanueva, Augusto: and Democratic Current, 194, 196;

and Echeverría, 143; and López Portillo, 158, 161; and peasant land invasions, 134; photograph of, *195;* as political elite, 41; and Salinas, 213

González Blanco, José Patrocinio, 126, 150–151, 206, 214–215, 246n65

González Casanova, Pablo, 34, 75, 84, 141, 146, 236n29

González Guevara, Rodolfo, 44, 46, 193

grassroots strike wave, 25, 27, 67, 76–78, 109–111, 113, 128, 212

great man theory of history, 2, 10

Grindle, Marilee S., 43, 238n99

gross domestic product (GDP): and public sector budgets, 71, 72, *73,* 74, 131, 136, 154, 176, 177; and public sector deficits, 75, 78, *80, 87,* 89, *90,* 91, 99, 131, 168–169, 241n74, 254n58; and social sector spending, 136, *137*

grupos: change in politics of, 29–30; and *confianza,* 43–44; cooperative politics among, 78, 124; covert mobilization of, 50, 118; and economic policies, 204–205; emergence of, 31; and expectation of political survival, 13, 15, 118, 123, 124, 127, 147, 157, 161, 162, 163, 178, 181, 191, 224; fluidity of, 46, 47, 124; and ideological escalation, 129; and influence on president, 41; informal structure of, 43; and internal party contest for presidential nomination, 5, 13, 50–51, 53, 76, 86, 93, 102, 123, 153, 157–158, 169, 190, 251n88; mutual conflict management of, 30; and personnel changes, 44–46, 124, *125,* 126, 131, 248n32; and presidential power, 93, 118, 119, 123,

189; and prohibition of overt mobilization, 117; public spending of, 14, 51, 76, 93, 157, 169; secrecy of, 46–47, 50, 124; struggles among, 5–6, 14, 29, 76, 93, 157–158, 162–163, 178–180, 181, 190. See also *camarillas;* political elites

Gunther, Richard, 225

Gurría, Angel, 169

Haggard, Stephan, 22, 23, 29, 84, 244n1

Hank González, Carlos, 45, 175

Heath, Jonathan, 261n92

Henríquez Guzmán, Miguel: and Lázaro Cárdenas, 121–122; independent presidential campaign of, 84, 86, 92, 105, 123, 231; opposition party supporting, 48, 49, 53, 121, 123, 128

Hernández Galicia, Joaquín "La Quina," 39–40

Hernández Rodríguez, Rogelio, 43, 182, 191, 258n38

Higley, John, 225

Hirschman, Albert O., 129, 145, 217–218, 239n14, 248n1

Ibarra, David: and de la Madrid, 93; and deterioration of economic model, 251n70; and devaluation, 179; and Díaz Serrano, 165; and López Portillo, 163, 169, 171, 172, 173, 176, 177, 255n87; and Ortiz Mena, 245n24; photograph of, *174;* and public spending, 51; and Silva Herzog, 186; and Tlatelolco Square massacre, 147, 250n39

ideological escalation, 129, 145–148, 248n1

IMF. *See* International Monetary Fund (IMF)

import substitution: blocking of, 218; and economic growth, 60, *61*; exhaustion of, 58–60, 62–67, 217, 238n15; Solís on, 147

income distribution, 75, 81, 145, 147

India, 60

Indonesia, 18, 221

industrial subsidies, 59, 67

Industry and Commerce, Ministry of, 62

inflation: and business subsidies, 68; and devaluation, 108; and Echeverría, 83, 157–158; and economic crises, 20; and economic crisis of 1994, 15, 16; and López Mateos, 78; and macroeconomic policies, 76; and presidential succession, 157–158; and public sector deficits, 201, 254n58; and public spending, 115; and Ruiz Cortines, 105; and Salinas, 203, 209; and wages, 109

Institutional Revolutionary Party. See *Partido Revolucionario Institucional*

interest rates, 16, 25, 164

Interior Ministry, 6, 35, 36, 52, 95

international financial markets, 1, 18–19, 23

International Monetary Fund (IMF): and Argentina, 221; and Asian crisis of late 1990s, 21; and de la Madrid, 89, 184, 185; and economic crisis of 1982, 206; and economic crisis of 1994, 206, 221; and foreign loans, 97; and global financial architecture, 19; as lender of last resort, 17–18; and Moctezuma, 161; and Ortiz Mena, 109; and Salinas, 11, 26, 201, 203, 208; and stability of Mexican peso, 13–14

Investment Commission, 112, 113

Izquierdo, Rafael, 70, 102, 113, 160, 228

Japan, 13, 46, 50, 62

Kaufman, Robert R., 23, 29, 84, 217, 239nn11, 15, 244n1

Kennedy, John F., 102

Kindleberger, Charles P., 17

Korean War, 25, 105, 119, 245n31

Krauze, Enrique, 78, 111, 121, 122, 132

Krugman, Paul, 223, 263nn66, 72

Labastida, Francisco, 2, 48, 91, 182, 186, 190, 198, 200, 203

labor: and devaluation, 108; and Echeverría, 27, 81, 83, 134, 138; and grassroots strike wave of 1958–59, 25, 27, 67, 76–78, 109–111, 113, 128, 212; and labor insurgency of the 1970s, 27, 78–79, 81, 83, 138; and macroeconomic policies, 76–79, 81, 83–84; and Pact of 1958, 67; and wages, 77–78, 86, 242n3. *See also* strikes

Labor Ministry, 95

Lal, Deepak, 59, 63

Langston, Joy, 43, 46, 118, 124, 197–198, 210, 258n37

Larraín, Felipe, 244n2

Latin America: and agriculture, 55; and democratic corporatism, 22–23; and free markets, 198; and ideological escalation, 129, 145, 157, 218, 224, 248n1; and import substitution, 58, 59–60, 217; and Mexican economic crisis of 1982, 14; and public spending, 84, 230, 243n25; and social sciences, 204; and U.S. Federal Reserve interest rates, 25

Lawson, Chappell, 3, 236n25, 237nn51, 53, 239n13

Legoretta, Agustín, Sr., 98, 179, 190
lenders of last resort, 17–18, 19, 244n2
Levín, Óscar, 93
Liberal Democratic Party (Japan), 46, 50
Lombardo, Vicente, 37–38, 81
López Mateos, Adolfo: and cabinet secretaries, 126, 127, 131, 192; and Finance Ministry, 111; and grass-roots strike wave, 67, 78; and infla-tion, 78; and labor, 83–84, 108, 110; and Ortiz Mena, 102, 104, 109, 113; photograph of, *79;* politi-cal career of, *144;* and political expertise, 97; and political shock, 18; and presidential nomination, 52, 53–54, 238n102; and public spending, 78, 115
López Portillo, José: and business in-terests, 74, 158; and cabinet secre-taries, 124, 125, 126–127, 145, 157, 160, 180, 187; and de la Madrid, 44, 52, 160, 163–164, 168, 169, 191; and devaluation, 179–180, 209; and dismissals, 160–164, 178, 180, 252n19; and Echeverría, 46, 131, 141, 150, 153, 251nn86, 87; and economic growth, 66–67; economic policies of, 71, 74, 160, 161, 163, 164, 172, 182; and elite struggle, 157, 160–163, 165–166, 172–173, 178, 181; and Finance Ministry, 188–189, 190; and ideological polarization, 172–173, 175, 181; and Muñoz Ledo, 151, 154, 158, 161, 179; and older generation, 158, 192; and Pact of 1958, 68, 71, 74; photograph of, *159;* political career of, *144;* and presidential nomination, 52, 103, 154, 238n102, 251nn86, 87; and presidential succession, 165–166,

169–171, 176–180; and public spending, 89, 91–92, 154–155, 168, 169–172, 173, 175, 254n70; and restoration of order, 158–160, 181; and workers' real earning, 84, 242n16
López Portillo, José Ramón: and de la Madrid, 89, 164, 173, 178, 256n114, 258n22; and devaluation, 180; and economic crisis of 1982, 168; on presidential power, 160; on public spending, 169, 170–171; and Salinas, 200, 260n76
Lugo Verduzco, Adolfo, 192, 196
Lustig, Nora, 215, 235n35, 239n11, 257n6

macroeconomic policies: in Colom-bia, 218; and distributive conflicts, 21, 23; and economic crises, 19–20, 66, 67–71, 74, 76; and economic growth, 77; and labor, 76–79, 81, 83–84; and populism, 76, 131; and promise of political survival, 127; and Salinas, 26, 29; and spending of political elite, 84–89, 91
Maddison, Angus, 67, 240n23
Maldonado, Braulio, 85
Mancera, Miguel, 132, 142, 148, 166, 172, 207–208, 261n92
manufacturing: real growth of manu-factured exports, 62, *63,* 64; real manufacturing growth, *61;* trade deficits in, 64, 65, *65*
Margáin, Hugo, 68, 69, 70, 132, 152–153, 189
Martínez, Ifigenia, 141, 193
Martínez Corbalá, Gonzalo, 193–194
Martínez Domínguez, Alfonso, 135, 143
Martínez Manatou, Emilio, 139, 141
Marxist views: and dependency theory, 147; of political elites, 129;

and Silva Herzog (father), 41, 143; of structural economic problems, 55, 57

Maxfield, Sylvia, 99, 244n7

media: freedom of the press, 32; and labor, 77; and presidential power, 40, 121; and presidential succession, 51, 93

Menem, Carlos, 221, 222, 223, 225

Mexican Chamber of Deputies, 32, 36, 38, 47, 103, 158

Mexican Communist Party, 159

Mexican Council of Businessmen, 69

Mexican fiscal data, 227–228

Mexican Food System, 175–176

Mexican peso: and economic crises, 14; and economic crisis of 1994, 15; exchange rate of, 16–17, 234n6; stability of, 13–14, 24, *24*. *See also* devaluation; overvaluation of peso

Mexican Revolution of 1910, 11, 32–33, *33*, 34, 41, 119

Mexican Senate, 32

Mexican state: and centralization of power, 31–40; competing factions in, 205; and fiscal crisis of the state theory, 67–71, 74; and free financial flows, 24, 235n34; historical legacy of, 32–34; internal politics of, 14, 15; promotion of manufactured exports, 62

Mexican Workers Federation, 23, 37–38, 40, 194

Middlebrook, Kevin J., 242n17

military coups, 145, 217–218

Miranda Fonseca, Donato, 86, 113

Moctezuma, Julio Rodolfo: and devaluation, 115; and Díaz Ordaz, 88; and Echeverría, 141, 149–150, 151, 250n48; and interview process, 3; and López Portillo, 159–160, 161, 162–163, 171, 172–173, 175, 178; and Ortiz Mena, 102, 112

money supply, and economic crises, 19–20, 59, 234n19

Moreno Valle, Rafael, 7, 50–51, 52, 134, 142, 153

Moya Palencia, Mario, 52, 143, 144, 153

multinationals, 64, 81, 145

Muñoz Ledo, Porfirio: and de la Madrid, 194; and Democratic Current, 192, 193, 194, 196; and Echeverría, 81, 150, 151, 154; and López Portillo, 151, 154, 158, 161, 179; and restructuring economic model, 146

NAFTA. *See* North American Free Trade Agreement (NAFTA)

National Action Party, 2, 27, 135, 138, 194, 197, 214, 217

National Federation of Popular Organizations, 23, 37

National Iron and Steelworkers, 81

National Peasants Federation, 23, 27, 37, 38, 51, 194

National University: Economics Faculty of, 55; and political elite, 42, 43, 44, 47, 138, 142–143, 146, 193; and presidential succession research, 48; and Tlatelolco Square massacre, 138–139

Nava, Salvador, 49, 134

Newell, Robert G., 133, 138, 149, 172, 173, 255n83

North American Free Trade Agreement (NAFTA), 26, 64, 205, 210

North-South Conference, 166

Obregón, Alvaro, 120

O'Donnell, Guillermo, 204

oil revenues: and economic crisis of 1982, 19, 25–26, 164; and economic growth, 66–67, 74; and exports,

98, 185; and prices, 165–166, 168, 184, 185, 203, 253n50

Ojeda, Pedro, 163, 173, 177–178, 180, 191, 254n70, 258n37

Olivares Santana, Enrique, 179

OLS method, and coefficient estimates, 230–231, *230*

Olson, Mancur, 95, 244n3

Ortiz Mena, Antonio: and de la Madrid, 182; and devaluation, 108; and Echeverría, 152, 153; and economic plan, 112–113; and economic stability, 98; as Finance Minister, 55, 67, 98, 104, 109, 113, 114, 115, 142, 187–188, 189, 217, 248n3; and inflation, 78; interview with, 4, 7; and Izquierdo, 160; photograph of, *56*; as possible presidential contender, 8–9, 100, 102–103, 113, 245n24; and presidential succession, 243n39; and public spending, 86, 114; and tax reform, 69–70

overt mobilization, 49, 50, 53, 117, 194

overvaluation of peso: and economic crises, 59; and economic crisis of 1994, 15, 214, 215; inflation leading to, 20; and manufacturing trade balance, 65, *65*; and Salinas, 26, 207, 208–209

Pact of 1958, 67, 71

Partido Revolucionario Institucional (Institutional Revolutionary Party; PRI): changing relations in, 6; and Corona del Rosal, 44; and distributive conflicts, 23; dominance of, 31, 76, 135, 158; and election of 1988, 11, 27, 29, 31, 197; and election of 2000, 2–3; fracture in, 191–194, 196–199; and interview process, 7; lack of

electoral competition for, 84; lack of independent power in, 31–32; National Executive Committee of, 31, 35, 54, 155, 192, 196; as political system, 34–35, 96; presidential power in, 31–32, 34, 35, 36; and presidential succession, 47–49, 52, 53, 54, 88, 89, 118, 121, 123, 210–211; and prohibition of overt mobilization, 117, 194, 196; and Salinas, 207, 212–213; social organizations incorporated within, 27, 31, 32, 37–40, 41, 84

Party of the Democratic Revolution, 2, 214

patron-client relationships, 37

Paz, Octavio, 31–32, 35, 75, 133

Paz Estenssoro, Víctor, 219–220

peak associations, 22

Pellicer de Brody, Olga, 123

Pemex: and interview process, 7; and labor demands, 78; and López Portillo's economic cabinet, 164; and presidential power, 35; and public sector income, 70, 74, 114; and public spending, 136, 175

Pérez Arce, Francisco, 38–39

Pérez Rios, Francisco, 81, 83

perfect dictatorship, 1, 2, 9

Petricioli, Gustavo, 186–187, 189, 202

Planning and Budget Ministry: and Beteta, 187; and de la Madrid, 51, 89; and interview process, 4, 6; and López Portillo, 160, 163, 188–189; and public spending, 89, 169–170; and reorganization plan, 112

Plan of Promotion and Growth, 201

political-academic relationship, 42

political elites: buying support of, 12; cooperation among, 5, 10, 13, 14, 15, 94, 107–109, 111, 117–118, 124, 127–128, 129, 130, 156, 191,

205–206, 209, 224; and economic policies, 205; elite settlement, 225, 264n82; elite struggle, 5, 14, 15, 93, 111–116, 129, 138–139, 141, 145, 146, 148, 152, 156, 157, 165–166, 181, 187, 191, 200–203, 206, 209; and emphasis on peace and order, 34, 85, 95–96; and ideological escalation, 145–148, 157; interviews with, 1–2, 3, 4–5; and nationalism, 41–42; and political cohorts, 192–193; and presidential succession, 41, 48–51, 52, 53, 54, 85, 86–88, 89, 91, 92, 93, 102, 165–166, 205, 206, 243n39; rebellions of, 92; relations among, 6, 9–10, 14, 205, 218; separation from corporatist structure, 47; social characteristics of, 6, 41, 142–143; and Tlatelolco Square massacre, 8, 131, 138–139, 141. See also *camarillas; grupos*

political shocks, 18, 212, 244n2

political spending, 11–13. *See also* public spending

pre-electoral spending cycle, 229–231

Presidency, Ministry of the, 4, 6, 86, 111, 112–113

presidential power: and budget authority, 103–104; and Calles, 34; centralization of, 31–32, 35; and corporatist structure, 37–40; de jure powers, 35; and economic crises, 105, 117, 245n31; and economic stability, 95, 116, 117; and elite cooperation, 129, 224; extra-constitutional powers, 35; and Finance Ministry, 187; and *grupos*, 93, 118, 119, 123, 189; historical legacies of, 32–33, 117; and legitimate use of force, 36–37; and media control, 40, 121; and military, 236n29; and political-academic

relationship, 42; and political culture, 33–34; and presidential succession, 47–54, 85, 102–103, 118–119, 123, 127, 224–225

president's cabinet: career stability of, 124, 150; comparison of political careers, 143, *144;* and elite struggle, 111–116; López Portillo's organization of, 160, 187; role of, 150–151; secretary replacements, 124–127, *125,* 131–132, 138, 143–145, 150, 152, 153, 155–157, 191; specialists in, 96

PRI. See *Partido Revolucionario Institucional* (Institutional Revolutionary Party; PRI)

private sector: and devaluation, 108; and Echeverría, 71, 74, 134, 148; and economic policies, 205; and López Portillo, 158, 164, 166; and political shock, 18; and presidential succession, 52; public/private sector division, 42, 47, 189; and tax reform, 69

protectionism: gradual lowering of, 205; and industrial efficiency, 57, 58, 60, 62, 63, 66, 240n23; lack of evidence linking to economic crises, 59–60, 62–67; problems with, 63–64

public/private sector division, 42, 47, 189

public sector budgets: and GDP, 71, 72, 73, 74, 131, 136, 154, 176, 177; and Planning and Budget Ministry, 160

public sector deficits: and capital flight, 165; and de la Madrid, 184; and Echeverría, 99, 131, 153; financing for, 97, 99; and GDP, 75, 78, *80, 87,* 89, *90,* 91, 99, 131, 168–169, 241n74, 254n58; level of, during 1960s, 68, 71, 72; and

López Portillo, 158, 168, 171; and macroeconomic policies, 76; and Salinas, 201, 208, 262n20
public spending: conventional use of term, 234n3; and Echeverría, 74, 75, 89, 91, 99, 131, 132–133, 135, 136, 138, 154–156, 162; growth in, 78, *80*, 85–86, *87*, 89, *90*; of *grupos*, 14, 51, 76, 93, 157, 169; and Latin America, 84, 230, 243n25; and López Mateos, 78, 115; and López Portillo, 89, 91–92, 154–155, 168, 169–172, 173, 175, 254n70; and overspending, 58, 66; and political elite, 84–89, 91; and pre-electoral spending cycle, 229–231; and presidential succession, 86–88, 169, 171, 176–180; and Salinas, 11–12, 26, 89, 93, 170, 184–185, 186, 200, 201, 257n13; social sector spending, 136, *137;* and Social Security Ministry, 87–88, 99, 114, 115, 127, 243n36; sources of data on, 255–256n94
Public Works Ministry, 96, 111, 249n32

Rabasa, Emilio O., 143
Radelet, Steven, 18
Reagan administration, 206
real growth of manufactured exports, 62, *63*, 64
real manufacturing growth, *61*
Reyes Heroles, Jesús, 155, 161, 163, 258n37
Reyna, José Luis, 76–77, 242nn1, 3
Reynolds, Clark W., 57
Riding, Alan, 100
Rodrik, Dani, 22, 59, 240n19
Roeder, Philip G., 204
Rojo Gómez, Javier, 50–51
Romero Kolbeck, Gustavo, 98, 102, 115, 172, 173, 179, 254n70

Romero Pérez, Humberto, 107, 108, 126, 127
Rubin, Jeffrey W., 32
Rubio, Luis, 133, 138, 149, 172, 173, 255n83
Ruiz Cortines, Adolfo: and cabinet secretaries, 126, 131, 259n42; and Carrillo Flores, 102, 104; and devaluation, 107–108, 109, 127; and economic growth, 66; and Finance Ministry, 111; and grassroots strike wave, 77, 110; and interview process, 7; photograph of, *106;* political career of, *144;* and political expertise, 97; and presidential succession, 122, 123, 259n42; and threat of economic crisis, 105
Russia, 14, 22, 41, 223

Sachs, Jeffrey, 18
Salinas, Carlos: and cabinet secretaries, 126, 192; and cause of economic crises, 57; and de la Madrid, 182, 184, 187, 189, 190; and Democratic Current, 198–199; dynastic ambitions of, 10, 206–207, 209–210, 212; and economic crisis of 1987, 200; and economic policies, 200, 201–202, 205, 208–209, 260n79; and elite struggle, 157, 209, 210–211; and Finance Ministry, 189; *grupo* of, 29, 91, 200, 205; and Hernández Galicia, 39–40; and inflating securities market, 13, 91; macroeconomic policies of, 26, 29; and Mexican fiscal data, 228; photograph of, *183;* and political elite, 205; and presidential nomination, 190, 191, 197, 198, 200, 202, 203; and presidential power, 157; and presidential succession, 1, 53, 92, 130, 205, 206, 209–210, 213; and public spending, 11–12, 26, 89,

93, 170, 184–185, 186, 200, 201,
257n13; and rational expectations,
186; and Silva Herzog, 11–12, 26,
182, 184–186, 187, 191, 192, 193,
198; and Urquidi, 4, 202, 206–207,
208; and Washington Consensus,
193, 199
Salinas, Raúl, 207, 209
Salinas Lozano, Raúl, 4–5, 108, 210
Sánchez Díaz, Antonio, 215
Sánchez Navarro, Juan, 107, 108, 158,
245n37
Schamis, Hector E., 224
Serra, Jaime, 199, 215
Silva Herzog, Jesús: and de la Madrid,
182, 184, 185–186, 189, 190,
257n2; and foreign debt, 200–201,
260n76; and López Portillo, 173;
and Ortiz Mena, 245n24; photograph of, 12; and presidential
nomination, 11, 192; and Salinas,
11–12, 26, 182, 184–186, 187, 191,
192, 193, 198
Silva Herzog, Jesús (father), 41, 143
Smith, Peter, 42, 43, 158
social conflict, 22, 25
Socialist Workers Party, 159
social sector spending, 136, 137
Social Security Ministry, 7, 87–88,
99, 114, 115, 127, 243n36
socioeconomic development, 26, 133,
135
Solana, Fernando, 35, 104, 139, 160,
163, 177
Solidarity, 26, 207, 209
Solís, Leopoldo, 69, 70, 132, 147, 229
South Korea, 19, 22, 23, 67, 164
Soviet Union, 204
State Industries, Ministry of, 4, 6, 44,
68, 111, 112, 152
Stepan, Alfred, 38
strikes: and conciliation and arbitra-
tion boards, 38, 78; and devalu-

ation, 108; federal jurisdiction
strikes, 84, 242n17; grassroots
strike wave, 25, 27, 67, 76–78,
109–111, 113, 128, 212. *See also*
labor
structural industrial problems: arguments against, 59–60, 62–67; and
economic crises, 21, 55, 57, 66, 76,
239n11; and exhaustion of import
substitution, 58–59; free-market
view of, 55, 57, 58, 60; Marxist
views of, 55, 57; perceptions of,
74–75
Suárez Farías, Francisco, 43, 118,
247n23
Suárez Mier, Manuel: and de la Madrid, 104, 164, 169; and Echeverría, 141, 161; and Finance Ministry, 97; and Ortiz Mena, 245n24;
on protectionism, 63–64; on tax
reform, 69
Summers, Lawrence H., 208
Supreme Court judges, 36, 81, 83

taxation, 67–71, 115
Teichman, Judith A., 173
Tello, Carlos: and Echeverría, 132,
141, 146–147, 149; and labor, 83–
84; and López Portillo, 159, 161,
162–163, 164, 169, 171, 172–173,
178, 257n116; and structural economic problems, 239n11
Thailand, 18, 164
Tlatelolco Square massacre: and
Echeverría, 81, 131, 133, 135–136,
141, 148; effects of, 133–134, 147;
and Federal Security Directorate, 36; and Ibarra, 147, 250n39;
and interviews, 8; and political
cohorts, 193; and political elites, 8,
131, 138–139, 141; public spending
following, 26–27, 133
total-factor productivity, 59, 62, 64

transparency, and economic crises, 19
trustworthiness, 43–44, 46

Urquidi, Victor: career of, 3–4; and
    Coquet, 88, 108; and Echeverría,
    133, 148; and Ortiz Mena, 102;
    on presidential power, 35; and
    Salinas, 4, 202, 206–207, 208; and
    Silva Herzog, 186; and tax reform,
    70, 115; and Tlatelolco Square
    massacre, 36, 139, 141
Urrutia, Miguel, 218–219
Uruchurtu, Ernesto P., 44, 124
U.S. Constitution, 10, 35
U.S. Export-Import Bank, 18, 109
U.S. Federal Reserve, 17, 20, 21, 25,
    164
U.S. State Department, 119
U.S. stock market crash of 1987, 26,
    91, 200, 203
U.S. Treasury, 109, 215

Vallejo, Demetrio, 77, 78, 111
Vargas Llosa, Mario, 1
Vatican II Council, 147
Velázquez, Fidel, 27, 28, 78, 82, 83, 151
Vernon, Raymond, 18, 60, 147
violence: and elite struggle, 210, 212;
    of Mexican Revolution of 1910,
    32–33, 33, 34, 41; and overt mobi-
    lization, 49, 50
Volcker, Paul, 201

wages: and Alemán, 119; and de la
    Madrid, 184; and devaluation, 108;
    and Echeverría, 70; and economic
    crisis of 1994, 15–16; and infla-
    tion, 109; and labor's demands for
    raises, 77–78, 86, 242n3; and lack
    of strikes, 38; and López Portillo,
    84, 180, 242n16
Washington Consensus, 157, 191, 193,
    199
wealth, distribution of, 145, 152
Weingast, Barry R., 225
World Bank, 97, 145, 201
World Trade Organization, 205, 210

Zapata, Fausto, 75, 132, 139, 141, 142,
    148, 251n86
Zapata Consortium factory, 81
Zedillo, Ernesto: and Camacho
    Solís, 212; and cause of economic
    crises, 57; concession speech of,
    3; and dismissals, 215, 217; and
    election of 1994, 214–215; and
    Finance Ministry, 189, 217; and
    López Portillo, 168; and Mexican
    fiscal data, 228; photograph of,
    216; and presidential nomination,
    213; and Supreme Court judges,
    36; and Washington Consensus,
    199
zone of vulnerability, 19